The Encyclopedia of
LAND WARFARE
in the 20th Century

DON'T IMAGINE YOU ARE NOT WANTED

EVERY MAN between 19 and 38 years of age is WANTED!

Ex-Soldiers up to 45 years of age

"YOUR COUNTRY NEEDS YOU"

MEN CAN ENLIST IN THE NEW ARMY FOR THE DURATION OF THE WAR

The Encyclopedia of LAND WARFARE

in the 20th Century

a Salamander book

Published by

SPRING BOOKS

London · New York · Sydney · Toronto

A Salamander Book

This edition published 1977 by
The Hamlyn Publishing Group Limited
London · New York · Sydney · Toronto
Astronaut House, Feltham
Middlesex, England

ISBN 0 600 33145 8

Second impression

© Salamander Books Ltd 1977
Salamander House,
27 Old Gloucester Street,
London WC1N 3AF
United Kingdom

Credits

Editor: Ray Bonds

Design director: Chris Steer

Designer: Barry Savage

Colour drawings: Gordon Davies; Peter
Sarson/Tony Bryan; John W. Wood

Line drawings: Gordon Davies

Maps: Richard Natkiel

Filmset by SX Composing, Leigh-on-Sea,
Essex, England, and Adtype Limited,
29 Clerkenwell Road, London EC1, England

Colour reproduction by Metric
Reproductions Limited, Chelmsford, Essex,
England

Printed in Belgium by Henri Proost et Cie,
Turnhout

The Authors

Brigadier Shelford Bidwell
Military historian, military commentator and author, specialist in
warfare in the 20th Century. He was for five years Editor of the
Journal of the Royal United Services Institute for Defence
Studies.

Brian Bond
Lecturer in War Studies at King's College, University of London,
and well-known as a military historian. He is the author of
numerous articles, including the chapter on World War I in the
New Cambridge Modern History (Vol. XII), and several books, the
latest entitled *France and Belgium 1939-40*. He is also senior
editor of the Yearbook *War and Society*.

Dr M. L. Dockrill
Lecturer in War Studies at King's College, University of London.
He is the author of several historical articles and co-author of *The
Mirage of Power: British Foreign Policy 1902-1922*.

Christopher F. Foss
Author of *Armoured Fighting Vehicles of the World, Artillery of
the World, Jane's Pocketbook of AFVs* and other books; weapons
correspondent for *Defence* magazine, and contributor to many
other military publications.

William Fowler
Contributor to numerous publications on military history, Editor of
many military books, member of The Royal United Services
Institute for Defence Studies, London.

Charles B. MacDonald
Deputy Chief Historian for Southeast Asia, US Army Center of
Military History, Washington (currently directing preparation of
the official US Army history of the war in Vietnam). He is the
author of several books and contributor to other volumes, and
was assistant to General William C. Westmoreland in the
preparation of his memoirs, *A Soldier Reports* (1976).

John Marriott
This is the pen name of a retired officer who has been writing on
defence for many years and is Deputy Editor of the Journal,
NATO's Fifteen Nations.

Billy C. Mossman
Following participation in Leyte (Philippine Islands) and Okinawa
campaigns in the Pacific during World War II, he was Military
Historian with HQ Eight Army, HQ Army Forces, Far East, during
the Korean War. He is the author of, and contributor to, many
official US Army military history publications, especially with
reference to the Korean War, including *American Military History*
(1968) and *US Army in the Korean War* (being prepared).

Michael Orr
Senior Lecturer in War Studies and International Affairs, Royal
Military Academy, Sandhurst, and author on military history.

Dr Ronald Spector
Historian with the Department of Army Center of Military History,
Washington, currently writing a history of US Army involvement
in Vietnam during the 1950s, and served as field historian in
Vietnam with the US Marine Corps, 1967-1969. He is the author
of *Admiral of the New Empire: The Life and Career of George
Dewey*, and many articles on military affairs.

John Terraine
Following many years as a political broadcaster and producer for
the British Broadcasting Corporation, he wrote more than half the
scripts for the BBC's *The Great War* series, contributed to the
BBC's *The Lost Peace* series, and was sole scriptwriter to the
Rediffusion (ITV) 12-part series, *The Life and Times of Lord
Mountbatten*. He is also the author of several books on aspects
of World War I.

Colonel John Weeks
Project Manager, Infantry Weapons, British Ministry of Defence;
Lecturer in infantry weapons at RMCS, Shrivenham, England;
military adviser for *Jane's Weapon Systems, Jane's Infantry
Weapons* and *Brasseys Infantry Weapons;* author of many books
and contributor to numerous international military periodicals.

Toby Wrigley
Military historian and commentator, military correspondent to
Defense and Foreign Report (USA), contributor to *Defence
Attache* (UK) and contributor to many other periodicals.

The publishers wish to acknowledge the valuable assistance
given by **Bill Gunston**, authoritative writer on military and
technical subjects, in the initial planning of this book.

Contents

Foreword

Events in land warfare have consistently surprised observers and confounded forecasters: small armies with inferior weapons have routed seemingly superior forces; major powers with massive military might have been able only to contain smaller fanatical armies, even after several years of expenditure in men and equipment. Today, with the prospect of a third and probably final World War menacing mankind, two nations cannot wage a "small" war with one another in isolation from the rest of the world. Nor is it possible for a super-power to crush into total obliteration or surrender another nation which is fanatically dedicated to succeed even if it takes 100 years.

Recently we have seen great armies do battle in South-East Asia and the Middle East. Years of destruction — of lives and lands — have led to mere interim victories, stalemate or ignominious withdrawal, but not to final solutions. "Small" wars continue to be waged, however, and soldiers continue to fight for "freedom" (from what, for whom?) in armies or in terrorist units.

Two devastating World Wars, and numerous conflicts around the globe, have inevitably led to great advances in the technology of warfare. Indeed, there have been many occasions when observers imagined that the ultimate weapon had been introduced to the battlefield. But for every new threat there has been a counter, and so there were born the anti-tank weapons, the anti-aircraft guns and anti-missile missiles. Recently new armour has been developed which is said to be proof against even the Soviet-built AT-3 Sagger anti-tank missiles used so effectively during the 1973 Arab-Israeli war; how long will it be before a super-armour-piercing missile is seen in action?

In 1897, a Polish banker and amateur war student, Ivan Bloch, stated: "The soldier, by natural evolution, has so perfected the mechanism of slaughter that he has practically secured his own extinction." Yet, eighty years on, soldier still shoots soldier, no more totally but with more

sophistication. With the most advanced weaponry that scientists can devise zinging round his ears, a soldier still clambers from a bunker or trench, sights an enemy soldier and engages him in combat. There will always be a need for the infantryman in land warfare; who else can advance into territory gained by machines and control it until peace reigns?

The soldier himself is a weapon used by political leaders. But, whether he be infantryman or general, he is an individual who can perform feats of great valour while stricken with justifiable fear.

Both horror and glory are elements of the evolvement of land warfare throughout the 20th century. This book does not set out to be an absolutely comprehensive history of warfare on land since 1900 — one volume could not do justice to the many facets, about each of which there are probably hundreds of books. But, using great battles as the backdrop before which evermore sophisticated weapons and tactics play their part, this encyclopedia describes the major events evaluating the armies and equipment and their performance in combat. The profound and far reaching changes which have occurred make fascinating reading.

Ray Bonds

Editor

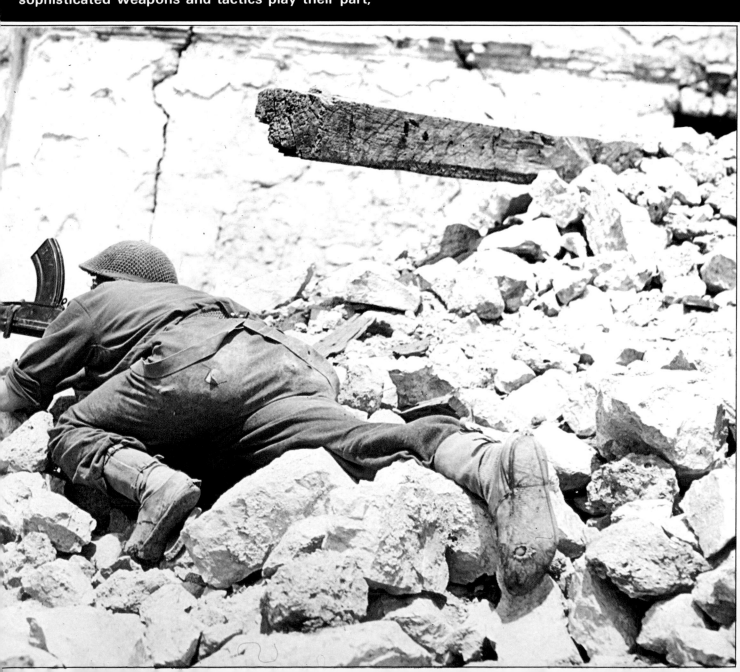

arms

Up to the end of World War I, most European armies were concerned with the development and tactical use of late 19th century weapons. But appearing in the background were the tank and aircraft.

The revolution in military technology which gave an enormous temporary advantage to the defensive and transformed the appearance of the battlefield was virtually completed in the last quarter of the 19th century. By the 1870s the leading European armies were equipped with breech-loading magazine rifles which could be fired as fast as the marksman could operate the reloading mechanism and were lethal up to about one mile in range. Artillery underwent similar changes which greatly improved its range, accuracy and rate of fire but with two important additions. By the 1880s the invention of a sliding carriage recoil absorption system obviated the need for re-aiming after each round, while the development of a smokeless propellant greatly reduced fouling and removed the 'fog of war'. The excellent French 75-mm field gun could fire up to 10 rounds a minute. Perhaps most important of all was the perfection of a truly automatic weapon

in Hiram Maxim's machine-gun. Each gun was designed to fire from 200 to 400 rounds per minute, which meant that a single machine-gun could achieve a sustained fire power superior to that of 500 infantrymen armed with magazine rifles.

A simultaneous revolution was taking place in field defences and fortifications. The American Civil War witnessed the introduction of barbed-wire entanglements, barriers of logs and earth, and vast networks of trenches (around Richmond and Petersburg), which anticipated those of the Western Front by half a century. After the Franco-Prussian War (1870–1), the French and Belgians constructed new fortifications with rings of forts surrounding each stronghold at distances of 15,000 to 18,000 yards to keep modern artillery out of range. The redoubts were constructed of concrete two or three metres thick reinforced by three centimetres of steel. These modern fortress systems were built to withstand a 9-inch

howitzer shell, the largest in existence at the time. Guns were mounted in revolving turrets which could be raised mechanically out of concrete emplacements for firing. A labyrinth of trenches and tunnels surrounded the guns, and these contained powder magazines, repair shops and accommodation for the troglodyte garrison. Even these supposedly impregnable bastions, however, were to prove vulnerable to the heaviest German siege guns (42-cm or 16.5-inch) in 1914.

It was ironic that these devastating im-

Below left: A British tank advances accompanied by troops of the Canadian Mounted Rifles. Infantry had to learn to operate effectively with this weird newcomer to the battlefield.

Below: Artillery greatly improved in effectiveness during 1900-1918. Here a British 9.2 inch howitzer sees action in the ruins of Tilloy-les-Mofflaines, France, during the Battle of Arras in April 1917.

provements in lethal weapons occurred at precisely the time when the spread of railways and industrialisation enabled vastly larger armies to be transported to the theatre of war and maintained there with food and supplies. The prevalent military doctrine before 1914 was to place in the field the largest possible host of men in the shortest time with a view to overwhelming the adversary at once by sheer weight of numbers.

Military theorists did not ignore the implications of these momentous changes in firepower and transport; indeed the professional journals and publications show that between 1870 and 1914 they were obsessed by them. The more imaginative thinkers absorbed the lessons of the American Civil War and the Franco-Prussian War: it was suicidal for infantry to advance in close order in the fire zone, so skirmishing and infiltration by small units rushing from cover to cover seemed to offer a better solution. The continuing effectiveness of the bayonet was questioned and even more so the future of the cavalry's traditional role of the charge with lance or sabre. Most important of all, some tacticians realised that the infantry would seldom be able to advance under fire without close and powerful artillery support. The machine-gun had proved lethal in colonial wars in the 1880s and 1890s, but its potential for future European warfare was not yet fully grasped.

In retrospect, after World War I, even the more radical among pre-1914 military writers were seen to have underestimated the difficulties of overcoming problems posed by the revolution in firepower and entrenchments. Supporters of the cavalry charge, and believers in the superiority of the offensive spirit such as Colonel (later Marshal) Ferdinand Foch, who argued that every increase in firepower would aid the attacker, were to appear ridiculous. Perhaps the only prewar thinker who fully foresaw what was likely to happen when mass armies clashed on a fire-dominated battlefield was a Polish banker and amateur student of war, Ivan Bloch. Unlike the soldiers, however, whose task was to find tactical solutions, Bloch was free to declare that in these conditions war between great nations was futile.

By comparison with these new weapons and defences, developments in mobility by land and air which would eventually restore an advantage to the attacker, were still in their infancy by 1914. Already by that date the invention of the petrol engine threatened the role of the horse but World War I ended, as it had begun, with military transport still predominantly horse-drawn. Even in World War II the horse was still essential for transport in some theatres. In August 1914

Above left: A trench at the front line being manned by men of the Royal Naval Division and Australians. The man on the left is using a sniperscope, the man on the right a periscope.

Left: A British tank crashing through barbed wire at Wailly in October, 1917. The tank was the major factor in breaking the stalemate on the Western Front.

there was no more than a handful of motor vehicles in any army, but gradually the motor lorry was used more and more to transport the huge mass of material demanded by this static war. Motor transport did not affect the pace or range of operations, however, because it had no power of cross-country movement and could not penetrate far into the fortified and devastated battle zones. Even in 1918 the pace of advance was generally determined by the foot soldier.

The significance of air power for future land warfare should have become obvious in 1909 when Louis Bleriot flew the English Channel in half an hour. Aircraft were first used in war in Tripoli in 1911–12, when Italian aviators warned their generals of the concentration of Arab and Turkish forces.

They also tried dropping bombs but without much effect. The Balkan Wars of 1912–13 saw the further use of aircraft. In August 1914 Germany had the advantage of numbers with some 200 first-line planes, but British avaiators in the Royal Naval Air Service had shown more imagination, having already experimented with the use of aircraft for torpedo attack, hunting submarines, dropping bombs and aerial combat. In 1911 the first plane took off from the deck of an anchored cruiser. The high commands on either side, however, were slow to grasp the potential versatility of the aircraft in war. They regarded it primarily as a reconnaissance vehicle, designed to be the eyes of the ground forces rather as balloons had been in recent wars. But the very success of aircraft in reconnaissance duties inevitably led to the construction of fighter planes to deny this advantage to the enemy.

Within four months of the opening of World War I the trench deadlock, predicted by Bloch, had become a reality on the Western Front. The tactical problem, implicit in the developments mentioned above, must be briefly described. The basic problem was that a handful of machine-guns could destroy a concentration of men necessary to overwhelm the defenders before they could cover the fire zone between the lines. To allow the attacking infantry to cross no-man's land the artillery had to smash the defender's fieldworks, barbed-wire, machine-gun nests and artillery defences. Even when the attacker's artillery barrage was reasonably effective the infantry could only advance up to distances of about 3,000 yards under its protection. Beyond that, uncut wire and a few machine-guns were sufficient to check the advance, and anyway by then the attackers were morally and physically exhausted. Counterattacks would frequently drive the attackers back to their start line. A vicious circle was created, in that to ensure that the defences were smashed before the infantry went in, prolonged bombardments sometimes lasting for weeks were necessary. This method not only betrayed the location of the coming attack but also choked the rear areas with vast quantities of shells, thus handicapping the forward movement of reserves. Moreover heavy bombardment, by churning up the ground, often actually aided the defenders. Even when these ponderous blows succeeded in smashing holes in the enemy defences, a genuine break-through could not be achieved because the traditional exploiting arm, the cavalry, was hopelessly vulnerable to stray machine-guns and unbroken wire.

The onset of siege warfare on the Western Front from early in 1915 was reflected in the relative proportions of fighting arms. While the numbers and value of cavalry declined, the proportion of artillery to other arms was almost doubled and rose to about 10 guns for every 1,000 rifles. Although the infantry remained the principal arm it was increasingly immobilised by impedimenta such as grenades, gas masks, entrenching tools, ammunition and rations. British infantry in the Somme offensive carried as much as 66 pounds, often more than half their body weight.

In the brief mobile phase at the start of the war field artillery often engaged the

75mm field gun M-1897

Calibre: 75mm. **Maximum range:** 7500 yards (6858m). **Weight of HE shell:** 12lb (5.44kg). **Weight of shrapnel shell:** 16lb (7.26kg). **Weight firing:** 2657lb (1205kg). **Elevation:** −10° to +19°. **Traverse:** 6°. **Rate of fire:** 20rpm (rapid). 6rpm (normal).

The 75mm is perhaps the most famous of all French artillery pieces. It was introduced in 1897 and for some time was built in secret. The gun had a shield, fired a fixed round of ammunition, and the breech mechanism was of the Nordenfelt type, with a single pole trail with a spade and a recoil mechanism. The hydraulic recoil system was revolutionary for its time as it returned the barrel to its original position after the round was fired. Before, when the gun fired, the weapon moved to the rear and it had then to be relaid again. As soon as the French 75mm gun appeared, work started all over the world, to develop similar weapons. The success of the 75mm lulled the French into a false sense of security as they believed that the gun, which had a high rate of fire, was a good substitute for a heavier gun with a slower rate of fire. The early battles of World War I were to prove the French wrong. The weapon had one disadvantage and that was its pole trail, which limited elevation.

A total of 17,000 75mm guns was built and they remained in service with the French Army until World War II. It was also built in the United States as the 75mm M1916. The Americans also built the British 18 Pounder to take the French 75mm round and called this the M1917. Even today, there are still some French 75s in service in some parts of the world.

7.92mm model 1908 (MG08) Maxim machine gun

Calibre: 7.62mm. **System of operation:** recoil, automatic only. **Length of gun:** 3′ 10¼″ (1.174m). **Feed:** 100 or 250 rounds fabric belts. **Cyclic rate of fire:** 400/500 rounds per minute. **Weight of gun:** 40½ lbs (18.37kg). **Weight of mount (sled):** 83lbs (37.64kg). **Weight of tripod:** 65½ lbs (29.74kg).

Born in Maine, USA, in 1840 Maxim worked on automatic weapons in the early 1880s and his first successsful weapon was the Model 1883 .45-calibre machine gun. In 1884 he linked up with Vickers and formed the Maxim Company. The British Army purchased a number of Maxims and issued them on the scale of two per battalion. The gun's were used in a number of campaigns in the 1890s and proved very effective. The Russians also used .312 calibre Maxims in the Russo-Japanese war with great success. At that time the British did not realise the full potential of the weapon, although the Germans did and they developed a 7.92mm machine gun at Spandau known as the Model 1908. By the beginning of World War I over 10,000 were in service.

The Model 1908 normally needed a crew of four, two men to pull the weapon and two carrying the ammunition. The machine gun proved to be deadly when established in entrenched positions festooned with barbed wire and allied losses from machine gun fire were huge. The Model 1908 was followed by the Model 08/15, introduced because the earlier weapon was too heavy. The 08/15 had a shoulder stock, bipod and a modified receiver and a 50-round magazine could be used rather than a 100 or 250 round belt. Maxims were built in many countries including the US and Russia, the latter having the Maxim 1910 chambered for the 7.62mm round, which remains in service with some countries today, as does the Vickers .303 MG developed from the British Maxim.

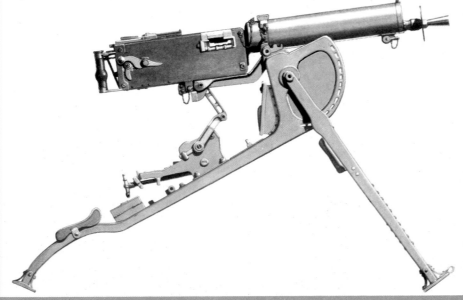

enemy over open sights at close quarters. Once the trench lines stabilised, however, it became clear that the artillery would have to blast a way through for the infantry. The Anglo-French artillery was ill-prepared for this role. The British assumption, for example, had been that an 18-pounder gun would require 1,800 rounds in the first six months, after which a further 500 rounds would be available. In the event some guns had fired more than 2,000 rounds by mid-September 1914 (after three weeks of campaigning), while in the battle of Neuve Chapelle (March 1915) more field ammunition was expended than in the whole of the Boer War.

Although the Allies were desperately short of ammunition in the first two years of the war, it was all too easy for the generals to regard this as the complete explanation of their failures, and so assume that more and more guns would eventually achieve a break-through. It took a succession of increasingly costly defeats, such as Aubers Ridge (10 March 1915), Loos (25 September–14 October 1915) and the Somme (July–November 1916) to show that by itself artillery could not provide the answer. The Allied artillery was lacking in range, mobility and above all a reliable system of observation and signal communications. Moreover, the larger part of the British artillery consisted of shrapnel-firing 18-pounders which were effective against men in the open but unsuitable as siege weapons: not that high-explosive shells were much more effective against the increasingly deep and ingeniously constructed German dugouts. In the later battles the infantry advance was covered by creeping barrage, a wide belt of fire moving forward in jumps of 100 yards every few minutes. This combination of fire and movement brought results so long as the infantry progressed steadily in long rows, but at best it could only make costly gains of a few thousand yards at a time into the miles-deep German defences. Then there were long delays while the

supporting artillery was moved up, dug in again and the dumps restocked with millions of shells. The series of offensives that comprised the 3rd Ypres campaign in 1917 witnessed the ultimate elaboration of these 'nibbling' tactics.

Among other weapons used to achieve tactical surprise, the one which acquired the most terrible reputation was poison gas. Although seldom mentioned in historical accounts, the Germans first used gas shells in Poland in 1914, but in the extreme cold they were completely ineffective. On 22 April 1915 the Germans tore a hole in the Allied front at Ypres by a surprise attack assisted by chlorine gas from cylinders, but they failed to exploit the breech and the Canadians quickly sealed it. That autumn the British employed gas in the ill-fated Loos offensive but most of it was blown back into their own front trenches. Although gas masks were quickly distributed, both sides went on using various gases throughout the war, including diphosgene, which has a marked tear-producing effect, phosgene, chloropicrin, hydrocyanic acid, which attacks the central nervous system, and the dreaded mustard gas, which causes slow-healing burns and affects the respiratory tract. Horrible though these gases were, postwar statistics show that they were far less lethal than more conventional weapons. Skilfully used gases could provide fleeting opportunities for infiltration but they were a failure in terms of a decisive break-through.

Another new weapon which was of

Right: The British 135th Siege Battery, Royal Garrison Artillery, with 8-inch Mark V howitzer, in action near Henin-Sur-Cojeul, France in May, 1917. This weapon entered service in 1915.

Below: A Vickers .303 machine gun team wearing gas masks on the Somme near Ovillers in July 1916. Gas was used by both sides during WWII, normally in artillery shells.

negligible importance in 1914 was the aircraft, but a variety of types were rapidly developed so that by 1918 the decisive potential of air power was becoming apparent. A desperate competition took place to gain command of the air over the static Western Front, each side seeking superiority in speed, firepower and manoeuvrability: in 1915 the Germans produced the Fokker *Eindekker*; in 1916 the Allies replied with fighters like the de Havilland 2 and the Nieuport 11; the Germans in turn responded with the Albatros D.I and Halberstadt D.I. By 1917 as many as 100 aircraft were taking part in air battles. In their great March offensive in 1918 the Germans concentrated no less than 900 aircraft, but even this was not enough to win control of the air from the Allies. By August 1918 the Allies had gained a decisive advantage in the air with about 2,000 planes against less than 400 German. The importance of this increasing aerial superiority is often neglected in accounting for the turn of the tide in the summer of 1918.

In long-range bombing the Germans took the lead with the hydrogen-lifted Zeppelins which terrorised London in 1916 but proved fatally vulnerable to explosive bullets. British fighter and anti-aircraft defences were at first utterly ineffective against 'conventional' bombing planes such as the Gothas and 'Giants', but by the spring of 1918 improved defence measures forced the raiders to turn against Paris. Meanwhile the British had built the Handley-Page 0/400 bomber for long distance raids against airfields, railway stations and Zeppelin hangars. Although in the last months of the war the newly created Royal Air Force was planning strategic bombing raids against targets deep in Germany, it must be stressed that the great majority of planes were used in close co-operation with the armies. By 1918 the aircraft had proved its tactical value and strategic potential, but it was by no means as yet a war-winning weapon.

The instrument that finally broke the trench deadlock and the dominance of the machine-gun in defence was the armoured fighting vehicle or tank. The component elements of this revolutionary new vehicle existed before the war, but it took the genius of a British Royal Engineer officer, Colonel (later Sir) Ernest Swinton, supported by Winston Churchill at the Admiralty, to bring them together. Armoured cars had been in military use for a decade before 1914 but had been confined to hard roads. The endless track had long been in service on caterpillar tractors on the great farms of North America. The first British experimental tank weighed 31 tons and was armed with two 6-pounder guns and four machine-guns. It was very slow (maximum speed 3.7 mph), cumbersome and prone to mechanical breakdown. British senior officers had displayed little enthusiasm for experimenting with tracked vehicles, and the tanks' first performance in battle served to confirm the doubts of the sceptics. Only 49 tanks were available when Sir Douglas Haig decided to use them in the middle of the Somme campaign on 15 September 1916, and of that number 17 broke down before reaching the start line. Of the remainder only nine were able to keep up with the infantry, and these

did make a good impression, particularly in clearing the village of Flers. Considering the crew's inexperience and the lack of time for mechanical overhaul, the tanks had not done badly, but given their limitations and the battlefield conditions at the Somme there was clearly no prospect of their achieving a decisive break-through in 1916.

The first real opportunity for tanks to display their potential as battle-winners occurred at Cambrai on 20 November 1917. Here the attack was launched without the usual preliminary bombardment and achieved complete tactical surprise. By this time nearly 400 tanks were available. They carried huge bundles of brushwood which enabled them to cross the three lines of German trenches. The tank spearhead achieved a remarkable break-in, advancing as deep as four miles in places and capturing 7,500 prisoners and 120 guns. Unfortunately reserves of tanks and infantry were lacking to exploit this brilliant success, while the two cavalry divisions available failed to grasp their fleeting opportunity. On 30 November a German counterattack regained most of the lost ground. In parenthesis it should be noted that despite their extremely skilful defensive tactics the Germans were slow to appreciate the value of tanks and used only a handful in their great March offensive in 1918. They had built only a few dozen by the end of the war, when Britain and France had several hundred each.

The Allied tanks' greatest success of the war was in the Battle of Amiens in August 1918, but even then their losses were heavy and favourable weather conditions were crucial. The battle, designed to lever the German forces out of France, began at dawn on 8 August. About 580 tanks were available, but only 420 were employed in the first attack. The lessons of the Battle of Cambrai had been carefully studied. Taking full advantage of a thick mist the tanks advanced as much as seven and a half miles by mid-day, but when the mist cleared approximately 100 were knocked out by anti-tank guns. These tactics were repeated on the following day with similar results: a successful advance under cover of mist but then heavy losses (39 out of 145 tanks leading the assault) to anti-tank guns. By 11 August the Tank Corps had suffered casualties of about 72 percent and the momentum of the advance had been lost. But although the tanks had not achieved a complete break-through into open country, they had spear-headed an advance of 12 miles; more important still they contributed to the

Austro-Daimler armoured car

Crew: 4 or 5. **Weight:** 3 tons. **Length:** 15ft 1in (4.6m). **Width:** 5ft 9in (1.76m). **Height:** 9ft 0in 2.743m. **Speed:** 28mph (45kmh). **Engine:** 4 cylinder petrol developing 40hp. **Armour:** 4mm.

The first armoured car with a turret was built in Austria in 1903 from an idea by a Captain Ludwig von Tlaskal-Hochwall. It was designed by Paul Daimler, anbd was built by the Österreichische Daimler Motoren Gesellschaft at Wiener-Neustadt. It consisted of a 4 x 4 (ie, all four wheels are powered) chassis with the engine at the front, driver and co-driver behind the engine and the turret at the rear could be traversed through 360° and was armed with two machine guns. Known as the 40 PS Panzerspähwagen, the vehicle had a turret. When shown to the Emperor Franz Joseph, it is reported to have scared his horses and that was the end of the project for a time.

The British used armoured cars from the beginning of World War I, in the hands of the Royal Naval Air Service. In 1914, a Naval Brigade and an RNAS squadron was sent to Antwerp, to be followed by a variety of armoured cars, with a number of chassis, from manufacturers such as Rolls-Royce, Lanchester, Delaunay-Belleville and Wolseley. These had two roles, first to protect air bases and second to rescue shot-down pilots. Within a short space of time trench warfare set in and armoured cars played no further part in operations on the Western Front until 1918, but they were used widely in Iraq, North Africa and Palestine by the British. The French and Germans also developed and used armoured cars in World War 1.

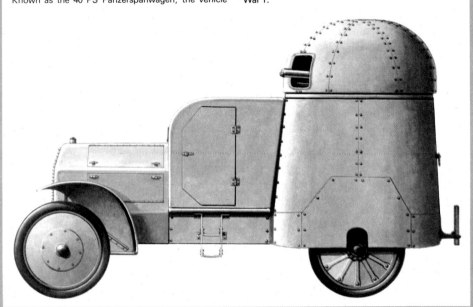

Above left: 2nd Lieutenant V. A. Browning firing a .30 Browning Machine in at Thillombois in 1918. His father was John Browning one of the greatest gun inventors of all time.

Left: A French Renault light tank returning from an attack on the Aisne Front. It had a crew of two and was armed with either a 7.92mm machine gun or a 37mm gun.

Above right: An artillery team of the Royal Field Artillery taking a bank on the Struma Front in 1916. Thousands of horses were used to move supplies to the front lines during WWI.

nervous collapse of General Ludendorff, who described 8 August as 'the black day of the German Army' and advised the Kaiser to open peace negotiations. Tanks continued to play a leading role in the remaining actions on the Western Front and may be fairly described as 'the weapon that finally revolutionised land warfare and brought an end to the stalemate'.

The period 1900–1918 witnessed the application of science and technology to the methods of waging war in a more intense fashion than ever before. Much of this effort was devoted to improving existing weapons: metallurgists and ballistics experts rendered

artillery and machine-guns more deadly; the telephone and wireless revolutionised communications; while logistics was transformed as railways and motor transport began to supercede the horse. In land warfare the three major innovations were poison gas, the aircraft and the tank. The first, thanks to a combination of practical difficulties and moral revulsion, never became a war-winning weapon; but by 1918 aircraft and tanks, sometimes in partnership, were providing glimpses of a new kind of mobile war which a few years earlier had been confined to the realms of science fiction.

The Russo-Japanese War 1904 to 1905

The Russo-Japanese War could be described as the first 'modern' war, but the shock of a non-European power defeating mighty Russia overshadowed its technical and tactical portents for World War I.

Major-General J. F. C. Fuller included the Russo–Japanese War (1904–5) in his *Decisive Battles* as constituting 'one of the turning points in Western history, for not only was it a trial of strength between an Asiatic and a European Power, but above all a challenge to Western supremacy in Asia'. In addition the conflict was of absorbing interest to contemporary students of land and naval warfare as a testing ground of new weapons and tactics. The Japanese navy had been largely built and trained by Britain, whereas her army inclined to Germany as its model. Representatives of the major powers' general staffs, together with war correspondents, flocked to Japan and Manchuria to study the performance of machine-guns, artillery, cavalry and numerous other innovations. Sir Ian Hamilton's *A Staff Officer's Scrap-book* is a good example of their reactions. For the next decade this war, together with the Boer War (1899–1902), provided the basis for professional analysis and prediction but were then superseded by World War I.

The root cause of the war was Russo–Japanese rivalry for control of southern Manchuria and Korea. In 1894–5 Japan had defeated China, but then the 'Great Powers' had compelled her to abandon all her claims on the Asiatic mainland and to give up the Liaotung peninsula with its great naval base, Port Arthur. In 1898, to Japanese indignation, China leased Port Arthur to Russia. Meanwhile Russia was competing with Japan for domination of Korea, which took on added significance to the former as a link between Vladivostok and Port Arthur. In 1904 Japan proposed to renounce her interests in Manchuria if Russia would give a similar undertaking about Korea. Receiving no reply, Japan broke off negotiations on 5 February and attacked the Russian naval squadron at Port Arthur without a declaration of war on 8 February.

Communications and geography played an even more decisive part in this conflict than in most wars. For Japan command of the Yellow Sea was essential since every single soldier had first to be ferried to the mainland and then supplied. This aspect of the war has been covered in the companion

Adjutant-General Kuropatkiny, Commander-in-Chief of the Manchurian Army, inspects troops commanded by General Gershelman in Manchura on 12 July 1904.

volume (*Encyclopedia of Sea Warfare*) so here it need only be mentioned that Japan never lost the initiative seized by its pre-emptive strike and, despite gallant Russian attempts to unite their Vladivostok and Port Arthur squadrons, retained command of the sea. When the Russian Baltic Fleet eventually arrived it was defeated, at Tsushima, in the most decisive naval battle since Trafalgar.

A single statistic highlights Russia's strategic problem; the distance between Port Arthur and Moscow is about 5,500 miles. This vast distance was spanned in 1904 by the Trans-Siberian Railway ending at Vladivostok, but when the war began a long stretch of it was single track and, worse still, there was still a 100-mile gap at Lake Baikal. It normally took over a month to transport a battalion from Moscow to Port Arthur. Thus the war was limited in the sense that both sides, but especially Russia, found it difficult to bring their military power to bear. It should be added, in Fuller's words, that 'few theatres could have been more unsuited to a struggle between highly organised armies'. The battle theatre possessed no good roads, much of it was mountainous and dense crops of millet made large tracts of the cultivated plains almost impassable. The climate is one of extremes, local provisions were scarce, and the tracks that sufficed for roads alternated between mud, ice and blinding dust.

When the war began, general world opinion expected Japan to be crushed. Russia had virtually unlimited trained man-power to call upon, but the question was how much of it could be concentrated in Manchuria. In 1904 Russia had east of Lake Baikal some 83,000 field troops and 196 guns, not counting 25,000 fortress troops. By contrast Japan could rapidly put the bulk of her standing army of nearly 300,000 men and 870 guns into the field. Both armies were raised by conscription, Japan's initial term of service being three years and Russia's five. Observers on the spot generally agreed that although in weapon power the contending armies did not differ greatly, in quality of both officers and men the Japanese utterly outclassed the Russians. At best the Russian solder obeyed unthinkingly like a goaded ox, whereas the Japanese troops were intensely patriotic and ready for self-sacrifice. Several commentators were converted to the view that the Japanese, in terms of organised courage, were the best soldiers in the world. In justice to the Russian troops, however, it must be said that they were wretchedly led. Most of the reinforcements were married peasants who had forgotten their training. They were despatched on the long journey across Siberia in cattle trucks lacking even primitive comforts, such as seats, and eventually reached the front tired, neglected and sullen. Utterly ignorant of what this war in a strange land was about, they regarded it as an incomprehensible tragedy.

Above: Part of the Russian defences of Port Arthur in the Far East which stood firm against repeated Japanese assaults until it finally surrendered on January 2, 1905

Right: Russian troops hurriedly assemble when an alarm is called at an advanced post in Manchuria, May 1904

The men's indifference was shared by many of the officers.

Japan's strategy was determined by the need to divide its armies between Port Arthur and the Russian field army concentrated at Liao-yang. The Japanese therefore planned to land three armies on the northern shore of the Bay of Korea, which would advance towards Liao-yang as the covering force. A fourth army would invest and capture Port Arthur before moving north to reinforce the others with a view to winning a decisive battle before the Russians could gain numerical superiority. What upset these calculations was the Japanese assumption that Port Arthur could be quickly rushed, as it had been in 1894, and that the loss of this vital base would shatter the enemy's morale.

General Tamesada Kuroki's 1st Army landed at Chemulpo (now known as Inchon) on 9 February 1904 and slowly moved up to the Yalu river, where on 1 May it decisively defeated a much smaller Russian force under General Zasulich, who had disobeyed his orders not to fight a pitched battle. Although only a small-scale affair, this victory was of enormous moral value to Japan since it demonstrated its ability, widely doubted, to beat a great European power.

With Korea under Japanese control, the next step was to isolate Port Arthur. On 5 May General Yasukata Oku's 2nd Army began an audacious landing at Pi-tzu-wo only 40 miles east of Port Arthur. The danger of a Russian naval attack was very great, particularly as the disembarkation took three weeks to complete, but the Russians missed the opportunity, presumably being demoralised by the recent loss of their excellent Admiral Stepan Makarov and the damage suffered by their fleet. On 26 May Oku, with four divisions, was checked by a Russian covering force with strong artillery support at Nan-shan. The Japanese assault was repulsed but that night the Russian artillery supply failed and the defence collapsed. This gave another important boost to Japanese morale, but significantly their losses were about four times greater than those of the entrenched defenders.

By the beginning of June the Japanese had succeeded in cutting off the land approaches to Port Arthur but found themselves in a difficult strategic situation. The siege of Port Arthur was now in the hands of part of General Maresuke Nogi's 3rd Army while the remainder acted as a covering force. The 2nd Army had begun to advance up the Port Arthur–Harbin railway line towards Te-li-ssu, faced by a Russian force of 33,000 men under General Stackel-

berg. The 4th Army under General Michitsura Nodzu would soon land at Ta-ku-shan, and the 1st Army remained near the Yalu faced by General Count Keller with 30,000 men. The Russian commander-in-chief, General Alexei Kuropatkin, with a reserve of 40,000 men near Liao-yang, had an excellent chance to exploit the Japanese forces' dispersion by holding one army while smashing another. He decided to contain the 1st Army and to drive the 2nd Army into the sea. In parenthesis it should be noted that Kuropatkin was an intelligent soldier with a high reputation as a staff officer and war minister. As a field commander, however, he proved to be hesitant and prone to half measures. His offensive movements were painfully sluggish, although in extenuation it must be said that this was partly due to incompetent subordinates. By contrast the Japanese commander-in-chief, Field-Marshal Iwao Oyama, was an outstanding and remarkably bold general, ably supported by three fine army commanders in Kuroki, Oku and Nogi. Oyama allowed his headstrong subordinates to take daring risks when he discovered that Russian reactions were invariably slow.

Kuropatkin failed to send Stackelberg adequate reinforcements, with the result that the latter was beaten in the first major land battle at Te-li-ssu (14–15 June) and began to retreat up the railway line towards Liao-yang on 15 June. By the beginning of August Oku and Kuroki had pushed the Russians back to Liao-yang while the 4th Army under Nodzu was advancing from Ta-ku-shan so as to come up between them. The outcome was still finely balanced: Kuropatkin was now under pressure to relieve the beleaguered Port Arthur, but on the other hand Oyama's communications

were dangerously stretched, as the Russian fleet's ineffective sortie from Port Arthur on 23 June emphasised. Port Arthur's determined resistance had completely upset the original Japanese plan to unite their armies before a major battle. It was in a desperate attempt to solve this latter problem that Nogi launched a series of terrific assaults over five days in mid-August. He captured two fortresses but only at the cost of 15,000 casualties as against the defender's 3,000. Clearly Port Arthur would be taken only after a prolonged siege.

Kuropatkin was thus able to launch the great battle of Liao-yang on 23 August with a superiority of 158,000 to 125,000 men. The battle foreshadowed those of World War I by lasting a fortnight. The first Russian offensive failed to outflank the Japanese outpost defences, and Kuropatkin withdrew into his defensive lines. He then concentrated superior numbers against the Japanese right but after a promising start this advance was also checked. Nevertheless the Russians appeared to be getting the upper hand when, on 3 September, Kuropatkin surprisingly decided to retreat towards Mukden. Admirably conducted though this retreat was, the Japanese had gained an enormous moral victory by driving a larger army from a strong defensive position. Kuropatkin had lost 16,500 killed and wounded to Oyama's 23,600.

In October Kuropatkin again took the offensive, at the Sha-Ho river, doubtless encouraged by the completion of the railway line round Lake Baikal. After checking the Russian offensive, Oyama launched a brilliant counterattack, leaving one division to contain six while he concentrated on the Russian centre. The battle cost the Russians

28cm howitzer

In February 1904 Japan attacked the Russian Fleet at Port Arthur in the Far East, to start the Russio-Japanese War. A Japanese attack in August was a failure but supported by almost 400 guns and howitzers, in September, they brought in twelve 28cm howitzers, guns originally part of Japan's coastal defences. They were used to bombard the decks of warships; 18 of these weapons had been sent earlier but were sunk by the Russians on route. Four months of heavy shelling by these and other weapons slowly reduced the Russian fortifications and, on January 2nd, 1905, the Japanese emerged victorious.

There were many lessons to be learned from this war, and as history was to show in 1914, the Germans learned most of them. One of the two important points was that the combination of machine guns and barbed wire could stop even the most determined enemy. The second was that no fort was safe from bombardment by heavy howitzers.

By early 1914 the Germans had thousands of 7.92mm machine guns in service and had also developed in secret two giant 42cm howitzers. In the first few days of the war, these two weapons proceeded to systematically knock out the Belgian forts around Liege.

Left: Dug-in Russian field guns prepare to fire against Japanese forces during the Russo-Japanese war of 1904/5

Below left: Three Chinese who spied for the Russians, being executed by a Japanese firing squad

40,000 casualties, twice the number of their opponent. Both sides were exhausted and dug themselves in, in another foretaste of World War I.

Meanwhile throughout the autumn Nogi continued to sustain heavy losses in prosecuting the siege of Port Arthur. The Japanese brought up heavy howitzers which did great damage to the fortifications and the town but were limited in their effects on the harbour by lack of an observation point. It was for this purpose that repeated assaults were launched on 203 Metre Hill in September, but the Russian garrison was magnificent in defence and beat them off. In November the news that the Russian Baltic Fleet was steaming towards the Far East made the Japanese even more determined in their efforts to destroy the squadron at Port Arthur before it arrived. A fifth general assault on 26 November was a costly failure, with the Japanese suffering three or four times as many casualties as the defenders. Nogi decided that 203 Metre Hill must be taken regardless of cost. The position was of tremendous natural and artificial strength: it comprised a huge redoubt with two keeps, completely surrounded by wire entanglements, and was held by a garrison of 2,700 troops commanded by an outstandingly brave officer in Colonel Count Tretyakov. The fortress eventually fell after a heroic

defence on 5 December. A British correspondent, Ashmead Bartlett, remarked that it would have been the ideal spot for a peace conference: he doubted if so many dead had been crowded into so small a space since the French stormed the great redoubt at Borodino in 1812.

This was the beginning of the end of the siege. In the days following the capture of 203 Metre Hill the Russian ships at Port Arthur were systematically reduced to wrecks, thus enabling Admiral Heihachiro Togo to steam home and refit ready to meet the Baltic Fleet. Shortage of food and the worsening situation caused the garrison commander, Lieutenant-General Anatoli Stësel, to summon a council of war as early as 12 December, but it was decided to fight on. Meanwhile the Japanese were steadily undermining the outer forts and when one of the most able and popular defenders, General Kontratenko, was killed by an explosion on 15 December, morale slumped appreciably. By the end of the month three important forts (Chi-kuan, Ehr-lung and Sung-shu) had been blown up and on 1 January the last real barrier, the historic Chinese Wall, was breached. Stësel, who does not emerge with much credit in most accounts of the siege, decided to capitulate and on 2 January 1905 the white flag was hoisted. It was then discovered that a considerable quantity of food remained, as well as over 500 guns and 82,000 shells. During the siege the Russians had lost 31,000 killed, wounded and missing, while 24,000 men marched out as prisoners of war. The Japanese lost nearly 58,000 killed, wounded and missing, not counting 34,000 sick, many thousands of whom also died. Thus ended one of the longest, most strategically significant and costly sieges in modern history.

After a brief rest Nogi marched his 3rd

Army north and took his place on the left of Oyama's line. He also transported some 28-cm siege guns, which played an important part in the impending battle of Mukden. The two sides were now facing each other entrenched on a front of some 40 miles with the railway bi-secting their lines. When the last and greatest battle of the war began on 23 February 1905 each side had approximately 300,000 men. Japanese intelligence seems to have been much better than the Russian, and Kuropatkin exhausted a large proportion of his reserves by marching and counter-marching them in dreadful conditions of frost and dust blizzards to meet a non-existent threat to his left. Meanwhile Nogi's 3rd Army was carrying out a wide outflanking march to bend back the Russian right wing and threaten Mukden from the west. When Kuropatkin belatedly awoke to the danger of his right flank he threw in his available reserves piecemeal but they failed to stop the advance which now began to threaten the vital rail communications through Mukden. Kuropatkin consequently abandoned Mukden on 8 March and after a night withdrawal of indescribable confusion established a new defence line some 20 miles north of the Manchurian capital. Although both sides were now exhausted the Japanese could count this as yet another victory: they had occupied Mukden, which was found to contain a large supply depot, and they had lost 70,000 men as against the Russians' 85,000 – staggering figures by the standard of the day. Kuropatkin was relieved of his command.

The loss of Port Arthur, the retreat from Mukden and the annihilation of the Russian Baltic Fleet at Tsushima on 27 May 1905 caused the Russians to despair of victory on terms they could afford, while strikes and riots in St Petersburg added urgency to their quest for a negotiated peace. Japan too, despite its remarkable successes, was also nearing physical and financial exhaustion. President Theodore Roosevelt managed to bring representatives of the two sides together at Portsmouth, New Hampshire and there a treaty was signed on 6 September. The effect of Russia's military failures was mitigated by skilful diplomacy and international support. Russia escaped without having to pay a war indemnity, but was forced to accept Japan's predominance in Korea and annexation of the southern half of Sakhalin island. Both belligerents agreed to evacuate Manchuria but Japan retained the Liaotung peninsula, including Port Arthur.

These may appear small gains and losses compared with the duration and intensity of the war, with the number of men killed and the wealth expended, but Japan's clear emergence as a Great Power foreshadowed immense changes in the political geography of the Far East. It could now only be a matter of a few years before Japan established a mainland empire at the expense of China. Also important, for those few observers who were not blinded by prejudice or a superiority complex, the fighting in Manchuria provided many valuable hints as to the likely characteristics of a future European war. It was perhaps too much to expect that these hints would be heeded and acted upon before the trench stalemate in World War I demonstrated their validity.

Illusion on the Western Front
1914 to 1915

World War I started in the west with great campaigns of movement. By the end of 1914, however, the trench lines had taken over, and few generals or planners foresaw the inevitable consequences.

The mass populations of the First Industrial Revolution made sure that World War I would be a war of masses, equipped and supplied by mass production, moved by machinery. The locomotives went to war: in Germany, there was a vast railway network purely for strategic purposes; in France, 4,278 special trains were earmarked for mobilisation; in Britain, to carry the Expeditionary Force across the Channel, as many as 80 trains a day ran into Southampton docks alone, and a daily average of 52,000 gross tons of shipping was required. But railways run to timetables, and timetables locked the strategic plans of all belligerents in an inescapable rigidity.

The plans varied from grandiose to trivial. The German object was simple: to

overcome the hazard of war on two fronts, threatened by the Franco-Russian military convention of 1894. The solution devised by General *Graf* Alfred von Schlieffen (Chief-of-Staff 1891–1906) was to hold the slow-moving Russians with slender forces, while a lightning offensive knocked France out of the war in 40 days. To achieve this, it was necessary to deploy great numbers: these were provided by Reserve formations. It was also necessary to avoid the French frontier fortress system, and to achieve this the overwhelming weight of the German array (54 out of 62 divisions) would sweep through Belgium, pass west to Paris and wheel to pin the French against their own fortresses, annihilating them in a gigantic

'Cannae' move. Even when watered down by Moltke, Schlieffen's successor, the scale and audacity of the German war plan in 1914 was breath-taking.

The French plan contained no subtleties and no surprises. Based on a belief in the 'Napoleonic offensive' and the inherent superiority of the French soldier in attack, it prescribed a headlong onslaught by the whole army across the common frontier. No manoeuvre could have suited the Germans better. And as an appendix to this French whirlwind, Britain had incautiously agreed to place an Expeditionary Force of one cavalry and six infantry divisions behind the French left. Every detail of embarkation and disembarkation was carefully worked

out, down to such trivia as half-hour halts for coffee; only the grim implications of continental war were missed.

In the event, the Schlieffen Plan was never carried out. Repeatedly Moltke wavered and tinkered, weakening the all-important right wing and contracting the plan's scope until all prospect of the intended annihilation faded. Nevertheless, enough force remained to inflict a terrible defeat on the French in the Battles of the

British soldiers in the trenches on the snow covered Western Front in 1915. Many men died because of the damp, cold and bad sanitation which prevailed in most trenches.

Frontiers. Four days sufficed to dispel all French dreams of advancing into Germany and make the harsh truths of superior German strength and superior equipment apparent. In Alsace and Lorraine, at the Battles of Sarrebourg and Morhange on 20 August, in the Ardennes on 21 and 22 August, and at Charleroi on 22 and 23 August, one by one the French armies met defeat.

Irreparable damage was done to France in this very first phase of the war. In the last 11 days of that fatal August, over 200,000 Frenchmen became casualties; worse still, some 10 percent of the entire officer corps was put out of action, one division losing as many as two-thirds of its officers on one day.

France's allies shared her defeat, though not her losses. The Belgian fortress of Liège had fallen disconcertingly quickly under the fire of 42-cm howitzers – a surprise weapon. The Belgian field army retired into Antwerp on 20 August, and three days later Namur fell. It was on that day, 23 August,

Right: A British WWI poster encouraging all men in all walks of life to join the ranks of the Army. As the casulties mounted replacements became vital to sustain the war effort.

Left: A German flame thrower team in action on the Western Front. These weapons were very useful when storming trenches and fortifications

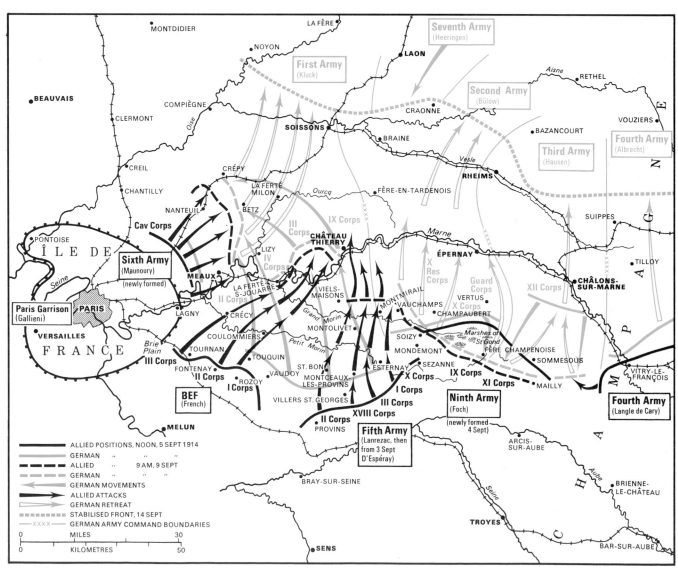

STEP INTO YOUR PLACE

PUBLISHED BY THE PARLIAMENTARY RECRUITING COMMITTEE, LONDON — POSTER No 104   PRINTED BY DAVID ALLEN & SONS Ld. HARROW MIDDLESEX

Lewis machine gun

Calibre: .303. **Weight:** 27lb (12.24kg). **Length:** 50½″ (1.282m). **Length of barrel:** 26″ (.66m). **Magazine capacity:** 47 rounds. **Muzzle velocity:** 2440fps (744m/s). **Rate of fire:** 500/600rpm (cyclic) 94rpm (practical). **Effective range:** 400 yards (366m).

The Lewis gun was the standard light machine gun of the British Army during World War I and was also used well into the second war. The weapon was designed by Samuel Neal McClean and further developed and marketed by Colonel I. N. Lewis, an American. It was first manufactured in Belgium and then in England and finally in the United States. For a number of reasons, the US Army did not adopt the weapon for some years, and chose the Chauchat, which gave no

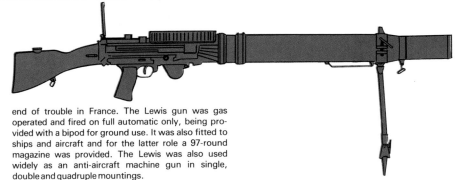

end of trouble in France. The Lewis gun was gas operated and fired on full automatic only, being provided with a bipod for ground use. It was also fitted to ships and aircraft and for the latter role a 97-round magazine was provided. The Lewis was also used widely as an anti-aircraft machine gun in single, double and quadruple mountings.

German 7.92mm karbiner 98K rifle

Calibre: 7.92mm. **Weight:** 9lb (4.08kg). **Length:** 43½″ (1.104m). **Magazine capacity:** 5 rounds. **Muzzle velocity:** 2600/2700fps (792/823m/s). **Range effective:** 600/800 yards (548/731m). **Maximum range:** 2000/3000 yards (1829/2743m).

The Mauser Kar.98K was the standard rifle of the German Army during World War II, although the Germans called it a carbine rather than a rifle. It was

bolt operated and used the same 7.92mm round as the MG-34 and MG-42 machine guns. The foresight was of the inverted V type and the rear sight was of leaf type with an open V notch sliding on a ramp, graduated from 109 yards (100m) to 2187 yards

(2000m). There were two types of grenade launcher, a spigot type which fired an anti-tank grenade, and the cup type firing an HE (G.Sprgr) or Armour-Piercing (G.Pzgr) grenade. A telescope could be mounted over the barrel for use by snipers.

.303 SMLE rifle

Calibre: .303. **Weight:** 8.62lb (3.91kg). **Length:** 44½″ (1.129m). **Length of barrel:** 25″ (.635m). **Magazine capacity:** 10 rounds. **Muzzle velocity:** 2060rps (628m/s). **Range, maximum effective:** 1093 yards (1000m).

The first Rifle, Magazine, Lee Enfield, Mark 1, was adopted by the British Army in November 1895, and in one version or another, it became the standard rifle of the British Army until replaced by the Belgian

7.62mm FN rifle in the 1950s. The first SMLE (Short Magazine Lee-Enfield) was adopted in December 1902. The rifle was built in many countries

including Australia, Canada, England and the United States and remains in service with many countries today.

that the British Expeditionary Force (reduced at the insistence of Lord Kitchener, Secretary of State for War, to four infantry divisions) had its baptism of fire. The Battle of Mons, by comparison with the great French battles, was a mere skirmish, fought by one British corps only, and costing no more than 1,600 casualties. It displayed the high qualities of the British regular army, but could not affect the main issue. At the end of the day's fighting the British were compelled to withdraw, to avoid encirclement and to conform with their allies.

During the next fortnight almost the whole of the Allied line was in retreat. Only on the right, from the Vosges to Nancy, were the French able to hold firm; there was hard fighting at Verdun, a fortress system which the French finally held, and which now became the pivot of the whole retiring left flank. There, on the 26th, the British fought a reasonably successful rearguard action at Le Cateau (casualties were nearly five times as many as at Mons) and on the 29th the neighbouring French 5th Army won a handsome, but small, victory at Guise. The effect of this was to check the German penetration westwards, and so narrow the scope of their great wheel; but their pressure on the Allied left continued remorselessly.

It was not, however, on the battlefields,

nor even on the long *pavé* roads where endless columns of infinitely weary men sweated southwards under a broiling sun, that the decision of 1914 took place. It was in the mind of Joffre, who had belatedly recognised the true state of affairs, and on 25 August took the first vital step to mend it: the formation of a new 6th Army on the Allied extreme left. 'My conception', he wrote, 'was a battle stretching from Amiens to Reims with the new army placed . . . in a position to outflank the German right.'

By 5 September, both Amiens and Reims had been left far behind: the Allies had been driven back south of Paris; but Joffre's concept held good. On that day the 6th Army, supported by the Paris garrison under General Joseph Galliéni, struck at the right flank of the German advance. The next day, the 5th Army turned on its pursuers, the BEF conforming. 'The happiest day in my life; we marched towards the rising sun,' wrote a British officer; the Battle of the Marne had begun. The battlefield stretched from just north of Paris to Verdun; fighting was violent and confused; and once again, the point of decision was in the minds of generals. Moltke was now in a state of depression. 'We have had successes,' he said, 'but we have not yet had victory. . .' The nerves of other German generals were also shaken; the apparition of the BEF

in the gap between him and his right-hand neighbour so affected General Karl von Bülow, commanding the 2nd Army, that he ordered retreat, and the whole German line began to give way. By 11 September Joffre was able to telegraph to the Minister of War: 'The Battle of the Marne is an incontestable victory for us.'

So far the war had been a war of movement: the German right flank had marched some 300 miles from the frontier to the Marne. It had been a war of generalship, good and bad: Joffre had dismissed no less than 50 generals by 6 September. There would still be some movement, some generalship; but the character of the war was about to change. The strong hint of things to come was received on 13 September, when the Allies reached the River Aisne, and found that the Germans had

Right: British troops of the 1st Cameronians in the front trench during the advance to the Aisne at St. Marguerite in September, 1914

Below right: At a hastily-rigged first aid and operation dug-out of the 42nd East Lancashire Division a soldier had just had a bullet removed from his arm

18 pounder QF Mk.1 field gun

Crew: 10. **Calibre:** 3.3in. **Maximum range:** 6525 yards (5966m). **Length:** 13' 8'' (4.165m). **Elevation:** −5° to + 16°. **Traverse:** 4° left and right.

The 18 Pounder Mk.1 was introduced into British Army service in 1904. In appearance it was similar to the 13 Pounder QF Horse Artillery Gun, but had a much longer barrel. Over 10,000 18 Pounders (this being the weight of the round) were built in Britain, India and America, the gun being adopted by the US Army.

The carriage was of the single pole type with the hydro-spring recoil system over the barrel. A Mk 2 gun was introduced in 1906 but the Mk.2 carriage which had a hydro-pneumatic recoil system, was not introduced into service until 1916.

In 1917 the 18 Pounder Mk.3 was developed, but not built. The 18 Pounder Mk.4 entered production in 1918, its main improvements being a redesigned breech and box-type trail which gave the gun an elevation of +30° and enabled it to fire 9,300 yards (8504m). This weapon remained in service until World

War II, by which time it had new carriages with rubber tyres.

At the start of World War I, an 18-Pounder Brigade had the following compliment: 23 officers, 772 men, 198 horses (riding), 548 horses (draught), 2 horses (heavy draught), 18 18-Pounder guns, 12 carts, 63 wagons and 5 bicycles. In the early days of the war, there were severe shortages in ammunition and at times the 18-Pounders were limited to just 10 rounds a day.

7.7cm Feldkanone C 96 n/A

Calibre: 77mm. **Maximum range:** 9180 yards (8.394m) **Weight:** 1930lb (875kg). **Elevation:** −12° to +16°. **Traverse:** 7° left and right. **Rate of fire:** 10rpm.

The 7.7cm Feldkanone C 96 n/a entered service with the German Army in 1896 and modified versions were developed in 1905 and 1906. It was the standard weapon of the field artillery batteries for the early part of World War I and in 1914, a German field battery had a compliment of 5 officers, 156 men, 6 guns, 6 ammunition wagons, one observation wagon and 4 other vehicles. A gun team consisted of the gun, limber carrying 36 rounds of ammunition and 6 horses. In 1915 the German artillery arm was greatly expanded and the basis for this expansion was achieved by reducing the batteries from six to four guns.

When the tank first appeared on the battlefield, the Germans introduced a modified version of the C 69 n/a with smaller wheels, which made the weapon much easier to conceal in the front line. Special armour piercing ammunition was provided for this weapon.

At the end of 1916 the K.i.H (Kanone in Haubitz-lafette) was introduced into service, being basically a C 96 n/a mounted on a field howitzer carriage. The FK 16, a development of the K.i.H., replaced the C 96 n/A towards the end of the war. This had a greater elevation and a maximum range of 11,264 yards (8504m). A modified version of the FK 16, the FK 16 n/A (neuer Artillerie) was used in World War II, and this saw service to the end of the war, by which time however, it was mainly used in the coastal defence role.

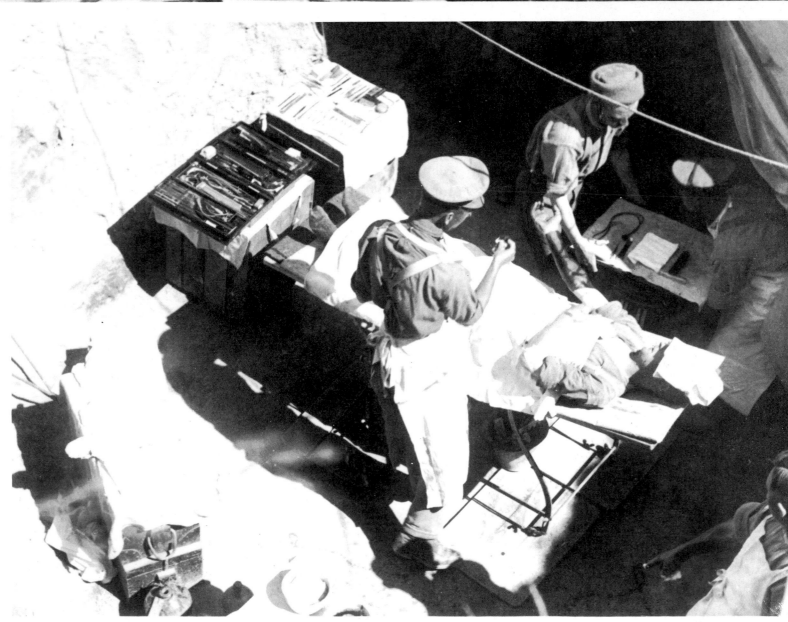

halted their retreat along the Chemin des Dames ridge on the north bank. Now trench warfare made its first appearance; the lethal combination of machine-guns and barbed-wire was experienced; trench mortars started their lethal careers. The Allied advance came to a full stop.

He was not the only one to perceive this. As stagnation set in along the whole front from Switzerland to the Aisne, both sides began feeling for the enemy's open flank, and kilometre by kilometre the battle line edged up towards the coast. This was the so-called 'Race to the Sea' – in fact, the last turning movement that would be open to the generals of either side. It ended at the River Yser, which runs into the Channel at Nieuport. There the French joined up with the retreating and somewhat demoralised Belgians from Antwerp (which fell on 9 October), while to the south the BEF, transported from the Aisne, assembled between La Bassée and Armentières. The arrival of the British I Corps at Ypres on 19 October coincided with orders from General Ferdinand Foch (co-ordinating the Allied forces in the north) to attack in order 'to exploit the last vestige of our victory on the Marne'; it coincided also with a German offensive aimed at rolling up the Allied left. Thus the 1st Battle of Ypres began as an encounter but, as the Germans developed their strength, became a defensive epic for the Allies. Once again it was the French who bore the brunt, finally holding twice the length of front of the British, yet for Britain this battle held particular significance. By the time the last German attack was stopped (14 November) the BEF's 58,000 casualties meant that 'The old British Army had gone past recall.' Soon the masses of a British citizen army would join the continental masses; hundreds of thousands of them would become familiar with the battlefield of Ypres.

It is normal, because it is easy, to think in terms of battles occurring between specific dates. But in World War I one battle often merged with another; frequently they overlapped. Thus, in 1914, no sooner was '1st Ypres' over than '1st Artois' began (14 December) and immediately after that '1st Champagne' (20 December). By both of these offensives, and another in the St Mihiel area in April 1915, Joffre sought to keep the front fluid and regain the initiative; nowhere did he succeed. The Artois battle was broken off after 10 days; the Champagne offensive lasted until March, costing some 90,000 French casualties; at St Mihiel fighting continued for over three weeks. At Neuve Chapelle the British made their own small, only moderately successful contribution (10–13 March). Nor were the Germans idle; this period between the 1st and 2nd Battles of Ypres is regarded as a period of vain and costly French attacks; broadly, this is true, but it is salutary to remember that out of 150 days, 70 were marked by German attacks or counterattacks, some on a very substantial scale.

Christmas, 1914, was marked at certain points along the front by truces and fraternisation. This would never happen again; henceforward the sentiments of the belligerents would be as rigid as the battle-lines themselves. These, at the end of the winter battles of 1914–15, had settled into the shape which – give or take a few miles where various offensives made their marks – remained until movement returned in 1918: the extraorindary phenomenon of a continuous entrenched front some 450 miles long, without flanks. 1915 was the year in which trench warfare evolved its style, dictated by a temporary technological equilibrium. To a well-constructed, stoutly-held trench system, amply protected by barbed-wire and defended by machine-guns, there was no answer but artillery until technology supplied a new weapon. The war became an artillery war, with the Germans, in 1915, enjoying the advantage in the all-important heavy calibres; their 5.9-inch (15-cm) howitzer was widely regarded as the best gun of the war. On the other hand, the first recorded use of a 'barrage' was by the British, and of a 'creeping barrage' by the French. Aerial observation, by aeroplane and balloon, and aerial photography helped the ever-increasing numbers of guns to establish their supremacy (despite universal ammunition shortages): 59.5 percent of all wounds inflicted on British troops during the war were by artillery fire, only 38.9 percent by bullets. But the defect of artillery was that in destroying the enemy's defences, it also turned the ground into a crater-field which, in wet weather, became a swamp – an obstacle more insuperable than the trenches themselves.

Both sides applied themselves indefatigably to breaking this deadlock. On 22 April 1915, at Ypres, the Germans tried chlorine gas released from cylinders; they achieved only local success, and the 2nd Battle of Ypres then dragged on for 40 days without further results except heavy loss to both sides. In a 2nd Battle of Artois in May, and a 3rd Battle in September, coinciding with a 2nd Battle of Champagne, the Allies tried all the available techniques to break through: gas, flame-throwers, trench mortars of all sizes, hand grenades, anything that was there – but all in vain. During this year the French bore the main burden of the fighting and the loss: by 31 December their casualties totalled 1,961,687, compared with a British total of just over 500,000. Although basically on the defensive throughout the year in the West, the German principle of bitterly disputing every inch of Allied gain ensured that, for them too, the butchery would be severe.

By the end of 1915, Britain was at last beginning to put forth her potential strength; the BEF had grown to 38 divisions (including two Canadian) organised in three armies. The failure of the attack at Loos in September brought a change in command. General Sir Douglas Haig replacing Field-Marshal Sir John French as Commander-in-Chief. Haig was already clear in his mind that France would not be able to go on carrying her heavy load for much longer; for him the problem of the new year would be to try to avoid committing his raw troops until they were ready for battle, while at the same time bringing relief to his allies.

Men of the 2nd Battalion, Royal Warwickshire Regiment being transported by requisitioned London buses, passing through Dickebach on their way to Ypres in November, 1914

The Eastern Front
1914 to 1917

Russian masses and determination pitted against German and
Austrian skill and training produced on the Eastern Front a war
of huge losses . . . and undreamt-of political consequences.

In 1914 Russia boasted that it could mobilise a peacetime army of two million men. The Minister of War, V. A. Sukhomlinov, had already drawn up Plan 19, whereby the Russians would launch an offensive into East Prussia in the event of war with Germany, in order to relieve Russia's ally, France, from German pressure in the West. Although Russia's armed forces were not as badly equipped with arms and ammunition as contemporaries supposed, the Russian war effort was consistently hindered by faulty and inadequate communications, the jealousies and rivalries of the officer corps, and poor planning and staff work. Russia's problems were increased by a decision to launch an additional offensive into Austrian Galicia, which meant dividing its forces between the northern and the southern theatres.

On the outbreak of war the Tsar appointed the Grand Duke Nicholas as commander-in-chief of the Russian armies, with General Yanushkevich as his chief-of-staff. Neither had any knowledge of the war plans which Sukhomlinov had drawn up: both were largely figureheads and planning, such as it was, was organised by the Quartermaster-General, General Danilov. General Yakov Zhilinkski was appointed commander of the front against Germany, but was on bad terms with his army commanders, and was frequently out of touch with military developments on his front.

In response to desperate French pleas for a Russian advance into Germany to draw German forces away from the Western Front, Zhilinski ordered an offensive into East Prussia on 17 August. The Russian 1st Army, commanded by General Pavel Rennenkampf, with three corps, was to advance towards Koenigsberg, and the 2nd Army, led by General Aleksandr Samsonov, was to attack the Germans from the southwest. This division of his forces at the outset resulted from the obstacle of the Masurian Lakes, but Zhilinski hoped that the two armies would soon join up on the coast at Koenigsberg.

Russian troops move forward through barbed wire entanglements on the Eastern Front during World War I. The unrest in Russia at that time lowered the effectiveness of the Russian Army.

Rennenkampf advanced slowly into East Prussia. The German 8th Army under General Max von Prittwitz attempted to stem the advance at Gumbinnen on 20 August but was brushed aside. Prittwitz lost his nerve and ordered his forces to retreat to the lower Vistula, and as a result he was replaced by Generals Paul von Hindenburg and Erich Ludendorff, who arrived at the 8th Army's headquarters at Marienburg on 23 August. Ludendorff adopted plans drawn up by the head of the operations department, Colonel Max Hoffmann, for a German counter-offensive in the south.

Samsonov's poorly provisioned force of 200,000 men had, meanwhile, moved slowly across the frontier in the direction of Allenstein. Samsonov made little effort to keep in touch with Rennenkampf's army which, by the 26th, had resumed its advance towards Koenigsberg. Ludendorff, who learned of the Russian dispositions from uncyphered Russian wireless messages, decided to deal with Samsonov's army first. using his superior railway network Ludendorff concentrated the bulk of his forces against the Russian 2nd Army on the 26th. Samsonov's forces were strung out along a 60-mile front and, near Tannenberg, the German army tore into the exposed Russian forces. By the 30th Samsonov's army had been crushingly defeated. Samsonov shot himself.

Rennenkampf, who had halted his advance, did nothing to assist Samsonov. His army lay in fortified positions between the sea and the Masurian Lakes. Ludendorff, whose forces soon arrived at this front after defeating Samsonov, was able to exploit a Russian weak spot at the Loetzen Pass. The German break-through on 9 and 10 September resulted in the collapse of Rennenkampf's army, which, having lost 125,000 men, retreated in considerable disorder to the Nieman river, closely pursued by the Germans. Tannenberg/Masurian Lakes was a brilliant German victory. East Prussia had been cleared of the Russians in a few days. But a German advance into Russia was repulsed and in the ensuing battle the Germans lost 10,000 men, with neither side gaining the upper hand.

Ludendorff's attention was distracted by the difficulties of his Austrian ally in Galicia. Conrad had decided to embark on an offensive in this theatre, rather than remain on the defensive along the San river, which was what the Germans desired. Towards the end of August three Austrian armies advanced from north-east Galicia in the direction of Warsaw and Brest Litovsk. Conrad planned to envelop the Vistula fortresses and occupy Russian Poland. At first his advance was successful, but the Austrian right flank ran into a Russian offensive in eastern Galicia, broke up and fled southwards. By 3 September General Alexei Brusilov's Russian 8th Army had captured the Galician capital of Lemberg (Lvov). Conrad's left flank was in turn defeated at Rava Russka on 10 September. By the 11th the Austrian armies were in retreat on all fronts, and were crossing the San. The Russians captured the Austrian fortress of Jaroslav and besieged Przemsyl, which was garrisoned by 150,000 Austrians. By mid-September Brusilov had driven the Austrians out of the Bukovina, and reached

the Carpathian passes which guarded the plains of Hungary. During these battles the Austrians lost 400,000 killed, wounded and taken prisoner; the Russians 250,000 men.

Ludendorff, in response to Conrad's appeals, was forced to send German reinforcements to assist his ally. In the latter part of September the German 9th Army was despatched from East Prussia to Breslau. Ludendorff planned a new Austro-German offensive into Poland with the object of capturing Warsaw. This offensive opened on 28 September, but the Russian high command had prudently withdrawn its forces from west Poland to the Vistula, in the hope of organising a new counter-offensive.

Early in October the Austrians counter-attacked in Galicia, driving the Russians beyond the San and relieving Przemysl on the 9th. By 12 October the German 9th Army had advanced rapidly and was about seven miles from Warsaw. In the south of this front heavy fighting on the Vistula resulted in a Russian repulse, although the Russians managed to hold the area around Ivangorod. Conrad sent Austrian reinforcements to Ivangorod, but these were defeated. On 18 October the Russians launched a counter-offensive in Galicia, which forced the Austrians to retire from the San and retreat to Krakow. As a result Ludendorff ordered the 9th Army, in danger of being cut off, to abandon its efforts to take Warsaw. The Russians did not pursue the retreating 9th Army with much vigour, and Hindenburg and Ludendorff were given time to prepare a new offensive in north Poland.

They requested General Erich von Falkenhayn, German Chief-of-staff, to send

them reinforcements from the Western Front, but the latter refused to do so until December. He had more confidence in the staying power of the Russian armies than his Eastern commanders, and he was convinced that a decisive defeat could be inflicted on the Entente's armies on the Yser river. Ludendorff concentrated General August von Mackensen's 9th Army at Thorn (Torun) in the north. He planned a southward thrust to smash the Russian flank at Lodz, enabling the Germans to move to the north of Poland to capture Warsaw. The German advance began on 11 November. The Russians were caught off guard and Mackensen broke through the Russian 2nd Army covering Lodz and forced it to retreat into the city, where its destruction was threatened by the encirc!ing German armies. The Russian high command ordered Rennenkampf's 1st Army from the north to relieve the 2nd Army. A fierce battle ensued from 18 to 25 November, and the 50,000-strong German 9th Army was trapped by the arrival in its rear of the Russian 5th Army from the south. The Germans escaped to the north. Heavy fighting continued for a month, when the arrival of German reinforcements from the Western Front enabled the Germans to capture Lodz on 6 December and to advance about 30 miles. Strong Russian entrenchments, however, held the Germans from further progress until July 1915.

There was considerable activity on the Carpathian front in January and February 1915, but neither side made much progress. Here Ludendorff, Hindenburg and Conrad agreed that a new offensive should be launched north of the Carpathians, between the Vistula and the San, in order to relieve

Above: Russian field artillery in action during World War I. Overhead flies an observation aircraft target-spotting for the guns

the Russian pressure on Krakow, and remove the threat to Hungary. The Russian high command also ordered a new offensive in this theatre in March 1915, with the intention of breaking through into the Hungarian plains. The German offensive wrecked these plans. Mackensen's 9th Army of eight divisions, drawn largely from the Western Front, was to spearhead the assault, which was launched on 2 May at Gorlica-Tarnow. After a shattering German bombardment the Russian defences collapsed, and by the end of May the Russians had fallen back in confusion to the San and Dniestr rivers. The despatch of Russian reinforcements to this theatre was hindered by a German advance in the north through Kurland towards the Dvina river, with the object of seizing Riga. By June the Russians had been driven out of Galicia, except for a small strip in the east which they held until 1917. Austro-German forces recaptured Lemberg on the 22nd, and Mackensen took Lublin and Kholm on 31 July. Warsaw fell on 4 August.

In their retreat the Russians adopted a scorched earth policy. On 25 August, after bitter fighting, the Russians abandoned Brest Litovsk, and with most of Russian Poland now under German control, Falkenhayn decided to halt further operations, his

Russian Renault-Mgebrov armoured car

The Russians became interested in armoured cars as early as 1899, but it was not until 1904/05 that they received their first vehicles. These were designed by a Russian and built in France. Three were ordered but only one eventually arrived in Russia, somehow the other two turned up some years later in Germany. The first Russian-built armoured cars were built from 1914 at the Russo-Baltic factory in St. Petersburg, and about 120 were completed by the end of 1918. As the Russian factories could not meet the army's requirements, a variety of armoured cars and armoured trucks were purchased from English firms, including Austin, Armstrong-Whitworth, Lanchester, Sheffield-Simplex and Peerless, France and Italy.

The Renault-Mgebrov armoured car was designed by a Captain Mgebrov and used a Renault chassis. The first prototype was built in 1915 with production vehicles following some years later. For its time, the car was very well armoured, especially in the front of the hull. It was armed with two machine gun turrets. The Russians made widespread use of their armoured cars both in World War I and in the Revolution that followed.

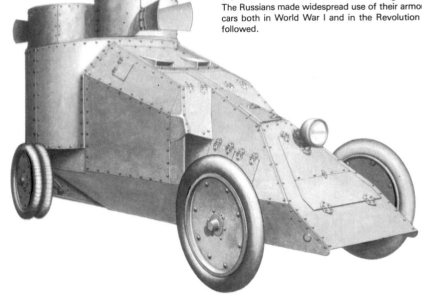

Cossack uniform

Cossacks — the word meaning guerilla or adventurer — first came from the Ukrainian plains. Shown here is the typical uniform — long smock which was either green or blue, felt hat and heel-less boots. Cartridges carried in breast holders. The sword, which had no hand guard, was slung from a shoulder belt. The dirk was mainly decorative. Main weapon was the lance — nearly 11ft long and weighing 5½ lbs. It was used like a sword, being thrust forward at the target.

Left: Russian infantry rest in the German trench they have just captured from the Germans. The unit commander Captain Lushenkov (standing), later died in action

forces having advanced into Belorussia and, in Lithuania, captured Kovno on 17 August. In the face of these disasters Nicholas II dismissed the Grand Duke Nicholas on 1 September, taking over personal command of the Russian armies, and appointing as his chief-of-staff the weak General Mikhail Alexeiev. This did not prevent the Austrians from capturing Lutsk at the end of September, or the Germans from taking Vilna in the Baltic on 9 September, although this was the limit of the German advance on this front.

There was little further activity in the East between October 1915 and March 1916. As a result of these tremendous battles Russia, whose forces heavily outnumbered those of her adversaries, had lost Poland and, between May and December 1915, had suffered casualties of two million men, one million of whom were prisoners. The Russian army, although severely shaken, was far from broken however, and in December 1915 the Russian high command promised the Entente that they would launch a major offensive in the East in June 1916. During the winter the Russians

mobilised two million men, and made successful efforts to increase the production of shells and armaments with which to re-equip their armies.

The morale of the Russian army was undermined by its defeat at the hands of the Central Powers at the Battle of Lake Naroch, east of Vilna, in March 1916, where it suffered losses of 100,000 men. The Russian high command, however, persisted with its plans for a summer campaign, which became even more urgent when the Italians appealed for Russian assistance in May after Conrad had launched his Trentino offensive. The energetic and capable commander of the Russian armies of the South-Western Army Group, General Alexei Brasilov, prepared for an assault by four armies along a 300-mile front in his sector, the objectives being to recapture Lutsk and Lemberg in Galicia, and to advance into the Bukovina, in the hope of encouraging Rumania to join the Entente.

He opened his offensive on 4 June. It was at first extremely successful. On 6 June the Austro-Hungarian armies at Lutsk collapsed and the Russians once again threatened Galicia. The Russian 7th Army entered Bukovina, and reached the Carpathians and the Rumanian frontier by the end of June. Only the German centre at Tarnopol held. The Austro-Hungarian army was completely

demoralised as a result of these Russian victories. On 2 July the Russian General Evert, commanding the Central Army Group, launched an attack towards Vilna but his forces were driven off with heavy losses near Baranovichi. Brusilov continued his offensive in Galicia until the end of September, but was unable to exploit his initial successes, especially when Ludendorff sent German reinforcements to stiffen Austria's forces in Galicia. Between June and September 15 German divisions were transferred to the East from the Western Front. Russia's offensives cost it a further million men, and its army never recovered from the terrible sacrifices it had endured.

In 1917 the political situation inside Russia declined to the point where a revolution in Petrograd led to the abdication of Nicholas II on 12 March, and the establishment of a provisional government. The Entente hoped that the new regime would inspire the Russian armies to prosecute the war more vigorously, a vain hope in view of the war-weariness and demoralisation which was affecting the rank and file. The provisional government could see no alternative but to continue the war. Many units were on the verge of open mutiny, indiscipline and desertion among the troops was widespread, and there was a growing feeling against further blood-letting for the sake of the Entente. Inflation and economic chaos added to the mounting dissatisfaction against the war within Russia. The Minister of War, Aleksandr Kerensky, appointed Brusilov as commander-in-chief of the Russian armies and tried to inspire the troops with anti-German zeal. Brusilov managed to scrape together about 200,000 men for an offensive against the Austrians in Galicia which opened on 1 July. The Russians advanced into Galicia but were met by an Austro-German counter-offensive on 19 July, which threw them back across the frontier.

Internally the situation deteriorated even further when the Bolsheviks attempted an uprising in Petrograd in July. This was crushed by Kerensky who, for a short time, became virtual dictator of Russia. He appointed General Lavr Kornilov commander-in-chief, but the latter attempted a *coup d'etat*, which was foiled by Kerensky. In August Ludendorff ordered a German offensive towards Riga, and although the Russians put up considerable resistance at first, the Germans broke through, and threatened Riga and Petrograd. The Russian army disintegrated, and on 7 November (or 25 October using the old calendar) the Bolsheviks seized power in Petrograd, forcing Kerensky to flee from the Russian capital. The Bolsheviks signed an armistice with the Central Powers, and on 3 March 1918 the Germans and their allies exacted huge territorial gains from Russia at the Treaty of Brest Litovsk.

Russia's departure from the war enabled Ludendorff to transfer German forces from the East to the Western Front to reinforce his offensive there in March 1918, which came close to destroying the Entente armies. The Entente powers might protest at the perfidy of their former ally, but they had long since written Russia off as an effective power in the East, despite the massive sacrifices the Russians had made since 1914.

The war outside Europe

Whilst World War I's bloodbath continued in Europe, the British were fighting a number of bloody and interesting wars in Gallipoli, the Middle East and parts of tropical Africa.

With the possible exception of the Dardanelles operation in 1915 it is a mistake to regard the British Empire's extra-European campaigns simply as 'sideshows' which made little if any contribution to the defeat of Germany on the Western Front. Most of them had some limited local object, such as depriving Germany of naval bases, or were regarded as useful bargaining counters in the event of a German victory. As the latter became less likely an imperialist element became evident; namely an ambition to extend British possessions, protectorates and spheres of interest in anticipation of major territorial changes in the postwar peace settlements.

Britain's early-established command of the sea enabled her and her Allies to seize Germany's overseas colonies with little expenditure of force in most cases. In August 1914, for example, a New Zealand expedition captured Samoa, and in the following month an Australian expedition took New Guinea as well as several German wireless stations in the Pacific. The German fortress of Tsing-tao on the coast of China put up a stronger resistance to a Japanese division assisted by a small British contingent, but eventually capitulated on 7 November 1914.

In Africa, Togoland was occupied in August 1914, but only at the beginning of 1916 did Anglo-French forces gain control of the densely forested Cameroons. Britain's recent Boer opponent General Louis Botha rendered the Empire a great service, first by putting down a rebellion by a section of his disaffected countrymen, and then by organising a force which conquered German South-West Africa. The exception to comparatively easy British successes concerned Germany's largest and richest colony, East Africa, where after a tragi-comic British Indian Army landing was repulsed on 3–4 November 1914, a brilliant guerrilla leader emerged in Colonel (later General) Paul von Lettow-Vorbeck.

After the rebuff at Tanga more than a year elapsed before a force could be assembled under the South African General Jan Smuts to subdue the last German resistance in East Africa. Smuts planned to drive a central wedge through the difficult interior, while a Belgian force under Tombeur was to advance eastward from Lake Tanganyika and a small British force under Major-General Sir Edward Northey was to march

A Turkish cavalry patrol passes through a village on the Macedonia Front.

in from Nyasaland in the south-west.
Lettow-Vorbeck's small force of Germans
and native troops were used with great skill
in 1916 to delay Smuts' movements designed
to cut the railway from Dar-es-Salaam on
the coast to Ujiji on Lake Tanganyika but
eventually, in September, he had to give
way and seek refuge in the Uluguru mountains to the south. After the Belgians and
British had cleared the western regions
Lettow-Vorbeck was steadily pressed back
into a small area in the south-east of the
colony. Early in 1917 Smuts departed to
London leaving the final round up to his
fellow countryman, Van Deventer. Lettow-
Vorbeck, however, remained elusive and
active to the end by skipping across the
frontier into Portuguese East Africa. From
there he maintained a guerrilla campaign
throughout 1918 until after the Armistice.
With an original force of only 5,000 troops,
about five percent of them Europeans, he
had caused the employment of 130,000
Allied troops and the expenditure of about
£75 million.

The Dardanelles campaign was originally
prompted by an urgent Russian request for
a diversion to help their hard-beset forces
in the Caucasus. Though the aim of the
campaign was 'To bombard and take the
Gallipoli peninsula with Constantinople as
its objective' these tasks were assigned at
first entirely to the Royal Navy, assisted by a
French squadron. During February 1915
the British War Council gradually came
round to the idea that troops would be
needed; but it was only after a major naval
attempt to force a way through the Narrows
had failed on 18 March that the naval
commander, Vice-Admiral John de Robeck,
admitted that further progress was impossible without troops. Thus the services' roles
were suddenly reversed: the army's task was
to seize the tip of the peninsula to open the
Straits for the navy. The army was ill-
prepared for this role. The commander,
General Sir Ian Hamilton, had only just
arrived from London with vague instructions and an inadequate staff; worse still he
had no suitable advanced base, so the
transport ships had to be sent to Alexandria
for the stores to be properly arranged.

Although it was a tribute to inter-service
co-operation and staff work that the landings
took place on 25 April, the delay proved just
sufficient for the Turks, under German
command, to augment the garrison and
prepare a defensive plan. Since Hamilton's
task was to clear the way for the navy, he
decided to make his main effort at the tip of
the peninsula with the aim of reaching the
dominating height of Achi Baba on the first
day. The narrowness of the few feasible
landing places caused Hamilton to choose
five beaches, two to the east and three to the
north of Cape Helles – an unorthodox but
unavoidable dispersion of force. A French
contingent was to create a diversion at Kum
Kale on the coast of Asia Minor, while about
10 miles to the north the Australian and
New Zealand (ANZAC) Corps was to land
near Gaba Tepe to cut off Turkish reinforcements on the way to Cape Helles. Finally,
further to the north again, the navy would
make a feint landing at Bulair, the narrow
waist of the peninsula.

One eminent historian, Dr. C. R. M. F.
Cruttwell, has called the execution of this

An NCO of the German Colonial forces (Kaiserlich Schutztruppe), East Africa, WWI. Standard sand-coloured uniform worn in the area, with pith helmet. The cockade on the helmet was common to all German forces, comprising the national colours — black-white-red. The rifle is a GEW 98.

Basic uniform of ANZAC forces with distinguishing bush hat. Puttees common to British forces of WWI. Loose fitting jacket worn under webbing, which was usually olive green. Tunic buttons were often blacked over to prevent glare, The ANZACs fought in France, Egypt and Palestine.

Khaki was adopted by the Turkish Army by 1909 and WWI uniform style was similar to that of Germany. This trooper wears a Kabalash peakless cap, Turkish religion forbidding the shading of the eyes. Equipment was also German, the rifle shown being a Mauser ·312 cal.

Above left: An Australian soldier gives a drink to a wounded Turkish soldier during the World War I Gallipoli campaign, which ended with the Allies withdrawing

Left: British troops of the 2nd Battalion The Black Watch armed with Lee Enfield rifles and Lewis machine guns man defences at Arsuf in June, 1918

plan on 25 April 1915 'the most dramatic day of the whole World War'. The feint at Bulair and the demonstration at Kum Kale both achieved their diversionary effect. The ANZAC landings also began brilliantly with 8,000 men safely ashore in the first three hours, but by a tragic error the troops were deposited a mile too far north against steep scrub-covered cliffs, with the result that they never obtained complete possession of the dominant Sari Bair Ridge. At Helles two of the landings (at 'Y' and 'S' Beaches) were unopposed, but those between, particularly at 'W' and 'V' Beaches, were the scene of epic fighting all day. The shallow half-moon cove at Sedd el Bahr ('V' Beach) provided a perfect position for the defenders. The Turks waited until the landing craft had almost touched shore and then blasted them out of the water. Half of the 2,000 men in

the hold of a converted collier, *River Clyde*, were unable to leave the ship and most of those who did were killed in the shallows, turning the waters red. Under such conditions the bare success of landing and seizing tiny beach-heads was a fine achievement, but with many senior officers killed and the troops exhausted, the Turks had just sufficient time to rush up reinforcements and consolidate a defensive line.

By the end of April the dreadful possibility of being driven into the sea had been overcome, but the Allies had fallen well short of their objectives and the cramped, widely-separated beach-heads at Helles and 'Anzac Cove' allowed little room for manoeuvre. The Allies, against all expectations, found the trench warfare conditions of the Western Front repeated at Gallipoli, with the enemy commanding the heights and better placed to receive supplies and reinforcements. Desperately short of guns and munitions, Hamilton fought a series of costly actions throughout the summer in a vain attempt to reach Achi Baba. After mid-May naval support was greatly reduced as a result of hostile submarine activity.

Political indecision in Britain caused a delay in meeting Hamilton's request for reinforcements, but by early August he would have five new divisions at his disposal. The leading role in Hamilton's elaborate new plan fell to the ANZACS who, con-

siderably reinforced under cover of darkness, were to seize the commanding heights of the Sari Bair Ridge after complicated approach marches by night. Meanwhile a strong holding attack at Helles was to pin the enemy down and draw off his reserves. Lastly, Hamilton planned a dramatic new landing in Suvla Bay, some three miles north of Anzac Cove, which was correctly believed to be virtually unfortified and unoccupied. The original idea was that fresh divisions landed at Suvla would surge forward on to the heights of the Anafarta range, link up with the ANZACS, and turn the whole Turkish position. The highest points on the ridge command a fine view of the Dardanelles Narrows for the observation of naval gunfire.

Unfortunately the elderly and ultra-cautious generals sent out by Kitchener at the War Office watered down the Suvla plan even before the landings, and Hamilton failed to impose his authority. The initial stages of the operation went well at both Anzac and Suvla on 6 August. Complete surprise was achieved but then inertia triumphed: 'Counter-orders succeeded one another; the commanders evaded responsibility by delay, the brigadiers quarrelled. Numbers of intact troops lay along the shore bivouacking or bathing.' Forty-eight hours elapsed before the tiny Turkish force at Suvla began to be reinforced from Bulair, but the Allies wasted the time. The Turks just won the race for the heights and the disorganised, dispirited new divisions were driven into the plain, never to attack again.

By the end of August this offensive, which had begun so promisingly, had clearly failed. Hamilton's request for nearly 100,000 reinforcements, with the frightful prospect of a winter clinging to the inhospital cliffs, confirmed the British government's growing pessimism. The latter was now committed to an autumn offensive in France, while the French government was anxious to transfer its contingent from Gallipoli to Salonika. Bulgaria was mobilising on the side of the Central Powers. Consequently, after a protracted, agonised debate the British government decided to cut its losses and evacuate, first from Suvla and Anzac and later (in January 1916) from Helles. Ironically, after a series of mismanaged offensive operations, these withdrawals were unexpectedly successful. Although enormous quantities of stores were abandoned, almost all the guns were removed and scarcely a casualty was incurred. Nevertheless the campaign had tragically failed to achieve its objectives and thereby discredited 'sideshows' for the remainder of the war.

The Mesopotamian campaign provides a classic example of the tendency of small military commitments to develop a momentum of their own. The original idea was that a brigade or two from India would suffice to drive the Turks out of Basra, thereby safeguarding the Anglo-Persian oil pipeline which joined the united Tigris and Euphrates rivers about 30 miles above their mouth. This was easily accomplished by 23 November 1914 and there seemed to be no reason for advancing further up the rivers. By March 1915, however, the political and military advisers with the force, now an incomplete corps commanded by General Sir John Nixon, persuaded the Government of India that the whole province of Basra should be occupied, with the eventual aim of an advance on Baghdad. Amara was taken

easily and on 22 July 1915 Nasiriya was captured after a hard fight. Despite the euphoria of Nixon and his chief lieutenant, Major-General Charles Townshend, the advance was already putting a strain on the tenuous line of British river communications. This was first evident in the mishandled evacuation of sick and wounded from Nasiriya. Despite these ominous hints, the ever-optimistic Nixon now set his eyes on Kut-el-Amara as the next objective. Kut was taken by a skilful manoeuvre on 2 October but the bulk of the Turkish garrison escaped.

Baghdad, now within Nixon's reach, seemed a tempting prize, particularly in view of the Allied failure to take Constantinople. Nevertheless the British cabinet made a colossal blunder in sanctioning the advance, which one historian has described as 'perhaps the most remarkable example of an enormous military risk being taken, after full deliberation, for no definite or concrete military advantage'.

Nixon and Townshend paid the penalty for overconfidence; they underestimated Turkish numbers and fighting spirit, and wrongly assumed that the sick and wounded would be cared for in Baghdad. At Ctesiphon, 16 miles south of Baghdad, 20,000 Turks awaited Nixon's 12,000 veterans in a well-prepared position. At the close of four days of terrible fighting on 26 November the British had lost about 4,500 men and the Turks twice as many. The former's situation was desperate, for to remain where they

Right: Feizal and Ageyl bodyguard mounted on camels during the Allied advance on Palestine in 1918

Below: Arab regulars of the Hejaz Camel Corps dealing with Bedouin pillagers after the capture of Damascus in 1918, when the Allies turned over the city to the Hejez authorities

were was to invite annihilation. Townshend, who was commanding the field force, resolved to retreat to Kut and there withstand a siege. Several determined attempts to relieve him were foiled by the Turks aided by rain, flood and mud. In March 1916 a 20,000 strong relief force actually got within sight of Kut but Townshend failed to break out to meet it. Attempts were made to drop food from aeroplanes but this failed, like the far greater airlift to Stalingrad in World War II. On 29 April 1916 starvation forced Townshend to surrender after destroying all his guns and ammunition. He went into an honourable and even comfortable internment, but seldom has any captor – except the Japanese – treated prisoners more sadistically. Ten thousand went into captivity; less than a third survived Turkish treatment.

In contrast with the Dardanelles campaign, the disaster at Kut did not cause the British government to cut its losses. The reconquest of Mesopotamia south of Baghdad was entrusted to an excellent commander in General Sir Stanley Maude. Unlike his predecessors he left nothing to chance. When his advance began at the end of 1916 his lavishly equipped force outnumbered the enemy by four to one. Making use of a strong flotilla of river boats he repeatedly outmanoeuvered the Turks from defensive positions and entered Baghdad on 11 March 1917. Despite its romantic associations, the ancient capital proved to be little more than a fetid and insanitary slum. For months on end the daily temperature reached 110°–115° Fahrenheit. In terms of sickness and privation the campaign was probably the worst fought by British and Imperial troops in World War I. Maude himself died of cholera on 18 November 1917 and it was left to his successor, General Sir William Marshall, to drive the Turks from most of the remainder of the country by the Armistice. The campaign, although nominally a success, failed to draw Turks from other theatres. Maude and Marshall were seldom opposed by more than 20,000 Turks.

Egypt, although not a British possession, was of vital importance to Imperial strategy and seaborne communications. From the outbreak of war the Suez Canal was guarded by British troops, who easily repulsed the only Turkish attack on it across the Sinai desert in January 1915. By the end of that year an enormous garrison (about 300,000 at its peak) had been assembled in Egypt. Gradually its role changed from the defence of the Canal to the invasion of Palestine. By the end of 1916 El Arish was in British hands and the whole of the Sinai peninsula had been cleared of Turks. The commander-in-chief, General Sir Archibald Murray, came under pressure from Lloyd George's new government to win a 'political victory' to offset the disastrous record of the past year. In March 1917, however, Murray bungled two attempts to take Gaza: the first was a daring venture robbed of success by muddled communications; the second an unnecessary frontal attack repulsed with 6,400 British casualties as against 2,000 Turkish. Murray was recalled and replaced by a dynamic cavalry commander, General Sir Edmund Allenby, whose temperament was perfectly suited to open desert warfare.

Allenby arrived to find the bulk of the British force tied to the railway and water pipeline in the coastal strip before Gaza. Rather than attempt another frontal attack on the latter, he planned a bold encircling manoeuvre to seize Beersheba at the eastern end of the Turkish defences with a view to cutting off the Gaza garrison from the rear. This plan was successfully implemented on 31 October 1917 by a force which outnumbered the Turks by two to one in infantry and ten to one in cavalry. Jerusalem was occupied after very little resistance on 9 December 1917.

Meanwhile the scattered Turkish garrisons east of the Jordan river were increasingly harassed by Arab irregulars inspired by Colonel T. E. Lawrence. In his culminating battle of Megiddo Allenby entrusted to the Arabs the capture of the crucial rail junction at Deraa which would sever communications with Damascus to the north. His main idea was to roll up the Turks' defensive line in the coastal plain of Sharon from west to

Model T Ford truck

Crew: 3-4. **Length:** 11′ 4″ (3.453m). **Width:** 5′ 8″ (1.727m). **Height:** 7′ 6″ (1.828m). **Engine:** Four cylinder petrol developing 20 HP.

After hundreds of years of battlefield service, in the late 1800s the horse began to be challenged by other forms of transport. The British were among the first to use mechanized transport at that time and the first British Motor Transport Company was formed in 1903. By the start of World War I, the British Army had quite a number of vehicles and by the end of the conflict there were over 165,000 trucks, cars and steam wagons in service. In comparison America

had just 35 trucks in 1914 and had to start a crash programme when she entered the war. The German Army also took an early interest in vehicles and it had about 50,000 (including motorcycles) in use by the time the war ended. The British Army used many versions of the Ford Model T, "Tin Lizzy" as it was also known, and by the end of the war, some 19,000 were on charge. They were used for a wide variety of duties including ambulances, staff cars, cargo carriers, kitchens, machine gun carriers and some were even adopted to run on many of the light railways which were used to carry supplies behind the front lines. The British also used them in Mesopotamia and Palestine for reconnaissance purposes.

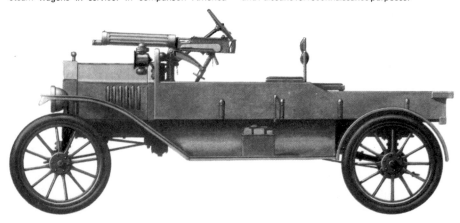

east, thereby forcing the Turks into the hills. To cut off their escape northward a 15,000 strong cavalry force would have to seize the railway line between El Affule and Beisan within 48 hours.

The offensive began at dawn on 19 September 1918. Overwhelming air and ground forces quickly overran the dispirited Turks, while the cavalry force provided the 'stop line' along the railway by covering 70 miles in 34 hours. The pursuit was relentlessly continued from the air where Allenby enjoyed complete command. The Arabs not only took Deraa as ordered, but also massacred a Turkish army isolated east of the Jordan. The fall of Damascus on 2 October heralded the end of organised Turkish resistance. Even this triumph was something of an anti-climax because Bulgaria's surrender three days earlier cut off Turkey from Germany and made its speedy capitulation on 30 October certain.

Whether or not these Middle Eastern conquests were worthwhile can be endlessly disputed. The verdict, however, should be based not on their influence on the outcome of the war in Europe (which was minimal), but on the political advantages and disadvantages which they brought to Britain in the postwar world.

Attrition on the Western Front

On the Western Front in France, Germany and the Allied powers were bleeding each other to death during 1916 and 1917 at places such as Verdun, the Somme and Passchendaele just outside Ypres.

By February 1916 over 5,800,000 soldiers had been assembled on the Western Front. They were brought by endless trains to their railheads; from here, however, their mobility was only what a limited number of primitive motor lorries, a large number of draught- and pack-horses or mules, and their own feet could make it. Technology had created greater mobility than ever before behind the battelfield, but on the battlefield had reduced mobility to that of the siege warfare of the Middle Ages or the eighteenth century. This was the conundrum that generals faced, although its solution could only lie with scientists, designers and manufacturers.

Meanwhile, with the weapons that were available, it was the task of the generals to end the war as victoriously as possible. For General Erich von Falkenhayn, who had succeeded Moltke as German Chief-of-Staff after the Battle of the Marne, the problem was relatively easy: all he had to do was to persuade the Allies to allow Germany to retain a substantial part of her great gains in 1914 and 1915. For Joffre, French Commander-in-Chief and virtual Generalissimo on the Western Front, it

was a more difficult matter. 'The best and largest portion of the Germany army was on our soil,' he wrote, 'with its line of battle jutting out a mere five days' march from the heart of France. This situation made it clear to every Frenchman that our task consisted in defeating this enemy, and driving him out of our country.'

The question was how to do it. Fortunately for Joffre, his new British colleague, Haig, approaching the matter from a different point of view, had reached the same conclusion. As early as March 1915 he had concluded: 'We cannot hope to win until we have defeated the German Army.' The experience of two world wars showed him to be right; in each case the mass of the German army had to be beaten – in 1914–18 in the West, in 1941–45 in the East. In each case this proved to be no light matter. In 1916 and 1917 Joffre and Haig learned this lesson painfully; but it was also in those years that the first suggestions of the necessary technological breakthrough were seen.

For the Allies, in every theatre of war, 1915 had been a year of frustration. Joffre diagnosed 'that the principal reason for this state of affairs lay in the disconnected fashion in which the Allies had conducted the war – each upon his own front and each according to his own ideas.' At an inter-Allied military conference at Joffre's headquarters (Chantilly) in December, it was accepted that the solution lay only in co-ordinated action, preferably simultaneous offensives, on the Eastern, Western and Italian fronts, to begin as soon as possible. This conference, said Joffre, 'marks a vital date in the history of the conduct of the war'. It meant that 1916 would be the first – and as it turned out, the only – year in which all the Allies would try to bring their superior strength to bear at once upon their enemies.

It is one thing to plan, another to execute. In 1916, once more, the Germans stole the initiative and threw all Allied planning into disarray. Working out his strategy for the year, Falkenhayn concluded: '. . . the strain on France has almost reached breaking point – though it is certainly borne with the most remarkable devotion. If we succeeded in opening the eyes of her people to the fact that in a military sense they have nothing more to hope for, that breaking point would be reached. . . . Within our reach behind the French sector of the Western Front there are objectives for the retention of which the French General Staff would be compelled to throw in every man they have. If they do so the forces of France will bleed to death – as there can be no question of a voluntary withdrawal – whether we reach our goal or not.' Falkenhayn's decision to adopt the strategy of 'bleeding to death' marks the true beginning of the war of attrition, and the place he selected for it was Verdun.

The German blow fell on 21 February, taking the French high command largely by surprise (French Intelligence throughout the war was poor, a long-term aftereffect of the notorious Dreyfus case of 1894). Joffre's

British gunners jacking and hauling a field gun out of the deep, strength-sapping mud. Terrible conditions such as this were typical on the Western Front.

reputation never recovered from the shock of the Verdun disasters – and disasters they were, giving a new dimension to the horrors of war. The real meaning of an artillery war was now seen: the Germans passed the French defenders of Verdun through a mincing machine of shell fire – in the course of this battle 1,000 shells fell to every square metre of ground.

On 25 February the Germans captured Fort Douaumont, believed to be the cornerstone of the defence. But on that day also General Philippe Pétain was appointed to command at Verdun, and by May, in a triumph of inspiration and organisation, he succeeded in stabilising the front – just. By that time Verdun had come to mean hell on earth: 'No fields. No woods. Just a lunar landscape. Roads cratered. Trenches staved in, filled up, remade, re-dug, filled in again. The snow has melted; the shell-holes are full of water. The wounded drown in them. . .'

It was not until July that British pressure on the Somme caused the Germans to abandon their offensive at Verdun. They discovered – as the Allies would later do – that it was easier to start a battle than to stop it; through the summer and autumn the French passed to the counterattack, finally retaking almost all the ground they had lost. The final losses of both sides totalled some 976,000 in 10 months of fighting. Germany had bled almost as much as France, and at the end of the sixth month Falkenhayn was replaced as Chief-of-Staff by Field-Marshal Paul von Hindenburg, with General Erich Ludendorff as First Quartermaster General.

In France, Germany had seized the initiative; in Italy it was the Austrians, attacking in the Trentino in May. Only in June did the Allied Chantilly Plan begin to be fulfilled, when the Russians launched their great offensive under General Alexei Brusilov. Meanwhile the British Expeditionary Force had increased to 56 divisions ($1\frac{1}{2}$ million men), and the pressures on Haig to relieve the burden of Verdun became irresistible. Aware that his army (now largely the volunteers who had responded to Lord Kitchener's call in 1914–15) was still unready for battle, Haig would have preferred to wait until August, but at French insistence he agreed that the Allied attack on the Somme should open on 1 July. This was the 132nd day of the Battle of Verdun.

1 July 1916, with its 57,000 British casualties (nearly 20,000 dead) for small gains, was probably the greatest single day's catastrophe of the whole war. There were many reasons for it: the inexperience of the troops and of many of their leaders, lack of trained staffs, breakdown of communications (a defect which technology would rectify),

Left: Well camouflaged British tanks with their infantry moving to the attack during the Battle of Polygon Wood on September 26, 1916. This was about 3½ miles east of Ypres

Right: The famous "Your Country Needs You" poster with the picture of Lord Kitchener on it. This poster was the rallying sign for the British in the early days of World War I before conscription

DON'T IMAGINE YOU ARE NOT WANTED

EVERY MAN between 19 and 38 years of age is WANTED!

Ex-Soldiers up to 45 years of age

MEN CAN ENLIST IN THE NEW ARMY FOR THE DURATION OF THE WAR

"YOUR COUNTRY NEEDS

YOU

RATE OF PAY: Lowest Scale 7s. per week with Food, Clothing &c., in addition

1. Separation Allowance for Wives and Children of Married Men when separated from their Families (Inclusive of the allotment required from the Soldier's pay of a maximum of 6d. a day in the case of a private)

For a Wife **without** Children	12s. 6d. per week
For Wife with One Child	15s. 0d. per week
For Wife with Two Children	17s. 6d. per week
For Wife with Three Children	20s. 0d. per week
For Wife with Four Children	22s. 0d per week

and so on, with an addition of **2s.** for each additional child.

Motherless children 3s. a week each, exclusive of allotment from Soldier's pay

2. Separation Allowance for Dependants of Unmarried Men.

Provided the Soldier does his share, the Government will assist liberally in keeping up, within the limits of Separation Allowance for Families, any regular contribution made before enlistment by unmarried Soldiers or Widowers to other dependants such as mothers, fathers, sisters, etc.

YOUR COUNTRY IS STILL CALLING.
FIGHTING MEN !   FALL IN !!

Full Particulars can be obtained at any Recruiting Office or Post Office.

insufficient artillery, bad ammunition, ill-judged tactics, daylight assault (a French demand) and, not to be ignored, a resolute, well-trained enemy in powerful positions.

Because of the shock of 1 July, and because this was the British citizen army's first great action, the full truth about the Battle of the Somme has been largely obscured. It cannot be grasped without paying due attention to the 140 days which followed that dreadful opening; during them the British army inflicted a major defeat on the Germans, a first stage in the process of grinding-down which ultimately brought Germany's collapse. In the course of this the British assumed a leading rôle on the Western Front, a fact which few had foreseen and whose cost would appal them.

There were good days and bad days as the battle wore on. 1 July was bad for the British, good for the French. 14 July saw a brilliant British dawn attack. August saw the Australian advance at Pozières. All the time incessant German counterattacks had to be beaten off. At last, in September, came the long-awaited co-ordinated effort of the Allies: finally Russians, Italians, French and British all attacked together. And in this attack, on 15 September, the technological means whereby the next generation would avoid trench warfare (but not mass casualties) made its début: the tank. Unfortunately, the 49 British Mark I tanks then available could bring a tactical success, but were quite unable to give a decisive advantage to the Allies. Tanks were for the future; meanwhile, the Battle of the Somme continued into a vile November. By the time it ended, the British had suffered 415,000 casualties, the French 195,000, the Germans an unknown number (carefully concealed) but probably not less than 650,000.

The statistics of 1916, the 'year of killing', are terrible, but they require careful interpretation. On balance, although the Allies had not won the hoped-for decisive victory, the year fell out to their advantage. At Verdun, the Somme and on the Eastern Front, Germany's admitted losses were 1,400,000. Her new leaders, Hindenburg and Ludendorff, agreed that 'the year 1916 spoke a language which made itself heard.'

'The Army,' said Ludendroff, 'had been fought to a standstill and was utterly worn out.' As early as September, they had made a drastic departure from existing German doctrine: the construction of 'powerful rear positions' behind the Somme front – a confession that Germany could not afford to fight another such battle. They went

Above right: British anti-aircraft gunners rush to man their 13 pounder 9cwt anti-aircraft guns mounted on lorries on the outskirts of Armentieres in March, 1916

Right: A captured British Mark IV tank being used by the Germans to support their own western front troops during an attack. The Germans used well over 20 captured British tanks in WW1

Far right: British machine gunners of the 11th Leicester Regiment (6th Division) in a German second line trench captured during the Battle of Cambrai, France on November 20, 1918

A British 6-inch siege battery in position at Memetz during the Battle of the Somme in August, 1916. This fired a shell weighing 100lb to a range of 14,200 yards

further: for 1917 they accepted a strict military defensive in the West for the only time, depending on unrestricted U-boat warfare to bring Germany victory. They even permitted the German government to make tentative suggestions of peace.

In November 1916 the Allied military leaders met again at Chantilly; their assessment of the situation matched that of the Germans. Joffre pointed out that co-ordinated action in 1916, although it had not produced final victory, had brought 'excellent results'. His new prescription was to press the Germans hard through the winter, and try another co-ordinated blow on all fronts as soon as possible in the spring – the very thing that Ludendorff most feared. But 1917 was not going to be the generals' year; it was the politicians' year.

Once more France had suffered heavy losses; for these, and the initial surprise at Verdun, Joffre was held responsible, and in December he was 'kicked upstairs' with the rank of Marshal of France. His successor was General Robert Nivelle, who offered a tempting alternative to attrition: a massive single blow which would end the war in 48 hours, on the principles of his recent dramatic successes at Verdun. Despite sceptics, the French government gratefully accepted this idea. Meanwhile in Britain a change of government had brought Lloyd George to power; Lloyd George was a bitter opponent of action on the Western

Front; he considered the Battle of the Somme to have been a 'bloody and disastrous failure'; he distrusted the high command which had planned and fought it. Yet he allowed himself to be persuaded by Nivelle, and by his underhand attempts to subordinate Haig to his French colleague created an antagonism between soldiers and statesmen which overshadowed the rest of the war.

The military proceedings of 1917 proceeded under this shadow. The Germans had begun constructing their rear position (the 'Hindenburg Line') in September 1916: a recognition of defeat on the Somme. In February and March 1917 they put it to unexpected good use: their unopposed withdrawal to it deprived Nivelle of a substantial part of his intended front of attack. Yet, ignoring his critics and the fall of the government which had appointed him, Nivelle optimistically continued his preparations. The British high command would have liked to make its effort in Flanders (as agreed with Joffre); Nivelle insisted that it should be further south, a preliminary to his own grand stroke.

The Allied offensive was opened by the British on 9 April; ironically, it was they who obtained the only outstanding success, the capture of the Vimy Ridge. Nivelle's own effort, starting on 16 April, did well (over 20,000 prisoners and 150 guns captured in a fortnight) but fell far short of the great victory which he had promised.

Deep gloom set in in France; Nivelle was dismissed, and replaced by Pétain; in May a large part of the weary and disappointed French army fell into mutiny; the British were forced to carry on the fight at Arras well into June at a final cost of some 150,000 casualties for no good result. The year took on a sombre look: Russia had collapsed in revolution; the French army was no longer reliable; America had come in, but was unlikely to make her presence felt for at least 12 months. Only the British, at a new peak of strength, well-equipped at last, and with high morale, could continue the fight on the Western Front, a prospect from which their government shrank.

The selected British battleground was Flanders: here the Germans (like the French at Verdun) could not afford to retreat, for the Belgian coast and its U-boat bases would be lost if they did. Unfortunately, time wasted over the Nivelle experiment meant that summer was already well advanced. Nevertheless, the brilliant opening of the British offensive, the capture of the Messines Ridge at small cost after the explosion of nearly a million pounds of explosive in 19 huge mines, promised great things. Before the promise could be fulfilled,

Mk. IV tank

Crew: 8 (commander, driver and 6 gunners). **Weight:** 62,720lb (28,450kg). **Length:** 26' 5'' (8.051m). **Width (with sponsons):** 12' 10'' (3.911m). **Height:** 8' 2'' (2.489m). **Road speed:** 3.7mph (5.95kmh). **Range:** 35 miles (56km). **Engine:** Daimler 6 cylinder petrol developing 105 or 125 BHP at 1000rpm. **Ground pressure:** 27.8psi (1.9kg/cm²). **Vertical obstacle:** 4' 6'' (1.37m). **Trench:** 10' (3.048m). **Armour:** 8 to 12mm.

Although a number of countries have claimed to have invented the tank, it was the British who first built them in quantity and used them in action. Foster's of Lincoln designed and built the first tank which was known as Mother, and fully completed by January 1916. Trials were so successful that 100 were ordered in February, 1916 and tanks were first used in action during the battle of Flers-Courcelette on September 15th. On this, as on many occasions during World War I, the tanks broke through the enemy lines but support troops were not quick enough to follow up the gaps made. British Tanks were either "males" or "females," the former being armed with 6-pounder guns and machine guns whilst the females had machine guns only. A variation of this theme was the hermaphrodite, which had one of each type of sponson. During the war eight basic Marks were built, as well as sub-types. Special vehicles included the Gun Carrier Tank Mark I and the Salvage Tank. The Mk.IV had many improvements over the earlier models, including thicker armour and sponsons that slid into the hull for rail transport. New 6-Pounder guns were fitted to the Mk.IV as were Lewis, rather than Hotchkiss or Vickers, machine guns.

Perhaps the greatest exploit of British tanks in France was the Battle of Cambrai on November 20th 1917. The Tank Corps used over 450 tanks to punch a five mile gap in the German line in less than 12 hours.

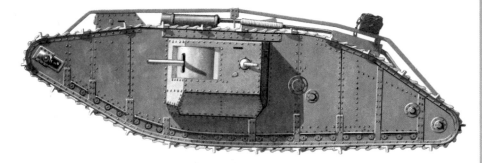

Whippet tank

Crew: 3 or 4 (driver, commander and 1 or 2 machine gunners). **Weight:** 32,360lb (14,678kg). **Length:** 20' (6.096m). **Width:** 8' 7'' (2.616m). **Height:** 9' (2.743m). **Road speed:** 8.3mph (13.35kmh). **Range:** 80 miles (129kmh). **Engines:** Two four cylinder Tyler petrol engines developing 45 HP at 1000rpm (each). **Ground pressure:** 15.8psi (1.1kg/cm²). **Vertical obstacle:** 2' 6'' (.762m). **Trench:** 7' (2.133m). **Armour:** 5 to 14mm.

First production Whippets arrived in France early in 1918 and saw combat from that March. A total of 200 Whippets were built, their official designation being Medium Mark A, and further development resulted in the Medium Mark B, C and D.

The Whippet was designed to follow and exploit gaps made in enemy lines by the heavier tanks such as the Mark 4. The most famous Whippet exploit was by a tank of the 6th Tank Battalion (B Squadron) of the Tank Corps, called "Musical Box" which caused havoc behind the German lines for nine hours before its crew were killed or captured.

The hull of the tank was rivetted, the engines being mounted at the front and the fighting compartment at the rear. As designed, each side of the superstructure had a ball mount for a Hotchkiss machine gun, but the rear hull gun was not normally installed. A total of 5,400 rounds of machine gun ammunition were carried.

Each track had its own engine with a flywheel, clutch and gearbox, and for straight running the cross shaft could be clutched together. Needless to say, the Whippet was a very difficult tank to steer.

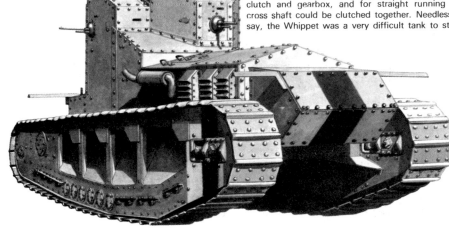

St. Chamond tank

Crew: 9. **Weight:** 50,706lb (23,000kg). **Length:** 25' 10'' (7.91m). **Width:** 8' 7'' (2.67m). **Height:** 7' 8'' (2.34m). **Road speed:** 5.2mph (8.5kmh). **Range:** 37 miles (60km). **Engine:** Panhard 4 cylinder developing 90 HP. **Armour:** 17mm maximum.

The prototype of the St. Chamond tank was completed early in 1916 by the Compagnie des Forges et Aciéres de la Marine et d'Hómecourt at Saint Chamond. The basis of the tank, like many vehicles of World War I, was the Holt tractor. The power unit consisted of a Panhard petrol engine, which drove an electric transmission. There was also an electric motor for each track.

The St. Chamond was armed with the standard French 75mm Model 1897 gun in the front of the hull and a Hotchkiss machine gun on the right. A further Hotchkiss was mounted in each side of the hull, with a fourth MG in the rear.

The St. Chamond made its combat debut in May 1917, and immediately its shortcomings became apparent when many became stuck in the first line of German trenches. By the end of the war however, it had taken part in almost 400 actions. Only 400 St. Chamonds were built as the French decided to concentrate on the small two-man Renault FT tank.

The other major French tank of World War I was the Schneider, designed in 1915 with the first production tanks being completed the following year. They first saw action in September, 1916, and 400 were built by the end of the war. Many of the early French tank operations were a failure due to both bad tactics (being sent in without infantry support) and their poor trench crossing capabilities compared to British tanks.

another six weeks went by, and when the main attack was launched on 31 July, it ran into an August rainfall twice the average for west Flanders. Disappointing progress in bad conditions persuaded Haig to transfer the control of operations to General Sir Herbert Plumer, the victor of Messines. By meticulous organisation, and aided by good weather, Plumer was able to win two notable successes in September, and on 4 October, at Broodseinde, yet another, described by the Germans as 'the black day'. But then the rain set in again, giving the shell-churned ground 'the consistency of porridge', and the offensive came to a halt with the capture of Passchendaele by the Canadians in November. Though less costly than the Somme, it had been a dreadful experience for all concerned, well described by a German officer as 'the greatest martyrdom of the war'.

The costly process of attrition was doing its work, in a manner unspeakably depressing to both sides. But before the year ended there was another glimpse of what the future might hold. On 20 November the British launched a surprise attack on the section of the Hindenburg Line south-west of Cambrai. The surprise was achieved by the sudden fire of 1,000 guns, a 'predicted shoot' without any preliminary registration or other warning, and the simultaneous advance of 324 'fighting' tanks (there were nearly 100 others for specialised purposes) in close conjunction with the infantry. The result was a spectacular success, but as so often, disappointment soon followed. The loss of 179 tanks on the first day showed that even the new Mark IV was no war-winner; the German counterattack on 30 November showed that the defeat of the German army was still some distance off. But on the credit side, it was clear that the Allied armoury would contain a formidable new weapon in 1918.

The Southern springboard

In the Mediterranean, Italy fought seemingly endless battles against the Austro-Hungarians and Germans before victory in 1918. Meanwhile the Balkans were also racked by grim campaigns.

After Austria–Hungary's humiliating ejection from Serbia in the summer of 1914, General Conrad von Hotzendorf planned a new invasion of the country in the winter which, he hoped, would restore the tarnished prestige of the Austro–Hungarian armies. This second invasion was, however, as great a fiasco as the first. Some 200,000 Austro-Hungarian troops under General Potiorek seized Belgrade at the end of October, but the main Serbian army, led by the skilful Marshal Putnik, had already withdrawn into the interior. The relatively inexperienced Austro-Hungarian forces, unfamiliar with the terrain, advanced towards Nish,

but met with a spirited Serbian flank attack near the Morava river. After a battle lasting from 3 to 6 December the Serbs gained the upper hand, and for a second time a shattered Austro-Hungarian army streamed back across the frontier into Hungary, leaving behind 40,000 prisoners and a substantial quantity of munitions.

Serbia's victory gained her only a brief respite. By early 1915 the German, as well as the Austrian, high command were determined to remove Serbia from the ranks of their opponents, particularly after Italy joined the Entente in May 1915. Serbia's eventual defeat seemed inevitable, since not

only were battle-hardened German forces transferred to the Austrian front, but also, in October 1915, Bulgaria joined the Central Powers. Bulgaria had neither forgotten nor forgiven its defeat by Serbia in 1913. The Central Powers offered it substantial territorial gains in Macedonia at Serbia's expense, promises which the Entente powers,

A patrol on the wintry slopes of Pizza Avostanis.

committed to Serbia, and humiliated by their military reverses in the East and in Gallipoli, were unable to match.

The German chief-of-staff, General Erich von Falkenhayn, was placed in overall command of operations, and devised a two-pronged assault on the country, with two Austro-German armies striking into Serbia across the Sava and Danube rivers, and two Bulgarian armies advancing from the east towards Nish and Uskub (Skopje). Serbia could only hope for assistance from Greece, with whom it had a defensive alliance. The Greek prime minister, Eleutherios Venizelos, was anxious to help Serbia and, with this in view, he mobilised the Greek army, and invited 13,000 Anglo-French troops to land at Salonika in the autumn. The Entente promised him that eventually their contingents would be raised to 150,000 men. The King of the Hellenes, Constantine, opposed the entire venture, which he thought could only lead to disaster for his country. In September he dismissed Venizelos, and proclaimed Greek neutrality.

In the ensuing campaign Serbia was overwhelmed by the forces opposing it in the north and east. Mackensen, the local commander, launched his offensive on 7 October and, after fighting a series of desperate rearguard actions, the remnants of the Serbian army escaped into Albania in November. After intense suffering from cold and disease, about 100,000 starving and exhausted Serbs were evacuated from the Albanian coast by the Anglo-Italian navies, and were taken first to Corfu, and later to Salonika. Meanwhile Austrian forces occu-

pied Montenegro and entered Albania. During Serbia's ordeal an Entente force had advanced from Salonika into Bulgaria, but had then been repulsed. The British government, fearing the effects on neutral opinion of the continued occupation of Salonika by the Entente, and seeing little point in remaining in Greece after the collapse of Serbia, wanted to withdraw. But the French prime minister, Aristide Briand, hoped for eventual success in southern Europe, and insisted that Allied forces not only remain in Salonika, but also that they be reinforced.

Earlier the Entente hoped that Italy, who declared war on Austria–Hungary on 23 May 1915, would be able to provide some assistance to the beleaguered Serbs. Although efforts had been made to repair the worst deficiencies in the Italian army since 1914, it still suffered from shortages of artillery, and the arrangements for recreational facilities and leave for the poorly paid Italian soldiers were lamentable. Furthermore, almost the entire Austro-Italian frontier was bounded by the Alpine ranges, which were well-defended by the Austrians. The Italian general staff considered that in these circumstances an advance towards the coveted Trentino would be suicidal. General Luigi Cadorna, the dictatorial chief of the Italian staff, decided instead on a campaign in the east, towards Istria, where there was a plateau between the mountains and the Adriatic along the Isonzo river. He hoped that a break-through in this sector would lead to the capture of Trieste, and he even had visions of a future juncture with Russo-

Serbian forces on the Danube. He therefore concentrated half his army on this front, placing the rest on the defensive to forestall any Austrian advance towards Lombardy and Venetia. Superior Austrian defences along the Isonzo, based on the two fortresses of Gorizia and Tolmino and the rocky terrain, wrecked Cadorna's calculations. As a result his 11 offensives on the Isonzo between 1915 and 1917 resulted in the loss of one million Italians, for the sake of advances, in places, of only 10 miles.

Conrad was equally determined to invade Italy, a country he had always despised. Although the Germans refused to send their troops to this front, the chief of the Austrian general staff managed to assemble, by the spring of 1916, 16 Austro-Hungarian divisions in the Trentino for an offensive towards the Po river. Delayed by bad weather, Conrad's forces were ordered into action on 15 May 1916, and managed to pierce the Italian defences at Asiago. The Austrians were unable to exploit their break-through, while elsewhere on this front the Italians held their positions. The

Skoda 75mm gun/howitzer

Calibre: 75mm. **Range:** 7700 yards (7041m). **Weight Firing:** 1330lb (603kg). **Elevation:** −9° to +50°. **Traverse:** 7° (left and right). **Ammunition:** HE weight 13.5lb (6.12kg), m/v 800fps (244m/s). Shrapnel weight 14.3lb (6.48kg), m/v 1180fps (360m/s).

Howitzers came into their own during the Austro/-Italian campaign, as much of the fighting took place in mountainous terrain and they could be broken down into small loads which could then be transported by men or mules. Howitzers were of much more use than guns in mountain warfare as their high angles of elevation enabled them to reach targets behind hills and on reverse slopes.

The word gun, although generally applied to cover all firearms from rifles to heavy artillery, when being applied to artillery normally refers to a weapon with a long barrel, low angle of

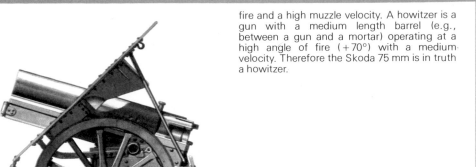

fire and a high muzzle velocity. A howitzer is a gun with a medium length barrel (e.g., between a gun and a mortar) operating at a high angle of fire (+70°) with a medium velocity. Therefore the Skoda 75 mm is in truth a howitzer.

Austrian schwarzlose M07/12 machine gun

Calibre: 8mm. **Weight (gun only):** 44lb (19.95kg). **Weight (tripod):** 43.75lb (19.7kg). **Length:** 42″ (1.066m). **Length of barrel:** 20¾″ (.527m). **Feed:** 250 round belt. **Muzzle velocity:** 2000fps (609m/s). **Rate of fire (cyclic):** 400rpm.

The Schwarzlose machine gun was developed by Andreas Wilhelm Schwarlose of Charlotten-Berg, Germany, in 1902, and entered production at the Steyr factory in Austria in 1905. The weapon was adopted by numerous armies and built in a variety of calibres including Austria (8mm), Bulgaria, Czechoslovakia, Germany, Greece (8mm), Holland, Hungary (8mm), Italy, Romania (6.5mm), Sweden (8mm) and Yugoslavia (7.9mm). It served in both world wars.

The first model was the Model 05 (1905), followed by the 07. The weapon has a place in the history of the machine gun as it was the only weapon of its time that used the retarded blowback system of operation with any success. The breech was held

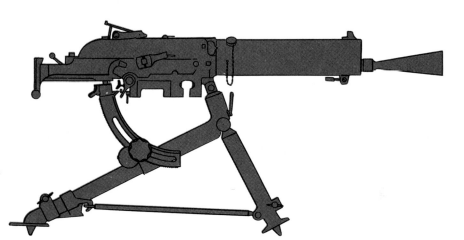

closed by a toggle lock which broke immediately upon firing and the weapon initially required a lubricated cartridge, although latter models had an oil pump. The weapon was then redesigned to need no lubrication. The Schwarlose had a very short barrel which was water-cooled and it was mounted on a heavy tripod.

Austrian offensive, weakened by the despatch of reinforcements to Galicia in June, collapsed. During the fighting the Italians lost 150,000 men; the Austrians 80,000.

The British prime minister, David Lloyd George pressed the French, in vain, to send Entente forces to the Isonzo, where he believed a decisive blow could be inflicted on the Central Powers. The French were thoroughly contemptuous of the fighting qualities of their Italian allies, and Cadorna was left to resume his offensives on the Isonzo, in May 1917, without Allied assistance. He achieved little beyond further heavy losses and the increasing demoralisation of his army. The eleventh, and final, Italian battle of the Isonzo was also the most stupendous, with 52 Italian divisions advancing on a front between Tolmino and the Adriatic. Despite an Italian penetration of the Austrian lines beyond Gorizia on the Bainsizza plateau, the Italian troops were too exhausted to exploit it, and the offensive ground to a standstill in September. The Italians lost a further 165,000 men without capturing the crucial fortress of Tolmino.

Now it was the turn of the Central Powers. The new chief of the Austrian staff, General Arz, was not confident that his forces could withstand a further Italian offensive, and so resolved to take the initiative by launching his own offensive in the autumn. This time the Austrians received German assistance, for Ludendorff, who had little faith in the fighting qualities of his ally, insisted that

the nine Austrian divisions earmarked for the campaign should be reinforced by seven well-trained German divisions, equipped with heavy artillery, gas and aircraft. The Austro-German army was placed under the command of a German, General Otto von Below. He decided to hinge the offensive on Tolmino and Caporetto in the Julian Alps, advancing on the Isonzo front between Tolmino and the Plezzo valley, with the objective of overrunning Italian communications in Friuli, seizing Udine, bottling up Italian forces on the southern Isonzo and pushing the rest of the Italian army beyond the river Tagliamento. Below and the Austrian high command did not think that their forces could accomplish much more in the immediate future; they believed, incorrectly, that the Tagliamento was well defended, and they also overestimated the morale of the Italian army.

On the Caporetto front the Italian 2nd Army, commanded by General Luigi Capello, had a slight superiority in men and heavy guns. The Austro-German operational plans had fallen into the hands of the Italian high command in September, and accordingly Cadorna ordered that Italian defences along the Isonzo should be reinforced in depth. Capello, who was on bad terms with his overbearing superior, ignored these instructions and, instead, planned a pre-emptive strike towards Tolmino. His army was, like the rest of Italy's armies, thoroughly exhausted, war-weary and demoralised. Many units were defeatist. Italy had made huge sacrifices for minor gains. The Italian general staff, isolated from the front-line troops, was in ignorance of these factors.

Hence, when the Austro-German assault opened on 24 October, the Italian 2nd Army was overwhelmed by the ferocity of the attack and disintegrated. The Battle of Caporetto was a disaster for Italian arms. Italian troops fled in panic, and by the evening the Austro-German forces had advanced 12 miles. On the 25th Cadorna ordered a retreat to the Tagliamento. On the 27th the Central Powers captured Udine. Cadorna did not lose his nerve. He now ordered a general retreat to the Piave, managed to extricate the Duke of Aosta's 3rd Army of 300,000 men from the lower Isonzo, and was able to reorganise a nucleus of the 2nd Army. After 1 November a measure of discipline was restored in the Italian army. Italian defences were stabilised on the Piave, which had been strengthened by Cadorna in 1916. Although the Austrians attempted to turn the Piave position by an abortive offensive from the Trentino, the line held, despite frequent Austro-German assaults. Venice and northern Italy were thereby secured from Austrian invasion. Five Anglo-French divisions were rushed to the Piave, and efforts were made by the new chief of the Italian staff, General Armando Diaz (Cadorna was dismissed on 9 November), to improve the conditions of Italian troops. Although at Caporetto Italy lost 10,000 killed, and 293,000 prisoners, together with about 400,000 deserters, the disaster for the first time in the war unified the Italian people and revived their patriotic spirit.

In 1916 the Entente collected a new ally, Rumania, who had designs on the Austro-Hungarian province of Transylvania. Rumania was persuaded to join the Entente after the initial success of Brusilov's offensive in Galicia in June 1916. It was also promised large territorial gains at Hungary's expense. However the Rumanian army of 600,000 men was poorly officered and poorly equipped, and its entry into the war on 27 August 1916 occurred just as the Russian offensive was grinding to a halt. Furthermore, like Serbia in 1915, Rumania's strategic position was precarious, since Bulgaria, to its south, was anxious to recover part of the Dobruja lost to Rumania in 1913, while Mackensen could send German troops stationed in Serbia to the Dobruja border to assist Bulgarian and Turkish forces poised for an offensive there. Nor did the Russians do much to assist Rumania.

Late in August 1916, a Rumanian army of 400,000 men advanced slowly into Transylvania, but after it had been checked by an Austro-German army of 200,000 men at Hermannstadt on 6 October, it retreated into Rumania. In the Dobruja Mackensen's forces captured Turturkai on 26 September and, later in October, Constanta on the Black Sea and Cernavoda on the Danube. By the end of October the whole of the Dobruja was in the Central Powers' hands. On 11 November Falkenhayn, commanding the Austro-German forces in Transylvania, broke through the Carpathians at the Vulcan Pass and advanced into Wallachia, towards the Arges river. Between 1 and 3 December the Rumanian army attempted an unsuccessful counter-offensive on the Arges, and then retreated (having lost 70,000 prisoners) during December to the Sareth line, in north-east Moldavia, where it was rein-

Above left: A battalion observation post in a trench in front of Vertojba, Isonzo Front August, 1917. Trench construction varied considerably on different fronts

Above: Italian troops moving up to the front line. The rough terrain on the Italian front made it difficult to keep the troops supplied with food and ammunition

forced by the Russians. Mackensen took Bucharest on 6 December. The Sareth line held, despite repeated assaults on it during December 1917, but Rumania had lost three quarters of its territory. Following the Treaty of Brest Litovsk in 1918, Rumania's position in Moldavia became untenable, and it was forced to sue for peace, losing territory to Hungary and Bulgaria, and becoming a vassal state of Germany. Rumania did not reopen hostilities against the Central Powers until a few hours before the armistice on 11 November 1918.

Rumania had hoped that its rear would be protected against a Bulgarian offensive by an Entente advance into Bulgaria from Salonika. In the event Rumania received little worthwhile assistance from the Entente. The French General Maurice Sarrail, appointed commander-in-chief of the Salonika forces in July 1916, was a radical-socialist intimate of Briand, and was loathed by Allied officers on the spot for his arrogance and bad temper. Early in September Sarrail ordered an Entente offensive against Bulgaria to assist the Rumanians, and although Franco-Serbian forces cap-

tured Monastir, British troops were forced on to the defensive in the Struma valley. This was the sum total of Entente assistance from the south to relieve the Rumanians. Indeed the Entente seemed to be more preoccupied with removing Constantine and reinstalling Venizelos as prime minister of Greece than with fighting the Bulgarians. Their relations with the king deteriorated rapidly as a result of their frequent interferences in Greek internal affairs, which ultimately threatened Greek independence. On 6 June 1917, after a series of Entente ultimata and armed incursions into Thessaly and Athens, the king was deposed and replaced by his second son, Alexander. Venizelos re-emerged as prime minister and promptly declared Greece an ally of the Entente.

The Entente remained relatively immobile on the southern flanks of Europe until the summer of 1918. Diaz had concentrated on re-equipping and reorganising his armies, and despite much Anglo-French pressure, had refused to undertake further offensive operations against Austria–Hungary. His hand was forced, however, when Arz, who was equally reluctant to expose his flagging army to a new offensive against Italy, succumbed to German prompting and embarked on a new campaign. He was persuaded by his army commanders to attempt, in June 1918, an over-ambitious three-pronged offensive, one from Asiago, the second towards Monte Grappa and the third from the Tonale Pass, near the Swiss border. Arz hoped to drive the Italians back to the Adige. Despite initial successes, these offensives were repulsed with the loss of

150,000 Austro-Hungarian troops. But the Italians failed to follow up their advantage, and the next move came from the Salonika front when, on 15 September, an Allied army of about 180,000 British, French, Italian, Serb and Greek troops, commanded by the French General Louis Franchet d'Espérey (Sarrail had been recalled in November 1917) invaded Bulgaria from Greece. The underfed and war-weary Bulgarian army of 160,000 men ceased to offer much effective resistance, despite frantic efforts to stiffen their morale by the few remaining German units on this front. Bulgaria surrendered to the Entente on 29 September, thereby exposing both Austria–Hungary and Turkey to Allied invasion, and contributing to Ludendorff's nervous collapse.

By October it was clear that the Habsburg Empire was on the point of dissolution, and on 24 October Diaz launched an attack on the Grappa front, in the region of Vittorio Veneto. Although the Austrians put up a spirited resistance, the British and Italians broke through and seized the Austrian headquarters at Vittorio Veneto on the 27th. The morale of the Austro-Hungarian army snapped, and by the 30th it was in headlong retreat, which soon became a rout. Italy entered the Trentino, recaptured Udine and seized Trieste, together with 500,000 Austro-Hungarian prisoners. Austria–Hungary capitulated on 3 November.

In a matter of weeks the Entente armies had accomplished what they had failed to do after almost four and a half years of appalling bloodshed and frustration on the southern front.

Victory on the Western Front

Worn-out, the Germans made their final pushes in 1918. But the Allies, reinforced by the Americans, held out and then at last launched their own offensives and ultimately secured costly victory.

In 1918 the initiative of the war passed to Germany for the last time. The collapse of Russia meant, said Ludendorff, that 'numerically we had never been so strong in comparison with our enemies'. So the German army would be able to resume the leading role which it had abandoned in 1917: the army, the nation and all its allies needed a quick victory, and there was no doubt in the minds of the German leaders that 'this was only possible on the Western Front.' Troop movements from East to West began in November 1917; by the end of December there were 171 German divisions on the Western Front; by 22 March 1918 British Intelligence had identified 190; by May there were over 200; at the armistice, even with the year's appalling losses, nearly 3½ million men.

The Allies were well aware of the threat which hung over them; unfortunately, political shadows still darkened their scene. The outstanding need of 1917 had been to restore a measure of co-ordinated control to the conduct of the war. Two changes of government in France, the dismissals of two commanders-in-chief, and the more or less open feud between the British prime minister and his responsible military advisers had prevented this. To end this frustration, Britain, France and Italy (America immediately joining them) set up a Supreme War Council consisting of political and military representatives of each power, with its headquarters at Versailles, 'to watch over the general conduct of the war'. Lloyd George was a prime mover in this, looking on the Supreme War Council as an opportunity of taking a strategic 'second opinion'. No other country saw it this way; every military representative except the British was the mouthpiece of the general staff responsible for conducting his nation's war. The result was that although Britain was playing the decisive role on the Western Front (in addition to a large role on other fronts and predominance at sea) she continued to speak with a weak and divided tongue.

The Supreme War Council proved unable either to foresee correctly or to counter the impending German effort. These duties therefore still had to be performed by the Commanders-in-Chief, General Pétain and Field-Marshal Haig. The French army, much rested and restored after its tribulations in 1917, was able to build a powerful reserve, which the steady inflow of Americans would increase. The British, on the other hand, were seriously weakened by the government's failure to resolve its manpower problems and by its distrust of the high command. The amazing spectacle was seen of the British army actually disbanding 141 infantry battalions (the equivalent

British Mark V Female tank of the 4th Battalion passing through Meaulte after it had been captured by the 5th Royal Berkshire Regiment during the Battle of Amiens on 22 August 1918

nearly 12 divisions) on the Western Front in the first three months of 1918. What made this the more astounding was the growing evidence that the German attack, when it came, would be against the British, although a clever deception plan persuaded Pétain that it would be against the French in Champagne.

The ever-increasing brutality of an artillery war came to a climax in Picardy on 21 March; 6,473 German guns, backed by 3,532 trench mortars of all calibres, subjected the fronts of the British 5th and 3rd Armies to a hurricane bombardment. Five hours later the German infantry came forward through a dense mist against the British positions, advance guards of a huge mass of 62 divisions, a battering ram by which Germany hoped to break through at last and end the war. Their first-day performance suggested that they had every chance of doing so. For the British 5th

Army this was a disaster of the first magnitude: casualties in all forward units were tragically high, and no less than 382 guns were lost. The army began a retreat which only the arrival of promised French support could bring to an end; the French, however, showed no sign of coming. Fortunately the British 3rd Army, to the north, which had been less heavily attacked, was able to hold on to vital positions.

Because of the drama of the great German bombardment; because whole units vanished in the first enemy onslaught; because nothing remotely like this had happened to the British army on the Western Front during the whole war, a myth of German brilliance has often surrounded the story of the 'March Offensive'. Quite to the contrary, however, the Germans made serious mistakes which soon robbed them of the success they needed. The worst was the absence of strategic direction: 'I forbid myself to use

the word *strategy*,' said Ludendorff. 'We chop a hole. The rest follows.' The result was that his army found itself attacking in divergent directions, nowhere strong enough for the task in hand. Secondly, for an offensive meant to be decisive, he provided no arm of exploitation: only nine tanks (five of them captured British vehicles), no armoured car units, no motorised machine-gunners, no cavalry. Pursuit of the British could therefore proceed only at an infantry-man's pace. And the best of the German infantry, creamed off into 'Storm Troop' units, quickly became casualties whose loss proved irremediable.

In fact the German success lay not in the amount of ground won, nor in the number of prisoners taken (70,000 British alone), but in the impact produced upon the mind of General Pétain. As the Allies withdrew, a potentially fatal gap threatened to develop between the British and French. Pétain

The Paris gun

In 1916, the Germans began the design of a long-range gun to bombard Paris, intended to have a range of 60 miles (96km). Development work was carried out by the Krupp Company and the German Navy. The design was almost complete when Ludendorf required that its range be increased to 74 miles (119km). The Paris Gun (it was also known variously as the Kaiser Wilhelm Geschutz, Long Max and Big Bertha) consisted of a 15'' (38cm) barrel bored out, and with an 8.3'' barrel, inserted and projecting beyond it, the whole unit reinforced with a barrel sleeve, onto which was screwed a smooth tube. The total length of the barrel was 112' (34m) and it weighed almost 140 tons. Special ammunition was developed for the gun and each round was numbered, the reason for this being that each time the gun fired the barrel expanded slightly bigger and therefore each round was slightly bigger than the last. The barrel only had a life of 60-70 firings. The weapon was transported by rail to a specially prepared firing position in a forest near Crepy-en-Laonnois, near Laon, late in 1917. The Paris gun fired for the first time on the morning of March 23rd 1918 and the shells took three minutes to arrive in Paris, and for several hours the Parisians thought they were under air attack. On the first day a total of 22 shells killed 22 people and injured 29. The shelling continued sporadically until May 1st, 1918 and began again from a new position on 27th May. The last of 367 shells was fired on August 18th, 1918, having killed 256 and injured 620 people. No trace of the Paris gun was found after Germany surrendered; even today the gun remains something of a mystery and full and accurate data on the weapon is still non-existant.

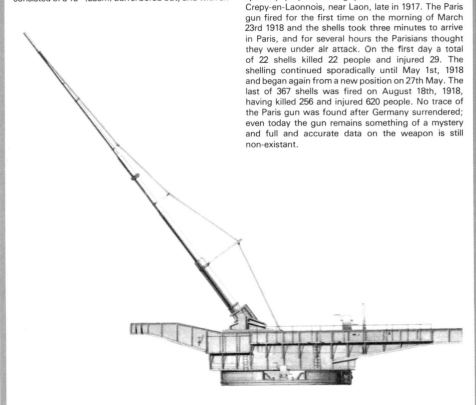

75 mm QF anti-aircraft gun

When aircraft first appeared on the battlefield in numbers during World War I, there was a mad scramble to find some sort of gun to shoot it down. The French first fitted their famous 75mm field gun on the rear of a standard Army truck, enabling it to be deployed quickly wherever it was required. Some of these were supplied to the British in 1915. The British requested additional weapons of this type but the French could not meet their own requirements let alone give the British more. They did, however, supply the British with a number of barrels and recoil systems. The Coventry Ordnance Works then quickly developed a mounting for the French 75mm gun and this was mounted on the rear of a De Dion lorry. Jacks were provided to stabilize the gun as it was being fired. The gun could be traversed 120° left and 120° right, elevation limits being from 0° to +70° The breech mechanism was of the Nordenfelt eccentric screw type with a percussion firing mechanism. The recoil system was of the hydro-pneumatic (Schneider) constant recoil type. These weapons remained in service with the British Army until 1920. The drawing shows the French 75mm Gun on a De Dion truck.

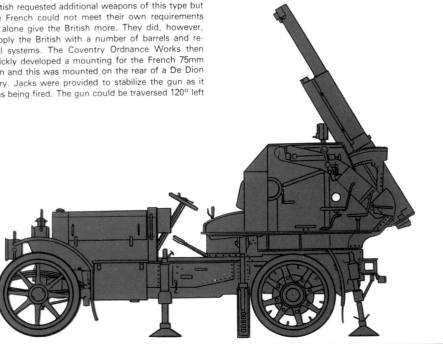

Above: US Government painting depicting American troops of the 30th and 38th Regiments reversing an attack from the Germans in three directions during July, 1918, near Meze, France, on the road to Paris.

admitted to Haig that in this event he would be more concerned to cover Paris than to maintain contact with his allies. Haig at once perceived that the only way to avoid defeat in detail was the appointment of what the next war would call a Supreme Allied Commander to co-ordinate the whole front. On 26 March General Ferdinand Foch was given this task.

By now, however, the impetus of the great German attack had died out. 'Friend and foe, said a British army commander, 'are, it seems, dead beat and seem to stagger up against each other.' French reserves were arriving fast. On 5 April Ludendorff broke off the first offensive, in Picardy, and

Above left: British Whippet light tanks of the 3rd Battalion at Maillet Mailly, France on March 20, 1918, being accompanied by infantry of the New Zealand Division

Above: Negro troops of the American 369th Infantry, 93rd Division, man a trench at Maffrecourt in May, 1918. The arrival of large numbers of American troops boosted the Allies

Left: British tanks carrying "Cribs" which were dropped into the trenches, enabling them to cross, and burst through the Hindenburg line in 1918

on 9 April he opened a new one, the second offensive, in Flanders (the Battle of the Lys) where he had always believed the decisive point to be. Once more the Germans achieved an opening success, this time against a weak Portuguese division in the front line. But once more the impetus of the attack soon died away. The last significant German progress was made on 11 April, when Haig issued his famous Order of the Day: '. . . There is no other course open to us but to fight it out. Every position must be held to the last man. There must be no retirement. With our backs to the wall and believing in the justice of our cause each one must fight on to the end. . .'

The battle continued until the end of April, but the Germans had really shot their bolt in the first three days. Their two

offensives against the British had cost them 348,300 casualties in 41 days; Allied casualties were 351,793. It was the British army which had borne the brunt; in these six weeks it had engaged 109 German divisions and lost 239,793 officers and men. The severity of of this loss may be judged by comparison with 244,897 casualties in the 15 weeks of the 3rd Battle of Ypres (Passchendaele). The German failure was complete: they had failed to knock out the British, failed to divide them from the French, and failed to win even the consolation prize of an important rail centre such as Amiens of Hazebrouck. But they still had strength enough for another try.

Ludendroff remained convinced that Flanders, where the British front ran dangerously close to the sea, was the decisive sector. He reasoned that their survival in April was due to French aid; if he could draw the French away, and damage them severely, they would not come to the help of the British again, and he might yet win Germany's victory. Accordingly, in May, he began a series of attacks on the French along the Aisne. On 27 May, for the third (and last) time, with the aid of another shattering bombardment by over 4,000 guns, the Germans won a brilliant success against the French in the third, Aisne, offensive, in the process capturing the whole of the famous Chemin des Dames ridge. By 3 June they had reached the Marne – an advance of 30 miles, creating, as in 1914, a direct threat to Paris. But the brilliance was all on the surface; yet again the Germans had gained no strategic object – indeed, their new

position was a dangerously narrow salient. To broaden and secure it, they launched a new attack on 9 June, the fourth or Noyon–Montdidier offensive; this time the opening success, though considerable, was not spectacular, and this time, too, French and American counterattacks followed immediately. By 14 June the battle was over, and there was a pause for breath on the Western Front.

During all this time Ludendorff never lost sight of his intended offensive in Flanders, and Haig never lost sight of its possible imminence. For Foch, the problem was to dispose reserves correctly between the front actually being attacked and the front threatened. Fortunately, relations between Foch and Haig were generally good; there were sharp disputes between them, but not many, and both were firmly agreed on plans for counterattacking as soon as possible. With American forces now rapidly building up in France (250,000 men came over in June, the same in July) it was clear that the sands were running out for Germany.

Ludendorff's final plan was to launch one last massive attack against the French around Reims, then turn on the British in Flanders for the knock-out blow. Fifty-two divisions struck east and west of Reims on 15 July. The attack east of Reims fell on empty positions and wasted itself in the air; to the west the Germans were successful enough to give Pétain a bad scare, but Foch was unmoved. As the German heavy artillery was making its way north, Ludendorff and his commanders sat down in conference at Mons to plan the details of the Flanders offensive. But its fate was already sealed: on 18 July Foch struck back on the Marne, and Germany lost her initiative once and for all.

The 2nd Battle of the Marne, like the 1st, was a decisive occasion of the war. French, Americans, British and Italians played their part in the fighting, which continued until 6 August. By that time the great German salient between the Marne and the Aisne had been eliminated; the Allies had taken over 29,000 prisoners, 793 guns and 3,723 machine-guns. But as so often, the real decision lay not in captures of ground or prisoners, but in the minds of the opposing generals.' Field-Marshal von Hindenburg wrote: 'We could have no illusion about the far-reaching effect of this battle and our retreat. . . . How many hopes, cherished during the last few months, had probably collapsed at one blow! How many calculations had been scattered to the winds.' And this was only the beginning.

No sooner had the thunder of battle died down along the Aisne than it was heard again on the Somme. A remarkable transformation had now taken place in the British armies: all the equipment lost in the great German offensives had been replaced, with more besides; three months' rest and some successful minor operations had fully restored morale; although still understrength, 59 out of 61 divisions were once more ready for battle, in the form of the Battle of Amiens. It started on 8 August, and was fought by the British 4th Army and the French 1st Army (temporarily under Haig's command). For this battle the British alone concentrated over 2,000 guns, more

A7V tank

Crew: 18 (commander, driver, gunner, loader, two engineers and twelve machine gunners). **Weight:** 73,920lb (33,530kg). **Length:** 26' 3'' (8m). **Width:** 10' (3.08m). **Height:** 10' 10'' (3.302m). **Road speed:** 8mph (12.85kmh). **Range:** 25 miles (40km). **Engines:** Two Daimler-Benz four cylinder water cooled petrol engines developing 100 HP at 900rpm. **Vertical obstacle:** 1' 7'' (.482m). **Trench:** 7' 6'' (2.286m). **Armour:** 15 to 30mm.

When British tanks appeared in 1916 the Germans took a much greater interest in tanks than they had hitherto and formed a A7V committee (Allgemeineine Kriegsdepartment 7, Abteilung Verkehrswesen or General War Department 7, Traffic Section). The committee looked at a number of possible designs and eventually ordered the first German tank, the A7V, the prototype of which was completed in December 1916. First production models were completed in May 1917. Although 100 A7Vs were ordered, only 20 or so were completed by the end of the war. In September 1917, the German Army formed the first eight tank units (Abteilungen) but only three of them were equipped with A7Vs, the rest using captured material.

The German's first used their tanks in March 1918 at St. Quentin and on April 24th, 1918, the first tank v tank action took place at Villers-Bretonneaux, when a British Mark IV encountered and knocked out a German A7V. The Germans used their tanks again until the end of the war but without much success. The A7V was armed with a 57mm gun (captured from the Russians) in the front of the hull, with two machine guns in each side and rear of the hull. Total ammunition supply carried was 250/500 rounds of 57mm and 32,000 rounds of machine gun ammunition.

Above left: American troops moving forward into action at Badouviller, France, in March, 1918. Most American troops were supplied with British or French equipment

Left: A German A7V tank attacking British positions at Villers-Bretonneux on April 24, 1918. This was the first German tank attack and took the British by complete surprise

than 500 tanks and nearly 800 aircraft. Aided (like the Germans on 21 March) by a dense mist, their attack came as a complete surprise; over 15,000 prisoners and 400 guns were captured, and the German official account of the battle says: 'As the sun set on the 8th August on the battlefield the greatest defeat which the German Army had suffered since the beginning of the war was an accomplished fact.' And this, too, was only a beginning.

Two big victories already gained, and a number of minor successes, determined Foch (now a Marshal of France) to give the enemy no respite. Yet it was a clear fact that the French army was once again showing signs of weariness after its exertions and losses in all the fighting since March, while the Americans, insisting on forming separate armies of their own, would not be ready to play a major part for some time. The onus of attacking thus fell, as in 1916 and 1917, on the British – but with this difference, that whereas in the earlier years they had faced a German army of high quality, now attrition and offensive failure had had their effect. The German infantry, in Luden-dorff's words, 'approximated more nearly in character to a militia, and discipline declined'. At Amiens, in four days, the Allies took 30,000 prisoners. In the next blow, delivered by the British 3rd and 4th Armies (the Battles of Albert and Bapaume) on 21 August, 34,000 prisoners were taken in a fortnight. Scenting real victory at last, Haig told his army commanders: 'Risks which a month ago would have been criminal to incur, ought now to be incurred as a duty.'

The next two months saw one of the most remarkable passages of British military history. In the words of Marshal Foch: 'Never at any time in history has the British Army achieved greater results in attack than in this unbroken offensive.' While the Battle of Bapaume was still being fought, the 1st Army joined in further north, taking 16,000 prisoners. Then, while the British closed up to the Hindenburg Line, the Americans struck their first blow on 12 September at St Mihiel. Here they caught the Germans in the act of withdrawing from a large salient, and harried them to the tune of 15,000 prisoners and 450 guns in 36 hours.

The fighting in the outlying defences of the Hindenburg Line began on the same day, and lasted for a week (Battles of Havrincourt and Epéhy); the British 4th and 3rd Armies took another 12,000 prisoners. The signs of a German break-up were by now evident, although German machine-gunners and artillery constantly put up a stout defence. There would be no walk-over. Indeed, as the Allies approached the main Hindenburg positions, there was understandable trepidation. Haig was warned that his government would look severely on heavy losses incurred in attack-ing this heavily-fortified line; undeterred, he calmly shouldered the responsibility. The result was the climactic triumph of the war.

The operations which now ensued be-tween 26 September and 14 October constituted the only fully integrated Allied offensive of the year, but it was enough. It began in the Argonne with a French/American attack, successful but costly, especially to the inexperienced Americans. On the 27th the British 3rd and 1st Armies joined in; on the 28th it was the turn of the Flanders Group (the Belgians, French 6th Army and British 2nd Army). In one day all the ground of Ypres so bitterly disputed for three months in 1917 was captured. And then came the attack of the British 4th Army on the Hindenburg Line itself, with the French 1st Army in support on the right. Success was complete, and the German high command recognised a crush-ing defeat. Hindenburg told a Council of War that 'the situation demanded an imme-diate armistice in order to save a catas-trophe'; on 1 October his representative told the *Reichstag* 'the war is lost', and he demanded that an immediate appeal should be made to the Allied governments for an armistice.

Victory caught the Allied statesmen as unprepared for peace as they had been for war. Another six weeks had yet to pass before the guns fell silent: six weeks during which all Germany's allies dropped away, but the German army itself continued a brave, stubborn resistance which slowed down but could not halt the Allied advance. The cost of this was always high; in the month of October alone the British army lost 5,438 officers and 115,608 other ranks. But mile by mile, battle by battle, the German army was being ground down. By 11 November, when the armistice at last came, the Germans had lost during the period of the Allied offensives beginning on 18 July:

	Prisoners	Guns
To the British	188,700	2,840
To the French	139,000	1,880
To the Americans	43,200	1,421
To the Belgians	14,500	474
	385,400	6,615

No army could stand a rate of loss like that.

So the war ended as it had begun. By committing their main forces to the Western Front in 1914, the Germans had made it the decisive theatre, and it was here that they met final defeat. In the process this front acquired a legendary notoriety. Mur-derous from the first, increasingly squalid as each year went by, thanks to medical science warfare on the Western Front nevertheless proved to be curiously 'healthy': just over 9.2 percent of deaths were the result of sickness or accidental injury, compared with nearly 66 percent in South Africa (1899–1902), some 75 percent in the Crimea (1853–56), and more than 61 percent in Mesopotamia (1915–18). In all other respects, however, the experi-ence of the Western Front between 1914 and 1918 was more damaging to the human body and mind than anything yet experi-enced, and in its duration even surpassed the bloodiness and terror of the Eastern Front in World War II.

Part 2: 1918 to 1939
Wars between wars

Between the two great world wars, other wars produced important political and military consequences in Russia, Ethiopia, Spain and China, and played their part in preparing for World War II.

No one now would call World War I 'a war to end wars'. Even as the peace-makers got together at Versailles a civil war was under way in Russia. The Versailles treaty contained within itself the seeds of the next world war, and the 20 years which separate the two were a very uneasy peace indeed, broken by numerous small conflicts. There were clashes between old enemies such as Greece and Turkey in the Greeco–Turkish War of 1920–22, border clashes such as the Gran Chaco War between Bolivia and Paraguay from 1932 to 1935 and colonial wars such as those fought by the British on the North-West Frontier of India and in Mesopotamia. Among all these wars four episodes stand out because of their par-

ticular political or military significance. They are the Russian Civil War and Russo–Polish War (1917–22); the Italo–Ethiopian War (1935–36); the Spanish Civil War (1936–39); and the first part of the Chinese Revolution (1928–37) and the Sino–Japanese War which followed it.

In 1917 Russia suffered two revolutions. In March (February in the old Russian calendar) Tsar Nicholas II abdicated. In November (October old style) the Provisional Government was overthrown by the Bolsheviks under Vladimir Lenin. The Bolsheviks had won power by promising peace and a redistribution of land, but they faced enemies on every side. In the west Germany was advancing into the Ukraine and everywhere else anti-Bolshevik forces were growing. The anti-revolutionary 'White' armies agreed only on the need to destroy the Bolsheviks, but they were supported by the Western Allies who wanted to establish a Russian government which would continue the war against Germany. During the winter of 1917–18 there were numerous clashes between Red volunteers and their enemies, but only the Germans

posed an immediate threat to the Bolshevik government. Having no answer to an organised army the Bolsheviks were forced to agree to the humiliating Treaty of Brest–Litovsk in March 1918, by which Germany occupied the Ukraine. But now the Bolsheviks were able to concentrate on the civil war which was now beginning.

On April 22 1918 the Red Army of Workers and Peasants was established and recruited by conscription. Numbers were not a problem, but morale was. Most peasants did not wish to go on fighting and would thus desert at the first opportunity. Fortunately the Bolsheviks had Leon Trotsky, a military organiser of genius, as their Commissar for War. He introduced 'Red Cells' into each unit. These were small groups of communist enthusiasts who were to provide moral and political leadership for the rest of the army and were concentrated wherever the situation was most serious. Many communist theorists would have liked to believe that enthusiasm could take the place of military training and discipline, but Trotsky insisted on incorporating former tsarist officers and NCOs into the army as

'military specialists'. To ensure their loyalty to the new regime, these officers were paired with communist 'commissars' under a system of 'dual command'.

Another problem facing Trotsky was shortage of equipment. By the end of 1918 the Red Army's manpower strength was about 600,000 but only 100,000 were front-line troops. Most of the rest were not even armed. Even in 1920, when there were $5\frac{1}{2}$ million men in the army, probably not more than 500,000 were armed. One consequence was that casualties counted for little in the Red Army: they could easily be replaced. The main Red advantage, however, was their central position in European Russia, where communications were comparatively easy. Trotsky made good use of this,

Japanese troops shout "Banzai" from the walls of the City of Nanking after they had captured it during the Sino-Japanese War.

Above: Armed force as an ingredient for the seizure of power. A pro-Bolshevik automobile and machine gun detachment patrolling the streets of Moscow during the 1917 uprising

Left: Japanese NCOs with drawn swords search the burning and wrecked buildings of Nanking during the Sino-Japanese War

switching reinforcements by rail to the most threatened front.

The White armies were originally composed mainly of ex-tsarist officers and Cossacks. As the war progressed the Whites had difficulty in recruiting, because their cause was associated with the old regime. Although they received support from Britain, America, France, Italy, Japan and the Czech Legion it seems doubtful that their force ever exceeded 300,000. Despite this the Whites made several gains during 1918 and seemed well placed for the 1919 campaign. However, they had no controlling brain to match Trotsky's. They adopted Admiral Aleksandr Kolchak as their supremo, but his plan for 1919 merely envisaged a general advance on Moscow and Petrograd. In the south Generals Anton Denikin and Piotr Wrangel were to advance north from the Caucasus and Crimea; in the east Kolchak would move out of the Urals and across the Volga. In the north British forces had landed in Archangel and Murmansk, and an attack on Petrograd was being prepared in Estonia. Polish forces were massing on the western border. As the circle tightened these forces might be able to support each other, but in the early stages of the campaign a mobile and flexible enemy had a chance to defeat them individually.

This was exactly what happened. Denikin had some early success, but not on the lower Volga, so he was unable to help Kolchak when Trotsky concentrated against him. In April the Reds began a series of attacks under Mikhail Frunze and Mikhail Tukhachevsky which broke through the White lines and captured the passes through the Ural mountains. In July the Red Army began its long campaign to clear the Trans-Siberian railway of Kolchak's troops and their Japanese allies; the campaign lasted until 1922.

Meanwhile Denikin had reached Orel, within 200 miles of Moscow. His success was largely due to his cavalry, but he had difficulty in consolidating their advance. Trotsky's solution was to organise his own mobile force, later the 1st Cavalry Army, under a former sergeant-major Semyon Budenny. Using the horse for mobility and the machine-gun for firepower, Budenny checked the White cavalry at Voronezh and a pincer attack on Orel in November destroyed Denikin's vanguard. His overstretched forces gave way and by January 1920 were split in two by the capture of Rostov. Denikin himself was forced into the Caucasus, from where part of his army were evacuated in March, leaving behind 100,000 prisoners.

1919 had also seen the failure of the attempts on Petrograd, and by 1920 most of the Whites' allies had lost interest in intervention in Russia. However a new enemy to the Reds appeared. Poland had only made a limited effort in 1919 but now decided on a determined effort to regain her old lands from Russia. Six armies, about 370,000 strong, trained and equipped by the French, were assembled for the invasion. The Pripet Marshes, in front of their centre, forced the Poles to divide in two and in the north they were met by a spoiling attack in May from Tukhachevsky. He had been too eager and a counterattack drove him back across the Russian border.

After these early checks the tide swung in Russia's favour. Budenny broke through in the south and Tukhachevsky launched a new attack which drove the Poles back and threatened Warsaw itself. It was now the Russian army which was split by the Pripet Marshes and Tukhachevsky was quarrelling with the southern commander, A. I. Egorov, and his commissar, Joseph Stalin. The nominal commander-in-chief, S. S. Kamenev allowed Tukhachevsky to plan a flanking attack on Warsaw from the north without ensuring that Egorov moved forces to cover Tukhachevsky's weakened southern flank. As a result a gap developed between the two Russian fronts, which was discovered by the Poles. A sudden attack cut off Tukhachevsky's southern army and another attack from Warsaw thrust his northern armies into East Prussia, where they were disarmed. Tukhachevsky's army fell to pieces and the Russians were only too willing to agree to the Poles' demands at the Treaty of Riga in October 1920.

While this was going on the west, the news was almost as bad in the south. General Wrangel broke out of the Crimea, but his resources were now limited and he was checked before he reached Rostov. Once the Polish war was over, reinforcements, including Budenny's much travelled army, were rushed south and Wrangel was forced back into the Crimea, where his forces were finally defeated.

In many ways the Russian Civil War was the most significant of the 'wars between the wars'. It established a communist government in Russia and so raised the Bolshevik spectre which helped the Fascists in their rise to power. It also moulded the Russian army in ways which are still apparent. The 'political officer' and the Party cell are still vital parts of every Russian unit. In part the roots of the army purges of 1937 lay in the quarrels between Stalin and Trotsky and Tukhachevsky. Militarily the importance of the Civil War lies in the fact that it was a mobile war and this experience coloured the approach of Russian generals towards armoured mobile warfare, just as their western counterparts were affected by four years of trench warfare.

During the 1920s and 1930s the League of Nations did have some success in settling international disputes. However, these were almost all between minor powers and after 1935 it rapidly became obvious that the League had little influence in quarrels involving a major power. The first of these wars was the Italo–Ethiopian War.

The war was begun by Mussolini as an act of aggressive colonialism, and justified as an attempt to bring the benefits of European civilisation to a barbarous and backward nation. The Italians had tried this once before, in 1896, but at Adowa they had suffered one of the most overwhelming catastrophes ever inflicted on a European army by non-Europeans.

In the two Italian colonies which bordered Ethiopia, Eritrea in the north and Italian Somaliland in the east, base facilities were prepared during 1934 and 1935 for a campaign which might last three years. From the depots roads were built to the borders where the troops were concentrated. The Italian commander-in-chief, General de Bono, concentrated his main forces in Eritrea, where supply was easier. There were basically three types of troops under his command, poor regular army units, inefficient 'Blackshirt' fascist militia formations formations and adequate regular colonial troops, called *Askaris* in Eritrea and *Dubats*

in Somaliland.

The Ethiopian army could not hope to match this technical superiority; its only assets were numbers and courage. The best trained and equipped part was the Emperor's bodyguard of about 4,000 armed with modern weapons. There was a 'standing army' of 100,000 with more or less obsolete rifles, and after mobilisation in October 1935 a militia of about 300,000 equipped mostly with museum pieces was available. Finally about 200,000 spearmen could be raised. A number of old artillery pieces completed the army's equipment. There were no anti-tank or anti-aircraft guns, very little mechanised transport and no air force to speak of. In organisation this was a feudal army commanded by rival 'Rases' who could not be relied on to support each other and had no formal military training.

De Bono's advance began in October 1935 with three columns moving from Eritrea and one under Rodolfo Graziani from Somaliland. There was little opposition and Adowa was captured without mishap. Mussolini ordered a halt while the League of Nations discussed an Ethiopian plea for help. Although the League took no effective action, Mussolini decided that the war must be finished before any other power could make up its mind to intervene. He therefore replaced de Bono with the more forceful General Pietro Badoglio. At the same time Ethiopian mobilisation was completed, but for his part the Emperor wanted to avoid a major battle and fight a guerrilla war. For both sides the opening of the rainy season at

the end of May was a key date, for it would delay the Italian advance and might provide the time the Emperor needed.

Unfortunately Haile Selassie could not restrain his chiefs, who insisted on advancing to meet the enemy, confident of another Adowa. Badoglio hurried his troops forward. They were not trained in mountain warfare, so instead of the conventional, and slow, process of clearing the heights before moving up the valleys, the Italians used aircraft to spray mustard gas ahead of their march and on the flanks. The Ethiopians had no defence against this weapon and suffered heavy civilian as well as military casualties.

The Ethiopian chiefs found it impossible to co-operate and Badoglio was able to exploit the superior mobility of his lorry-borne infantry and bare-foot Askaris. Within a month the three major Ethiopian groupings had been outflanked, encircled and annihilated.

Haile Selassie assembled a force of 30,000 men, including his bodyguard, but mostly very irregular levies. Badoglio watched this concentration and waited for the attack which came at Mai Ceu at the end of March 1936. Frontal attacks, however brave, made no impression on the entrenched Italians. The next day the Ethiopian retreat dissolved into another rout and the Emperor's prestige suffered an irreparable blow. Badoglio now decided to risk a 400-mile dash to Addis Ababa, led by a motorised column. The capital fell on 5 May and on 9 May Graziani's troops joined Badoglio's. The formal part of the campaign was over.

Few military lessons emerged from the war. It showed that the technological gap between European armies and their less well equipped rivals was too great to be crossed in conventional warfare. It also demonstrated that tanks could be used in mountainous areas. Otherwise the war revealed the weakness of the League of Nations, which boded ill for the future peace of the world.

The Civil War in Spain began in July 1936 with an attempt by a large proportion of the army's officers to overthrow the Republican government, which they believed to be too weak to withstand growing left-wing pressure from communists and anarchists. The plot misfired, but the government was too slow in reacting to prevent large areas of Spain falling into rebel hands. The Republican government kept the capital, Madrid, and most of the centre and east of the country. In the north Catalonia and a narrow strip along the coast remained loyal. The rebels, or Nationalists, had occupied most of the north and a small area around Cadiz and Seville in the south. Most im-

Japanese type 92 light tank

Crew: 2. **Weight:** 8595lb (3,900kg). **Length:** 11ft 2in (3.402m). **Width:** 5ft 4in (1.625m). **Height:** 5ft 6in (1.676m). **Speed:** 24.84mph (40kmh). **Range:** 124 miles (200km). **Trench:** 4ft 7in (1.397m). **Fording:** 2ft (.609m). **Engine:** One four-cylinder petrol engine developing 35hp at 2500rpm.

The Type 92 (it would appear from recent reports that this designation is incorrect and it should in fact be called the Type 94) was developed in the early 1930's and is based on the British Carden-Loyd carrier, some of which the Japanese purchased. It saw combat in China and was also used in the Malayan campaign, it was however withdrawn from service well before the end of the war. Although called a light tank it was in fact designed to tow ammunition trailers in the battle area, but it was more often used for the reconnaissance role. There were two basic models of the Type 92 and later in the war the second model had its 6.5mm machine gun replaced by a 7.7mm machine gun.

Carroveloce CV 33 (or L 3-33)

Crew: 2 (commander/gunner, driver). **Weight:** 7571lb (3,435kg). **Length:** 10' 4¾'' (3.16m). **Width:** 4' (1.4m). **Height:** 4' 2¾'' (1.28m). **Road speed:** 26mph (42kmh). **Range road:** 62 miles (125km). **Engine:** SPA CV 3, four cylinder, water cooled petrol developing 43 BHP at 2400rpm. **Vertical obstacle:** 2' 2'' (.65m). **Trench:** 4' 10'' (1.45m). **Armour:** 6 to 13,5mm.

In 1929, the Italians purchased a British Carden-Loyd Mk.VI and at the same time obtained a licence to manufacture the vehicle. The first was the CV 29 and 25 were built, to be followed by the CV3. The latter served as the prototype for the CV 33, or Carro Veloce 33. There were two basic models of this, the series I and II. The series Is were armed with a single 6.5mm machine gun and series II with twin 8mm machine guns. Eventually, all examples were brought up to series II standard. In 1936 the CV 33 was replaced in production by the CV 35 (or L 3/35), which was a development of the earlier vehicle. The hull of the CV 33 was of rivetted construction with the

driver on the right and the commander/gunner on the left. The machine guns had an elevation of + 15° and a depression of − 12°, traverse being 24°. There were many variants of this vehicle including a wireless tank, flamethrower, bridgelayer and recovery tank.

The CV 33 was used by the Italians in Ethiopia as well as the Spanish civil war and it also took part in the early battles of World War II. By that time however, it was outclassed and most were soon destroyed in combat.

portant of all, the army in Spanish Morocco declared for the Nationalists. The 'Army of Africa' was the best-trained part of Spain's forces and under command of General Francisco Franco, was ferried across the Straits of Gibraltar with German and Italian aid.

The Nationalists originally believed that they could capture Madrid quickly and that Republican resistance would then soon collapse. Four columns were advancing on the capital, and according to General Emilio Mola, Nationalist commander in the north, there was a 'fifth column' of Nationalist sympathisers within the city. Also on the Nationalist side were Italian and German 'volunteers', tanks and aircraft. But Republican resistance was much stronger than expected and in the nick of time they were joined by Russian tanks and aircraft and the first of the 'International Brigades' which the communists had organised.

The Battle for Madrid developed into a stalemate although Franco gained some ground. At Guadalajara in March 1937 the defeat of a Nationalist force which included an Italian mechanised column was used by observers as an argument against mechanised forces in general. However, the Italian force consisted mostly of motorised infantry with only a battalion of tanks in support. Heavy rain soon bogged down the tanks and grounded the Italian air support.

Setbacks such as this caused Franco to change his strategy and concentrate his main efforts in the north. In the fighting that followed the Nationalists gradually won the upper hand, beating off all the Republican counterattacks.

With this advantage in equipment Franco was able in May 1938 to split the Republican-held area in two. In December he launched a drive on Catalonia, which was subdued by February 1939. Only Madrid and thè centre of Spain now remained in Republican hands and in March fighting broke out between the communists and the other parties on the Republican side. Franco's strength was now overwhelming. Madrid was surrounded and surrendered on 28 March. By April only some isolated and ineffectual guerrillas continued the Republican struggle.

Franco's victory was not entirely the result of foreign aid. He gave greater unity and more efficient leadership to the Nationalists than was ever achieved among the variety of parties supporting the Republic. Nor were the Nationalists always better equipped. The Russian T-26B tank, with a 45-mm gun, was greatly superior to the German PzKpfw I and the Italian L3, both of which were thinly armoured and armed only with machine-guns. The Nationalists' main advantage was in the air: Germany's 'Condor Legion' had the Bf109, which was then the best fighter flying, and with the Ju 87 'Stuka' developed the techniques of air support which made possible the armoured 'Blitzkriegs' of 1939–41.

The theme of communist versus nationalist was also played out in China throughout the 1930s. In the 19th century China had been a country too weak to govern or protect itself and so had fallen a prey to exploitation by the European powers, America and Japan. However, by the early 20th century a new national spirit was emerging in China, typified by the Kuomintang movement. By the middle of the 1920s the Kuomintang was even receiving support from Moscow and had become the dominating force in Chinese life. But the Kuomintang leader, Chiang Kai-shek, remained suspicious of the Chinese communists working within the Kuomintang and in 1927 began a purge which almost eliminated them. Those who survived lost patience with their orders from Moscow and decided that the 'Chinese revolution' must come from within.

The basic disagreement between Russian and Chinese communists was that the Russians believed that a revolution must start among the industrial workers in the cities. It was a young Chinese party leader, Mao Tse-tung, who saw that the dominant element among the Chinese workers were the peasants and that the revolution must start in the countryside. Breaking with Russian ideas, the Chinese Communist Party after 1928 began to organise the peasants and established a government or 'Soviet' in the province of Kiangsi, an area of about 50 million inhabitants.

Chiang Kai-shek reacted in 1930 with the first of a series of 'bandit extermination drives'. Despite disadvantages of discipline and morale, but not of weapons, Chiang Kai-shek's five 'extermination drives' wore down the Kiangsi 'Soviet'. The Kuomintang army surrounded their enemies with lines of barbed-wire and blockhouses, which limited the communist army's mobility and introduced a strict blockade which restricted the supplies reaching the communists. Eventually it became clear that the communist cause in Kiangsi was doomed and decision was

taken to break out. Some 90,000 men began the 'Long March' in October 1934, but only 20,000 remained when the army reached the mountainous north-western province of Shensi a year later. Even these sacrifices only bought a temporary respite and one cannot be sure that the communists would have survived if it had not been for the Japanese attack on China in July 1937.

Mao seized his opportunity and announced his willingness to fight under Chiang against the foreign invader. During the war that followed the balance between Kuomintang and communists was reversed and when the civil war broke out again, at the end of World War II, the advantages were almost all with the communists.

In 1937 it was the Kuomintang which took the brunt of the early fighting against the Japanese; it achieved some successes, but was unable to prevent the Japanese from occupying large areas of northern China. By 1939 both sides were exhausted and a period of uneasy quiet followed. Chiang was confident that China was too big to be conquered quickly and he hoped for intervention from outside, especially from the United States. Mao, on the other hand, saw the war against Japan as an opportunity for the communists to show themselves as a national party and to consolidate their hold on large areas of the country.

By now Mao's doctrines of guerrilla warfare, based on his experience in Kiangsi, were well developed. These involved combining the communist army, in many ways a conventional army in training and organisation, with an armed population fighting a guerrilla war against the Japanese. These were classic tactics; if the Japanese dispersed their army to control the countryside, the communists could concentrate overwhelmingly against their isolated detachments. If the Japanese massed their troops, the communists withdrew to a secure base, leaving the Japanese to suffer the harassing attacks of the guerrillas. All the time communist party cadres were working among the people, convincing them that the communists, rather than the Kuomintang, had China's real interests at heart.

It is worth remembering today that these techniques, although they have been copied by guerrilla movements around the world in the 1950s and 1960s, might not have succeeded if the Japanese had concentrated their efforts in China. However in 1941 world opinion, horrified by Japanese atrocities in China, combined with western fears of Japanese southward expansion forced the introduction of sanctions against Japan. In particular, oil supplies were cut off, and the Japanese, faced with economic and military collapse, decided to seize the resources they needed in South-East Asia. Because of the threat posed by the United States, they decided to strike first at the American fleet in Pearl Harbor, and so in December 1941 the war in China became absorbed into the war which had begun in Europe in 1939 as another worldwide conflict.

Rebel soldiers take possession of the wrecked and smouldering town of Santander in August, 1937. The civilian casualties were very heavy

75

Technical advances in land warfare 1918-1939

Although few new weapons emerged between the world wars, the tank saw considerable development, and advances in transport and communications equipment portended the rebirth of mobile operations.

In any study of the military technology in the years between the two world wars one feature immediately becomes apparent above all others. This is the increase in the basic speed of warfare. The static warfare of the trenches had been broken already by 1918 as the German April offensive clearly showed. This was followed by the Allies' summer offensives, to counter which the Germans had in 1917 abandoned the linear trench-line theory entirely and taken to defence in depth with zones several miles deep. The plans for 1919 were all for movement. Military thinkers of the calibre of the British J. F. C. Fuller and the American W. Mitchell outlined their ideas for fast-moving deep penetration attacks with wide outflanking movements directed against headquarters and communications centres in the rear areas. Twenty years later this theory was called the *Blitzkrieg*, and the Germans showed how it should be done.

But wide-ranging attacks depend for success on two main requirements. The first is obviously the means of transport,

and this was to be provided by the internal combustion engine, which was still in its infancy in 1918. Tanks and vehicles were slow, heavy, unreliable and poorly suited to the fast moving, flexible assaults that were being planned. There was great scope for improvement in all aspects of vehicle design, and this was well known to the military. The second was communications. The generals in World War I were almost entirely isolated from their troops once the battle started. The only change in communication since the days of Wellington and Napoleon was the telephone, and to ensure that telephone lines survived shell-fire, they had to be buried more than nine feet deep. From the moment that the assault left the trenches the only way to pass messages was by runner or verey light signal, and no general ever knew exactly when to commit his reserves or when to follow up a successful breakthrough. In 1918 the infantry portable radio required nine men as a carrying party, It took over half an hour to be set up satisfactorily, and could only

communicate in morse code. The reliability was very low, the range short and the power output feeble.

In the 1920s the advances in radio were dramatic, as commercial radio improved and domestic sets were introduced. In 1931 there appeared crystal-controlled sets which permitted speech communication, and at once it became a practical proposition to give orders by radio. At the same time the size of radios had sharply decreased, so it was perfectly possible to carry a set inside the turret of a tank. Steady improvements in valve and component manufacture enabled the sets to survive in the difficult environment inside an armoured vehicle driving across rough country, and commanders learned to operate a radio set with

French Renault light tanks manned by US troops in France near the end of the war. Tanks had proven their worth at last and were to be greatly developed for the next major world conflict over 20 years later.

confidence while carrying out all their other tasks. At one stroke all the theories of the pundits became attainable. Field commanders could now move with their formations, yet remain in touch with general headquarters; all levels of command could be continuously fed with up-to-date information; and best of all, plans could be changed while forces were on the move. These changes did not come immediately (indeed there were many who still had to learn them when war broke out in 1939) but for those with the eyes to see it, the means were there. The tank became the symbol of mobile warfare, but radio was the voice that told that tank what to do and when to do it.

From 1920 onwards significant advances were made in all armoured fighting vehicles, but mainly in tanks. Armoured cars were for the most part treated as being of lesser importance: a few of the 1918 vehicles were still in service in World War II with the British army, taking part in some minor actions. However, no 1918 tanks survived to fight in 1939, except in the French army.

Development of the tank was the most obvious way of improving the fighting ability of any army, and much effort went into this development, though not in the country which invented it. British financial policy in the 1920s and 1930s handed over systematic improvement of tanks to the commercial attitudes of the firm of Vickers for whom, of course, sales came first. In

USA there was even less interest, and again the tank was in the hands of private enterprise. Only in Germany, Russia and Japan was there a coherent and steady government policy, although even in these countries progress was slow and sometimes followed blind alleys.

There would have been no tank development at all had it not been for the motor industry. As the one advanced, so did the other follow, and this was no more obvious than in engines and their power output. The first British tanks had used a simple and comparatively inefficient Ricardo engine specially designed to be built of readily-available materials. Size was not important, and the engine actually stood upright in the middle of the engine compartment with a walk-way all round it. The luxury of such an arrangement disappeared with the rhomboid shape of World War I tanks, and from then on there was difficulty in finding enough space inside the hull not only for the engine itself, but also for the ancillaries that go with it. The radiators, fans, batteries and exhaust systems had to be fitted into spaces smaller and less convenient than their designers had catered for, and had to be maintained by unskilled men.

The engines had to operate in extremes of temperature and altitude, in heavy dust, when tilted to great angles, through the widest possible range of revolutions from flat-out to tick-over, for long periods without repair, and not be vulnerable to fire. Very

Soviet tanks and aircraft on exercise near Kiev in 1935. Despite superior equipment, Stalin's purges of officers during the 1930s led to early WWII defeats by the Germans.

few achieved these levels of performance in the interwar years, but some came close to it. It was soon found that not many commercial designs offered the right combination of virtues for tank propulsion, mainly because commercial engines at that time were not meant to cater for such operating extremes. The best available engines with the power output for size were aircraft types, and from these several successful tank engines were developed.

Until the early 1930s tank engines ran on petrol with spark ignition. The complications of adjusting and tuning complicated multi-carburettor layouts turned attention to diesel fuels. The essential robustness of the diesel had caused some determined research for industrial uses also, so tanks were able to take advantage of this and several successful diesel engines were produced, most of which served well. Another argument which was found in favour of diesel was the lessened fire risk.

But power is of no use without the means of transmitting it, and all the aspects of taking the power to the ground safely and reliably were actively investigated. For the first 10 years after World War I the only gearboxes available to the tank builders were

The major difficulty with tracked vehicles lies in steering. The rhomboid tanks used two gearboxes and the lighter Whippet tanks used two engines, but neither of these solutions was tried again. The first postwar tanks used brake steering, in which the inner track of the turn was simply stopped with a brake and power transferred through the differential to the outer one. This is a most inefficient method, and it was improved with the CLETRAC steering introduced by the Cleveland Tractor Company in 1916. In this system there was some control over the differential and when one track was braked most of the power was transferred to the other. This was a big step forward, and it was still used in the Sherman of 1942, but it was by no means the ideal and was improved on in the Vickers A6 of the middle 1920s, in which Major Wilson fitted two epicyclic boxes interlocked so that they gave different ratios to the turning tracks.

The Wilson system was ultimately developed into the Merritt-Brown regenerative steering systems of today's tanks, in which power is automatically channelled in precisely correct proportions to either track as the steering brakes are applied. However, the Merritt-Brown came in just after war was declared in 1939 and so lies outside the scope of this survey.

Having taken the power to the driving sprocket, the next problem is to apply it to the ground. The first tracks had been taken directly from farm tractors and were not only flimsy, but also short-lived and inefficient. They lasted as little as 20 miles, but in 1928 Vickers produced a cast manganese steel track with a life of up to 3,000 miles and greatly improved strength.

There were difficulties with armour. The early tanks were protected with thin plates of easily handled soft plate, known to the trade as 'boiler plate'. This was soon seen to be insufficient, and thin plate of a harder texture was substituted. Thin armour plate is not too difficult to roll and bend, but when the tank designers began to call for thicker plate it was a different matter. The tanks of the 1920s and the early 1930s were angular and square in their outlines because the designers were having to use flat pieces of plate with as few joins as possible. It was difficult not only to shape the plate, but also to join it effectively.

The first tanks had their plates bolted together, and later models were riveted. Neither method was satisfactory. Both bolts and rivets tend to give way when the plate is hit by solid shot, and once a gap is formed fragments and bullet-splash can reach the crew. What was needed was a continuous join, but this could only be provided by electric arc-welding and this was not a commercial proposition until 1935. Although arc-welding had been known and used in World War I, it remained a technical curiosity and was only used for small scale production, partly because of the cost of installing the necessary plant. German firms installed the plant and German tanks from 1934 onwards were welded. It was only at

25 pounder gun

Calibre: 88mm. **Maximum range:** 13,400 yards (12,253m). **Weight:** 3968lb (1800kg). **Length, travelling:** 26' (7.924m). **Width, travelling:** 7' (2.12m). **Height, travelling:** 5' 5'' (1.651m). **Elevation:** −5° to +40°. **Traverse:** 4° left and right. 360° on turntable. **Rate of fire:** 5/10rpm. **Ammunition:** HE weight 25lb (11.34kg). Smoke weight 21.75lb (9.87kg). AP weight 20lb (9.07kg).

In the 1920s and 30s, the Royal Artillery issued a requirement for a new weapon to replace both the

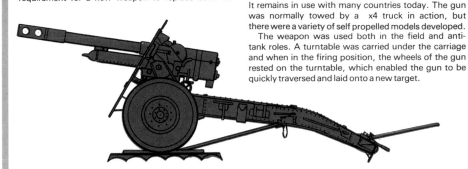

18-Pounder and the 4.5 inch howitzer. After various prototypes had been built and tested, the 25-Pounder (this being the weight of the HE projectile) was approved for production in December 1938, with the first guns being completed in 1940. To meet the army's urgent requirement for guns, many older 18-Pounders had their barrels removed and replaced with a new 25-Pounder barrel, under the designation 18/25-Pounder, or 25-Pounder Mk 1. The first production models were known as the 25-Pounder Mk 2 on Carriage Mk 1. By the end of World War II, over 12,000 had been built for service on all fronts. It remains in use with many countries today. The gun was normally towed by a x4 truck in action, but there were a variety of self propelled models developed.

The weapon was used both in the field and anti-tank roles. A turntable was carried under the carriage and when in the firing position, the wheels of the gun rested on the turntable, which enabled the gun to be quickly traversed and laid onto a new target.

German 88mm gun

Calibre. 88mm. **Maximum anti-aircraft range:** 34,770, (10,600m). **Effective anti-aircraft range:** 26,250, (8,000m). **Weight:** 15,129 lb (6861 kg). **Length:** 25ft (7.62m). **Width:** 7ft 7in (2.305m). **Height:** 7ft 11in (2.418m). **Elevation:** −3° to +85°. **Traverse:** 360°. **Rate of fire:** 15 to 20 rpm. **Time into action:** 2½ minutes. **Time out of action:** 3½ minutes. **Ammunition:** HE M/V 2690 fps (820m/s); APCBC M/V 2600 fps (795m/s); armour-piercing; HEAT; Starshell.

Without doubt, the German 88mm gun was the most famous gun of World War II and it remains in service in a number of countries today. Its development can be traced back to World War I when the German Army issued a requirement for a powerful anti-aircraft gun. Both Krupp and Rheinmetahl-Borsig designed an 88mm gun on a four-wheeled carriage and this was in service by the end of the war. In the 1930's a new

88mm gun was developed in secret and this entered service as the 8.8cm Flak 18. This was mounted on a four-wheeled carriage. This was followed by the Flak 36 and Flak 37; the latter could only be used in the anti-aircraft role. The 88mm gun was used in the Spanish Civil War and in the French and Polish campaigns. The British first encountered the 88mm gun in the anti-tank role when it stopped their counter-attack at Arras in 1940. From then on the 88 was used as an anti-tank gun in ever-increasing numbers. It was also the backbone of the German Air Defence System for the whole of the war. There were many other models including the Flak 41 anti-aircraft gun, and a number were mounted on special railway wagons. The Tiger 1 heavy tank was armed with an 88mm gun and there were many self-propelled models, including the Nashorn (on Panzer III and IV chassis), Elefant and the famous Jagdpanther. The 88mm gun was normally towed by a half-track which also carried the crew and ready-use ammunition.

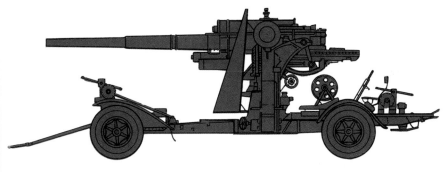

German 420mm howitzer (Big Bertha)

The use by the Japanese of their 28cm Howitzers during the siege of Port Arthur against the Russians in 1904, led the Germans to develop weapons of a similar type. The Germans already had howitzers for coastal defence, but these lacked mobility and they started a programme which resulted in the construction of a huge 420mm howitzer called Gamma. This had certain disadvantages—it weighed 140 tons, took almost two days to set up and required 10 railway wagons to transport it. Further development resulted in a new 420mm howitzer which weighed just 43 tons and this could be broken down into five loads for

ease of transportation and took about four hours to prepare for action. It fired a projectile weighing 1,800lb (816kg) to a maximum range of 10,200 yards (9373m).

The German operation for the invasion of France—the Schlieffen plan—included the elimination of the Belgian forts around Liege and Namur. To achieve this, the army sent in their 42cm howitzers, and Austrian 305mm howitzers. They first opened fire on August 12th 1914 on Fort Pontisse, which surrendered the following day. Over the next few days, the other forts fell one by one and within a few days the Germans were in Liege.

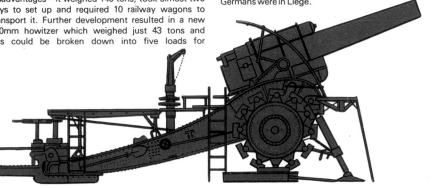

the insistence of the British government during the rearmament phase immediately before the war that British firms turned over to full-scale heavy arc-welding and the advantages of speed, lower cost and stronger armour resulted.

It was not only in welding that advances had to be made: armour plate itself needed much improvement, despite the technology inherited from warships. Tanks required thinner, lighter and more tightly shaped plate than was used on ships, and the processes of rolling, heating, hardening and quenching all brought out technical difficulties that had not been met before. Hard armour could neither be machined nor welded without great difficulty, but so-called 'soft' armour could be machined, and could also be cast. This brought about a cry for cast turrets, for the turret is the most vulnerable part of a tank, and the one most awkward to make. But plant did not exist for large castings of such a size, and had to be specially laid down at great cost. When they were operating, not only were turrets cast, but parts of the hull also.

The final improvement that tanks needed was better suspension. The tendency in early tanks was to run the track on a large number of small bogies, but these bogies were difficult to suspend on springs which allowed an adequate degree of travel. Much research went into spring systems, but the small bogie was never entirely satisfactory. Some were hung in pairs joined by a short axle. In the Vickers arrangement each pair was sprung by a vertical coil spring, later modified to two pairs compressing a horizontal spring as well as moving on a vertical one. This was the so-called 'scissors' suspension which also appeared on French models. Another French experiment featured pairs of bogies joined by axles and compressing three vertical springs, but none of these ideas allowed a cross-country speed of much more than 10 mph, so no matter the power of the engine or the efficiency of the transmission, maximum speed was strictly limited by what the bogies and tracks could accept.

It was an age when military men with a technical bent were often despised and frequently ignored, and much development work for the services was left to civilian firms. Into this arena came an American engineer, J. Walter Christie. Christie had been working on tank tacks and transmissions since 1921, and in 1928 he produced prototypes with which he demonstrated his design for a high-speed cross-country tracked armoured vehicle. Instead of small bogies, Christie used a few large wheels with the track passing over the top of the wheel on the return. Each wheel was suspended by a trailing arm held by a vertical coil spring. The vertical movement allowed by this system was considerable, and Christie added to it by putting rubber tyres on the wheels. He achieved record cross-country speeds with this method, easily reaching 40 mph, leaping obstacles and riding bumps with the track flapping in a highly dramatic manner. The American army was not greatly impressed, but bought some prototypes; more significantly so did the Russians, who developed the basic idea for widespread use. In time the developed Christie suspension gradually replaced all

others, and it is universal today in one form or another.

Another innovation brought forward by Christie was sloped armour. His light vehicles needed the most economical use of weight and he hit upon the idea of sloping the plates. At 50° the effective thickness of the plate is doubled, and again Christie was widely copied and developed. Once more the Russians took his ideas and today have become the masters of sloped tank armour.

The infantry, so often the poor relations of technological advances, gained little from the interwar years. Most armies went to war in 1939 with few changes from the equipment they had used in 1918, and in many cases it was exactly the same. The only significant newcomer to the infantry weapon family was the sub-machine gun. First introduced as a developed weapon in the Germany army in 1918, the sub-machine gun had been used basically for police work during the 1920s and its military applications were hardly recognised outside Germany, where the Treaty of Versailles forbade its use in the army. However, design slowly progressed in several countries, and some of the small South American wars showed the value of the weapon. So too did the Spanish Civil War (1936–1939), and from then on improvements were rapid.

In gunnery the advances were significant but scarcely any more obvious than in the infantry world. As always, the search was for more range from existing guns, and the simplest way of doing this is to put more propellant behind the shell and so fire it at a higher muzzle velocity. This works well enough for range purposes, but it was soon found that it entailed two highly undesirable features. The first was muzzle flash, and the second increased recoil. Muzzle flash meant that the gun lines were more easily spotted from the air (and aerial reconnaissance was improving rapidly), but the only effective cure lay in chemical research into improved propellant compounds. Much effort went into this field, resulting in a compound by the name of nitroguanidine, which came to be adopted by most nations as providing the best compromise between reduced flash and smoke without loss of power.

The problem of increased recoil was more serious, especially when the tendency was to try to cut down all unnecessary weight and thus produce guns and equipment that were more mobile than earlier ones. Here again Germany took a lead, the firm of Krupp of Essen doing much valuable research into fitting baffles on to the gun muzzle to deflect the emerging gases and cause them to pull the gun forward, or at least to deflect them sideways so that the recoil force was lessened. Other nations quickly followed the idea, and muzzle brakes became general for field guns and later, tank, AA and other high-velocity guns. Muzzle brakes were even put on to anti-tank rifles to reduce the push on the firer's shoulder.

More research was put into other ways and means of increasing the muzzle velocity, not only for more range, but also for better

A very early, lightly armoured car trundles through a village in Haiti, where it was operating with American Marines.

armour penetration against tanks. In France, Brandt experimented with what is now called Discarding Sabot shot for field guns. He put a small calibre shell into a large barrel and filled the space around it with light metal 'petals' which blew off at the muzzle. The shell then went on with an increased velocity combined with reduced drag, and so greater range. The idea was not particularly attractive for field artillery because it delivered only a small shell at the target, but it was taken and developed in Britain to become the most successful anti-armour projectile of all time, the APDS or Armour Piercing Discarding Sabot. However, that did not happen until late on in World War II.

The German approach to high muzzle velocities lay in tapering the bore, so that the projectile was progressively squeezed to a smaller size as it travelled to the muzzle – in a way rather like an extreme form of the choke in a shot gun. The shells for this type of gun had to have soft metal 'skirts' which

Right: A British field gun being used for registering ranges. During WWII the Allies soon found that shrapnel shells were useless against dug-in troops. Production of HE shells had to be increased.

Below: A knocked out Russian T-26A-4V light tank which was based on a British Vickers design. The frame around the hull is the radio aerial.

Panzerkampfwagen 1 (Pz.Kw.1) tank

Crew: 2 (commander/gunner, and driver). **Weight:** 5.4 tons. **Length:** 13' 2'' (4.02m). **Width:** 6' 9'' (2.06m). **Height:** 5' 8'' (1.72m). **Road speed:** 23mph (37kmh). **Range:** 90 miles (115km). **Engine:** Krupp M105, four cylinder air-cooled petrol engine developing 57 HP at 2500rpm. **Vertical obstacle:** 1' 2'' (.36m). **Trench:** 4' 7'' (1.4m). **Gradient:** 60%. **Armour:** 7 to 13mm.

In the early 1930s the German Army issued a requirement for a light tank to weigh about five tons, and be armed with two machine guns. Krupp was selected to develop the chassis and Daimler-Benz the turret and hull. The first prototype was completed in 1934 and production commenced. To conceal its true identity it was known as the Landwirtschaftlicher Schlepper (La.S), or Industrial Tractor. In 1938 it was finally called the Panzerkampwagen 1A (Sd.Kfz.101 Ausf.A), which was armed with twin 7.92mm machine guns and carried a total of 1,525 rounds of ammunition. The next model was the 1B, with a more powerful Maybach petrol engine which developed 100 HP at

3000 rpm, and increased speed to 25mph (40kmh). The 1B also had a slightly longer hull and modified suspension.

Pz.Kw.1s were used in the Spanish Civil War and in most the the early campaigns of the World War II. The type was finally phased out of front line service in late 1941.

A command model known as the Kleiner Panzer Befehlswagen had a crew of three, mapboards and radios and was armed with a single 7.9mm machine gun. The first German self-propelled gun used a 1B chassis, and its turret was replaced by a captured Czech 47mm gun. The chassis was also used to mount the 15cm heavy infantry gun.

British light tank Mk.IV

Crew: 2 (commander/gunner, driver). **Weight:** 9520lb (4318kg). **Length:** 11' 2''* (3.402m). **Width:** 6' 11½'' (2.12m). **Height:** 6' 8½'' (2.044m). **Road speed:** 36mph (60kmh). **Range:** 130 miles (210km). **Engine:** six cylinder Meadows petrol engine developing 88 HP. **Armour:** 4 to 12mm.

Before World War II, the Carden-Loyd Company (which was taken over by Vickers-Armstong in 1928), developed a variety of light tanks for both the British and a number of foreign Armies. The first of these was the Mk.I, followed by the Mk.II and Mk.III. The Mk. IV was a development of the earlier Mk.III and was armed with a Vickers .303 or Vickers .5 machine gun, which had an elevation from —10° to +37°, and the turret had a traverse of 360°. The Mk.V was the first of the light tanks to have a two-man turret and this entered service in 1935. The Mk.VI had a redesigned turret with radio in the rear and there were a number of sub-variants, including the Mk.VIA, B and C, the latter armed with a 15mm and a 7.92mm machine gun.

In 1939, some 80% of the tank strength of the British Army was composed of light tanks but

production of these stopped in 1940. The Mk.IV was used in action in France in 1940 as well as in most of the early battles in North Africa. Due to a shortage of heavier tanks, the light tanks were often used in the cruiser role with heavy casualties and by 1941 they were withdrawn from front line service. Some remained in use with training units in England and abroad as late as 1943.

Matilda Mark 1 infantry tank

Crew: 2 (commander/gunner and driver). **Weight:** 24,640lb (11,176kg). **Length:** 15' 1'' (4.584m). **Width:** 7' 6'' (2.286m). **Height:** 6' 1½'' (1.866m). **Road speed:** 8mph (12.85krnh). **Range:** 80 miles (128km). **Engine:** Ford V-8 petrol engine developing 70 HP. **Vertical obstacle:** 2' 1'' (.635m). **Trench:** 7' (2.133m). **Armour:** 6 to 60mm.

In 1935, Sir John Carden of Vickers Armstrong announced that he could build a small infantry tank for £5,000/£6,000. Work started on it late in 1935 under the designation A11 and the first prototype was completed in September 1936. The design was not considered satisfactory and a new one, the A12, was initiated by the Mechanisation Board and the Vulcan Foundry at Warrington. A production order was placed in December 1937, although the first proto-type was not completed until April 1938. The A12 was known as the Matilda 11 (or Infantry Tank 2) and almost 3,000 were built before production stopped in 1943. The Matilda saw extensive service in the early North African campaigns and became known as "Queen of the Desert."

A total of 139 A11s (or Matilda 1) were built and most of these, together with a few A12s saw action in France in 1940 with the 4th Battalion of the Royal Tank Regiment. On May 21st, 1940 the 4th and 7th Battalions of the Royal Tank Regiment and two battalions of infantry launched an attack on the German's south of Arras. According to the Divisional commander (Rommel), they caused havoc before the Matildas were stopped by the Germans' 88mm Anti-Aircraft Guns.

Above left: Highly mobile *Reichswehr* soldiers during manoeuvres in 1929. It was in these early years that the strategy and tactics of *Blitzkrieg* were evolved.

Above: Improved communications had a dramatic effect on the battlefield. Here a British soldier tries out a captured tandem cycle frame used by the Germans to generate electricity for a wireless set.

Left: New threats led to new counter-measures. Here US troops in France use a Model 1914 Hotchkiss machine gun in the anti-aircraft role.

deformed and wrapped around the centre core as the bore diminished. These were expensive to manufacture, but the increase in muzzle velocity was worth the extra trouble, and this idea was used in a small family of anti-tank guns. The drawback to the squeeze-bore was that the barrel quickly wore out, and the gun could not really be used for anything else except anti-tank work.

If the taper-bore guns were a blind alley, another German invention was more successful. In 1910 Commander Davis of the US Navy had invented a recoilless gun in which the recoil of the shell leaving the muzzle was exactly counter-balanced by a mass of lead shot fired out of the back of the barrel. The idea was never fully developed, and Krupp set to work to improve upon it in

the early 1930s. The lead shot was quickly discarded and replaced by a gas jet. This jet used gas from the propellant charge to balance the recoil force and the result was a very light gun which could fire a large shell at a useful muzzle velocity. These guns were developed for mountain and airborne troops and were highly successful. They were the forerunners of the lightweight infantry anti-tank recoilless guns which appear in practically every army today, and which have done much to bring the infantry-man in his foxhole a little nearer to parity with an advancing tank.

Other artillery improvements were less obvious and dramatic. The fusing of shells gave a lot of trouble in World War I and 'duds' were frequent. Up to 1918 time fuses worked by burning a powder train and these were erratic and inaccurate. Throughout the 1920s and 1930s there was continuous research to develop reliable clockwork mechanisms, and by 1938 these were generally successful and available. Not surprisingly in view of their exposed position in the centre of Europe, the Swiss took a leading part in this field, and the British army bought the Swiss Tavaro fuse for anti-aircraft artillery.

Anti-aircraft gunnery received a good deal of attention in the interwar years, for not only were better fuses needed, but also some reliable means of laying the guns. The air raids of World War I, although not very effective, raised quite justified fears for what might happen in World War II and it was realised that the AA fire plans of 1918 would be largely futile in preventing aircraft

flying wherever they chose. In World War I the height and speed of the target aircraft was assessed as best it could be from sound-detectors and observers, and the correct lay for the guns either guessed from experience or quickly worked out on paper. Corrections were made by observing the position of the burst, whereupon the target would turn or dive and the process would have to start all over again. The need for rapid and accurate estimation of all the many variables in aiming an AA gun brought about the first computers, known as predictors. Predictors were mechanical calculators which could answer a strictly limited number of mathematical problems, and they had to be driven by turning hand wheels and reading answers from dials, but nonetheless they were a great advance on guess-work.

Moreover, the predictor directly sponsored the search for electrical and electronic means to solve more complicated sums in even faster time, and from this search the modern computer science began. But electronic systems had entered the AA field as early as 1930. In that year the US Army built an experimental AA layout in which the output from the predictor was transformed into electrical power and fed directly to a gun which laid automatically on the bearing and elevation calculated by the predictor. The idea was not pursued, but it was an interesting indicator of what was to come within a very few years of the outbreak of war. The main difficulty was the fact that the target information came from highly inaccurate and misleading sound detectors, or from visual sightings which were naturally useless at night.

In their search for better target information the US Army Signal Corps at Fort Monmouth, New Jersey, also made some sketchy trials with a crude radar set, but apparently it gave such feeble results that it was abandoned until the British invented the cavity magnetron transmitter. The long-range equipment which was set up in 1938 for the defence of Britain gave course, speed and height only in general terms, but this information gave the guns a much better basis for their predictor calculations, with a consequent improvement in shooting. Radar was in fact one of the great technological advances of the years immediately before World War II and it is the one which has had the widest and most fundamental effect upon warfare since it was introduced. The story is too well known to bear repetition here, and in any case the early stages are generally taken as being part of the saga of air power during the 1930s, but the value of radar to AA gunnery should not be overlooked.

There was one other significant technological advance in land warfare between 1918 and 1939: the introduction of airborne troops. Although the techniques employed in the actual flying, gliding and parachuting of soldiers and their equipment more properly belongs to a treatise on aviation, the whole purpose was to increase the strategic mobility of ground troops. Russia made the first experiments and showed the way; Germany developed the idea and brought it to the point where airborne attacks formed a substantial and decisive part of the *Blitzkrieg*.

Part 3: World War II
The leaders and their armies

Like World War I, World War II was to be fought by mass armies. But this time the tactics were to be more fluid, and each major nation led by a man of forceful and pronounced individuality.

World War II in Europe might equally well be called the Hitler War,' for it came about because of this one man. The military history of the war can be summed up as an enormous and prolonged operation to crush Hitler and the first-class military instrument he had created to achieve his apocalyptic political goals – the creation of a Germanic empire in Europe, the conquest of the richest parts of Russia west of the Urals, the destruction of world communism and the liquidation or enslavement of 'inferior races' such as the Jews and Slavs.

Hitler came to absolute power as *Fuehrer* in August 1934, and from then on war was inevitable. But it was four years before it broke out, and in that period, when the new German army and air force were being organised, Hitler with consummate skill used this growing military power as a threat to test the resolution of the European powers. He judged it exactly right, and the Rhineland, the Czech Sudetenland and Austria were won without a shot being fired. This culminated in a game of bluff between the Germans and the Poles with the future of the port Danzig as a stake; a poker game

which included as unwilling participants the French and the British and, indirectly, the Russians. No one, not even Hitler, actually wished to go to war at that moment. But the Poles refused to give way, and Hitler, fortified by the non-aggression pact with Russia, (August 1939) became more daring. At 0600 hours on 1 September 1939 German aircraft bombed Warsaw. The luckless Poles were rapidly overrun by a modern but only half-prepared German army.

There are three important points to keep in perspective before going to look at the course of the war. The first is that never before had a war on this scale been fought against a world leader who was in a literal, clinical sense mentally deranged. Hitler was violently aggressive, had irrational fears and hatreds about whole groups of people, was totally indifferent to human suffering, had illusions about calculable military facts and could not follow, at least in the military field, the connection between cause and effect.

The second point is that the war was won and lost between the Germans and the Russians. The Russians bore the greatest

burden, fought the greatest number of Germans and finally entered the German capital. The Americans were most powerful, more advanced and fully as determined as the Russians, but never had to deploy their full strength in the West. Their entry simply made Hitler's defeat surer and sooner. Britain and her Commonwealth played a noble part, but it was of a bulldog hanging on to the nose of a bull while someone more powerful eventually came to despatch it.

The third point is that the war was

Below left: Hitler with his new field-marshals in September 1940. From left to right these are Wilhelm Keitel, Gerd von Rundstedt, Fedor von Bock, Hermann Goering, Hitler himself, Walther von Brauchitsch, Wilhelm Ritter von Leed.

Below: Churchill inspects a unit of the Home Guard in 1941. The Prime Minister's popularity among troops, at home and overseas, increased as the war drew on.

Above: Stalin's pre-war policy of ousting politically unsound officers severely weakened the effectiveness of the Russian forces early in WWII. Eventually, however, Soviet discipline prevailed.

Left: Hitler, visibly shaken by the almost successful attempt on his life on 20 July 1944, greets his old ally Benito Mussolini on the latter's arrival at the *Wolfsschanze*.

Above right: Hitler addresses the massed ranks of *Sturmabteilung* (SA) troopers from the podium. The SA was broken as an effective force in the 'Night of the Long Knives'.

decided by the economic strength of the Allies and the number of tanks, guns, aircraft, ships, bombs and shells their factories could turn out, the number of men they could put in the field and – grim factor – how many they could afford to lose.

Apart from these material considerations the course of the war was determined by the leadership at the top. The strategic direction of each of the major European powers was by the political head of the state, all three of whom acted as the war-lord or generalissimo of the armed forces, each approaching his enormous problems in a characteristically different way.

At the very top the problem is to be enough of a dictator to insist on the aims but at the same time keep the mind open to argument and, vitally, also to unpalatable information. This was Hitler's Achilles'

heel. His leadership at the top lacked rational direction – it remains a mystery to this day what he thought he was eventually going to do in Russia even if his invasion had been successful – and as it was he cut himself off from all advice.

In dealing with the army Hitler suffered from inverted snobbery, deeply resenting the combination of *Junker* aristocracy and intellectual strength which was the hallmark of the great general staff. He believed himself to be a better general than any of his professionals and took control on the operational level. He became a 'pins in the map' general – one who delights in the regrouping of armies and corps and the drawing of arrows showing thrust lines and encirclements. A clever man, in this he was dangerously proficient. But it distracted him from economic and political questions.

Winston Churchill's anti-Hitler strategy was based on a very simple plan firmly rooted in reality. He had to keep the war going until the United States was drawn in; his aims were first survival and then liberation. For this two springboards had to be retained for re-entry into Europe; Britain itself and the eastern Mediterranean together with the north African coast.

Neither Stalin nor Hitler were worried about expenditure of life. Churchill's military views were strongly influenced by the grim casualties of World War I, and all his strategy favoured a long-range, encircling counter-offensive from the southern flank of Europe as opposed to frontal, cross-Channel assault followed by a clash with the main German forces in France, which would only repeat the losses of 1916–17 which always haunted him. He was a great nuisance to his generals and also tended occasionally to meddle with operations, but his advisers were the best he could find and ones not afraid to speak their minds. His main objectives were correctly chosen and he pursued them with unwavering determination.

Stalin succeeded where Hitler failed totally; he functioned as the supreme head of state, the generalissimo and virtually the commander of troops in the field. His problems were appalling. The whole of Red Army's doctrine and plans were in disarray as late as 1940, and the overwhelming fact facing Stalin in 1941 was that nowhere could the ill-led Soviet divisions stand up to the magnificent German armies, and they surrendered in droves.

Stalin had first to check Hitler's advance and behind his defences build up industry and re-equip and retrain new armies, and then go over to the offensive and destroy the invaders. This was his single aim, and there is no reason to believe that he would have ever temporised even if Moscow and Stalingrad had fallen. Stalin was clear headed, with an enormous capacity for realities, in contrast to Hitler with his illusions, and the whole of his command system was geared to provide immediate operational information from every front. (One of the great difficulties in large-scale warfare is to find out what one's own troops are doing and what is their condition, let alone the equivalent information about the enemy.) In this way Stalin had a complete grip of the operational picture. Above all, he grasped fully the fact that the only way a generalissimo can influence the battle is by having an uncommitted reserve – altering the 'pins in the map' has little effect – and he created a huge one which he used with decisive effect.

The Americans kept a more orthodox balance between their head of state, constitutionally the Commander-in-Chief, and his service advisers. There was a clear-cut division between national policy and military operations. Roosevelt had no ambition to play the generalissimo, although he inevitably had to take the most important decisions. His advisers, led by General George C. Marshall, were unsurpassed, and where they differed from the formidable Churchill and his equally strong team, history will say that they were generally right. Professionalism was the hallmark of the senior US commanders, who ran their armies efficiently like successful business corporations.

The military instruments each of the belligerents had available differed markedly in character. The Germans were an advanced western society with a high level of education for all classes organised into an authoritarian society conditioned to unquestioning obedience and imbued with a deep-seated martial tradition. The army was monolithic, with a common loyalty and a common *esprit de corps*. There were, tactically speaking, two wings: one being

Left: A striking poster for the German Youth Festival of 23 June 1934. The Nazis were always at great pains to try to indoctrinate the growing generation of Germans.

Above: General De Gaulle inspecting a Free French Commando unit at Wellington Barracks. After the fall of the low countries many men found their way to England to carry on the fight against Germany.

Right: President Roosevelt and Prime Minister Churchill studying plans during the Casablanca conference which decided the Allied policy for the Invasion of Europe in 1944.

the modernised Panzer element and the other the rifle and machine-gun divisions with horse-drawn artillery on the pattern of World War I.

The Red Army, as it was then called, lacked all the German initiative and *élan*, being made up of a vast mass of illiterate peasant levies dragooned into action by the discipline of the communist party machine. In 1937–1938 its leadership had suffered a traumatic purge. (Three marshals and 400 odd general officers from divisional to brigade commanders were 'liquidated'.) In equipment the Red Army was not as backward as sometimes portrayed: it had excellent tanks and guns in the ever-increasing quantities which were exactly suited to the mentality of the Russian soldier, and its tactical doctrine was well-founded. There were eventually whole armies of tanks, but artillery was the Red Army's

principal weapon: 'The God of War' as Stalin called it. Discipline was draconian. Commanders were expected to drive their troops into action as long as a man remained standing.

The British started in a period of self-inflicted confusion about military doctrine and with the task of up-dating an imperial police force into a modern army. This was done with remarkable success, and the most flattering tributes paid to it came from its German opponents, but it took time. The number of fighting divisions was kept deliberately low by Churchill and it remained a small *corps d'élite* compared with

the colossal armies of the other powers.

The late comers to the conflict, the US armies, were regarded by the Germans as over-civilised and soft, but the basic US doctrine was to have the best weapons available and to use equipment and munitions to save lives. The US Army was highly successful, being admirably designed to make the best use of American technological know-how and of its well-educated, technically minded soldiers.

Such was the balance of military forces for the years of warfare ahead, but in 1939 and 1940 the military might of the Swastika cowed all Europe.

The Blitzkrieg conquers Europe

In 1939 and 1940 the German armies swept all before them with
uncheckable speed. But then Hitler turned against Russia,
leaving Great Britain undefeated and determined in his rear.

What, in fact, was the secret of the German victories of 1940–41? It is not enough to say that Hitler's Germany was geared to aggression and that his armoured divisions, supported by dive-bombers, were bound to carve through old-fashioned armies deployed in a linear defence.

As far as tactics are concerned, the Germans in 1917–18 had devised a new form of attack based on small groups of élite troops – the *Stosstruppen* and *Sturmabteilungen* – whose task it was to thrust without regard for flank security as deeply as their momentum would carry them into the heart of the enemy defence system, the officers leading from the front.

The invention of the tank and the tactical theories of Fuller, Broad and Liddell Hart caught the imagination of the men rebuilding the German army – notably Heinz Guderian – who never again wished to see the stagnation of French warfare.

The tactics of the *Blitzkrieg* were the result of uniting infiltration tactics with the tank and substituting dive-bombers for slow-moving heavy artillery. But the real secret was the combat training of the German soldier. It was not the tanks which counted so much as the men in them, and the infantry of the motorised divisions who worked with them.

The spearhead of the attack on the French in May 1940 was the eight out of 10 specially trained Panzer divisions.

A fish, as they say, begins to rot from the head, and in 1939–40 the leadership of France had neither the will nor the knowledge to fight a modern war; moreover, this weakness was compounded by vain confidence in the superiority of the French army over all others. The leadership of the French army and air force was decayed, the generals being old, cautious and expecting a repetition of the 1914–18 war. Their whole theory of war was wrong, being based on a linear defence and a fortified belt of frontier bulwarks of obsolete pattern, the expensive and useless Maginot Line. There was no large, properly organised reserve army, or *mass de manoeuvre*, for decisive use once the enemy's point of main effort had become clear.

German infantry move up through the lingering smoke of an artillery barrage. Often during the early stages of the war the Allies were overwhelmed by the superiority of forces and speed with which the Germans attacked small sectors of the front.

although in fact some 22 divisions were left over from the front line. As for modern weapons, there were few aircraft suitable for co-operation with the army and the command system in any case did not cater for it.

As regards tanks, the French had 3,100, of which 2,285 were modern and of which in turn 800 were the powerful Char-B and Somua types with 75-mm and 47-mm guns, to pit against 2,500 German tanks of all natures of which 1,400 were lightly-armed PzKpfw IIs, eked out by obsolete PzKpfw Is, and only 627 of the really battleworthy PzKpfw IIIs and IVs, with 37-mm and a short 75-mm gun tespectively. Unlike the Germans, the French tanks were distributed throughout the army formations, except a few in the newly formed *Divisions Cuirassés*, which in any case were wrongly organised. The whole command and control system was defective, right down to the tanks, few of which had radio sets.

These weaknesses they could all have remedied by vigorous training at all levels between the declaration of war in 1939 and the German onslaught on 10 May. Instead, absolutely nothing was done. No attempt to evaluate the lessons of the Polish campaign was made, and there were neither staff exercises nor manoeuvres. The staff, although highly intelligent and full of theory, sat at their desks and tried to run a war using peacetime office methods, with the result that the French formations proved to be

German artillery crosses the Marne river over a pontoon bridge. The German army relied to a very great extent on horses for heavy towing duties.

Range with tripod: 1968/2187 yards (1800/2000m).

The MG-34 was one of two standard machine guns of the German Army during World War II, the other being the later MG-42. The MG-34 could be used as a light machine gun with a bipod, heavy machine gun with a tripod, or as an anti-aircraft machine gun. Mainly mounted in armoured vehicles, it was also used as an aircraft machine gun (the MG-81).

The weapon was recoil operated (assisted by a muzzle booster) and the barrel could be quickly changed when it became too hot. The top of the trigger was used for semi-automatic fire and the bottom of the trigger for full automatic fire. The MG-34 was fed from a 250-round belt—which consisted of five 50 round belts joined together — or by a 50-round drum or a 75-round saddle drum.

German 7.92mm MG-34 machine gun

Calibre: 7.92mm. **Weight with bipod:** 26¼ lb (11.8kg). **Weight with tripod:** 68½ lb (31kg). **Length:** 4' (1.219m). **Muzzle velocity:** 2500/3000fps (762/914m/s). **Rate of fire:** 800/900rpm (cyclic). 100/120rpm (practical). **Range with bipod:** 656 yards (600m).

9mm MP40 sub-machine gun

Calibre: 9mm. **Weight with loaded magazine:** 10½ lb (4.763kg). **Length, stock extended:** 33¼" (.85m). **Length, stock folded:** 24¾" (.628m). **Magazine capacity:** 32 rounds. **Muzzle velocity:** 1040/1250fps (317/381m/s). **Rate of fire:** 520rpm (cyclic). 80/90rpm (practical). **Range:** 200 yards (182m).

The MP40 (Maschinen Pistole) or Schmeisser as it

was more commonly known, was developed from the earlier MP38 SMG, as it was found that the MP38 was too expensive to build in the large numbers required. Although designed originally for use of airborne troops, it was in fact used by most branches of the German forces. Over 1,000,000 MP40s were built by the end of the war, manufacturers included Erma, Haenel and Steyr and it is still used by a few countries. The MP40 is air-cooled and blowback operated and fires full automatic only. A folding metal stock was provided and the weapon was fired from the hip or the shoulder.

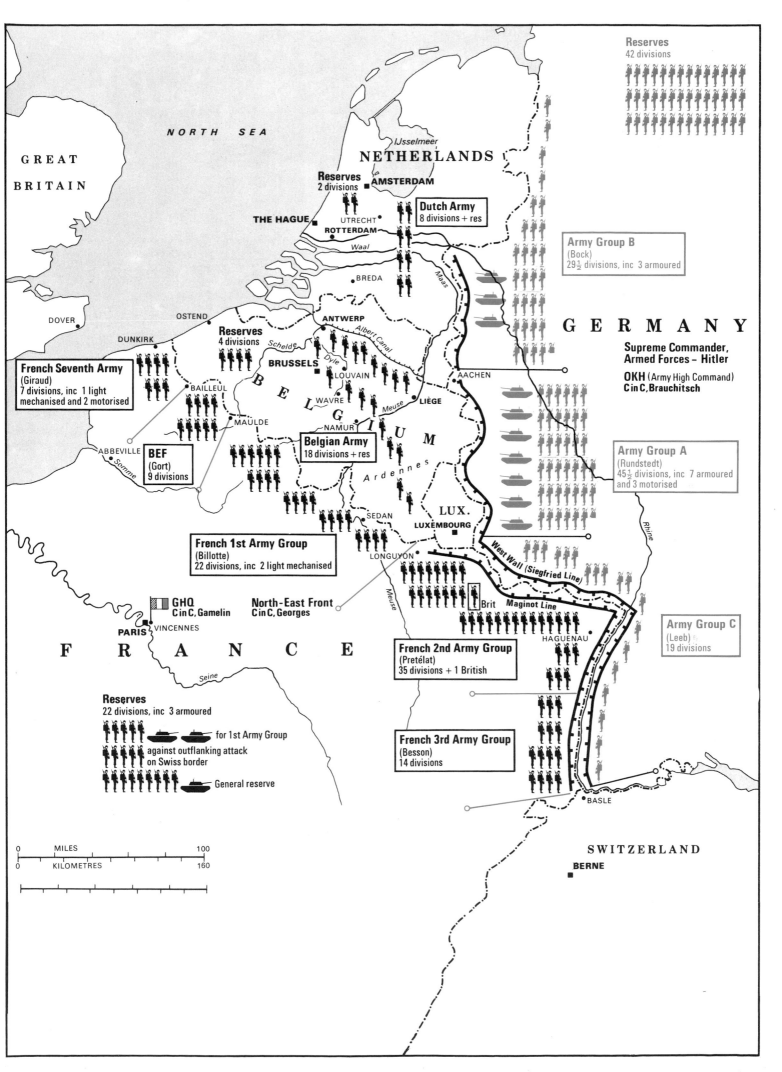

NORTH SEA

GREAT BRITAIN

NETHERLANDS

Reserves
42 divisions

Reserves
2 divisions

AMSTERDAM

THE HAGUE

UTRECHT

ROTTERDAM

Waal

BREDA

Maas

Dutch Army
8 divisions + res

Army Group B
(Bock)
29½ divisions, inc 3 armoured

DOVER

OSTEND

DUNKIRK

ANTWERP

Albert Canal

GERMANY

Reserves
4 divisions

Schelde

BRUSSELS

Dyle

LOUVAIN

AACHEN

Supreme Commander,
Armed Forces – Hitler

French Seventh Army
(Giraud)
7 divisions, inc 1 light
mechanised and 2 motorised

BAILLEUL

WAVRE

Meuse

LIÈGE

OKH (Army High Command)
C in C, Brauchitsch

MAULDE

NAMUR

B E L G I U M

BEF
(Gort)
9 divisions

ABBEVILLE

Somme

Belgian Army
18 divisions + res

Ardennes

Army Group A
(Rundstedt)
45½ divisions, inc 7 armoured
and 3 motorised

SEDAN

LUX.

LUXEMBOURG

French 1st Army Group
(Billotte)
22 divisions, inc 2 light mechanised

Rhine

West Wall
(Siegfried Line)

LONGUYON

GHQ
C in C, Gamelin

North-East Front
C in C, Georges

Meuse

Brit

Maginot Line

Army Group C
(Leeb)
19 divisions

PARIS

VINCENNES

F R A N C E

HAGUENAU

French 2nd Army Group
(Pretélat)
35 divisions + 1 British

Seine

Reserves
22 divisions, inc 3 armoured

for 1st Army Group

against outflanking attack
on Swiss border

General reserve

French 3rd Army Group
(Besson)
14 divisions

BASLE

SWITZERLAND

BERNE

MILES   100

KILOMETRES   160

incapable of the simplest manoeuvres. Worst of all, the vast mass of conscripts and reservists called up to the colours in 1939–40, and none too pleased about it or very clear about what this '*drôle de guerre*' was about, were left idle for months in a very cold winter. (By contrast the British Expeditionary Force was worked incessantly.) When battle was joined, therefore, the bulk of the French troops who met the superbly enthusiastic young German soldiers were bored, disillusioned, sullen and indisciplined. It was a recipe for disaster.

The French order of battle ignored the very reason for basing defence on a fortress line, which is to save men and free units for mobile operations. From Longwy, where the Maginot Line ended, south to the Allied right flank were stationed no fewer than 45 divisions, 10 garrisoning the forts, 30 lined up behind or between them, and five to watch the Swiss frontier. Opposite the Belgian Ardennes, which was regarded as

difficult country and an unlikely invasion route, the frontier was lightly held by cavalry – some still on horses – and a few second-rate reservist divisions. In the north there were 20 divisions of the French 1st, 7th and 9th Armies, plus the BEF, whose task was to enter Belgium and Holland the moment the latters' neutrality was broken and take up a defence line running from Dinant along the Dyle and then to Breda.

The German general staff had a clear idea of these French dispositions which, they guessed, were intended to forestall a giant right hook through Flanders on the pattern of the Schlieffen Plan of 1914. Their counter was to be a supremely daring variation, the brain-child of General Erich von Manstein and welcomed by General Guderian, who was determined to use *en masse* the armoured force he had helped to create. The breakthrough was to be in the centre by an advance southward via Luxembourg and the Ardennes, whose forests were

by no means the obstacle to armoured movement the French supposed it to be, and then across the Meuse on a front of some 60 miles, from Sedan to just north of Dinant. The Panzers themselves were to force the crossing and lead throughout: there was to be no pause, no time for the defence to mount a counterattack. Once across they were to swing right, carve a corridor through the rear areas of the Allied armies advancing into Belgium and Holland and drive for the English Channel, thus cutting the entire Allied defensive system in two – a sickle sweep or *Sichelschnitt*. Behind the Panzers would come the infantry divisions marching on foot to form secure flanks to right and left, and to consolidate the gains. After this, first the group of French armies cut off in the north could be rounded up, and then a sweep to the left would pen up the mass of French divisions in or behind the Maginot line.

None of the French armoured divisions were used in action in one piece, the British had no armoured divisions, while seven out of the 10 Panzer divisions, or some 1,500 tanks, formed the cutting edge of the sickle.

Faced with an accelerating catastrophe, with roads jammed with fugitive soldiers, some of whom had abandoned their guns under the shock of dive-bombing, and floods of refugees, among whom counterattack forces ordered up became jammed or melted away, French staff work broke down until all control was lost. Little emerged from the top except rhetorical 'orders of the day' to do or die, of which soldiers as a rule take not the slightest notice.

On 15 May Guderian was over the Meuse, and the Dutch had surrendered; by 25 May the Allied armies in the north were fairly surrounded; on 27 May the Belgians capitulated; on 28 May the British began to embark at Dunkirk; by 7 June the Germans, having cleaned up in the north, were across the Somme and fighting south and south-west – the Panzers still leading; Paris fell on 14 June; and on 21 June the German terms for peace were dramatically and vengefully dictated in the very place the French had dictated theirs in 1918.

It was a resounding victory. In the whole history of war there has never been such an occasion when a new philosophy of warfare has been carefully thought out, the correct military instrument to realise it created and the philosophy then so triumphantly carried out.

The valid military question then to be asked was, how would the *Blitzkrieg* work against an opponent who also had tanks, powerful anti-tank guns, an effective air-defence against the terrifying Stukas and, above all, commanders and staffs who did not fall into hysteria at the first disaster? Not all the defenders had panicked: in many places there had been determined French resistance. As a result the Germans lost 156,492 men, of whom 27,074 were killed. Military history properly read shows that a challenge eventually produces the appropriate response and counter-weapons. The

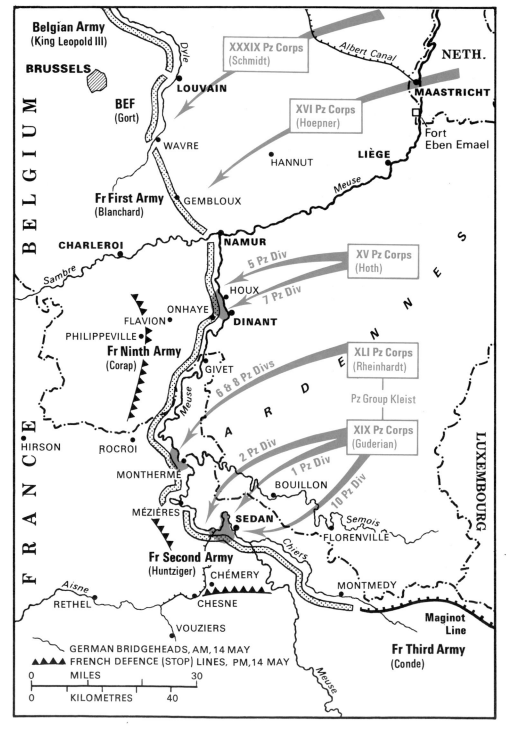

PzKpfw III tanks are swayed down from a transport ship onto Tripoli dock for Rommel's *Deutsches Afrikakorps*. The DAK was far from an elite formation.

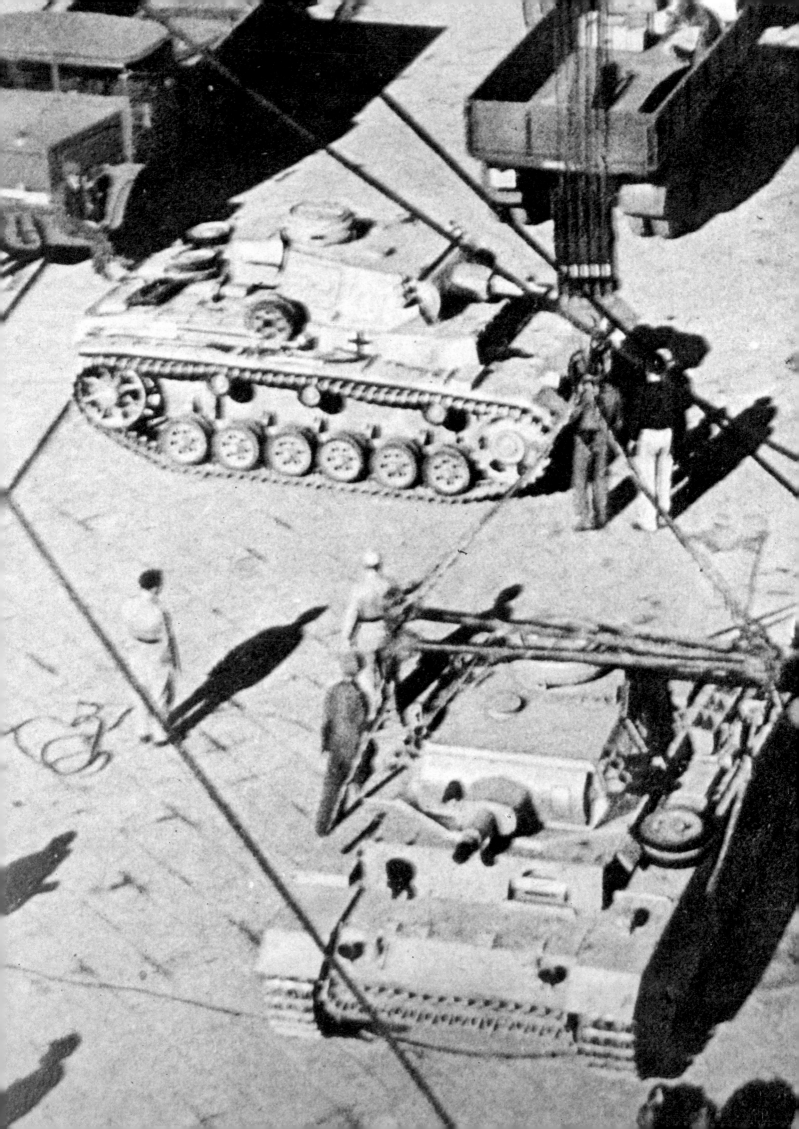

answers to such questions Hitler was to learn in Russia.

As to the strategic or political exploitation of his victory Hitler had not given a thought. For him the climax was dictating the surrender terms in the railway carriage at Compiègne. At this stage he actually damped down arms production, and released some army man-power to industry.

Half-heartedly Hitler considered invading England. Postwar studies lean to the conclusion that Operation 'Sea Lion' would never have succeeded, but there was just a chance that it might had some anticipatory planning been done and the Channel crossing been mounted as soon as possible after the evacuation of Dunkirk. Certainly those who can remember the state of the British Home Forces in the early autumn would not have backed them confidently against the veterans of Poland and France, and the fate of surface ships elsewhere under concentrated air attack was not, in retrospect, encouraging for a naval defence. In fact it was the German admiralty which was against 'Sea Lion'. In the Norwegian campaign the navy had lost half its destroyers, and it had a healthy respect for the Royal Navy which, it was only too sure, would make every sacrifice necessary to cut the sea communications behind the landing. And as for getting the troops to England by water, the German navy feared that the river and canal barges commanded by civilian freshwater skippers would all founder in the strong tides of the Channel. All the same, great as the risks were they did not compare with the dangers of following Napoleon's road to Moscow. But nevertheless, without any coherent plan in his crazed brain, it was in that direction that Hitler's thoughts began to turn.

He had first to enlarge and consolidate his position in the remaining portions of Europe. He sought to draw Franco's Spain into the Axis, or at least to obtain right of passage for his troops so as to capture Gibraltar and block off the whole Mediterranean. In Spain he failed signally, and as a result the British were able to keep open a precarious life-line to Malta and Alexandria. He had better success in the east, and by March 1941 Hungary, Rumania and Bulgaria were firmly in the Axis camp. (Czechoslovakia had been annexed as a German 'protectorate' in March 1939.) There remained Greece, at war with the Axis in the shape of Mussolini's Italy, and Yugoslavia, which had revolted against its rulers when they agreed to accommodate Hitler. He declared war on both Greece and Yugoslavia on 6 April 1941.

In the meantime a British Commonwealth army (Australians, Africans, British, Indians, New Zealanders and South Africans) in a minor *Blitzkrieg* of their own had set about dismembering the Italian African empire and removing its threat to their Middle East base. Mussolini was in deep trouble, unable to make any headway in Greece and routed and humiliated by the British in Africa. Hitler decided to reinforce the Italians in Tripolitania by air and land. On 14 April the reconnaissance unit of the German 5th Light Division disembarked in Tripoli and Lieutenant-General Erwin Rommel seized command of operations.

The British government had decided to go to the help of Greece with some 100,000 men, drawn from the Middle East theatre. They were duly 'blitzed' and forced to re-embark after 13 days, leaving all their equipment and 11,000 casualties behind. Yugoslavia had fallen, so the Balkans were now completely in Hitler's hands. It was hoped at least to hold Crete and control the Aegean from there, and a garrison was hastily organised from the troops evacuated from Greece, under a redoubtable New Zealander, Major-General Bernard Freyberg.

The German reaction was a unique operation and their first – and last – major airborne assault. On 20 May, after a heavy bombing, 1,500 troops were landed, more bombing stifled the counterattacks to recapture the landing ground and the German build-up continued, under cover of more intense bombing, using parachutists, gliders and finally troop-carrying Ju 52s.

The Royal Navy destroyed every seaborne convoy bringing reinforcement and supply, but lost no fewer than three cruisers and six destroyers in the process, and the outcome after 10 days' fierce fighting was another defeat and another evcuation. The Germans had won a narrow and bitter victory, but 12,970 useful British soldiers were left in Crete to add to those lost in Greece. The Australians suffered particularly heavy losses: 3,573 out of 6,486 in Crete alone.

Things went almost as badly in Tripolitania, where the effect of the diversion of so many good troops to Greece had left the Italians with a foothold which should have been liquidated long before. Rommel on arrival in March had been given permission to probe the British defences, and finding them weak rapidly converted his reconnaissance in force to an all-out offensive and fairly routed them, capturing two generals in the process and locking up the 9th Australian Division in Tobruk while his advanced units drove the British outposts back to the Egyptian frontier. Suez, he thought, was almost in his grasp.

It was in this outwardly discouraging period that the weakness of the *Blitzkrieg* as a magical formula for success first became apparent, even if dimly. The *Blitzkrieg* could only work against poorly trained and badly led troops of low morale.

Tobruk was an impossible place to defend,

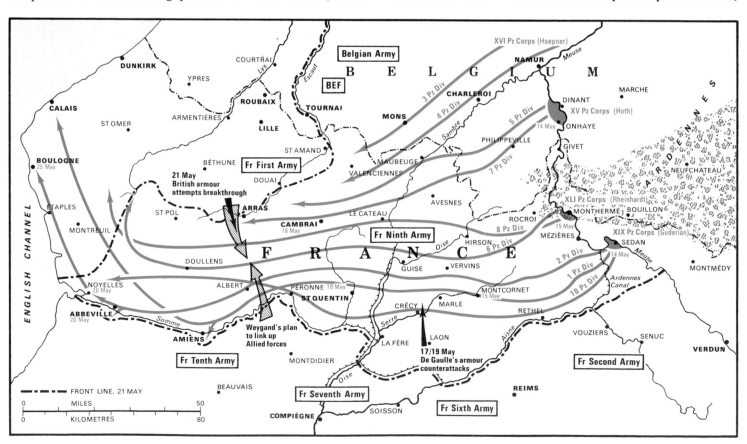

lying in a basin overlooked from all sides once the long perimeter was breached, and the troops in it should by rights, after such a disorganised withdrawal, have been easy meat for the typical Panzer rush Rommel ordered on 14 April. To his chagrin the Australian infantry refused to budge, keeping German infantry in play forward, while the tanks careering on unsupported and unattended ran into the British and Australian artillery, plus a few British tanks, in the heart of the defences and were badly mauled. Another better organised attack

made later fared little better. These were minor actions but straws in the tactical wind. Rommel, as it turned out, was not to march to Suez but to spend the rest of 1941 defending himself against British counter-offensives.

So by mid-summer Hitler's land empire was contained, in an unlikely manner, by the sea-coast in the north, the Pyrenees in the west and a few British divisions on the frontier of Egypt in the south. It is tempting to speculate what might have been the outcome had Hitler chosen to make his next

Above: German troops march in empty triumph down the deserted Champs Elysées after passing the Arc de Triomphe.

major effort in the Middle East with all the glittering strategic benefits it offered him, but fortunately communist Russia was his obsession. On 22 June he embarked on Operation 'Barbarossa', leaving the British still gripping the cornerstones of their land strategy – their island and Egypt.

Barbarossa– Germany invades Russia

At first Hitler's gamble in Russia seemed to have paid off. Then the arrival of winter in 1941 halted his forces. 1942 proved moderately successful, but then came disaster at Stalingrad.

Long before he came to power Hitler had concluded that part of his mission was the destruction of communism and its base in Soviet Russia. The Russians, whom he lumped together in his uneducated mind as one, inferior, race, were to be eradicated and enslaved under German colonial rule, and the wealth of the Ukraine and the Caucasus farmed for Greater Germany. His notional strategic goal was Russia as far east as a line running from Archangel to Astrakhan, but he refused to admit to any remaining danger from the vast expanse of the Soviet Union which extended into Asia, it being

typical of his mental condition that no doubts from the real world were allowed to challenge his fantasies. No appreciation was made of Soviet industrial and economic capabilities. The Soviet armaments industry was in fact capable of producing 12,000 tanks and 21,000 aircraft per year. The peacetime strength of the military power he was challenging was 5 million men organised into 303 divisions plus other field formations, fortress troops and frontier guard units, 24,000 tanks of all sorts and some 7,000 largely obsolete, but still useful, aircraft.

The western defences of the Soviet Union were soundly planned on conventional lines, bearing in mind that the first strategic aim in defence is to retain intact as much of the national territory as possible. (It is specious to pretend that operationally it is correct to trade the lives and homes of millions of civilians in exchange for an elastic withdrawal and the use of space or some such tactical shibboleth. Even the ruthless Soviet leaders did not at first think in such terms, any more than does NATO today.) Essentially there was spread out along the frontier a covering force consisting of three elements – special frontier troops, a fortified belt consisting of machine-gun and artillery emplacements in concrete (arranged in depth and manned by fortress troops), backed by field divisions stationed in each military district and ready to deploy to their battle stations on mobilisation. Behind this covering force stood three armies and a rifle corps totalling 28 divisions, whose task was an immediate counter-offensive. The role of this numerically formidable defence system was to gain time for general mobilisation. Its total strength in the frontier defence zone was 2.9 million men, 12,000 modern tanks plus some 6,000 obsolete ones, 35,000 guns and heavy mortars (excluding pieces of 50-mm calibre and under) and 1,500 aircraft. It should be noted that the Soviet T-34 and KV-1 tanks with their

A Russian reconnaissance unit peer across the battle-torn Mtsensk area on the Bryansk front in August 1943.

long 76.2-mm guns outclassed and out-gunned the German battle tanks, although few of these latest Russian vehicles were available at the outset of the Russo–German war.

The Soviet weakness lay in the quality of these troops at every level. The terrible Stalin purges had reduced the numbers of the officer corps and left the survivors badly shaken, the junior officers were of poor quality, the training of the armed forces had lagged and some war-games held under Stalin's own eye had revealed that the Red Army's tactical doctrine was confused, notably over the question of the organisation and use of armoured formations.

Stalin, a complete realist, feared war and the terrible damage Hitler's war-machine might inflict on his country. He knew that 24 years of Bolshevik rule had not been enough to weld the diverse Russian peoples together or to develop fully the country's whole economic potential. No one knew better than he its political, economic and military weaknesses. While preparing for inevitable war he was determined to avoid its premature outbreak.

Stalin was not totally deaf to the various Intelligence warnings that reached him, but for fear of provoking Hitler he delayed

mobilisation and the deployment of the covering force to its battle stations. The result was that orders only went out on the night of 21 June. Operation 'Barbarossa' was launched by Hitler at dawn on Sunday, 22 June, and the Panzer spearheads rolled into a peaceful countryside unresisted, the defenders caught in their barracks or bemusedly filing off to their positions. Surprise was complete. The collapse of the covering force and the first deep penetrations of the German army was the fault of Stalin's vacillation, but it was the only moment in the war that followed when he faltered.

The German operational plan ignored the problems of time, space, topography and relative strengths, and these were crucial, because at the back of Hitler's cloudy notions of warfare there was the hope that the strategic absurdities of his plan would be covered by its operational success.

Western Russia was a backward forest and arable country, whose towns and cities were connected by dirt roads impassable at the first burst of wet weather. (It is ironic, in a way, that the backwardness of the German army's first line transport, which was almost all horsed, proved a positive advantage when the Panzers and all wheeled transport were immobilised.)

The lines of communication of an invading force would stretch 600 miles from Brest-Litovsk to Moscow and eventually 1,200 to Stalingrad on the Volga. The front was 900 miles at the start line but would expand to 1,500 on the proposed final pause line.

In terms of time, the whole conquest of western Russia had to be complete before the autumn rains, after which there was the Russian winter. For the whole of this gigantic task, the smashing of the Soviet war-machine and the subjugation of half a continent, the operational plan relied upon 3,550 tanks (the bulk upgunned 50-mm PzKpfw IIIs and PzKpfw IVs with the short 75-mm) and some 2,000 aircraft. Reserves of all sorts were deficient, and if the Russian rail network was to be used it had to be converted from broad to narrow gauge to accommodate German rolling stock.

The invasion was to be by three army groups: Army Group 'North' under Field-Marshal Wilhelm von Leeb was directed through the Baltic states on Leningrad; Army Group 'South' under Field-Marshal Gerd von Rundstedt was to advance through Bessarabia on Kiev; and Field-Marshal Fedor von Bock's Army Group 'Centre' was to push along the line of main effort – the axis Minsk-Smolesnk-Moscow. Of the 19 Panzer and 14 motorised divisions, Bock was allotted two Panzer 'groups' (equivalent to 'armies', as indeed they were later designated) out of four, one under General Hermann Hoth and one under Guderian, the architect of the Panzer arm. (Guderian in fact denies that there was a point of main effort and criticised the plan, as he criticised any plan which did not use

Left: The Germans were completely unprepared for the freezing conditions on the Eastern front. But these German troops look cheerful enough as they warm themselves in the snow.

ARMOURED DIVISIONS

OTHER DIVISIONS, including motorised infantry (in Panzergruppen) and cavalry

the whole Panzer might in one concentrated blow.) A significant part of the plan was that Bock was not to drive all out for Moscow, which was both strategically and operationally the real prize, but had first to turn aside to help Leeb mop up and capture Leningrad, to which Hitler for some reason attached great importance.

Behind the Panzer spearhead 116 marching infantry divisions with horse-drawn artillery and transport were committed to 'Barbarossa', plus one useful anachronism in the form of a cavalry division, to operate in the trackless Pripet Marshes.

The tactics to be followed were the 'double envelopment', or to use the graphic German phrase the *Keil und Kessel* (literally 'wedge and kettle', or *Kesselring*, a hunting term in which a shrinking circle of beaters drives the game on to the waiting guns.)

The idea was to break through in a few narrow Panzer *Schwerpunkte* (point of main effort) whose heads would meet far behind the enemy defensive positions, cutting them off. The infantry divisions would then destroy or pound the mass caught in the 'kettle'. These were to be really bold manoeuvres: the junction point for the first of Bock's encirclements was Minsk, and the second Smolensk.

By 16 July these vast operations had three-parts succeeded, and in terms of sheer numbers the Germans might have concluded that the war was won. Some of the Russian units fought hard, but a great many simply dissolved under Panzer and air attack after the Russian command and control system broke down from top to bottom, leaving the Germans the tactical problem of mopping up and marching on.

The encirclements in the centre netted 590,000 prisoners and 5,500 tanks, while Rundstedt in the south pulled in another 130,000 prisoners. The German casualties by this date were 102,000, or 3 per cent. All Hitler's predictions seemed true, but the view from closer to the front was less encouraging. Only Army Group 'Centre' had totally destroyed its opposing West Front. ('Front' is the Russian equivalent of 'army group'.) Leeb had advanced successfully and was approaching the outskirts of Leningrad but having to fight hard, while Rundstedt in the south was facing two battered but unbroken Fronts and threatened by a major counter-offensive from his left, or north-east.

To harvest the fruits of the operational victory it was essential to keep moving and give the Soviet high command no respite to stabilise the front or mount counterattacks. The supply and replacement situation was beginning to cause anxiety, especially in tanks and tank spares. The German range of tanks was mechanically reliable, but long grinding away in low gear in dust and soft ground for hundreds of miles were inevitably taking its toll. Artillery ammunition was running short, and sooner or later, when there was bound to be some protracted, static fighting, this was going to count.

We can see now, with the advantage of hindsight, that the German invasion was historically doomed from the start, but it was at this point that Hitler, sticking his pins in his map far away in his headquarters in East Prussia, took the fatal step which ensured the eventual defeat of his armies – he turned away from Moscow.

In all operations it is a good rule to reinforce success, and success had been in the centre, where Bock's army group was only 200 miles from Moscow with nothing in front and its soldiers, flushed with easy success, panting to go on.

The capital had great symbolic value in war, and it also was the main rail communication focus in western Russia. Its capture would split north from south and make the movement of reserves and the building-up of fresh fronts extremely difficult. These advantages were thrown away for the sake of an operational success. One of Bock's panzer groups (Hoth) was ordered to break way and march 400 miles north to assist in the capture of Leningrad (which was never achieved), and the other (Guderian) 400 miles in the opposite direction to assist Rundstedt to trap and destroy the South-West Front in a great *Kessel* 130 miles wide and deep north-east of Kiev. There 665,000 prisoners were taken, but it was a barren victory, for while theoretically it is sound sense to make the enemy armies, and not places, the objective, there remained the stubborn facts of military arithmetic.

Left: A Russian 85mm anti-aircraft gun being used in the anti-tank role on the Eastern Front in 1941. It fired an APHE round which would penetrate 100mm of armour at 1000m

Right: Winter-equipped German troops. Until the arrival of such equipment, the Germans had to strip Russian dead for winter clothing and snow suits, especially overboots.

Enormous as Soviet losses were, yet more armies would appear out of Siberia in a seemingly endless procession.

The significant thing about the whole battle of Moscow was its date: 9 September. Bock's total success against West Front was completed by 16 July, and it was not until 23 August that Hitler, his weathercock mind spinning at every minor operational change, as his generals groaned to observe, decided to scatter his Panzer striking force and declare that his true strategic objectives lay far away to the south-east. Then, while the battle of Kiev was in progress, he abandoned his set aim of capturing Leningrad and ordered a frontal attack to capture Moscow.

The preliminary break-in battle of Vyazma-Bryansk was fought in the first week of October. In Russia the first rain and snow of autumn is expected at the beginning of the second week of October, and it was punctual. The onset of winter is then marked by mud which arrests all movement, and its proper arrival by unimaginable cold, which freezes unprotected men to death and stops machinery – the very lubricants solidifying to a gum.

What is astounding about the German army in that first winter is that it did not break down. It was not as if the German and the Red armies were wearing each other down equally: the same German army, eked out by a few reinforcements, fought successive, fresh Russian contingents, and however great the defeat inflicted on each, it cost both sides casualties in terms of men, tanks and, what is often forgotten, thousands of starved and overworked horses which died in harness, until the whole forward transport system was almost paralysed. From an initially desperate position the Russian defence recovered by superhuman exertions to the point that by November the militarily frugal Stalin could once more pull out formations to build up his reserves. By mid-

November massive reinforcements, including 2,000 guns, were available for the West Front, whose counter-offensive was to go on throughout the winter.

What Hitler had lost was six weeks of dry weather, as a result of the Yugoslav and Greek campaigns, and delays to Bock's efforts, and all the track mileage wasted in motoring Hoth and Guderian on a round trip of 1,000 miles in opposite directions. In a static position, or when attacking after preparation, the Red Army could fight well. What put it right off balance was manoeuvre:

once enveloped or surrounded its commanders were bemused and control collapsed. This was now impossible. Once the autumn rains fairly started, all wheeled transport bogged down. There was not petrol for the tanks, and the war became an infantry/artillery affair fought at foot pace, with double teams or even 16 horses trying to drag a single 105-mm howitzer through the mud. To exploit the Vyazma-Bryansk victory, where some 670,000 men, 1,200 tanks and 4,000 guns had been trapped, proved impossible, and the battle of Moscow

T-34/85 tank

Crew: 5. **Weight:** 70,548 lbs (32,000kg). **Length overall:** 26ft 8in (8.076m). **Length:** 20ft 3⅜in (6.19m). **Width:** 9ft 10in (2.997m). **Height:** 9ft 0in (2.743m). **Road speed:** 31 to 34mph (50 to 55kmh). **Range:** 186 miles (300km). **Engine:** Model V-2-34, V-12, water-cooled diesel developing 500hp at 1,800rpm. **Ground pressure:** 11.8psi (.83kg/cm²). **Vertical obstacle:** 28¾in (.73m). **Trench:** 8ft 2½in (2.5m). **Gradient:** 60%. **Armour:** 18 to 90m.

The Soviet T34 tank is considered by many to be the best all-round tank of World War II and it remains in service with about 30 nations. The first model to enter service in 1940 was the T-34/76, which was armed with a 76mm gun. Just over 1,000 of these were in service when the Germans invaded Russia in

June 1941. The T-34/85 was introduced in 1943 and proved to be capable of defeating most German tanks. Production continued until 1964 and it is estimated that up to 100,000 were built. The hull front and sides of the T-34 are well sloped to give maximum possible protection and the turret is of cast construction with the roof welded on. The main armament consists of an 85mm gun which was developed from an anti-aircraft weapon and has an elevation of +25° and a depression of −5°. It can fire the following types of ammunition: — HE with projectile weighing 9.5kg, APHE with projectile of 9.3kg and HVAP of 5 kg, the latter being able to penetrate 130mm of armour at a range of 1,093 yards (1,000m). A 7.62mm Degtyarev MG is mounted in the bow of the tank. Some T-34s had a 7.62mm machine gun mounted on the turret roof. Total ammunition carried is 56 rounds of 85mm and 2,394 rounds of 7.62mm.

and the war was lost – at least such is the German view.

Historically it is more correct perhaps to say that the battle for Moscow was the first milestone on the way to Hitler's defeat, with two more to come – Stalingrad and Kursk.

The final phase of the battle for Moscow concluded with Army Group 'Centre', over-extended, below strength and exhausted, being driven back some 60 miles by furious counter-attacks converging from either side of Moscow. All military common sense dictated that the only sane course open to the Germans once the Moscow offensive had failed was to break cleanly away on to a shortened fortified defensive line to rest, reorganise and re-equip. No such policy was allowed. Hitler, who on 29 December sacked Field-Marshal Walther von Brauchitsch and assumed direct operational control as commander-in-chief himself,

forbade any withdrawal, with the upshot that his exhausted armies were driven slowly back in a costly running battle to the line their commanders had asked to occupy in the first place. Fighting went on and on, as Stalin realised that whatever the cost, his troops knew how to fight in the winter and the Germans did not. He was right, and it is doubtful if the army which had so brilliantly won the 'three weeks offensive' of that summer was ever to be the same instrument again. After much confused and bitter fighting, in which the encirclers were encircled and the encircling rings broken again, the battle for Moscow ended with the Russians victorious and both sides immobilised by sheer exhaustion and the mud of the spring thaw.

This was a great victory, but the actual turn of the tide was at Stalingrad. Balked completely in the north, Hitler for his 1942 campaign decided to sweep down to the

Caucasus, cutting off all Soviet resources in the Don basin and oil supplies in the Caucasus, thus ending the war economically.

Two armies, one Panzer and one marching, were to race to the line of Baku-Batum (Army Group 'A') while Army Group 'B' of one Panzer and two marching armies, driving all before them, were to establish a defensive flank over 600 miles long from Voronezh along the upper Don as far as Stalingrad and thence along the Volga.

Behind these all German spearheads there were to follow an Italian, a Hungarian and a Rumanian army (with two more armies in the Crimea), the whole expedition totalling six motorised, 10 Panzer and 44 infantry German divisions plus – grimly indicative of the German manpower situation – 43 non-German divisions. The total seems enormous, but at the maximum point of advance this front alone, measured round the bends, would be some 1,200–1,400 miles,

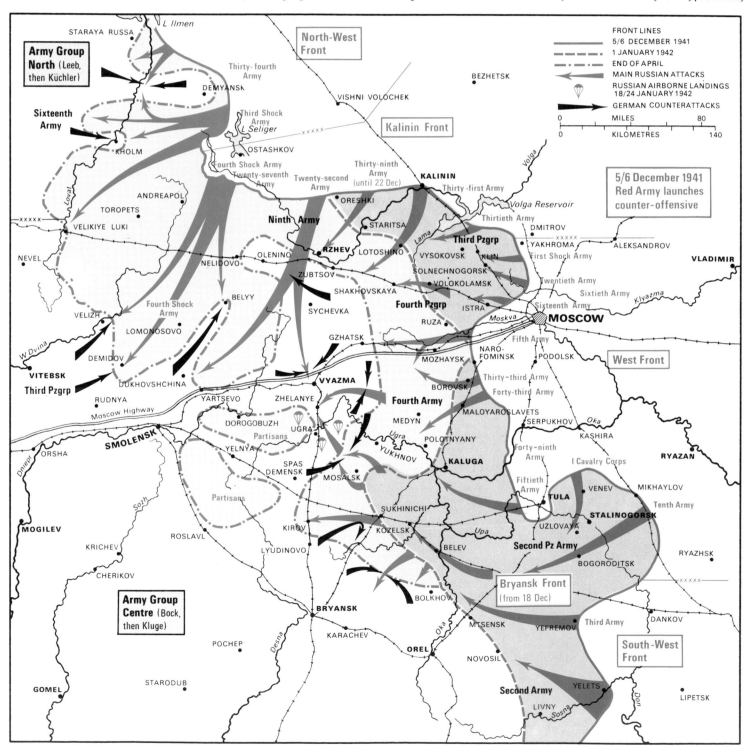

A mixed armour-infantry team moves up towards an objective outside Moscow. The swastika flag is for identification by ground-support aircraft.

with tenuous lines of communication over 1,000 miles long exposed to constant partisan attack. Hitler may rightly have assumed that the Soviet divisions could not yet stand up to the Panzers, but he could not understand that distance diluted the latters' strength, that fighting caused casualties he could not replace and that the further this rash invasion advanced the more it was exposed along its long north-eastern flank to a deadly counter-offensive.

This is in fact what happened, and the significance of the battle of Stalingrad was that first it sucked in troops which could have been employed better elsewhere, and then gave vital time for the Russian counter-stroke to be mounted.

The sequence of events at first repeated the pattern of 1941. The Crimea fell to Manstein and his German–Rumanian group. Army Groups 'A' under Field-Marshal Wilhelm List and 'B' under Bock rolled forward over all opposition. Again the Red Army suffered enormous losses, two armies and part of another being encircled in May. Voronezh was lost in July, and by August the Don had been crossed in force and List's Army Group 'A' had reached Maykop and Krasnodar in the Caucasus, and Novo-rossiysk by mid-September.

The significant date was 23 August. On that day General Friedrich Paulus's 6th Army reached the suburbs of Stalingrad, on the west bank of the Volga. If Stalingrad fell all rail and river transport to the north would be severed. But instead of pinching it out, Paulus was committed to direct assault, and if there was one thing the Red Army was able to do as well as the Germans it was fight a dour defensive battle from the cover of ruined buildings. The German 6th Army was stuck.

Stalin's immediate reaction to this chain of fresh disasters was to put his trouble-shooter, the ruthless and immensely competent General Georgi Zhukov, in overall operational command and demand that counter-offensives be mounted at once. They were, and they failed, except insofar as they tempted Hitler to draw on his Caucasus striking force for reinforcements for the front on the Volga, including most of List's aircraft.

Zhukov had his customary battle with Stalin (so like the struggles British generals had with Churchill). He read the position as being outnumbered 1.4 to 1 in bayonets, more or less equal in artillery but desperately short of artillery ammunition, without which he could not fire the heavy preparation needed to soften the Germans to the point when the Red Army could face them on equal terms, 2 to 1 in tanks and 3.5 to 1 in aircraft. He needed above all time to train and prepare. Finally in November he was ready to launch a giant double envelopment with General Konstantin Rokossovsky in the north and General Andrei Evemenko in the south, which trapped Paulus and 200,000 combat troops. The Germans were now tasting their own medicine. Paulus could have broken out, but Hitler was deaf to all

7.5cm PAK.40 anti-tank gun

Calibre: 75mm. **Effective A/Tank range:** 1968 yards (1800m). **Weight:** 3142lb (1425kg). **Length:** 20′ 3½″ (6.185m). **Width:** 6′ 10″ (2.08m). **Height:** 4′ 1″ (1.245m). **Elevation:** −5° to +22°. **Traverse:** 65°. **Rate of fire:** 10rpm (practical).

The Pak.40 (or Panzerabwehrkanone 40) was developed from 1939 by the Rheinmetall-Borsig company as the—then current 50mm anti-tank gun did not have sufficient penetration capabilities. The Pak.40 entered service late in 1941 and served on all German fronts continuing in service with a number of countries after the end of the war.

The weapon had a split-trail carriage with a spade on the end of each trail and the barrel was provided with a muzzle brake. The breech mechanism was of the semi-automatic horizontal type. The Pak.40 fired an armour piercing projectile weighing 14.99lb (6.8kg) with a muzzle velocity of 2,600fps (792m/s), which would penetrate 4.57 inches (116mm) of armour at a range of 1,093 yards (1000m). There was also a HE and a special tungsten-corded projectile, the latter able to penetrate 5.24 inches (133mm) of armour at a range of 1,093 yards (1000m). A variety of self-propelled models were also developed.

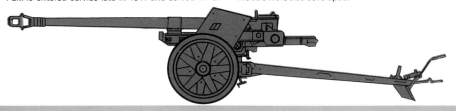

pleas and the survivors of the 6th Army surrendered on 2 February 1943, all attempts at relief having failed against the gathering Russian strength.

At the end of December Hitler was persuaded that to leave Army Group 'A' in position was to ensure its total loss, and in a series of dogged and brilliant rearguard actions the Germans, fighting not only Russians but once more temperatures of −20° and −30° Centigrade, escaped eastward, but utterly defeated. The whole of their southern front was open to the enemy. The Russians had not only worn them down but at last had learnt how to beat them. And Kursk, the clinching battle of the war, where the newly-equipped Panzers were to be smashed on their start-lines and the *Blitzkrieg* finally tamed, was the disaster to come.

'Torch' to the Alps

The campaign in North Africa culminated in 1943 with the invasion of Italy. But then dissension in the Allied camp hampered the development of one of the hardest fought campaigns of World War II.

Throughout 1941 and 1942 a curious little war swayed back and forth along the Mediterranean coast of Africa, with the famous Erwin Rommel and the Axis forces on one side and what became the British-Commonwealth 8th Army of Australians, British, Free French, New Zealanders, South Africans and Indians under a succession of commanders on the other. Compared with the vast scale of the war in Russia the battles were tiny, mere skirmishes. At the crisis of the campaign, when General Sir Claude Auchinleck came forward to take command in the field himself to win the 1st Battle of El Alamein, the units were counted in brigades and mere handfuls of wornout tanks on both sides, but although the board was small, the play was often brilliant and the stakes high. Initially Hitler had intervened to prop up his inept partner Mussolini, only to perceive later the possibilities of inflicting a crushing moral defeat on the British in their Middle East bastion and just possibly of opening a southern route to the Caucasus. The Allies had so far agreed a Mediterranean strategy in that they had resolved to clear up Africa and take the war to Italy pending the final cross-Channel invasion.

A Bren gunner in action at Cassino, Italy, in 1944. The Germans successfully repulsed many allied attacks with heavy casualties before it finally fell after an attack by allied bombers. It was finally captured by the Polish Army on 18th May, 1944.

On 3 November 1942 the 8th Army under Grneral Bernard Montgomery cracked the Axis defences at El Alamein and began its long advance westwards. And 7 November was D-day for Operation 'Torch', the first of the four major landings in the Mediterranean, in which some 850 naval vessels and transports disembarked American and British armies in French North Africa. Soon afterwards, paratroops and a small mechanised force were sent off to capture Tunis.

The German general staff, or rather the Commander-in-Chief South, Field-Marshal Albert Kesselring, reacted with their usual speed to block them and establish their own bridgehead in Tunisia by forming, in their inimitable way, small battle-groups from every available unit or individual as fast as they could be flown in. After some dashing operations by both sides the Germans won the race by a week or so, just as the autumn rains began. But in spite of all their efforts, the Axis venture in Africa was doomed. The Allies had control of the air, so the Axis sea routes were cut and their armies trapped

between Montgomery's and General Dwight D. Eisenhower's forces advancing irresistibly from east and west. There was much hard fighting yet to be done, but today the final battles are of professional interest only. Long before the Axis forces were liquidated the Allied staffs were preparing for the landings in Sicily and the Italian mainland.

On 9–10 July the British 8th and the US 7th Armies invaded Sicily. A pointer to the extreme complexity of such operations, and to the room for error inherent in them, was the terrible mishap to part of the airborne forces which inadvertently flew over the supporting fleet en route to its dropping zones and was engaged by the naval AA fire.

Left: German ground troops watch the effect of artillery shells pounding a typical Italian mountain terrain.

Right: A heavily armed jeep patrol of the Long Range Desert Group. These patrols carried out daring reconnaissance missions and raids deep behind the German lines.

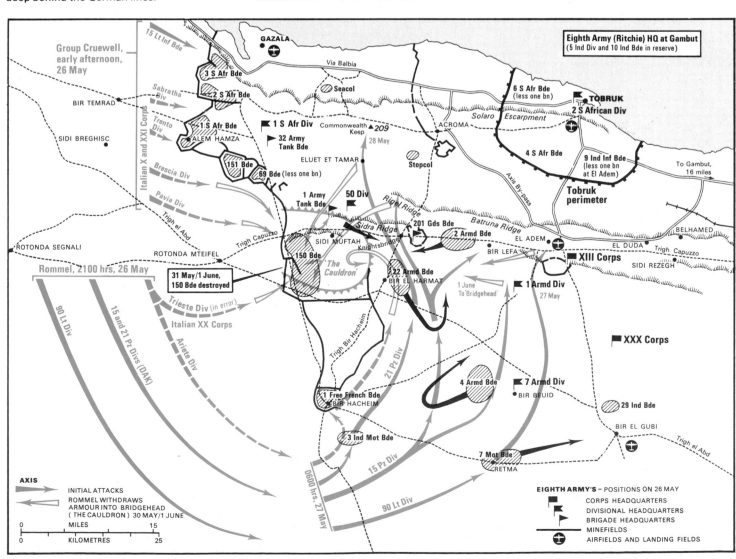

Tactically, Sicily was a warning of the defensive potential of the Italian terrain, so different from the flat expanses of Russia or the undulating Western Desert. The tank was no longer supreme, and slow, bitter 'winkling' attacks by infantry with powerful artillery support were required to turn the skilled and dogged German battle-groups out of the little villages or off the rocky ridges where they were ensconced. This pattern was to persist for month after long month until the spring of 1945.

All resistance in Sicily ended on 17 August, the very day on which Churchill and Roosevelt met in Quebec to agree the final strategy for the liberation of Europe.

Churchill saw strategy as a preparation for the political goals he saw as necessary in the ensuing peace, the foremost of which was to prevent central Europe falling under Soviet control. Operationally he favoured the 'indirect approach' and never ceased to press for a far-reaching encircling thrust from the south with perhaps Vienna as its objective.

To the Americans both these ideas were anathema on two grounds. It was politically unacceptable to use American lives and war

matériel to further Britain's aims – always suspect – in Europe, and strategically the United States chiefs-of-staff favoured the exact opposite: invasion by the shortest, cross-Channel route and a deliberate clash with the enemy main forces, which would be destroyed in the field, so as to free the United States to concentrate on the war against Japan. Coming from the major partner, the American view inevitably prevailed (and, as many would argue, rightly). The agreed aim of the Italian campaign was to contain or distract as many Axis troops away from the main area of decision in France after which, in due course, a proportion of the Allied divisions in Italy would be switched to subsidiary invasion of the French Riviera. This was the general idea. There was never a 'master plan' for Italy, with precise objectives, and there continued to be a tug between a purely holding operation, and the ambitions of the theatre commanders to exploit to the maximum – perhaps even to Austria. Generals in command of large forces are seldom content to accept a passive or secondary role, and Field-Marshal Sir Harold Alexander and General Mark Clark were no exceptions.

As it happened, Hitler, an 'indirect approach' man himself, saw the Italian situation and its dangers to his position through Churchill's eyes, and decided to reinforce Italy regardless of its surrender on 8 September, from then on treating it simply as an occupied country.

Two German armies were organised, initially of 16 divisions, eight in the south to fight a long delaying action, and eight to prepare a final defensive position in the Appenines, running approximately from La Spezia to Pesaro, known as the Green Line or, to the Allies, as the Gothic Line. These 16 divisions were later reinforced to 19, but the Germans were under-strength (divisions holding 10 miles or more of front), outgunned (except in tanks and anti-tank guns) and had lost control in the air.

The German defence in Italy was to prove one of the most remarkable professional feats in military history, bearing

Right: German paratroopers in defensive positions at Cassino in Italy. These were the elite of the German Army and were last used as paratroopers in the invasion of Crete.

DUKW amphibian

Crew: 1. **Weight:** 19,570lb (8876kg). **Length:** 31' (9.448m). **Width:** 8' 2⅞'' (2.51m). **Height:** 8' 9¾'' (2.686m). **Speed road:** 45mph (72.5kmh). **Speed water:** 6.3mph (10kmh). **Range road:** 220 miles (354km). **Range water:** 50 miles (80kmh). **Engine:** GMC 6 cylinder liquid cooled developing 94 HP at 3000rpm.

The DUKW was developed by the US National Defence Research Committee (NRDC) with the assistance of Sparkman and Stephens and was essentially a standard GMC 6×6 truck chassis fitted with a watertight body. It was standardised in October, 1942, and 21,147 were manufactured by the Yellow Truck and Coach Manufacturing Company by the end of the war. The designation DUKW-353 was arrived at as follows:— D for 1942, U—amphibious, K—6×6 all wheel drive, W—rear wheel axles and 353 was the chassis designation. After the war, the Russians built a vehicle similar to the DUKW, the BAV-485. The DUWK was used for transporting supplies from ships to beaches as well as overland. On land it was powered by all six wheels (or the driver could select just the rear four wheels) and in water by a single propeller at the rear, steering being by combined use of the front wheels and rudder.

Some DUKWs had an M36 ring mount above the cab, with a .50 Browning machine gun for antiaircraft defence. The vehicle could carry 25 fully

equipped troops or 5,000lb (2268kg) of cargo. A winch with a capacity of 10,000lb (4536kg) was mounted at the rear of the hull for self-recovery operations.

Jeep

Crew: driver and three passengers. **Weight empty:** 2453lb (1,113kg). **Length:** 10' 11'' (3.327m). **Width:** 5' 2'' (1.574m). **Height (hood up):** 6' (1.828m). **Road speed:** 55mph (88kmh). **Range:** 225 miles (362km). **Engine:** Willys 441 or 442 four cylinder petrol engine developing 65 BHP at 4000rpm.

In the late 1930s Captain Howie and Sergeant Wiley of the US Army built a semi-cross country vehicle called the Howie-Wiley machine gun carrier, or the "Belly Flopper" as it became known. At about the same time the Bantam Motor Company loaned three of its vehicles to the Army for trials, which were quite successful. In June 1940, Bantam designed a vehicle combining the best features of both types and the Army put out a requirement for 70 for trials. The Bantam Company and Willy-Overland responded to the tender and Bantam won the contract. The first prototype was delivered to the Army on September 23rd 1940. In the meantime however, both Ford and Willy built prototypes to the same specification as the Bantam model. Production contracts were awarded to all three companies but Bantam lost out and they built their last of 2,675 Jeeps in December, 1941. Of the total of 639,245 Jeeps built, the vast majority were made by Ford and Willy.

There are various suggestions as to how the name Jeep came about, the most common that it is derived from the designation GP (General Purpose), the full name of the Jeep being Truck, ¼ ton, 4×4, command and reconnaissance, or Truck, ¼ ton, 4×4 utility.

The Jeep was used on every Allied front (many were supplied to the Russians), and for a variety of roles including cable laying, towing, wireless communication, observation, reconnaissance, ambulance and so on. Development continued after the war and the current model is the M151 series.

in mind that it was not simply superior fire-power and a mass of *matériel* which drove them back. The German infantry, not long before the terrors of Europe and Russia, now met opponents who, platoon for platoon, were as good at the game as themselves. To take the 8th Army alone, its forcing of the Gothic Line defences in the autumn of 1944 was one of the finest feats of its multi-national infantry, for the credit was not confined to the Americans and British: there were 26 nationalities in the 5th and 8th Armies – including Brazilians, Canadians, French and French Moroccans and Algerians, Gurkhas, Indians of a dozen castes and ethnic groups, New Zealanders and Poles. Allied strength fluctuated, but after four French and three US divisions had been withdrawn Alexander still had 20 divisions.

From the Allied side Italy can be seen as the war of lost opportunities. After Sicily the 8th Army hopped over the Straits of Messina and established bridgeheads round the foot of Italy and then began, rather slowly, to work inland. On 9 September the 5th Army landed in strength south of Salerno, initially lightly opposed, but the German reaction was characteristically rapid and Clark was not able to break out until the 24th. Thereafter the autumn and winter were spent with the 8th Army in the east and the 5th in the west slowly grinding away against the German intermediate lines and through a maze of mines and demolitions. Every river line and every ridge ran athwart the Allied line of advance, was skilfully defended and determinedly forced. It was an engineer's war as well as an infantryman's war and, surprisingly in the mid-century, a muleteer's war as well; by the end of the campaign no fewer than 30,000 mules were occupied in first line supply and casualty evacuation from ground where not even a Jeep could go.

In October the Allies then came up against a solid belt of defences based in the west on Cassino and the Rapido river, and then what the German commanders feared more than anything else happened. On 22 January 1944 the Allies used their amphibious capability to land behind the German right flank, at Anzio, and so turn their whole position. This opportunity was muffed through feeble leadership, and the Anzio detachment was kept penned up in its bridgehead until 23 May, when it broke out as the 5th Army broke through the Gustav intermediate line at Cassino. (None of these lines, it must be said, were seen as 'intermediate' by the troops on the ground: to clear each required an intense bombardment by 1,000 or more guns, massive air-strikes and costly hand-to-hand combat.)

A further chance to trap the southern echelon of the German armies was then

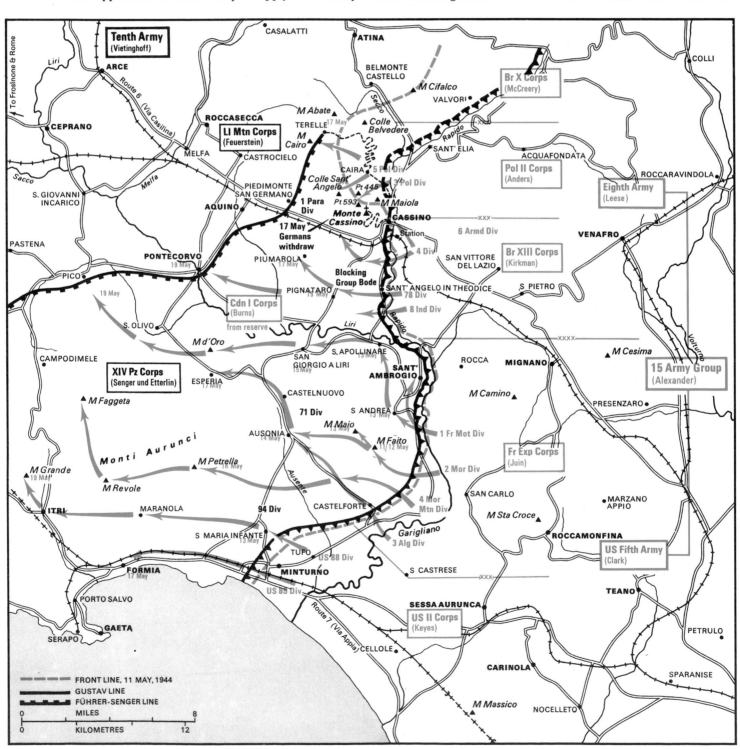

Sherman tank

Crew: 5 (commander, gunner, loader, driver and hull gunner). **Weight:** 71,175lb (32,284kg). **Length, overall:** 24' 8'' (7.518m). **Length:** 20' 7'' (6.273m). **Width:** 8' 9'' (2.667m). **Height w/o A/A MG:** 11' 3'' (3.425m). **Road speed:** 30mph (48.2kmh). **Range road:** 100 miles (161km). **Engine:** Ford GAA v-8 petrol developing 450 BHP at 2600rpm. **Vertical obstacle:** 2' (.609m). **Trench:** 7'5'' (2.26m). **Gradient:** 60%. **Armour:** 19 to 64mm.

Before World War II, the US Army had very limited funds for tank development, but in the 1930s a tank known as the T5 was developed and used as the basis for the Grant/Lee tanks which served the British Army so well in North Africa. This in turn served as the basis for the T6 Medium Tank, or the Sherman as it became known. It took just nine months to design and build and at the same time a factory was being built to build the tank. The Sherman became the most widely used allied tank and was eventually built by a number of car and locomotive manufacturers. By the end of the war, 48,000 had been built.

One of the last models to enter service was the M4A3E8, which was commonly known as the "Easy Eight." This was armed with a 76mm gun and a co-axial .30 Browning machine gun. Another .30 MG was mounted in the hull with a .50 MG on the turret for anti-aircraft defence. A 2'' mortar was also provided. Total ammunition supply consisted of 71 rounds of 76mm, 6,250 rounds of .30 and 600 rounds of .50cm. The suspension on the E8 model was of the HVSS (Horizontal Volute Suspension) type and gave a much easier ride, hence the name Easy Eight.

As a tank, the Sherman was by no means out standing; it was however available in vast numbers, was very reliable and backed by an efficient logistical system. The Sherman chassis was used for a whole range of variants including the M10 and M36 tank destroyers, M40 (155mm) and M41 (8'') self-propelled weapons and a variety of other vehicles.

lost through a decision by Clark to go for the prestige goal of Rome instead of swinging from the Anzio perimeter round behind the defenders of the Gustav Line and so cutting off a major portion of the 10th Army, and from then on the two Allied armies were committed to a laborious northward crawl, led by their engineers building bridges, with one frontal attack after another until they at last came up against the Gothic Line.

The decision to force the Gothic Line was a bold one. Alexander had only a marginal superiority in numbers (although by the nature of mountain warfare he could concentrate at will against one pass after another), it was late in the season and he had no reserve. Moreover, his planners were mistaken in the notion that behind the Appenines there was country suited for a classical armoured breakthrough, and they continued to believe that a breakthrough might yet after all permit a glorious strategic thrust through the Ljubljana 'gap' to Vienna.

It was a vain hope, for once the divisions for the landings in southern France were withdrawn, there were no reserves for rapid exploitation. The Gothic Line was indeed pierced in a series of company and battalion battles in which both sides showed self-sacrifice and heroism, but the British armour was stopped cold, there were no replacements for casualties, the supplies of artillery ammunition were cut down to keep the insatiable guns in France supplied and then it began to rain. Napoleon's 'fifth element', the mud, stopped the war until the spring of 1945.

Kesselring, the German commander-in-chief, could at least grimly congratulate himself that he had kept his word to Hitler and held the Allies penned in Italy.

Left: Italian refugees crossing the Ponte Alle Grazie bridge over the River Arno in August, 1944. The bridge was extensively mined by the retreating Germans.

Overlord– Germans are swept from France

Allied plans for the liberation of Europe from the German yoke led in June 1944 to the greatest seaborne invasion of all time: the landings in Normandy, otherwise Operation 'Overlord'.

That the shortest and surest way to defeat Hitler and liberate Europe was to launch an invading army across the English Channel was never in doubt, but all involved perceived that the dangers were immense. Churchill was not a man given to fear, yet he dreaded the prospect. On a lower plane, late in 1943 during a Staff College discussion of the purely technical problems, one speaker referred facetiously to 'Operation Bloodbath', and a shudder went round a room full of veteran officers.

How it was done, and done successfully, was a triumph of imaginative planning and technology applied to apparently insoluble military problems.

The German defence in France and the Low Countries, under Rundstedt, totalled 10 Panzer and *Panzer-grenadier* divisions – as ever the *élite* and spearhead of the army – and 38 other divisions. The coast was guarded along its whole length and the most likely landing areas strongly fortified in depth, with underwater obstacles, mined beaches, tank traps and ditches and a chequerboard pattern of heavy anti-ship guns and anti-tank guns in concrete emplacements, infantry pill-boxes and field artillery. This was the so-called '*Westwall*'. Only one uncertainty divided the minds of the German command. Was the best plan to hold the perimeter and maintain the bulk of the armour in reserve so as to mount a counter-offensive when it became clear which landings were feints and which were the ones on the point of main effort; or should the defence forces rely on a rigid linear defence of the beaches, gambling on eliminating the assaulting troops when they were most vulnerable?

Rommel, whose Army Group 'B' was to defend the invasion coast, believed that the Allied air forces could interdict any large-scale move by a central reserve, and Hitler supported him, so the second course – the more favourable from the attacker's point of view – was adopted, with one reservation: the armoured reserve, Panzer Group 'West' under General Geyr von Schweppenburg, was held back for use at the high command's discretion.

The difficulties of an opposed landing can be simply explained by comparing it with a purely land attack on a highly organised defensive system. The attackers in the latter

A mighty Sherman tank rumbles ashore during a massive Allied beach landing. The rugged Sherman was used to great effect during WWII. Over 45,000 were built eventually.

case could – exactly as their ancestors had when attacking a fortress – start from the cover of their own defence works with massive pre-planned supporting fire, and were faced with only a short advance in the open before close combat inside the enemy defences began. If checked they could try again or, at worst, disengage and dig in. By contrast, an amphibious attack was like attacking the same system across a dead flat plain without cover from assembly areas 50 or 100 miles off.

This was the accepted picture, and in classical strategy its worst elements were to be avoided by a surprise landing on some undefended stretch remote from the objective, taking the coastal defences in reverse and capturing a working port through which the build-up of the invaders could continue.

It was not tactics that were to provide the solution to the problem but technology and the enormous industrial potential of the United States. The fortified assembly area was provided by the whole island of Britain, and the 'artillery preparation' and covering fire on the vast scale and intensity required were provided by aircraft based on the 'unsinkable aircraft-carrier'. The success of 'Overlord', the most famous of operational code-names and now a proper noun in its own right, rested on four technological bases.

Specialised landing-craft were produced so that tanks, guns and infantry could be

Above: American troops wade ashore in France from a landing craft manned by men of the United States Coast Guard on D-Day, June 6, 1944

Right: German medium artillery, part of the much-vaunted, but still largely imaginery 'Atlantic wall' beloved of the German Propaganda Ministry.

carried up to the very beach, where the craft were deliberately stranded so as to allow the troops to wade ashore.

The second was air power, used offensively on a vast scale.

The third was a very simple British invention called a 'DD', or duplex drive, tank: ordinary tanks fitted with canvas floating gear and a marine propeller, which swam in until their tracks touched bottom. They were supported by engineer-manned specialist tanks for breaching obstacles and clearing mind-fields, and self-propelled armoured artillery, which started firing as their landing craft ran in. Without the DD tanks it was doubtful whether or not the infantry could have survived on the beach, let alone moved inland decisively.

The fourth was a piece of breath-taking 'lateral thinking'. Capturing a port and putting it in working order would take too long. Instead, two prefabricated ports were prepared in England and towed across the Channel to serve the British and American beach-heads.

To this can be added a fifth. It was not possible to outflank the *Westwall*, but it was possible to jump over it. An effective part of the operational plan was the use of

three airborne divisions – one British, two American – to land in the Germans' rear and block the likely routes for immediate counterattack.

The operation plan was simple enough, but as always in war the problems lay in the details of managing and manoeuvring such large forces in a novel operation of such size and complexity. The essentials of the plan were as follows.

The first phase was a sustained air offensive prior to D-Day to cripple the German transportation system and wreck the coastal batteries and radars.

The assault would be made on a 70-mile front with 15 divisions organised in two armies, plus other combat troops, amounting to two equivalent divisions, and the three airborne divisions.

Of these, five (the US 1st and 4th, Canadian 3rd and British 3rd and 50th were to be the spearhead divisions on the selected beaches.

Once the beaches had been joined up and the bridgehead deepened to its first objectives, the British and Canadians on the left were to pound and grind away around Caen so as to draw in all the German reserves in a battle of attrition, while the Americans on the right broke out westwards, clearing the Contentin peninsula and thrusting down to Brittany until the German forces containing the beach-head were outflanked, and so allowing a great armoured operation to develop in the open and then move east.

This was the 'master-plan', developed by Montgomery and given to him to execute as the overall commander in the field. There has been much controversy about the Battle of Normandy, but in fact, allowing for the accidents of war and the fact that the enemy does not always oblige, it went almost exactly according to plan.

Finally, as soon as time and space permitted, another US army was to be deployed and Eisenhower would take command of all the operations in France. But Montgomery can be fairly credited as the planner and victor of the Battle of Normandy. It was his greatest feat and one of the great battles of the war.

Only figures can give an idea of that vast operation. Before D-Day on 6 June 1944 the combined air forces dropped 66,000 tons of bombs, of which some 14,000 were directed on the coastal defences, knocking out all the heavy guns and radar stations. Some 14,600 offensive sorties were flown on D-Day itself. The airborne assault was carried in 2,395 aircraft sorties and 867 gliders. When it was light enough at dawn on 6 June 1944 the astonished defenders could see some 4,000 landing-craft in the bay, only part of a combined fleet of 6,000 vessels.

The fire-plan for the run-in used 7,600 tons of bombs, augmented by naval bombardment, followed up by bombarding craft with multi-rail rockets and the self-propelled field batteries firing while still afloat in the approaching landing-craft. By 12 June there were 326,000 troops, 54,000 vehicles of all kinds and 104,000 tons of warlike stores in the beach-head, which was then proof against any counter-offensive.

The reaction was typically dour, but unfortunately for the Germans the harder they fought and the more sustained their forward defence, the more they became trapped in Montgomery's meat-grinder and the more they served to further his 'masterplan'. Their only hope would have been a phased withdrawal keeping their armies in being, but this was vetoed by Hitler when he actually made one of his rare visits (on 17 June) to a theatre commander.

On 3 July Lieutenant-General Omar Bradley's US 1st Army began to clear space for a break-out at St Lô, while the British and Canadians went for Caen, the anchor position of the German right, which Rommel and Rundstedt saw as their most dangerous flank. The British attacks were made after intense bombing, with results similar to the ponderous artillery bombardments of World War I: the craters and the damage done blocked the advance of the assaulting troops, and provided cover for the defenders. On 18 July another advance was attempted under cover of a further huge aerial bombardment, which was to be followed up this time by three British armoured divisions. But the bombing failed to include the German anti-tank belt deployed in depth and, as was now the trend in armoured warfare, the guns won the day and stopped the British tank attack with heavy losses. Nevertheless these attacks served their purpose in attracting the German reserves and wearing them down.

The US 1st Army, using similar tactics at St Lô, made better progress against reduced resistance. On 28 July Coutances was captured and Lieutenant-General George Patton's newly-formed 3rd Army took up the hunt. He captured Avranches, by 10 August Nantes was in Allied hands and the whole of the Brittany peninsula was cut off. Patton was now directed to turn east, and on 4 August set off with objective Paris.

It was at this point that Hitler, looking at his map as usual and playing military chess, perceived the theoretical vulnerability of the inner, or left-hand flank of Patton's eastward swinging hook, and ordered every Panzer formation which could be disengaged to attack from Mortain westwards towards Avranches. Bradley rapidly and

competently countered this, deploying eight US divisions, and as General Paul Hausser's German 7th Army threatened to cut into Patton's flank, the Americans in turn cut into Hausser's with an attack directed on Vire.

Away to the east, the British had cleared as far south as Villers Bocage on one side of Caen and on the other the Canadians had thrust down towards Falaise. It was slow progress, but they achieved their objectives and Montgomery's objects by bashing and battering away, supported by massive air and land fire-power. Meanwhile Patton, out in the open, was already south of Hausser's left rear.

The 7th Army, with its head at Mortain and its communications running back 40 miles to the narrow gap between Falaise and Argentan was, therefore, doomed. That the net was not pulled tight has been the

Left: White phosphorus shells explode close to American soldiers as they dash across a street in Brest, France, while searching for German snipers in surrounding buildings in 1944

Below: The dreaded flamethrower was a weapon invented in WWI, improved and almost universally adopted for close-range anti-personnel and anti-tank work in WWII.

Infantry tank mark IV Churchill

Crew: 5 (commander, gunner, wireless operator, driver, hull gunner). **Weight:** 87,360lb (39,626kg). **Length:** 25' 2'' (7.67m). **Width:** 10' 8'' (3.251m). **Height:** 8' 2'' (2.489m). **Road speed:** 15½mph (25kmh). **Range:** 120 miles (193km). **Engine:** Bedford 12 cylinder (ie 2 × 6), petrol developing 350 BHP at 2200rpm. **Vertical obstacle:** 2' 6'' (.762m). **Trench:** 10' (3.048m). **Armour:** 10 to 88mm.

In 1940, design work commenced on a British heavy infantry tank known as the A20. Prototypes, built by Harland and Wolff of Belfast, were completed that year and Vauxhall Motors were then asked to redesign the tank as the Infantry Tank Mark IV, or A22. The first prototype was completed in November 1940, with the first production tanks being completed in June 1941. After initial problems had been over-

come, the Mark IV, or Churchill as it became known, gave excellent service throughout the war. In the early 1960s, the last models in service were those of the AVRE (Armoured Vehicle Royal Engineers). A total of 5,640 Churchills of all marks were built. One of the virtues of the Churchill was that it was capable of being fitted with heavier armament as it became available, apart from the 17-Pounder gun. The first Churchills were fitted with a 2-Pounder gun in the turret and a 3'' howitzer in the hull. In 1942, a 6-Pounder was fitted in place of the 2-Pounder and in 1943, some were fitted with a 75mm gun.

The Churchill Mark III had a 6-Pounder (57mm) gun with a co-axial 7.92mm Besa machine gun, a similar weapon being mounted in the hull front. A .303 Bren was mounted for anti-aircraft defence and a 2'' bomb thrower was mounted in the turret roof. Total ammunition carried consisted of 84 rounds of 6-Pounder, 42 boxes (each of 225 rounds) of 7.92mm and 30 2'' bombs.

There were eleven basic marks of the Churchill.

subject of much military criticism, but in fact it was partly due to the accidents of battle, what Clausewitz calls 'friction', and the disobliging behaviour of the 2nd Panzer Division which, battered though it was, refused to play the part of the passive enemy to oblige theoretical strategists. It tore a gap in the enclosing Allied cordon and held it open for just long enough to enable a substantial fraction of the wrecks of the 7th Army formations to slip through to temporary freedom. Those that remained inside this *Kessel* of Hitler's own creation became the victims of some of the most horrifying scenes of destruction of the whole war. All the roads were jammed three abreast and miles deep with tanks, artillery and transport from 15 German divisions, and up and down them the combined air forces flew remorselessly, bombing, rocketing and cannon-firing. The Germans left west of the Seine some half million men, 3,000 guns, 1,500 tanks, 2,000 wrecked aircraft and 20,000 vehicles. The Falaise pocket was full of wrecked tanks and guns, and of dead men and horses.

Such was the end of the Battle of Normandy.

Hitler's other contribution, apart from ordering the hopeless Mortain counter-attack, had been to sack Rundstedt (who, asked on 23 June what should be done, with disasters occurring thick and fast, replied 'Make peace you fools!') and Geyr von Schweppenburg, the Panzer corps commander, and replace them by his stooge Field-Marshal Guenther-Hans von Kluge, who was later replaced by General Walther Model. Rommel was *hors de combat*, wounded, wo not only was the German defence smashed but also its effective leadership. All France was now open to Eisenhower.

As a battle, 'Overlord' lives up to its resounding title. It was a masterpiece which General J. F. C. Fuller (*The Decisive Battles of the Western World*) classes among the decisive battles of history.

Over its strategic exploitation there is less agreement. On 15 August, at the climax of the battle, the landings in the French Riviera took place, elaborately planned in every detail and executed with barely a shot fired. This operation, some argue, was a classic violation of the principle of economy of force: the resources taken from Italy rendered the Gothic Line battles sterile for lack of power to exploit, and landed so late in France they had no effect on the operations there either. (The chief advantage was the gain in port facilities to speed the US build-up.)

Others again argue that Patton's spectacular dash could have been better directed to a deep encirclement of the remaining German formations instead of motoring off to register a glittering list of liberated French cities. The chief critics of Eisenhower's strategy, of which Montgomery was the most vocal, argue that if all the logistic resources had been concentrated on one selected army, stripped down to its fighting echelons so as to make it fully mobile, a rapid pursuit in classical style might have prevented the shattered German forces from ever rallying again, allowing the war in the West to be ended in 1944.

To be effective such a move would have

had to be planned long before 'Overlord' was launched, commanders briefed and acclimatised to the idea and national rivalries concerning who was to have the leading role assuaged. There were also purely technical considerations. The Western divisions were so lavishly equipped with vehicles that they had reached a point at which over-mechanisation had actually made them less mobile than leaner formations.

After bitter argument the Eisenhower strategy was followed, and the five armies rolled forward against light resistance in line abreast: the US 7th coming up from the south of France directed on the Vosges, Patton's US 3rd on Verdun, the US 1st

astride Paris rowards the Ardennes, the British 2nd crossing the Somme at Amiens and the Canadian 1st moving along the Channel coast. In this way the German forces were swept out of France tidily enough, but were given what no prudent commander ever gave German generals – time. With their marvellous resilience they were able to organise another defensive front and even stage a counter-offensive before the year was out.

Right: A German gun in a counter-battery shoot. At Kursk the German artillery was outclassed and outnumbered by that of the Russians on higher ground.

M1 2.36 inch anti-tank rocket launcher

Crew: 2. **Weight of launcher:** 13.25lb (5.96kg). **Length:** 5′ 1″ (1.549m). **Length of rocket:** 19.4″ (.492m). **Weight of rocket:** 3.4lb (1.52kg). **Muzzle velocity:** 270fps (83m/s). **Range (effective):** 182 yards (200m). **Maximum range:** 700 yards (640m).

The M1 Rocket Launcher was developed in the early days of World War II and was first used in action by American forces in Tunisia in 1942. It was usually called the "Bazooka". The first model to enter service

was the M1, followed by the M9, which be broken into two for ease of transportation. The M18 of aluminium construction entered service towards the end of the war.

The weapon was used in the following manner. A rocket was loaded into the rear of the tube and then connected to an electric wire. When the operator pressed the trigger, a connection was made with the two batteries in the grip, the circuit was completed, and the rocket was launched. The rocket had a HEAT warhead which would penetrate 5-6 inches (127-152mm) of armour. Smoke and incendiary rockets were also available.

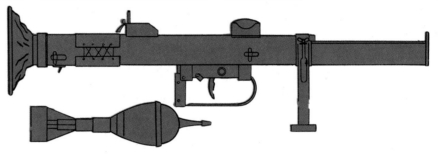

PIAT anti-tank weapon

Crew: 2. **Weight:** 32lb (14.4kg). **Length:** 3′ 3″ (.99m). **Weight of bomb:** 3lb (1.35kg). **Muzzle velocity:** 250/450fps (76-137m/s). **Effective range:** 100 yards (91m). **Maximum range:** 750 yards (685m).

The PIAT (Projector, Infantry, Anti-Tank) was the replacement for the Boys anti-tank rifle which was the standard light anti-tank weapon at the start of World War II. The PIAT was designed by Lieutenant Colonel Blacker and remained in use with the British Army for some years after the war. It fired a hollow

charge grenade, although smoke and High Explosive grenades were also available.

The weapon was fired in the following manner. The bomb itself was laid in the tray at the front on the weapon and when the trigger was pressed a steel rod, driven by a powerful spring, was driven into the rear of the bomb to ignite the cartridge which sent the bomb on its way. The blast of the bomb blew the spigot back into the weapon and thus re-cocked it ready for use again. Its main drawback was that if it did not cock automatically, it had to be done manually, which was difficult and often required two men.

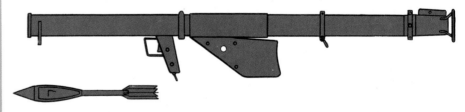

German Panzerfaust anti-tank gun

Weight complete: 11.5lb (5.1kg). **Muzzle velocity:** 98fps (30m/s). **Range:** 33 yards (30m).

The Panzerfaust first entered service in 1942 and it essentially consisted of a bomb with a tail which was inserted into a long tube. Once the weapon was fired, the bomb left the tube and four steel fins unfolded to guide it to its target. The first model to

enter service was the Panzerfaust 30 (Klein), soon followed by the Panzerfaust 30,60 and 100, the numbers referring to their effective range in metres. They were fitted with a hollow charge warhead which would penetrate 7.87 inches (200mm) of armour. The Germans also developed a whole range of "Bazooka" type weapons including the RP43, RP54, RP54/1 and so on. Although these weapons were cheap, easy to use and were built in large numbers, they could not stop the flood of allied armour in the final years of the war.

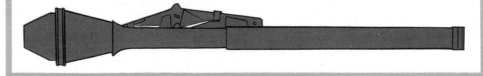

Unconditional surrender

With the Western Allies pushing on from France and the Russians from the east, Germany's end in the spring of 1945 was certain. But its death throes exacted a terrible cost on both sides.

When we look at the whole strategic picture of the war in Europe in August 1944 the great question that springs to mind is: why should it have taken another eight months of bitter fighting to subdue the German war-machine? Why did the Germans fight on and not follow Rundstedt's brutal advice to make peace; or why would not the Allies choose some less uncompromising alternative to 'unconditional surrender'?

The German defensive system in the West had ceased to exist. Even the original *Westwall*, or 'Siegfried Line', was without a garrison and its weapons, shifted to the Atlantic Wall (the later *Westwall*), had all been lost. In the East there had been a series of appalling disasters, starting with the

unheard of surrender of a whole German army at Stalingrad in 1943, the retreat from the Caucasus and the defeat at Kursk (an event as significant as Stalingrad). Offensives up and down the Eastern Front, checked only with great difficulty, were followed in the last week of July 1944, when the Normandy battle was at its height, by the virtual destruction of the German Army Group 'Centre', which momentarily left a great gap in the line running from Riga to Sandomierz.

The Germans no longer had any true reserve. The best they could do was to shuttle divisions from one part of a front to another, or between the two major fronts.

The short and simple answer to these

questions is that the war was not being fought for any coldly weighed considerations of political profit and loss, but to destroy a wholly evil and destructive entity. Looking

Russian soldiers installing the Red Banner on the Reichstag in Berlin on 1 May, 1945. The final Russian attack on Berlin started on 16 April; the city was encircled by 16 April.

15cm Nebelwerfer 41

Calibre: 158.5mm. **Weight loaded:** 1698lb (770kg). **Weight empty:** 1125lb (511kg). **Length travelling:** 11' 10" (3.6m). **Width travelling:** 5' 5" (1.66m). **Height travelling:** 4' 7" (1.4m). **Range at 45°** elevation: 7723 yards (7062m). **Range at 30° elevation:** 7018 yards (6417m). **Range at 6½° elevation:** 2710 yards (2478m). **Traverse:** 27° **Elevation:** +5° to +27°. **Rate of fire:** 6 rounds in 90 seconds.

The Nebelwerfer consisted of the carriage of the 3.7cm Pak.35/36 anti-tank gun fitted with six rocket tubes. The carriage had split trails with a spade on each end, and when in the firing position a jack supported the front of the carriage. Each barrel had three guide rails and a latch to hold the rocket in position after loading.

The rocket was fired electrically by remote control in the order 1, 4, 6, 2, 3 and 5, a sequence adopted so that the projector would not be overturned.

A variety of rockets could be fired, including HE weighing 70lb (31.8kg), Smoke weighing 79lb (35.9kg) and chemical. The Nebelwerfer was normally used against area targets as the rockets had too much dispersion for use against point targets. Allied troops called the weapon the "Moaning Minny" because of the sound the rockets made whilst in the air. The Germans had a variety of other rocket projectors, including the 28/32cm and the 21cm Nebelwerfer 42.

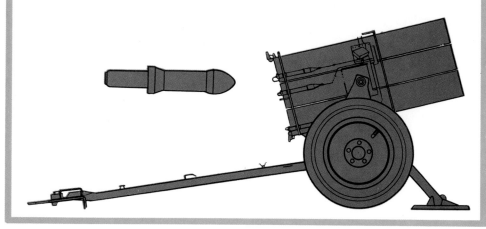

back now, it is possible to regret a military outcome which has divided Europe and Germany, but it must be remembered that as far as the Soviet Union was concerned, an unprovoked aggression had devastated their country and cost untold lives, and so they were not going to stop until the last German soldier was dead or disarmed and Berlin in their hands. The British and American leaders were equally determined to destroy Hitler and his war-machine, and talked of the dismemberment of the German *Reich*. This no doubt hardened the will of the ordinary Germans to resist, but at the time it echoed what the ordinary people of the West felt.

Hitler himself in any case was immovable and irremovable. He still held his followers in a hypnotic grip, and was by 1944 completely demented and thus determined to immolate the Germans as a punishment for their failure to achieve the aim he had given them. He still possessed a huge and still extraordinarily responsive army whose leaders, driven by a complexity of motives

Right: A German 21cm Mörser 18 firing on Russian positions on the Eastern Front. This weapon fired an HE shell weighing 113kg (249lb) to a range of 16,700m (18,263 yds).

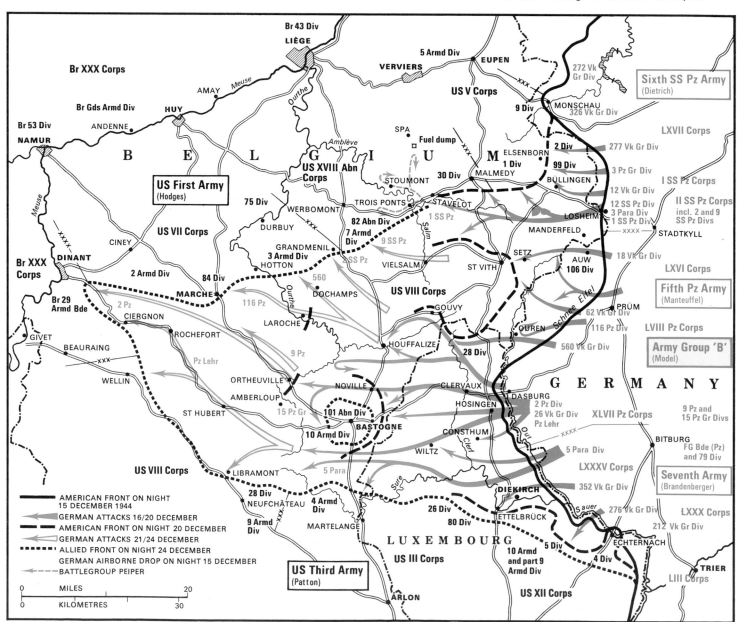

ranging from faith in Hitler bringing off a miracle, their own soldierly traditions, to fear of defeat, grimly continued in battles which their professional judgement told them they could not possibly win.

It must be remembered that in the summer of 1944 the German army still had in being some 325 divisions. Admittedly they were under-strength, there was a dearth of ammunition, petrol and, as a result of chaotic planning policies, weapons in general and tanks in particular. But these divisions carried little administrative fat, their middle and junior leaders in spite of frightful losses were still very good, and the extraordinary alchemy of German training turned their last remaining recruits, some mere boys and some elderly and often sick men, into tough and resilient fighters. Right to the end no Allied soldier in his senses ever tackled a German position except with great circumspection and maximum fire-support.

In 1944 the Russians appreciated that they faced 179 of these divisions, together with 49,000 guns and 5,250 tanks. They knew of only one way of dealing with this huge and still formidable force, which was to build up their own resources. In 1943 alone the Russians had raised 78 new divisions. They had organised whole tank armies, as well as artillery divisions intended to provide the enormous bombardments which preceded every attack. In 1944 their armaments industry produced 90 million shells, 29,000 tanks and 40,000 combat aircraft. These were to be used in a succession of well planned, deliberately mounted offensives, first on one sector and then on another, with local superiority of 4:1 and 100–250 guns and mortars per kilometre of front, until the last German reserves were used up, their whole Eastern Front cracked and the way to Berlin open. The Russians' final grand offensive was timed for January 1945, and that was their aim and that was their time-table. As for the Allied armies in the West, it is argued to this day whether or not they could have conquered Germany in 1944. All that is certain is that their victory in France caught them unprepared militarily and mentally.

Some German generals believed that a dash at the Rhine crossings before a defensive crust had time to harden might have reached the Ruhr. This was the policy advocated by Montgomery but, as has been said, for perfectly good political and logistic reasons Eisenhower, as soon as he had assumed command in the field, had decided on a broad-fronted advance.

This at first was against the lightest of resistance. The British arrived in Brussels

on 3 September and the US armies reached the Dutch and German frontiers by the 11th. Then there was the pause which gave the Germans breathing space for Hitler's last operational plan to be put in hand. First both fronts had to be stabilised, using every possible expedient, then an armoured force was to be assembled for a spoiling attack through the Ardennes against the long, weak cordon the broad-front policy had lined along the German frontier and after that, when the British and Americans had been thrown back on their heels, the main effort would be switched back to the East.

In the meantime Montgomery, balked in his original plan for a single *Schwerpunkt* tried, with Eisenhower's approval this time, a new move. In the United Kingdom there was unemployed an army of at least one British and two American airborne divisions. His way forward to the Ruhr was barred by three canals, the Escaut, the Wilhemina and the South Willemsvart, and three rivers, the Maas, the Waal and the lower Rhine. Against any sort of resistance each crossing would be a slow, methodical business. Montgomery thus proposed to drop the three airborne divisions along the axis Eindhoven–Nijmegen–Arnhem, with the task of capturing the bridges intact and holding them while the British XXX Corps, with the famous Guard Armoured Division in the lead, followed up on the ground to relieve them, and the US 1st Army on the right moved up in step and covered the flank. As has been often told, the race was lost at Arnhem, the last fence, where XXX Corps was held up south of the Rhine by a stiffening German defence and the British 1st Airborne Division was overrun by armour. The 'Market Garden' operation is justly celebrated for the heroism of the airborne troops, and has been equally justly condemned for a number of serious mistakes in planning and execution. But its real weakness lay in the fact that it was an after-thought, and by the time it was launched, on 17 September, the door to the Ruhr had been firmly closed. The luckless British 1st Airborne Division dropped into an area occupied by two Panzer divisions.

The final German offensive was also late. It was timed for mid-November, but it was not until December that the 5th and 6th SS Panzer Armies could be re-equipped, and so the attack was not launched until 16 December. The plan, a revival of old memories, was to attack from assembly areas in the Eifel hills north-west through the Ardennes and across the Meuse with objective Antwerp, so separating the northern wing of Eisenhower's forces into two parts

Left: A German Racketenpanzerbüchse 54 anti-tank weapon. The Germans had hundreds of thousands of light anti-tank weapons but could not stop the flood of Allied armour.

Above right: British troops firing at German snipers in Arnhem in April, 1945. The first Allied airborne assault on Arnhem in September, 1944, was a failure

Right: Troops of General Patton's Third Army pass a fallen comrade during heavy street fighting which resulted on the fall of the German town of Coblenz early in 1944

and cutting both off from their new supply base, after which the northern segment would be eliminated. It was far too ambitious for the forces available, and doomed from the start, but it gave the British and Americans an unpleasant shock. Surprise was complete, but the defence put up by the American troops (notably by the 101st Airborne Division at Bastogne) was obstinate, the British 2nd Army redeployed promptly to establish a stop-line along the Meuse, and swift and aggressive reaction by the US formations south of the salient created by the offensive soon threw the Panzers back on the defensive. The Germans were never a soft touch, and it took the Americans a month's hard fighting and some 75,000 casualties to clean up the situation, but at the end all that had been achieved by this last military inspiration of Hitler's was a further, fatal reduction of his armoured mobile troops.

The Ardennes offensive was the last unpredictable and therefore militarily interesting operation of the war in Europe, the last flicker of mobility and manoeuvre, and the last of the *Blitzkrieg*. The operations of 1945 were uniformly dull and depressing, savouring as they did of an execution prolonged by the struggles of the victim. The German army was methodically destroyed by opponents with apparently limitless resources. The astonishing fact is that the resistance it offered lasted four long months. Some idea of what it took in the way of punishment can only be given by figures. On D-day of the operation to clear the *Reichswald*, merely the preliminary to their final crossing of the Rhine, the British used 1,050 guns and fired 6,000 tons of ammunition. Hostile batteries received some 1,000 rounds apiece and 50 guns were knocked out. For the final offensive directed on Berlin the Russians brought forward seven million rounds of artillery ammunition and assembled 68 infantry divisions, 3,155 tanks

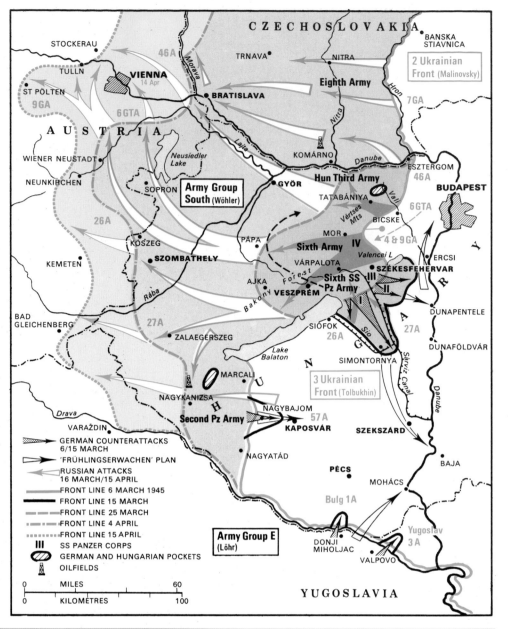

Tiger tank

Crew: 5 (commander, gunner, loader, driver, hull gunner/radio operator). **Weight:** 125,440lb (56,899kg). **Length overall:** 27' 9'' (8.457m). **Length hull:** 20' 8½'' (6.311m). **Width:** 12' 3'' (3.733m). **Height:** 9' 4¾'' (2.863m). **Road speed:** 23mph (37kmh). **Road range:** 73 miles (117km). **Engine:** Maybach HL 230 P45, 12 cylinder petrol developing 700 HP at 3000rpm. **Trench:** 13' (3,962m). **Gradient:** 60%. **Armour:** 26 to 110mm.

In May 1941, both Henschel and Porsche were awarded contracts to design a new 45 ton tank armed with an 88mm gun. The Henschel design was known as the VK.4501(H) and that from Porsche as the VK.4501(P). Both were completed early the following year. The Henschel tank was judged the best and placed in immediate production, known as the Tiger (Sd Kfz-181). Between August 1942, and August 1944,

1,350 Tiger 1s were built before it was replaced in production by the Tiger II (or King Tiger as it was also known). The Tiger was one of the most powerful tanks of World War II, but as with a number of other German tank designs, it was not suited to large-scale production and its heavy weight caused transportation problems. The Tiger had two sets of tracks, a narrow set for transport, 20½'' (.52m) wide and a wide set for combat, 28½'' (.723m) wide. When the narrow set was used the outer set of road wheels had to be removed. The Tiger also had a very short

operational range—only 42 miles (68km) in rough country.

The Tiger was armed with an 88mm KwK 36 gun which was a development of the famous 88mm anti-aircraft gun, with elevation of +11° and a depression of −4°. A 7.92mm MG 34 was mounted to the left of the main armament and a similar weapon was mounted in the bow of the tank. A total of 92 rounds of HE and APCBC 88mm ammunition were carried as were 5,700 rounds of machine gun ammunition.

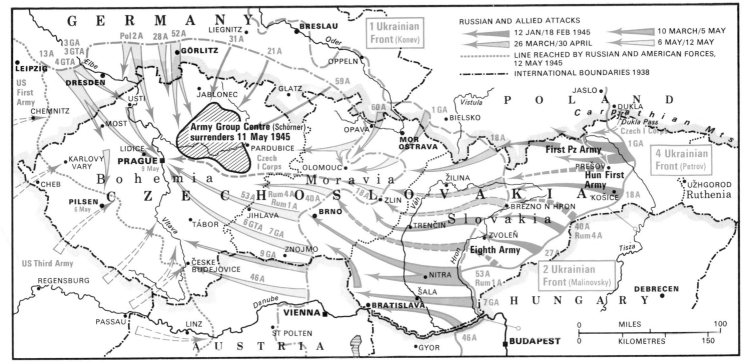

and self-propelled guns and 42,000 guns and mortars, these last being at a density of 250 per kilometre of front at the point of main effort. When the advance was held up by minor resistance on the Seelow ridge barring the way to Berlin Zhukov simply threw in two tank armies.

An account of the final battles can be little more than a catalogue of dates and offensives. The aim of the Allies, firmly adhered to by Eisenhower in the spirit of the Yalta agreements, was to meet on the Elbe, crushing all resistance between them. The Red Army led off on 12 January, and the caption attached to the operational sketch in Guderian's memoirs is sufficient comment – 'The Catastrophe'.

In February the British 21st Army Group and the US 9th Army broke into the 'Siegfried' Line and were finally poised along the Rhine after very heavy fighting in the *Reichswald* and the Hurtgen forest, eliminating some 19 German divisions. They then forced a passage over the Rhine covered by more massive bombardments and the last airborne attack of the war, after which the British turned north and east, the Americans cleared the Rhur and their 1st Army cut another eastward swathe farther south.

German resistance in the west was dour: in the east it was fanatical. It was not until 25 April that the 1st Belorussian and the 1st Ukrainian Fronts linked up to the west of Berlin. On the same day the Red Army and the US Army met at Torgau on the Elbe. Hitler committed suicide on 30th, Berlin surrendered on 2 May, and on 7 May General Alfred Jodl signed the instrument of unconditional surrender at Eisenhower's headquarters in Reims.

The end of the war in Europe and the final destruction of Hitler's war-machine took place officially at one minute past 2300 hours, Central European Time, 8 May 1945.

Right: German graves in the summer of 1941. There were to be many more graves like this on the Eastern Front before 1945.

Developments in land warfare
1939-1945

Initially taken by surprise by German weapons and tactics, by the middle of the war the Allies had remodelled their armies and were equipping them with the best of modern weapons.

In 1943 a marked change came over the nature of warfare on land, a change induced almost wholly by technology. The *Blitzkrieg* which had been seen, over simply, as a war between tanks and dive-bombers against out-dated World War I armies, appeared marvellously advanced in 1940–41, but in fact the vast number of back-up divisions used by both sides on the Eastern Front differed very little in essence from those of 1914–18.

The new British and American armies were by contrast fully mechanised, with a far more elaborate structure for command, control and logistic back-up. The US armoured divisions, in particular, with all their infantry and artillery on tracks, were the most advanced in organisation of any. Only their tanks remained inferior to the German ones in terms of armour and gun-power).

At the same time a change came over the status of the tank, so far as its position as the decisive battlefield weapon was concerned. It remained (and still remains) so, but there was a natural and inevitable growth in counter-weapons. In the air the Allies, bypassing the dive-bomber, adapted high-performance fighter aircraft to strike roles, with bombers and fighters to control the air space above the armies. Soon it was impossible for the Panzers even to move by daylight.

On the ground the Germans themselves – always ready to use a defensive weapon offensively – had started to use high-velocity towed guns in the forefront of the battle to destroy enemy tanks. In a number of small but significant actions in North Africa, notably Medenine, and the great defensive/counter-offensive battle at Kursk, the way to use guns to defeat tanks was clearly demonstrated and the Panzers, while remaining formidable, ceased to be a bogey.

In what many thought much later was a retrograde move, massed field artillery came back into fashion, using highly sophisticated techniques pioneered by the British Royal Artillery. (Only the Soviet artillery remained through lack of educated personnel and resources anchored to slower, battering techniques of 1916.) The fire-power of the British and US armies was, probably, quantitatively less than that of the Red Army, but its powers of concentration and the speed of its response to the ever-fluid situations of mechanised warfare multiplied its effect several times.

The Allied divisions were designed primarily for offensive operations against the best army so far seen in modern times, and this combination of fire-power and technology enabled such operations to be sustained without a pause from Operation 'Torch', the North African landings of late 1942, onwards.

In 1940 the German navy, probably wisely, had balked at any hastily improvised amphibious operation across the English Channel. The Allies devoted two years to the problem (including a disastrous experiment at Dieppe in 1942) and by 1943 had devised in great and elaborate detail the fire support and other tactics required to put large, armoured forces ashore almost anywhere on the long perimeter of *Festung* 'Europe' (Fortress 'Europe'), and proceeded to do so. What had been in former history one of the hazardous operations of war now became a standard technique. (A British officer in 1945 was naively asked if he had been at 'D-Day'. He asked tartly in reply, which one: Sicily, Salerno, Anzio or Normandy?)

German tanks advancing through France in the spring of 1940. The speed of the German advance took the Allies by surprise and France and Belgium fell in a matter of weeks.

Both the British and the Americans, undeterred by and absorbing the lessons of Crete, developed large airborne forces of parachute and glider troops which opened a new vertical 'flank', to be used in major operations with decisive effect.

The great advantage the British and Americans had over the Russians was that they were free to plan, equip and train their new armies from general down to private until they were ready and launch their invasion to liberate Europe. Then all the advantage of surprise, and the initiative they refused to be hurried into by the urgent Soviet demands to open a 'second front', were in their favour.

The Western arsenals were seemingly inexhaustible: some measure of their capacity is that during all this preparation Soviet Russia was sent as aid 427,000 vehicles, 10,000 tanks, 300 other armoured fighting vehicles and 19,000 aircraft, without affecting Western needs.

Both the British and the Americans were ingenious and inventive, but the strength of the alliance lay in the American genius for realising technological ideas in terms of engineering, and then mass-producing the result. Quite apart from basics like tanks, aircraft and landing craft of every kind, the combination was able to produce less eye-catching but vital equipment: radar and radio sets down to the 'walkie-talkie', better artillery fuses, the marvellous 'jeep' and new life-saving drugs.

The transportation of the liberating armies to Normandy, seen purely as a feat of logistics and engineering, was of itself an astonishing feat even when all the tactical considerations of an opposed landing are excluded.

It is not as if the Germans were without ideas. They produced two good new tanks (PzKpfw V and VI), three operational jet aircraft and two long-range surface-to-surface missiles, guided surface-to-air missiles and an air-to-surface missile, but they lacked the industrial capacity and, as a result of Hitler, the policy makers and skilled managers to realise their own inventions. There was no co-ordination, no priorities, no attempt to create a coherent 'family' of weapons, even if there had been time.

It can therefore be said without exaggeration that 1943 saw another watershed in the 'art' of war, which transformed it to the 'business' or 'industry' of war.

In 1940–41 the army of Fuller's '1919' vision totally defeated armies whose ideas were rooted in the 19th century. In 1943–44 this momentarily revolutionary military force was in turn crushed by the industrialised armies of the New World.

There was one other factor inherent in the overrunning of Europe by a racialist conqueror: the growth of partisan warfare. Since 1945 there has been a great vogue for guerrilla warfare among military commentators, and it has been elevated to a revolutionary form of warfare in its own right. This is as may be. In World War II partisan warfare in fact varied from incompetent to highly effective in terms of the numbers of German or Axis (or Russian turn-coat) divisions absorbed in trying to cope with it. The significant point is that it existed, and afforded a man-power force which, when

Above: A good example of Germany's *matériel* problems: an artillery unit, with some of its guns drawn by horses, and others by the excellent *Schwerer Zugkraftwagen* 12t prime-mover.

Left: British Royal Marine Commando machine gun teams in action during the closing months of World War II. The Vickers machine gun served the British Army well for over 50 years

contacted, equipped and controlled by competent military authorities, opened a 'fourth' flank or, rather, involved the Germans in a war without a front in certain areas. There has been much romantic literature about special and raiding forces whose contribution remains a matter for debate, and anyway was marginal.

Partisan warfare, made possible by air-power and radio-control, was the far more significant in that it roused whole populations behind the German lines. As the Allied armies advanced into Italy, the partisans became a nuisance to the Germans, while in Yugoslavia they tied down large German and Italian forces in full-scale operations.

Thus, as the campaigns of 1943 opened, Hitler's forces found themselves out-numbered and outclassed on the ground, their tank weapon blunted, and their air-borne tactics turned against them. More-over, their conquests had served no other purpose but to generate new enemies in their own rear.

KV heavy tank

Crew: 5. **Weight:** 103,620lb (47,000kg). **Length, overall:** 22′ 8″ (6.908m). **Length, hull:** 22′ 2″ (6.755m). **Width:** 10′ 11″ (3.327m). **Height:** 9′ 7″ (2.921m). **Road speed:** 21mph (33.8kmh). **Range:** 95-140 miles (153-225km). **Engine:** V-2K, 12 cylinder liquid cooled diesel developing 600 BHP at 2000rpm. **Ground pressure:** 11.4psi (.8kg/cm²). **Vertical obstacle:** 3′ (.914m). **Trench:** 9′ 3″ (2.82m). **Gradient:** 60%. **Armour:** 32 to 100mm.

The KV heavy tank was developed from 1938 by a design team lead by I. S. Kotin. It entered production in 1939, was in service the following year and first saw action in Finland. The KV was in fact named after Klementy Voroshilov, Marshal of the Soviet Union. The first model was the KV-1, this being followed by the KV-1A and the KV-1B, the latter having additional armour on both the hull and turret. The KV-1C had a turret of a new design with thicker armour and the

KV-1S was a redesign with much thinner armour which reduced its weight to 42½ tons. The KV-85 had a new turret with an 85mm gun, but it appears that this was not built in large numbers. The most unusual member of the family was the KV-11, with a huge flat-sided turret and armed with a 122mm or 152mm howitzer, the turret increasing weight to 57 tons. About 10,000 KVs were built.

The KV-1C was armed with a 76.2mm M-1940 gun (which was also fitted to the T-34/76), which could fire Armour Piercing, High Explosive and Shrapnel rounds. A 7.62mm DT machine gun was mounted co-axially with the main armament and a similar machine gun was mounted in the hull. An unusual feature of the KV-1C was the 7.62mm DT machine gun in the turret rear, and a similar MG was some-times mounted on the roof of the tank. Total ammunition supply was 110 rounds of 76mm and 3024 rounds of 7.62mm, the latter being in drums of 63 rounds each.

Part 4: War in the Pacific
Surprise attack by Japan

Japan's period of conquest after her devastating attack on
Pearl Harbor was marked by ruthlessness and skill, and seemed
irresistible until the great US naval victory off Midway island.

Years before the war in the Pacific began, a 1929 US Army staff study had observed that at the beginning of each of its major conflicts the United States had found itself unprepared and 'this condition has eventuated in some cases in humiliating and disastrous reverses'. Not even the most far-sighted military strategist, however, could have foreseen the staggering defeats and disasters which the United States was to suffer during the first half year of the war against Japan.

The war began with a surprise attack by the Japanese on the major American military and naval base at Pearl Harbor, in the Hawaiian Islands. In late November 1941 a Japanese task force comprised of six of her largest carriers, accompanied by supporting ships, under the command of Vice-Admiral Chuichi Nagumo secretly left Japan for Hawaii. Sailing by a circuitous route through the North Pacific, the Japanese fleet reached a point some 200 miles north of the island of Oahu, Hawaii, by the morning of 7 December, and headed for Pearl Harbor.

Within hours of the Pearl Harbor attack Japanese forces moved to knock out the other principal American bases in the Pacific. The island of Guam, in the Marianas, was occupied easily but at Wake Island, farther east, the Japanese suffered a sharp reverse.

Wake is a tiny V-shaped atoll in the central Pacific, and in December 1941 it was manned by a defence battalion of 450 US Marines under the command of Major James P. S. Devereux. The battalion was 50 per cent under strength, but it had some useful artillery in the form of six 3-inch anti-aircraft guns as well as some 5-inch coast defence guns and a squadron of Grumman F4F Wildcat fighters attached.

After repeated bombings of the island a small Japanese invasion force of about 500 men, escorted by eight cruisers and destroyers, approached Wake Island on the morning of 11 December. Holding their fire until the enemy had closed to only 3,500 yards, the 5-inch batteries on Wake suddenly opened fire on the Japanese. Despite the fact that much of their range-finding equipment had been disabled in the bombings, the Marines' fire was accurate and deadly. Four 5-inch shells ripped into the Japanese flagship *Yubari*, which limped away under a cloud of smoke. The destroyer *Hayate* was almost blown in two by a 5-inch salvo and her sistership *Oite* was damaged. Two

Below left: The magazine of the destroyer *Shaw* explodes during the Japanese air attack on Pearl Harbour on 7 December, 1941.

Below: US Marines defend their positions against a surprise attack by the Japanese. It took the Americans just over a year to stop the Japanese advance and start pushing them back.

transports and another destroyer were also hit and by 0700 the entire Japanese squadron was in full retirement. The few remaining planes on Wake pursued the task force and inflicted further damage, sinking the destroyer *Kisaragi*.

The Japanese had lost over 500 men and two warships, but they moved quickly to make good their losses. On 22 December a much larger task force, which included two aircraft-carriers and six heavy cruisers, escorted a new assault force of about 1,200 men to Wake Island. Around 0230 in the early morning of 23 December Japanese forces began landing on Wake. The Marines resisted fiercely, but by daylight it was clear that the enemy had succeeded in landing a superior force on the island. Although several isolated positions were still holding out and one Japanese landing force at the extreme western tip of the island had been virtually annihilated, Major Devereaux and Commander W. S. Cunningham, the senior naval officer present, decided that further resistance would be useless. A relief expedition from Pearl Harbor with additional troops and aircraft had turned back a few hours before and no further relief attempts could be expected. At 0730 in the morning Major Devereaux left his command post with a white flag to find the Japanese.

The surrender of Guam and Wake gave the Japanese control of the American line of communications across the central Pacific. The Commonwealth of the Philippines, whose defence was the responsibility of the United States, was now completely cut off from reinforcement except from the south, where the swift Japanese conquest of Borneo and the Dutch East Indies soon made this route extremely perilous.

During the 1920s and 1930s American strategists had tacitly recognised that in a war with Japan the Philippines would probably fall before a relief expedition, which would have to fight its way across the Pacific, could reach the islands. It was hoped that the defenders would at least be able to hold the entrance to Manila pending the arrival of the American fleet, but the small size of American forces in the islands made even this a doubtful proposition.

During 1941, however, as American war *matériel* became more plentiful, the defences of the Philippines had been steadily augmented with modern tanks and with planes, most notably by a small force of Boeing B-17 heavy bombers. American military leaders believed that the B-17s, whose long range made them capable of reaching Japan itself, would serve as a powerful deterrent against attack. In addition, General Douglas MacArthur who had assumed command of all US and Filipino land forces in the islands in 1941, believed that the Philippine Army of some 100,000 men would be sufficient, together with the 23,000 odd US Army forces in the Philippines, to put up a successful defence of the entire archipelago. Scrapping the old defence plans, MacArthur expected to meet all enemy attacks at the beach-head and force them back into the sea.

The first days of war quickly demonstrated the hollowness of MacArthur's assumptions. As a result of a series of mistakes, delays and miscalculations which have never been adequately explained, MacArthur's air force was caught on the

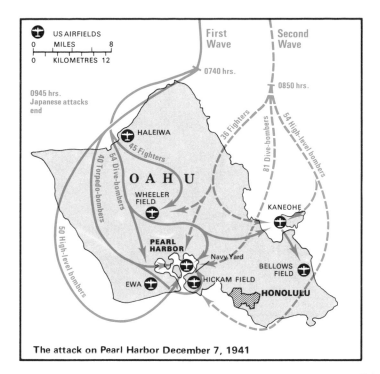

The attack on Pearl Harbor December 7, 1941

US AIRFIELDS

First Wave
Second Wave

0740 hrs.
0850 hrs.
0945 hrs. Japanese attacks end

36 Fighters
45 Fighters
54 Dive-bombers
40 Torpedo-bombers
50 High-level bombers
81 Dive-bombers
54 High-level bombers

HALEIWA
OAHU
WHEELER FIELD
KANEOHE
PEARL HARBOR
Navy Yard
BELLOWS FIELD
EWA
HICKAM FIELD
HONOLULU

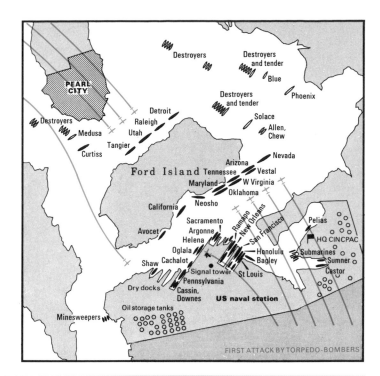

FIRST ATTACK BY TORPEDO-BOMBERS

Left: Japanese with flame throwers attack the fortress island of Corregidor. The fall of Corregidor was a major defeat for the Americans and was the end of Philippine resistance

Below left: Captured American troops are given a brief rest during the notorious "March of Death" from Bataan to the Cabana prison camp. Many Americans died on this journey

Type 97 medium tank

Crew: 4. **Weight:** 33,060lb (15,000kg). **Length:** 18' 1'' (5.516m). **Width:** 7' 8'' (2.33m). **Height:** 7' 4'' (2.235m). **Road speed:** 25mph (41.8km/hr). **Range:** 130 miles (210km). **Engine:** Mitsubishi 12 cylinder air-cooled diesel developing 170 HP at 2000rpm. **Gradient:** 60%. **Armour:** 8 to 25mm.

After World War I the Japanese acquired a number of tanks from Europe including the British Mark IV, and Whippet Mark A, and Renault FT light tanks from France. In the early 1920s they also purchased a Medium C and some Carden-Loyd tankettes from Britain and some Renault NC-1s from France and in the latter part of the decade, Japan built her first tank. From an early stage the diesel rather than the petrol engine was adopted and Japan built a variety of tanks but total production amounted to well under 4,000 of all types. Japanese tanks saw extensive action in China, Malaya and in many of the Pacific island campaigns of World War II.

The Type 97 (or CHI-HA) was developed by Mitsubishi and the first prototype was completed in 1937. At least six companies built the tank including Mitsubishi, Hitachi and Kobe Seikosho. The Type 97 had its turret offset to the right and was armed with a Type 97 57mm gun, with a 7.7mm Type 97 machine gun mounted in the turret rear whilst a similar weapon was mounted in the nose. Total ammunition carried consisted of 120 rounds of 57mm (80 HE and 40 APHE) and 3,825 rounds of machine gun ammunition. The Type 97 Special had a new turret mounting a 47mm gun and it's chassis was used as a basis for a variety of vehicles including a ram tank known as the Ho-K, various mine clearing tanks, the TG-Ki bridge-layer, and Shi-ki command tank. The Ho-ki APC used components of the Type 97 and the Japanese Navy built a number of self-propelled guns on the Type 97 chassis including both a 120mm and a 200mm weapon.

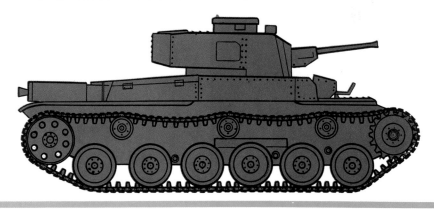

ground by Japanese bombers many hours after word of the Pearl Harbor attack had reached the Philippines. Over half of the modern aircraft, together with part of the repair facilities, hangars and fuel storage areas, were destroyed.

On 22 December the principal Japanese invasion force, Lieutenant-General Masaharu Homma's 14th Army, landed on the shores of Lingayen Gulf, on the island of Luzon, about 100 miles north-west of the Philippine capital of Manila. Two days later an additional 7,000 troops of the Japanese 16th Division landed at Lamon Bay, 70 miles south-east of Manila. In both areas the defences swiftly crumbled.

MacArthur quickly realised that he could not hope to defend all Luzon and that if he attempted to defend Manila he would be caught between the closing pincers of the Japanese forces advancing south-east from Lingayen Gulf and north-west from Lamon Bay. On 23 December, therefore, Mac-Arthur declared Manila an open city and ordered his forces to withdraw into the narrow peninsula of Bataan lying between Manila Bay and the South China Sea. Just off the tip of the Bataan peninsula was the island fortress of Corregidor, which guarded the entrance to Manila Bay, and here MacArthur established his headquarters.

Meanwhile American and Filipino troops under Major-General Jonathan M. Wainwright were fighting a desperate battle to cover the retreat of MacArthur's forces into Bataan and to gain time for the preparation of defences there. Stubborn fighting and good luck on the part of Wainwright's troops, combined with a half hearted pursuit on the part of the Japanese who were pre-occupied with the capture of Manila, re-sulted in the successful withdrawal of the bulk of MacArthur's forces into the Bataan peninsula.

The defenders of Bataan occupied a position at the base of the peninsula in the rugged jungles on either side of a high mountain, Mount Natib. To the west, between Mount Natib and the South China Sea, were three Philippine Army divisions and a regiment of Philippine Scouts under Wainwright. The Philippine Scouts were tough, well trained Filipino soldiers who formed a part of the regular US Army. On the east, or Manila Bay side, of the mountain,

were four more Philippine Army divisions and another scout regiment under Major-General George M. Parker. In the rear, in reserve, was the so-called 'Philippine Division' made up of scouts and other regular army troops, plus some light tanks and the heavier artillery.

All of these forces were short of food, and supplies of all types, particularly medicine, were very low. MacArthur's ill-fated plan to defend all of the Philippines had necessitated the stocking of forward defence positions with large amounts of food and equipment. Once the invasion began and these positions collapsed there was little time and less transport available to move these supplies back to Bataan. The supply problem was

The situation in the Pacific December 1941

JAPANESE EMPIRE, 1933
OCCUPIED BY JAPAN, JULY 1937/DECEMBER 1941
MILITARY BASES ESTABLISHED BY JAPAN, SEPTEMBER 1940
ABDA (American, British, Dutch, and Australian) COMMAND

MERCATOR'S PROJECTION

further complicated by the unanticipated presence of over 25,000 civilian refugees on the peninsula. By 5 January 1942 MacArthur's forces on Bataan were already on half rations, and these were to be reduced still further in the coming weeks.

The first Japanese attack against the defenders of Bataan began on 9 January. The Japanese assaulted both flanks of the American line, only to be repulsed. But other Japanese troops were able to infiltrate between Parker and Wainwright by crossing over the supposedly impassible heights of

Mount Natib. Emerging behind Wainwright's forces, the Japanese infiltrators set up a road block on the only usable road, while other elements threatened to outflank Parker. With their line of communications thus threatened, the American defenders withdrew to a more defensible position farther down the peninsula, the Bagac-Orion line.

There now began two weeks of vicious fighting during which Homma attempted to penetrate the new line by frontal attacks and to outflank it by an amphibious assault

against the so-called 'points'. Each point is a narrow finger of land pointing out into the South China Sea at the south-west corner of the Bataan peninsula. A heterogeneous force of sailors, Marines and grounded airmen together with elements of two scout regiments managed to contain the Japanese landings near the beach-head and then wiped them out in the so-called 'battle of the points'.

On the Bagac-Orion line a Japanese regiment was able to slip through the American defences and form two defensive

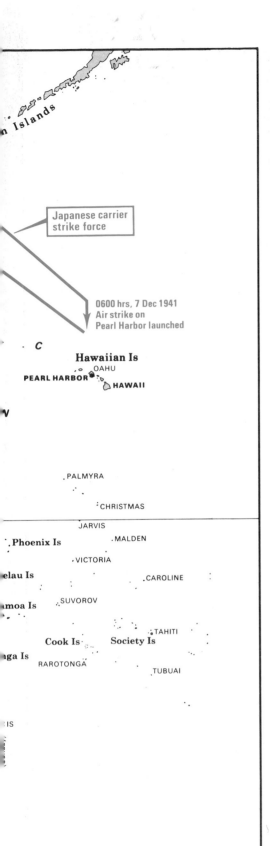

Japanese carrier
strike force

0600 hrs, 7 Dec 1941
Air strike on
Pearl Harbor launched

C

Hawaiian Is
OAHU
PEARL HARBOR
HAWAII

V

. PALMYRA

. CHRISTMAS

JARVIS

. Phoenix Is   . MALDEN

. VICTORIA

elau Is

. CAROLINE

moa Is   . SUVOROV

. TAHITI

Cook Is   **Society Is**

ga Is   RAROTONGA

. TUBUAI

IS

**Above right: A poster displayed by the Dutch
in the Dutch East Indies (now Indonesia)
warning of the impending threat of a Japanese
advance in the Pacific**

rings of 'pockets' behind Wainwright's
corps. In a hard-fought series of actions,
lasting until 17 February, the Americans
finally succeeded in destroying the pockets
as well as a Japanese relief force which had
attempted to reach them.

INDIE MOET VRIJ !
WERKT EN VECHT ERVOOR !

75mm mountain gun model 94 (1934)

Calibre: 75mm. **Maximum range:** 8,939 yards
(8173m). **Weight:** 1,181lb (436kg). **Length travelling:**
12′ 9″ (3.885m). **Width:** 4′ 5″ (1.346m). **Height:**
2′ 11″ (.889m). **Elevation:** −10° to +45°. **Traverse:**
20° left and 20° right. **Rate of fire:** 15rpm (for 2
minutes). 4rpm (for 15 minutes). 2rpm (sustained).

The Japanese 75mm Model 94 replaced the earlier
75mm Model 41 (1908) mountain gun in the 1930s.
The new weapon was designed for easy transportation
in the jungle and could be broken down into 11 loads
for carriage by mules or men. A mountain artillery
(pack) regiment of the Japanese Army had 36 guns
and consisted of an HQ, three battalions and a
regimental train. Each battalion in turn had an HQ
(of 100 men), three gun companies each with four
guns and a battalion train.

The hydro-pneumatic recoil system of the Model 94
was of the French Schneider type whilst the breech-
block was of the German Krupp horizontal sliding-
wedge type. The trails were of the split type, although
the gun could be fired with the trails closed. The
main drawback of the weapon was its lack of elevation
which was a major disadvantage when operating in
mountainous terrain.

A variety of ammunition could be fired including
High Explosive M94 with a range of 7,960 yards
(6974m) and the M90 with a range of 8,938 yards
(8173m), Armour Piercing, Shrapnel, Incendiary,
Illuminating and Smoke.

By now both sides were exhausted. The Japanese had suffered over 7,000 casualties and had about 10,000 incapacitated by tropical diseases. American casualties had been somewhat lower but the physical condition of the Americans and Filipinos was far worse as a result of their long days on an inadequate and unbalanced diet.

In late February MacArthur was ordered by President Franklin D. Roosevelt to leave the Philippines and proceed to Australia where he was to assume command of a new South-West Pacific Theatre. Wainwright replaced MacArthur, and Major-General Edward P. King took over command on Bataan.

During March Homma had been strongly reinforced with an additional division and other infantry elements as well as more artillery. On 3 April the Japanese renewed their attacks. The American–Filipino defences, manned by men near the starvation level, rapidly crumbled and on 9 April King surrendered his forces on Bataan.

The island of Corregidor and the smaller islands of El Fraile (Fort Drum), Caballo (Fort Hughes) and Carabao (Fort Frank), which together guarded the entrance to Manila Bay, remained in American hands, but the Japanese at once began an intense air and artillery bombardment of these positions. Designed for naval defence, most of these islands had their batteries above ground where they were easily pinpointed by Japanese observers on the high ground on Bataan or in spotting planes. On 5 May, having destroyed most of the artillery on Corregidor and its satellite islands, Japanese forces landed on the southern end of the island. The American defenders, supported by the remaining artillery, inflicted heavy casualties on the attackers but the outcome was never seriously in doubt. By the morning of the 6th the last American reserves had been committed and the Japanese were closing in on Wainwright's underground command post and the hospital in the Malinta tunnel. At 1000 Wainwright radioed Washington that he had regretfully decided to surrender.

By the time that Wainwright went to meet Homma, Japan had achieved all of her objectives in South-East Asia and the Pacific. Singapore had fallen. All of Malaya, most of Burma, and all of the Netherlands East Indies had been overrun. The islands of the Central Pacific were in Japanese hands and the line of communications to Australia threatened.

Both sides now undertook to revise their strategy and reorganise their forces. At the start of the war in the Pacific the American, British, Dutch, Australian and New Zealand governments had all been involved in defending their territories and possessions against the advance of the Japanese. After a few weeks these governments had established a unified command known as ABDACOM (American, British, Dutch and Australian Command) under the British General Sir Archibald Percival Wavell to co-ordinate the defence of South-East Asia and the Pacific against the Japanese. With the fall of Malaya and the Dutch East Indies, however, it became clear that the Allied forces in South-East Asia and the Pacific could no longer operate as a single command. Instead the British and American

governments agreed to establish separate spheres of responsibility in the war effort against the Japanese.

The American Joint Chiefs-of-Staff were assigned responsibility for the Pacific Ocean including Australia and New Zealand. But the Joint Chiefs did not, as might have been expected, establish a single supreme commander for the Pacific. MacArthur, a soldier of almost legendary stature in the United States, was already on the scene and was the logical choice for such a command. Yet the campaign against Japan in the Pacific would obviously require the use of large naval forces and the United States Navy was unwilling to entrust the command of its fleet to MacArthur, or indeed to any army officer. The US Navy, on the other hand, had no officer of the prestige or seniority of MacArthur to offer as a candidate.

The result was a decision by the Joint Chiefs to divide the Pacific theatre into two commands. MacArthur was designated Commander-in-Chief of the 'South-West Pacific Area' comprising Australia, New Guinea, the Bismarck Archipelago, the Solomon Islands, the Philippines and most of the Netherlands East Indies. Admiral Chester W. Nimitz, of the US Navy, was designated Commander, Pacific Ocean Areas. Nimitz's areas encompassed most of the Pacific Ocean except the South-West Pacific and included Hawaii, New Zealand and the many small islands of the South and Central Pacific, most of which were in Japanese hands.

While the Americans were reorganising, the Japanese high command had been pondering their next move. Two lines of action appeared especially promising. One was to continue their advance on the large island of New Guinea, directly north of Australia. Japanese forces had landed at Lae and Salamaua near the narrow south-east 'tail' of New Guinea known as Papua in March. Japanese strategists now planned to seize Port Moresby on the southern side of the Papuan tail as well as the Solomon islands chain to the west of New Guinea. From these positions they could menace Australia and threaten its line of communications with the United States. The second course of action was to extend the Japanese defensive perimeter in the Pacific by seizing Midway Island, east of Hawaii, and the Aleutians south-west of Alaska. Planning and preparations for both these new projects commenced at once.

The attack on Port Moresby got under way at the beginning of May 1942. A troop convoy carrying the invasion force started from the Japanese base at Rabaul escorted by the small carrier *Shoho*, four heavy cruisers and some destroyers. The large carriers *Zuikaku* and *Shokaku* with more cruisers and destroyers provided general support for the expedition. The Americans, who had by this time broken the Japanese naval code, knew of the impending invasion and sent Rear-Admiral Frank Jack Fletcher, with a task force built around the carriers *Yorktown* and *Lexington*, to intercept the

A 37mm anti-tank gun manned by men of the 129th Regiment, 37th Division (United States Army), opens fire on Japanese positions on the west wall of the Intramuros, Manila, in the Philippines.

Japanese 38 (1905) 75mm

Calibre: 75mm. **Transportation:** 6 horses. **Maximum range, HE shell:** 8,938 yards (8,173m). **Maximum range, pointed shell:** 13,080 yards (11,960m). **Weight:** 2,500lb (1,134kg). **Length travelling:** 29ft 4in (8.94m). **Width:** 5ft 2in (1.574m). **Height:** 4ft 10in (1.473m). **Elevation:** −8° to +43°. **Traverse:** 3° left and 3° right. **Rate of fire:** 15 rounds per minute maximum. **Ammunition:** HE with muzzle velocity of 1640fps (499m/s); pointed shell with a

muzzle velocity of 1977fps (603m/s); APHE; shrapnel; smoke and illuminating.

During the First World War the Osaka Arsenal modified one of the Japanese Army's standard artillery pieces, the Model 1905. These modifications were quite extensive and included the modification of the plain box trail into an open box trail, this allowed the gun to have a much greater elevation. Equilibrators were added and the hydro-spring recoil mechanism was modified so that it was variable, this enabled the weapon to be fired at the higher elevation. After these modifications the weapon became known as the Model 38 (1905) Improved Field Gun, and the data relates to this weapon. This remained in service until the end of World War II although more modern artillery pieces were in service by then including the 75mm Model 90 (1930) and the 75mm Model 95 (1935).

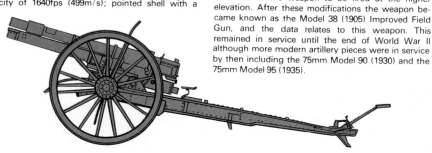

Model 89 (1929) 50mm grenade discharger

Crew: 2. **Calibre:** 50mm. **Length:** 24″ (.609m). **Length of barrel:** 10″ (.254m). **Weight:** 10¼lb (4.762kg). **Range of 89 shell:** 770 yards (704m). **Range of 91 grenade:** 175 yards (160m).

The Model 89, commonly called the Juteki by the

Japanese, was a development of the earlier Model 10 (1921) weapon. It consisted of a pipe-like rifled barrel attached to a small base plate. This plate was curved so that it could be fitted over a log or tree-trunk and many allied soldiers thought that it was designed to be fired from the knee. The bombs were dropped down the barrel and when the trigger was pulled the bombs were launched. Types of bomb included HE, incendiary, smoke, signal and flare.

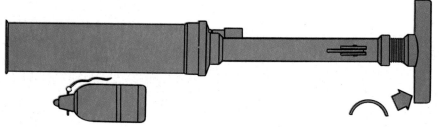

M3 sub-machine gun

Calibre: .45. **Weight loaded:** 10.3lb (4.7kg). **Length, stock extended:** 29.8″ (.757m). **Length, stock retracted:** 22.8″ (.579m). **Magazine capacity:** 30 rounds. **Muzzle velocity:** 918fps (280m/s). **Rate of fire:** 450rpm (cyclic). 120rpm (automatic). **Range:** 220yards (200m).

When America entered World War II, the standard SMG was the famous Thomson M1. This was how-

ever expensive and difficult to build in large numbers. In 1942 a new weapon was developed and was standardized as the M3 SMG in December 1942. This fired the standard .45 round, some were built to take a 9mm round, and there was also a special silenced model. Over 600,000 M3s were built, and a later model of the M3 was known as the M3A1. The weapon is provided with a sliding stock and a sling and is blowback operated and fires on full automatic only.

M1 Garland rifle

Calibre: .30. **Weight with bayonet:** 10.5 lb (4.8kg). **Length:** 43.6″ (1.107m). **Magazine capacity:** 8 rounds. **Muzzle velocity:** 2838fps (865m/s). **Rate of fire:** 30rpm. **Range:** 650 yards (600m).

The M1 Garland rifle was designed by John C Garland in the 1920s and was in full scale production

by the time World War II started. Over 5,500,500 Garlands were built and many consider it to be the best rifle of the war. The weapon is gas operated and self-loading. It remained in US Army use until being replaced by the 7.62mm M14 in the 1950s, but it is still used by many armies today. It has also been built in Italy by Beretta in 7.62mm calibre, in which form it is known as the BM59.

Japanese.

On the morning of 7 May American carrier planes found the *Shoho* and sank her. The following morning the *Shokaku* and *Zuikaku* and the American carriers made contact and launched their planes against each other. Both American carriers were damaged and the *Lexington* sank shortly afterward. The *Shokaku* was badly damaged and both Japanese carriers suffered such heavy losses in planes and aircrews that they were unavailable for operations for several weeks. This Battle of the Coral Sea frustrated Japanese plans to seize control of southern New Guinea.

Despite this setback, preparations for the Midway operation went forward on schedule. The Americans, again alerted to Japanese intentions through reading their code, rushed reinforcements to Midway and the Pacific Fleet under Fletcher deployed north of the island. Fletcher had three carriers, the *Yorktown*, hastily repaired, and the *Hornet* and *Enterprise* under Rear-Admiral Raymond Spruance.

On 3 June a small Japanese force eluded the American naval forces guarding the Aleutians and successfully landed an invasion force on the islands of Kiska and Attu. Meanwhile the main Japanese fleet under Yamamoto advanced on Midway. Yamamoto was confident that the Americans had been diverted to the Aleutians and that his attack would come as a surprise.

Nagumo, who commanded the carrier striking force of four large carriers, was unaware that powerful American forces were lurking in the area when he launched his first strike against Midway on the morning of 4 June. The island base was heavily damaged but the attackers reported by radio that another strike would be necessary. While the Japanese planes were being armed for this second strike Nagumo received word that American warships were in the area. He immediately ordered that the planes be rearmed again, this time for a naval attack.

While the Japanese were in the midst of this second rearming the American carrier planes appeared. Japanese fighters took a heavy toll of the attackers and none of the American torpedo planes hit their targets. But a group of dive-bombers from the *Enterprise* and *Yorktown* broke through and scored bomb hits on three of the Japanese carriers, all of which were soon in sinking condition. The fourth Japanese carrier, *Hiryu*, which had not been damaged, launched a strike against the *Yorktown*, inflicting severe damage. (She was later sunk by a submarine.) Planes from the carrier *Enterprise* then found and sank the *Hiryu*.

The Battle of Midway deprived the Japanese of most of their formidable carrier striking force. It was, as Sir Basil Liddell Hart observes, 'the most extraordinarily quick change of fortune known in naval history'. The Japanese advance in the Pacific was slowed to a crawl and the initiative soon passed to the Allies.

Right: A 75mm pack howitzer of the United States Marine Corps opens up on Japanese positions somewhere in the Pacific

War within a war: India, China and Burma

The war centred on China's vital link with the outside world,
the Burma Road, was fought with a savagery rarely equalled in
World War II, and in some of the world's worst fighting terrain.

The term 'World War II' is a misnomer. There were really two quite separate wars, one in Europe and one in Asia, whose fortunes were linked basically by the fact that the United States was involved in both, and all strategy turned on which theatre she decided to give priority. Fortunately for Europe she favoured the West, but this did not mean Japan could be left alone to consolidate her conquests in the East. The American strategy for defeating Japan was simple but sound: to hold the over-extended Japanese perimeter, which by 1943 embraced parts of eastern China, the Dutch and British empires in South-East Asia, and to concentrate on thrusting at the heart of Japanese power, Japan itself.

In the meantime it made sense to encourage any opponent who could attract Japanese forces away from her Pacific flank and wear them down. British India was one obvious choice, but the Americans rated British fighting power and determination there very low and, moreover, the Americans were emotionally anti-imperialist and quick to suspect proposed British operations merely as veiled attempts to reconquer their lost territories. By contrast, a Sino–Japanese war had been festering for years, and although important parts of eastern China were sporadically under Japanese control, so vast was China and Chinese strategy so suited to her circumstances that Japan could not 'win' in any military sense. To assist China made strategic sense and was also politically shrewd, because there were strong cultural ties between the Americans and the Chinese and such a policy would have public backing.

The basic American plan, therefore, was to provide the Chinese with American advisers and American weapons and so modernise their ramshackle rifle-and-bayonet divisions, and to mobilise China's man-power effectively. Figures of 20, 30 or even 50 Chinese divisions were thought of, but the Americans with their magnificent self-confidence and idealism underestimated the political difficulties of using brash, alien advisers with the chauvinistic and xenophobic Chinese, the appalling state of the Chinese army and the corruption of the Chiang Kai-shek regime. In the event United States aid and the operations of the US 14th Army Air Force kept the Sino–Japanese war in being, at great material cost, but Chaing Kai-shek proved reluctant to co-operate in any Allied operations. He had enough to contend with in mainland China. Moreover, the Chinese concept of strategy was timeless, and fundamentally opposed to the American urge for rapid results.

There was also the US Army Air Force lobby, which considered that China offered better scope for a purely air strategy. Air support for Chinese troops would enable them to hold the Japanese, and if a defensible zone could be established in eastern China then American air-power could be exerted on Japan from that direction as well as from the Pacific. The proponent of a land strategy was Lieutenant-General Joseph Stilwell, a ruthless man of uncommon ability and determination, and deeply versed in Chinese ways. He was commander of all US troops in the theatre, chief-of-staff and adviser to Chiang Kai-shek, was to be deputy of all the Allied forces assembled in South-East Asia under Admiral Lord Louis Mountbatten as a result of the 1943 Quebec Conference, and also *de facto* commander of a Chinese corps of his own creation.

Stilwell had been caught up in the debacle in Burma in 1942 and after reaching India on foot had assembled as many Chinese troops as he could collect at Ramgarh, where they were organised and trained along US lines. This force was to prove the most effective, indeed the only effective, Chinese formation.

A Bren gun team cover an infantry advance across a railway line at Prome in Burma. Prome was the third city of Burma and also the railhead on the Irrawaddy near the oil country.

Wary of snipers, Australian troops advancing through the jungles of Burma whilst fighting the Japanese in 1944

Whichever strategy, air or land, was adopted depended on an uninterrupted flow of supplies to China, but after the sea routes had been lost and the Burma Road cut, the only link was a costly and tenuous air-lift from India, which had to fly over ranges up to 12,000 feet high to avoid Japanese-held territory.

The chosen American operational goal, therefore, was to clear and secure the extreme north of Burma using Stilwell's Chinese troops, and to drive a road and fuel pipeline from Ledo via Myitkyina to China, a proposal typically American in its size and scope.

The British viewed all this with irritating cynicism; they did not believe that the Chinese cock would fight. They themselves had to bear some delicately balancing factors in mind, not least of which was that all that they did depended on American good will and support. Behind them their Indian empire was a powder keg: the events of 1919, when there had been a rebellion in the Punjab, were never far from British minds, and a substantial part of their armed forces were therefore locked up in India in internal security duties. They were determined eventually to reconquer Burma and Malaya and wipe out the shame of their defeat, but they were doubtful of the feasibility of a long advance back into Burma through a country riddled with disease, without roads and with large rivers and mountain ranges covered with tropical rain forest. To the British a sea-strategy striking directly at Singapore or even Sumatra came more naturally and so seemed preferable. Above

all, the British commanders in India were determined not to challenge the Japanese in the field again until they had re-equipped, re-trained the British–India army and re-inspired it with self-confidence.

None of this was viewed by the Americans with any sympathy, and as far as amphibious adventures were concerned they held the whip hand as they controlled the supply of landing-craft.

As a result, a succession of operational plans were made after much debate only to be modified and discarded one after another. Here it is only possible to concentrate on what in fact happened, which was that the Japanese took the initiative and committed military suicide when, in 1944, they gambled on the assumption that Japanese ferocity, combat skill and self-sacrifice could overcome all obstacles of numbers, weaponry and geography, crossed the Chindwin and attacked the British 14th Army at Imphal-Kohima.

The Allied plans for 1944 as they eventually took shape were for Stilwell's Indian-based Chinese force to operate south from Ledo, along the Hukawng valley and then east to the key objective of Myitkyina, so clearing the way for the US Army engineers and labourers following behind them. This was already well under way by the beginning of the year. In support of this the British were to launch a large air-transported force of, initially, some 14 specially trained battalions (or 28 'columns') to cut all Japanese supply routes to the north along the line Bhamo–Indaw – the celebrated 'Chindits'.

The operational merits of this scheme have been hotly debated ever since, but it was a bold and imaginative concept and the Americans, depressed by the apparent refusal of the British so far to get on with the war or even to fight, except at some remote date, welcomed it and its originator, the guerrilla warfare expert Brigadier Orde Wingate, with enthusiasm. They made the whole operation possible by providing the necessary resources to carry it out, especially a 'commando' of transport, strike and light communication aircraft.

Looked at on the map and counting numbers (the three Chindit brigades were backed by a further three ready to reinforce them) a rapid and encouraging success might have been predicted, but there were divided minds and divided objectives. The British high command, alarmed at seeing so many of the best British units converted to quasi-guerrillas, objected to the whole project and agreed to it only on direct orders from Churchill and the British chiefs-of-staff. On the US side Stilwell had one disastrous disqualification for high command in an alliance: he despised and hated the British and was incapable of co-operating with them. The inevitable result was that what should have been one single operation diverged into two imperfectly co-ordinated ones.

Wingate cannot be blamed for this, because he was killed shortly after his operation began, but there is much evidence to show that he himself was more concerned with demonstrating how Burma could be reconquered using his peculiar methods than in playing second fiddle to Stilwell. As it turned out neither his nor Stilwell's activities much influenced the outcome of the war in Burma or in China.

In the meantime General Sir G. Giffard, and his subordinate General William Slim, in command of the 14th Army, had been methodically reorganising and strengthening their positions west of the Chindwin river and in the Arakan when the Japanese struck.

Their first attack, in February 1944 in the Arakan, was a diversion intended to draw the 14th Army's reserves away from the Imphal front, and was delivered with the utmost impetus. The result might have sounded a warning note for the Japanese. At the battle of the Nyakyedauk Pass in the Arakan they met the revitalised British and Indian troops, and their offensive was savagely handled then thrown back. The Japanese did, however, succeed in drawing Slim's reserves away from the vital Imphal sector, but never guessed that it was possible to fly a whole division north again to meet their main thrust over the Chindwin river.

In fact, the Japanese had made two serious errors. They had underestimated their enemy, and they had not kept abreast of military development. In March 1944, when they crossed the Chindwin in strength to challenge an expectant 14th Army, they were an all-infantry army of a previous age, without heavy artillery or tanks, with little air support and relying almost entirely on animals and coolies for transport. Their artillery consisted of no more than 17 light guns. Their undoubted courage and combat ferocity proved incapable of balancing the material superiority the British possessed, and even this was underestimated. They did not realise that British and Indian soldiers were amongst the best in the world, with a tradition of courage and devotion equal to their own, having met previously in Malaya and Burma only hastily expanded wartime units whom they had easily defeated. In 1944 they encountered the same soldiers, well led, fighting from well-prepared positions and lavishly supported by guns, tanks and aircraft, and who were not prepared to budge, whether they were encircled or not.

The result was the extremely hard-fought battle of Kohima-Imphal which, nonetheless, had moments of great anxiety for both sides. The Japanese had mounted their offensive without any real reserves and without regard for the massive intervention by the Chindits or Stilwell which was apparent in March, and elected to fight with over-extended communications and a large river behind them, on ground of the enemy's choosing already well stocked with supplies. They themselves were to be starved for ammunition and food.

The weakness of the British position lay in the fact that their supply routes lay parallel to their front. The Japanese thrusts isolated Kohima and therefore Imphal by cutting the road from rail-head, and had their penetration been deeper the Japanese could have cut the railway as well and so starved all the US and Chinese

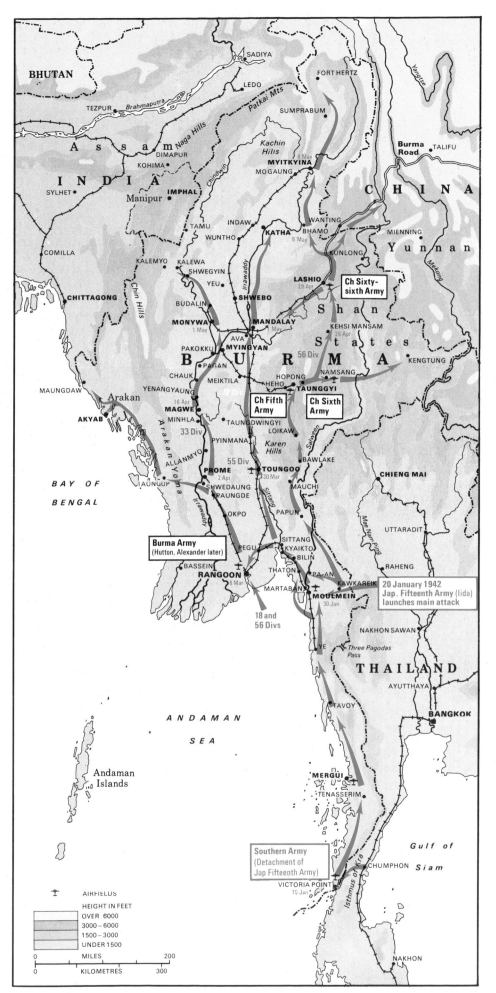

The Japanese attack on Burma 15 January to 15 May 1942.

troops supplied through Ledo. (This possibility alarmed Stilwell greatly, as he had no confidence in the staying power of British troops, and he offered to Slim, who refused it, a Chinese regiment to secure the rear areas.) For Slim, therefore, all hinged on holding the Japanese around Kohima and Imphal while his garrisons lived on their stocks or were supplied by air, throwing the Japanese in turn on the defensive, wearing them out and then destroying them in a series of counterattacks.

Imphal was first encircled at the beginning of April and not relieved until 22 June, but in the course of the fighting the Japanese army which had so confidently crossed the Chindwin was totally destroyed as a fighting force. The 14th Army had confounded its critics, and to clinch the point, regardless of the exhaustion of its units and the onset of the monsoon rains, plodded after the Japanese remnants in pursuit. By 5 August it was into Burma and by 20 August was able to announce that there were no Japanese troops left in India, and that it was still going forward.

In the meantime Stilwell's Chinese had had considerable success, and a surprise march led by his Chindit-trained 'Marauder'

regiment had captured the airfields outside his objective Myitkyina in early May. But it was not until August that the town itself fell, as the Chinese–American troops lacked both the skill and the heavy weapons required to dislodge the Japanese by direct assault from a strong position they had determined to hold until the bitter end. The new Burma Road was finally opened in January 1945, a tribute to Stilwell's ruthless determination and to the US Army Engineer Corps. But Stilwell himself, whose relations with the prevaricating Chiang Kai-shek had sadly deteriorated, had been relieved in October.

The Chindit operation proved a tragic failure, bedevilled by conflicting aims, by being organised for one role and employed in another, and by its mission being altered in mid-operation. It has excited controversy ever since, the Chindit veterans maintaining that their failure was due to misuse, and the orthodox soldiers that it was an expensive diversion that achieved little in proportion to its cost. On the credit side it had offered in 1943 timely proof to the Americans that the British were really prepared to fight the Japanese and offered the chance of Anglo-American co-operation in a theatre where

relations were strained and tainted with suspicion. The opportunity was unfortunately missed as a result of Stilwell's violent anglophobia.

It is also, of course, a remarkable tribute to the Imperial Japanese Army as a purely fighting instrument. Its strategy may have been misguided, but in 1944 it fought an offensive operation on one front and defensive operations on two others (dealing very roughly with any Chinese who crossed the Salween river) and broke about even in battles with the scattered Chindits who had landed in their midst. The Chindit 77th Brigade scored two notable successes at Mawlu and Mogaung. The 14th Brigade (less conspicuously) and the West Africans operated successfully to the bitter end. The 16th and 111th Brigades were both heavily defeated, and the 16th was evacuated complete at an early stage. The Chindits were worn out more by long marches, short rations, lack of rest and disease than by enemy action.

The fact remains that the harder they fought in 1944 the more ripe they were for the *coup de grace* to be delivered in 1945 by Slim and the 14th Army – not so much 'forgotten' as badly underestimated, even by

Widely-used Douglas C-47 Dakota transport aircraft being loaded with men and supplies ready for an air-drop somewhere in Burma

the British — who gave an astonishing demonstration of how to conduct modern war in an undeveloped country over mountain and through jungle, crossing two of the great rivers of Asia in the process. Rangoon fell in May and the surviving Japanese troops, after suffering fearful casualties and hardships, were persuaded to surrender in August.

To see World War II in perspective it is necessary to realise that these huge, costly and prolonged operations, which were virtually a war within a war and fought, ironically enough, largely by Asian troops were in the phrase of World War I merely a 'side-show'. With hindsight we can see that it was an unnecessary effort. Japan would have fallen in any case, and a passive defence might have saved many lives and much misery, but warfare has a momentum of its own and the mere fact that hostile armies are in contact seems to generate offensive action.

American M3 (Grant/Lee medium tank)

Crew: 6 (commander, driver, 2 loaders and 2 gunners). **Weight:** 60,000lb (27,216kg). **Length:** 18' 6" (5.638m). **Width:** 8' 11" (2.717m). **Height:** 10' 3" (3.124m). **Road speed:** 26mph (41.8kmh). **Range:** 120 miles (193km). **Engine:** Continental R-975-EC2, 9 cylinder air-cooled radial developing 340 HP at 2400rpm. **Ground pressure:** 13.6psi (.95kg/cm²). **Vertical obstacle:** 2' (.609m). **Trench:** 6' 3" (1.905m). **Gradient:** 60%. **Armour:** 12 to 37mm.

The M3 Medium Tank was a development of the earlier M2 and was in production by the time the United States entered World War II. Over 6,000 were built by the time production was completed in December, 1942. The tank was first used in combat by the British Army in North Africa and its arrival there turned the tide for the 8th Army. It was also used by the US Army in North Africa and by the Allies in the Far East. The tank was declared obsolete in 1944 and many were converted to specialised roles such as armoured recovery and command vehicles.

The M3 was armed with a 75mm gun on the right side of the hull, and had a traverse of 30°, elevation limits being −9° to +20° The turret had a 37mm gun with an elevation from −7° to +60° A .30 machine gun was mounted co-axially with the 37mm gun. On top of the 37mm turret was second small turret with a .30 machine gun for anti-aircraft use, and there was also a .30 machine gun in the hull. Total ammunition supply consisted of 46 rounds of 75mm, 178 rounds of 37mm and 9200 rounds of .30-calibre.

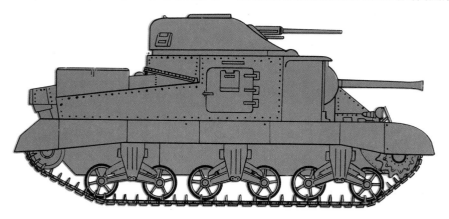

Japanese "lunge" anti-tank mine

Length of mine body: 12in (304mm). **Diameter of base of body:** 8in (203mm). **Length of handle:** 4ft 11in (1.498m).

The "lunge" anti-tank mine was a suicide weapon used towards the end of the World War II by the Japanese. It consisted of a conical-shaped hollow charge encased in a steel container and a long wooden handle. Three legs were equally spaced around the base of the charge, these provided the stand-off distance. The well in the apex of the charge contained the detonator. The firing mechanism consisted of a needle type striker, a shear pin, and a safety pin, this being housed in a metal sleeve.

The mine operated as follows. The soldier removed the safety pin and then waited for the tank to pass. He then "lunged" forwards and struck the tank with the mine squarely. As the legs of the mine hit the tank, the handle went forwards, breaking the shear pin, and the striker was driven into the detonator, initiating the explosion. According to American reports, this mine would penetrate between four and six inches (101 to 152mm) of armour.

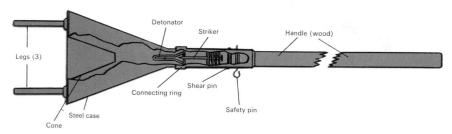

Japanese land mine Model 93 (1933)

The Model 93 weighed 3lb (1.36kg) and was 6¾in (171mm) in diameter and 1¾in (44mm) deep. The body consisted of a cylindrical sheet metal container with a threaded hole in the domed top for seating the fuze. A brass cap with a leather washer screws over the fuze well hole. The bursting charge weighed 2lb (91kg) and had a hole in the centre which formed a fuze cavity. Around this hole was a booster of powdered picric acid. The booster and bursting charge were encased in a paper cover glued to the explosive. The paper-encased pellet was further protected by a heavy cotton cloth bag. The Model 93 mine had two safety devices. The mine was pressure-activated and detonated when a pressure of between 7lb (3.175kg) and 200lb (90.72kg) was applied.

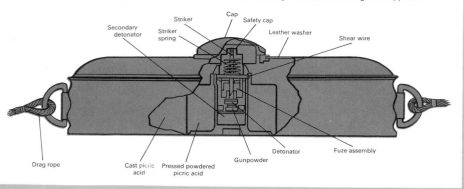

The setting sun

It took the American forces almost three years to retake what Japan had taken in six months. The campaign was marked by heavy casualties on both sides during the famous island battles.

After the great American victory in the Battle of Midway the American high command (the Joint Chiefs-of-Staff) was anxious to seize the initiative against the Japanese. General Douglas MacArthur, commander of the South-West Pacific Theatre, and Admiral Ernest J. King, Chief of Naval Operations, suggested a campaign aimed at the capture of the great Japanese base at Rabaul on the island of New Britain in the Bismarck Archipelago north-east of New Guinea.

After much discussion and debate over the question of whether the projected operations would be under navy or army control, the Joint Chiefs-of-Staff issued orders for a three-stage operation. The first stage was to be under the command of Vice-Admiral Robert L. Ghormley, commander of the South Pacific Area of the Pacific Theatre, and the subsequent stages to be under the direction of MacArthur. In the first stage Ghormley's forces would seize bases in the southern part of the Solomon Islands, south-east of New Guinea. In the second stage Ghormley's forces would advance north through the Solomons while MacArthur's command cleared the north coast of New Guinea as far as the villages of Lae and Salamaua. In the third stage the two commands would co-operate in an attack on

US troops on Marshall Island take cover amid shattered palm trees, evidence of the ferocious resistance the Japanese put up before surrendering.

Rabaul itself.

Operations began with landings by the reinforced 1st Marine Division under Major-General A. A. Vandegrift on the islands of Guadalcanal and Tulagi, at the southern end of the Solomons, on 7 August, 1942. The Marines achieved complete surprise, quickly overcoming the small number of Japanese defenders on the islands and capturing the still-unfinished airfield on Guadalcanal, which they renamed 'Henderson Field' after a Marine aviator killed at Midway.

The Marines' position soon became precarious, however, when on the night of 9 August Japanese cruisers under Vice-Admiral Gunichi Mikawa slipped down undetected from Rabaul and sank one Australian and three American heavy cruisers which were covering the invasion convoy. American aircraft-carriers covering the operation had already been withdrawn because of fear of Japanese air attack, and now the transports and supply vessels were also forced hurriedly to withdraw although they had not been completely unloaded. The Marines were thus left short of supplies and ammunition and with little air support. But they possessed two advantages which, in the end, were to prove decisive. They held Henderson Field, which was speedily rushed to completion, and their strength had been drastically underestimated by the Japanese.

As a result of this latter miscalculation, Japanese forces were fed into the island piecemeal. The first detachments were annihilated by the Marines in futile attacks on Henderson Field and, in September, a major Japanese effort to seize the high ground south of Henderson was beaten off in the 'Battle of Bloody Ridge'.

During September and October air and naval battles continued around the island as both sides sought to reinforce their troops. Ashore Marines fought the jungle, mud, heat, torrential rain and tropical diseases as well as the Japanese. A three-day battle in late October marked the high tide

of Japanese efforts to retake the island and was beaten off with heavy losses by the Americans.

Following this the Americans took the offensive. The 1st Marine Division was relieved by the 2nd Marine Division and two US Army divisions, the 25th and the Americal. In three more months of hard fighting the Japanese were gradually forced back to Cape Esperance, at the extreme western end of the island, from which 13,000 were successfully evacuated during the first week of February 1943.

If 'Task One' had proven much more difficult than anticipated, MacArthur's 'Task Two' was forestalled completely. On 21 July a Japanese force landed near Buna on the northern side of the Papuan peninsula of New Guinea and pushed south across the rugged Owen Stanley mountains toward Port Moresby, the principal town of New Guinea still in Allied hands. By September the Japanese had advanced to within 30 miles of Port Moresby when growing supply problems and incessant Allied air attacks finally brought them to a halt.

Australian forces under General Sir Thomas Blamey stubbornly fought their way back across the Owen Stanleys but were halted by strong Japanese defences around the villages of Buna and Gona on the north New Guinea coast. In what was to be one of the most costly operations of the war, in proportion to the forces engaged, Australian troops reinforced by the Ameri-

Right: A Japanese soldier surrenders to an American Marine on Okinawa (in the Ryukyu Islands) in June, 1945.

Below: American casualties being treated just behind the front line during fighting on New Georgia Island. Unless given immediate treatment, wounded soldiers often contracted even more serious, gangrenous, conditions.

can 32nd Division gradually reduced the
Japanese strongholds at a cost of about some
8,500 killed and wounded and thousands
more incapacitated through disease. The
Japanese force was almost totally destroyed.

The bloody battles in the steaming,
disease-ridden jungles of Papua and Guadalcanal had been far longer and more costly
than anyone had anticipated. Yet the
Allied victories there had shown that
Australian and American troops could engage the Japanese soldier in jungle warfare
and defeat him. By the conclusion of the
Guadalcanal and Papuan campaigns the
initiative clearly lay with the Allies. Both
sides had lost heavily in warships and planes,
but while the immense industrial capacity of
the US insured that its losses would be
more than replaced, the Japanese losses

could not be made good so easily.

While MacArthur and Vice-Admiral
William F. Halsey, who had replaced
Ghormley as the South Pacific Area commander, prepared to resume their campaign
against Rabaul a debate raged among Allied
strategists as to the proper long-range
strategy to be pursued against Japan. During
the spring and summer of 1943 American
forces had cleared the Japanese off the
islands of the Aleutians which they had
occupied during the Midway operation, but
any further advance along this line was
ruled out by the severe weather of the region
and the lack of adequate bases. Logistical
problems also ruled out any major offensive
operations from China, leaving only two
practical routes of approach to the Japanese
home islands.

**Above: Supported by a Sherman medium
tank, US troops move forward on Kwajalein
Atoll in January 1944. Even after heavy
shelling, Japanese positions were very
difficult to capture.**

The first route was by way of the island
chains of the Central Pacific, the Gilberts,
Marshalls, Marianas and Carolines to either
the Philippines or Formosa and thence to
Japan itself. This was the route long con-
templated in the American prewar 'Orange
plans' for war against Japan. This route
would allow the US Navy to employ the
growing strength of the Pacific Fleet, which
by late 1943 had been reinforced with
modern fast carriers and battleships. Moreover the Japanese garrisons on the small
central Pacific islands were far apart and

M3 Stuart light tank

Crew: 4 (commander, gunner, driver and co-driver bow gunner). **Weight:** 27,400lb (12,429kg). **Length:** 14' 10¾" (4.54m). **Width:** 7' 4" (2.235m). **Height:** 8' 3" (2.514m). **Road speed:** 36mph (60kmh). **Range road:** 70 miles (112km). **Engine:** Continental W-670-9A 7 cylinder petrol engine (some had a diesel). **Ground pressure:** 10.5psi (.74kg/cm²). **Vertical obstacle:** 2' (.609m). **Trench:** 6' (1.828m). **Gradient:** 60%. **Armour:** 10 to 51mm.

The M3 Stuart light tank was a development of the earlier M2A4 light tank that entered service in 1940 as a result of the fighting in Europe. It was standardised in July 1940, and entered production early in 1941, when it replaced the M2A4. As a result of combat experience, the M3 was followed by the M3A1, M3A2 and M3A3. The most significant change occurred when the rivetted hull and turret gave way to an all-welded hull and a cast/welded turret. The M3 was built by the American Car and Foundry Company and 8,548 were built.

The Stuart was widely used in the reconnaissance role and large numbers were supplied to the British Army. It first saw combat in North Africa, where it was affectionately known as the "Honey" and the Americans used the Stuart in both Europe and the Far East.

The M3 was armed with a 37mm gun which had an elevation of +20° and a depression of −10°; a .30 machine gun was mounted co-axially with the main armament. A .30 Browning machine gun was also mounted in the bow and a similar weapon was provided on the turret roof for anti-aircraft defence. Early M3s also had a single .30 machine gun in each

sponson firing forwards. Total ammunition supply consisted of 103 rounds of 37mm and 6400 rounds of .30 ammunition.

The M3 was replaced in production by the M5 Stuart, a direct development. The Stuart was officially declared obsolete in 1944 and many examples had their turrets removed and were used to tow anti-tank guns.

Landing vehicle tracked (LVT)

Crew: 4. **Weight, empty:** 27,000lb (12,247kg). **Weight, loaded:** 32,200lb (14,605kg). **Length:** 26' 1" (7.95m). **Width:** 10' 8" (3.251m). **Height:** 8' 1" (2.463m). **Road speed:** 20mph (32kmh). **Water speed:** 7.5mph (12kmh). **Engine:** Continental W670-9A air-cooled radial developing 250 HP at 2400rpm. **Vertical obstacle:** 1' 6" (.457m). **Trench:** 5' 4" (1.625m). **Gradient:** 60%. **Armour:** 12.7mm.

In the 1930s, Donald Roebling, an American, developed an amphibious tracked vehicle for use in the Florida Everglades, about the time that the US Marines were looking for a vehicle which could 'swim' from ship to shore. In 1940, Roebling re-designed such a vehicle (then unarmoured) for the Marines and it became known as the LVT-1, entering service in 1941, to be followed by the LVT-2. The LVT-1 was first used at Guadalcanal for carrying troops and supplies ashore. In November 1943, LVTs were used in the assault role. They proved such a success that almost every amphibious operation in the Far East after this used LVTs in this specialised combat role.

There were many LVT variants: the LVT(A)1 had a light tank turret and was used for close support; the LVT(A)2 was the LVT-2 with armour protection,

the LVT(A)4 had the same turret as the M8 75mm self-propelled howitzer, whilst the LTV(A)5 was similar but had a stabiliser fitted. The LVT-3 and -4 had redesigned hulls with a ramp at the rear to enable artillery and vehicles to be carried — LVTs were propelled through water by their tracks. The LVT-4 was armed with two .50 machine guns and two

.30 machine guns in single mounts and there was a third .30 weapon in the bow; 5,000 rounds of .50, and 4,000 rounds of .30 ammunition were carried. A total of 18,620 LVTs of all types was built by five companies and some were issued to the British, who used them on a number of operations at the end of the war.

---

could easily be isolated and overwhelmed.

MacArthur and his staff strongly challenged the Central Pacific approach. They pointed out that the old Orange plans had never taken into account the possibility that Australia would be an ally in the war against Japan. The considerable military resources of Australia and its potential as an advance base could best be exploited by following a line of advance along the coast of New Guinea and then through the Philippines to the Japanese home islands. This South Pacific drive could be supported by land-based air forces, while forces operating in the Central Pacific would be totally dependent upon carrier-based planes for their support.

In the end Allied strategists decided to use both routes. At the British–American

'Trident' Conference at Washington in May 1943 it was agreed that MacArthur and Halsey should proceed with their campaign against Rabaul while Admiral Chester W. Nimitz's force would open the central Pacific drive with an assault on the Marshall Islands (later changed to the Gilberts.)

A few weeks after the conclusion of 'Trident' the South-West Pacific forces resumed their drive on Rabaul. This operation, now called 'Cartwheel', consisted of a series of alternating co-ordinated attacks against the Japanese as MacArthur's forces advanced west along the New Guinea coast and Halsey advanced north-west up the 'ladder' of the Solomon Islands.

The campaign began with the invasion of the unoccupied Trobriand Islands, off the New Guinea coast, by elements of the US

6th Army under General Walter Krueger. Halsey followed this up with an invasion of the island of New Georgia, the principal Japanese air base in the Solomons. The landings were accomplished with little opposition but Major-General John H. Hester's 43rd Division was inexperienced in jungle warfare and faced stubborn opposition from the Japanese. A second US Army division eventually had to be committed, and Hester was replaced by Major-General Oscar Griswold. Fighting dragged on for almost two months before the airfield at Munda was secured and Japanese resistance overcome.

Wishing to avoid a repetition of the 'slugging match' on New Georgia, Halsey and his commanders decided to bypass the next island, Kolombangara, and instead attack

the lightly held island of Vella Lavella. This was accomplished successfully against little opposition and an airfield was constructed for an attack against the island of Bougainville at the top of the Solomons ladder.

Meanwhile MacArthur's forces began their advance along the New Guinea coast, capturing Lae and Salamaua in mid-September. One week later a brigade of the 9th Australian Division landed at the Port of Finschhafen and held out against determined Japanese counterattacks until the end of October. By January 1944 Allied forces controlled the New Guinea coast as far west as Sio on the Huon peninsula.

The Joint Chiefs-of-Staff now adopted the tactics of 'leap-frogging', or bypassing and cutting off strongpoints and attacking weak ones, which Halsey had employed after New Georgia. MacArthur and Halsey were ordered to encircle Rabaul and destroy it through air attack and blockade rather than by a direct ground attack, which would have proved very costly against Rabaul's 100,000-man garrison.

Halsey's part in the isolation of Rabaul was completed in the autumn and winter of 1943 when troops of the 3rd Marine Division landed at Empress Augusta Bay on the west coast of Bougainville. The Japanese reacted violently to the invasion. Planes and ships from Rabaul attacked the invasion forces but Allied planes from New Georgia successfully interdicted most of the Japanese air attacks while carrier task forces, lent by Nimitz's Pacific Fleet, took a heavy toll of Japanese warships at Rabaul. By the end of

1943 the Marines had been reinforced by a US Army division, and Allied air bases were in operation on Bougainville. The remainder of the island was finally secured the following spring.

The encirclement of Rabaul was completed at the end of February 1944 when the US 1st Cavalry Division landed on Los Negros Island in the Admiralties. The Japanese forces on the island initially outnumbered the invaders but the island commander fed in his forces piecemeal against the increasingly large American forces. By 23 March the island was secured. Rabaul, with its large garrison, naval base and airfield was now surrounded by a ring of Allied bases and left to 'wither on the vine'.

While MacArthur and Halsey had been closing the ring around Rabaul, the long-planned Central Pacific drive got under way with an attack on Tarawa and Makin in the Gilbert Islands in November 1943. Convoyed by one of the largest naval armadas ever assembled, under the overall command of Vice-Admiral Raymond Spruance, the invasion forces arrived in the Gilberts on 20 November. Makin fell with little difficulty but the attack on Tarawa developed into one of the bloodiest battles of the Pacific war.

The Japanese had converted Tarawa into a small fortress with a formidable array of light and heavy guns protected by concrete bunkers. The entire island was ringed with beach defences and anti-boat obstacles. Yet the island's most deadly defence proved to be a shallow coral reef where many of the landing-craft carrying the assault troops of

Above: American troops of the 163rd Infantry Regiment, 41st Division, storm ashore from Higgins boats during the invasion of Wakde Island in May, 1944.

Above right: American Marine flamethrower teams attacking Japanese positions holding up the advance on Iwo Jima's Mount Suribachi in February, 1945.

Right: New Zealand troops use a captured Japanese boat to cross a deep river in the Solomon Islands in the South Pacific.

the 2nd Marine Division ran aground, forcing their occupants to wade ashore under murderous fire from the Japanese.

By nightfall on the first day almost a third of the Marines on the beach had been killed or wounded, but the remainder hung on tenaciously and the following day, with the help of reinforcements, pushed back the Japanese defenders. In three days of hard fighting the Marines cleaned out the enemy bunkers and pillboxes and virtually annihilated the defenders. Almost 3,000 casualties were suffered by the Marines in the battle for the tiny 300-acre island.

Despite the appalling casualties, the Tarawa campaign proved of considerable value to the US Marines and Navy in improving their techniques of amphibious warfare. The lessons learned on the subject of air and naval gunfire support, the need for better communications arrangements,

and the need for improved amphibious assault vehicles were to stand the Allies in good stead in later campaigns in the Central Pacific. In addition, the seizure of the Gilbert Islands gave Nimitz's forces air and supply bases to mount their assaults against the Marshall Islands, next on the schedule of the Central Pacific drive.

The campaign in the Marshalls proved unexpectedly easy compared with the ordeal of the Gilberts. Nimitz directed Spruance's invasion forces to bypass the most easterly islands and attack the atoll of Kwajalein, in the centre of the island chain. On 1 February 1944, after a three-day air and naval bombardment, an Army and Marine division of General Holland M. Smith's V Amphibious Corps were landed on different islands of the atoll. Japanese resistance was stubborn but ineffective and the atoll was secured in less than a week with relatively light losses. The westernmost atoll of Eniwetok was then attacked by about 10,000 men of Smith's corps reserve.

To cover the assault on Eniwetok, Spruance's fast carrier task forces carried out a devastating series of raids on the Japanese fleet base at Truk, in the Carolines on the south-western flank of the Marshalls. Truk was the principal central Pacific base of the Imperial Japanese Navy and had long been considered an impregnable fortress. The American carrier raids revealed Truk to be surprisingly vulnerable. Half a dozen Japanese warships, many more auxiliaries and more than 250 planes were destroyed at small cost to the attackers. Eniwetok fell four days later and Truk was unusable as a

Above: American Marines show weapons and captured Japanese Rising Sun Flag after a battle on Guadalcanal in 1943. Guandalcanal was the turning point in the battle for the Pacific.

Left: Marines of the 6th Marine Division use smoke grenades to flush out hiding Japanese troops on Okinawa in June, 1945.

fleet base for the remainder of the war. Like Rabaul, Truk had been effectively neutralised and could be safely bypassed in the Allied march toward Japan.

The campaign in the Marshalls had proved so successful and been brought to such a swift conclusion that Nimitz was able to advance considerably his timetable for his next objective. This was the Marianas, the long island chain south-east of Japan. Over 1,000 miles from the nearest American air base at Eniwetok, the Marianas formed part of the inner ring of Japan's defences. From bases on the three large southern islands. Tinian, Saipan and the former American-held island of Guam, Boeing B-29 long-range bombers could attack Japan itself.

The Japanese were well aware of the importance of the Marianas and committed all their available forces, including the Combined Fleet, which had been kept out of the Gilberts and Marshalls, to defend them.

The invasion of the Marianas began on 15 June 1944 with the landing of Holland M. Smith's V Amphibious Corps on Saipan.

Saipan was a much larger island than those that had previously been encountered in the Marshalls and Gilberts. Smith's two Marine divisions, soon reinforced by the US Army's 27th Division, were obliged to fight their way from south to north on a broad front through extremely rugged jungle country studded with sheer cliffs and narrow ravines. Army and Marine commanders sometimes blamed each other for the slow progress of the advance and at one point Holland Smith (a Marine general) relieved the Army general commanding the 27th Division. Saipan was finally secured in mid-July at a cost of some 3,126 American and 27,000 Japanese dead. Guam and Tinian fell during the next few weeks.

News of the American invasion of Saipan brought Vice-Admiral Jisaburo Ozawa hastening to the area, with a large fleet built around nine carriers, to attack the American invasion forces. The Japanese made contact with Spruance's fleet west of Guam on the morning of 19 June. In the ensuing Battle of the Philippine Sea the Japanese naval air arm was virtually wiped out and Ozawa lost in addition three of his best carriers. American losses were negligible. The carrier-based striking force, Japan's most potent weapon of the Pacific war, had now ceased to exist.

While Nimitz's forces had been advancing across the Central Pacific, MacArthur, in one of the most brilliant operations of the war, had leap-frogged more than 500 miles along the New Guinea coast, bypassing the Japanese strongpoints at Madang and Wewak, to capture the major supply base at

Hollandia. Hollandia was outside the range of Allied land-based air support but MacArthur managed to borrow the fast carrier force of the Pacific Fleet, under Vice-Admiral Marc A. Mitscher, long enough to support his assault on Hollandia and an intermediate position at Aitape. From Aitape MacArthur's land-based planes, under Lieutenant-General George C. Kenney, could support further operations in western New Guinea. So as not to alert the Japanese to his objective, MacArthur directed that Aitape and Hollandia be attacked at the same time.

In late April 1944, while Australian forces kept the Japanese at Madang occupied, the American 24th and 41st Divisions, covered by Mitscher's carrier planes, landed on beaches east and west of Hollandia. Other forces, covered by Kenney's planes, seized Aitape. Within two days American aircraft were operating from Aitape and on 27 April, Hollandia was secured.

The Japanese 18th Army, cut off from its supplies at Hollandia, attempted to break out during the summer of 1944 but the Japanese attacks were beaten off with heavy losses by American and Australian forces. MacArthur, meanwhile, continued his advance westward, capturing Biak Island on 29 June after one of the bloodiest battles of the Pacific war. By the end of July 1944 American forces stood on Cape Sansapor, at the extreme north-west tip of New Guinea, and all Japanese forces on the island had been isolated or destroyed.

MacArthur now proposed to proceed with his long-planned invasion of the Philippines, but some Allied strategists had come to favour bypassing the Philippines in favour of an attack on Formosa, followed by an invasion of the south coast of China. In the end, however, considerations of strategy and logistics, the military weakness of China and the fact that an invasion of the Philippines could be launched long before an attack on Formosa, dictated the decision to proceed with the Philippine operations.

In October 1944 forces from both Pacific and South-West Pacific Theatres converged on the island of Leyte, in the central Philippines. Four US Army divisions comprising the 6th Army under General Walter Krueger were put ashore on the Leyte beaches in the largest invasion of the Pacific war.

The Japanese reacted vigorously to the Leyte invasion. All that remained of the Combined Fleet was ordered to Philippine waters to attack the invasion forces. In the ensuing Battle of Leyte Gulf, the largest naval engagement in history, the Japanese lost most of their navy but almost succeeded in decoying part of the American fleet's fast carriers away from the invasion beaches.

Meanwhile American troops on Leyte were making slow progress against determined resistance. Heavy rains hampered American ground and air operations and allowed the Japanese to slip in reinforcements. But the Americans had also been reinforced. On 7 December the 77th Division made an amphibious landing on the west coast of Leyte, and by 20 December the Japanese were surrounded by three US Army divisions and cut off from all access to the sea. By Christmas Day the back of the Japanese resistance had been broken.

While mopping up actions continued on Leyte the bulk of Krueger's 6th Army moved on to Luzon, landing at Lingayen Gulf, north-west of Manila, on 9 January 1945. General Tomoyuki Yamashita, who commanded the Japanese army forces defending Luzon, did not intend to imitate MacArthur's ill-fated attempt to defend the entire island. Nor did he intend to be bottled up in the narrow Bataan peninsula. Instead he concentrated his forces in the rugged mountain country of northern Luzon where they could conduct an effective defensive campaign against the superior American forces.

Japanese naval ground forces on Luzon, only nominally under Yamashita's command, insisted on conducting a stubborn defence of the capital city, Manila, which Yamashita had ordered abandoned. It required almost a month of bitter house-to-house fighting before the capital was again

in American hands. Bataan and the islands of Manila Bay fell by mid-March, but operations against the Japanese strongholds in north Luzon continued until the end of the war.

With the successful invasion of the Philippines accomplished, Allied forces closed in on the Japanese home islands, the invasion of which was scheduled to begin in November 1945. On 19 February 1945 Marines of Major-General Harry Schmidt's V Amphibious Corps landed on the tiny island of Iwo Jima, south-east of Japan. From Iwo Jima fighter planes could escort B-29s in their strikes against the home islands and damaged bombers could make emergency landings there for repairs and fuel.

Defended by more than 22,000 men, Iwo Jima was probably the most strongly fortified island attacked by the Allies in the Pacific war. Its brilliant commander, Major-

General Tadamichi Kuribayashi, did not throw his men away on suicide attacks but skilfully and stubbornly defended every yard. Iwo Jima soon became a symbol of carnage and gallantry. Nearly 25,000 Marines were killed or wounded in five weeks of savage fighting before the island was secured.

A final preliminary to the invasion of Japan was the capture of Okinawa, a large island in the Ryuku island chain just south of the southernmost Japanese island of Kyushu. Two Army and two Marine divisions under Lieutenant-General Simon B. Buckner attacked Okinawa on 1 April 1945. Japanese resistance on land was savage and at sea swarms of 'kamikazes', or suicide planes, attacked the invasion fleet supporting the landings. Yet the overwhelming superiority of the Americans in air and fire power and their ability to bring in superior numbers of support weapons,

Above: Lt. Col. Ross raises the American flag on a Japanese flagpole on Shuri Castle Okinawa, after it had been captured by a spearhead battallion of the 5th Marine Regiment in May 1945.

Above left: Men of G Company, 2nd Battalion, 22nd Regiment of the Marine Corps, fire on Japanese troops holding out in buildings on Okinawa in May 1945.

Left: A Stuart light tank with Marine infantry cover moves forwards on Bougainville in the Solomon Islands. Tanks, when used without infantry, were usually knocked out by the Japanese.

especially tanks, doomed the defenders to defeat. Okinawa was secured on 22 June at a cost of almost 50,000 American and over 100,000 Japanese casualties.

Allied commanders now began the final planning and preparations for the assault on the Japanese home islands, but this operation was to prove unnecessary. On 6 August 1945 a single B-29 bomber dropped an atomic bomb on the city of Hiroshima. Two-thirds of the city were destroyed and over 78,000 people killed. Three days later the Soviet Union entered the war against Japan and a second bomb was dropped on the city of Nagasaki.

Although die-hard militarists in the Japanese government wished to fight on, the novelty and destructiveness of the bomb gave Japanese moderates a chance to seize the initiative and, with the staunch support of the Emperor, end the fighting. On 10 August Japan signified her readiness to surrender, and on 15 August the guns ceased firing throughout Asia and the Pacific. The Allies had reached the end of their long and bloody road to Japan.

Asian wars of Imperial succession

With the end of World War II the colonies of Asia returned to the struggle for independence, and as soon as they had secured this they set about numerous small wars of their own.

The Allied victory over Japan and the destruction of the short-lived Japanese Empire also heralded the end of the three older imperial systems in Asia, those of the Dutch, the French and the British. Notwithstanding the British reconquest of Burma and Malaya and the liberation of Indo-China and the East Indies, the sweeping and conclusive nature of the Japanese victories in 1941–2 had shattered for ever the fatalistic belief in western superiority on which, in the last analysis, the imperial systems had rested. It was clear enough to the leaders of the emergent eastern nations that it was one eastern nation – the Japanese – which had defeated their colonial masters, and another – the Chinese – which, alone and encircled, had remained unconquered after years of invasion by the Japanese. They also perceived that it was the Americans who, in fact, had bailed out the colonies' western masters and they were in no way disposed to restore the European imperialists to their former eastern property. The British alone

perceived this clearly and withdrew in as orderly a fashion as possible, but an aftermath of conflict was to continue nearly 30 years.

It might have been thought – indeed it was thought by some high-minded but simple idealists – that all that was required in the aftermath of the defeat of Japan was to establish a new system of autonomous, democratic states, whose boundaries and composition had been established by the free choice of their inhabitants, and that perfect peace would then follow. This ignored the nature of war and the lessons of history. Wars do not always die down immediately a cease-fire is officially declared; they continue like imperfectly quenched forest fires; smouldering on obstinately here and suddenly bursting into fresh flames there. No doubt the actual eastern peoples, that vast mass of long-suffering and durable peasants extending from the Indus to the Red River and from the Tibetan plateau to the East Indies, would have been only too

thankful to devote themselves to the business of staying alive without the added hazards of war ('If the rains come and the tax-gatherer stays away who cares who reigns in Delhi?' runs the Hindi proverb). But their new rulers proved just as belligerent as their old ones.

One fatal lesson the British, abetted by the Americans, had taught the eastern peoples was the use of guerrilla tactics and insurgency to overcome a more sophisticated and better-equipped enemy. Of the post-imperial conflicts the internal struggles in

Below left: Indian troops searching for Pakistani infiltrators who were destroying Kashmiri villages in Jammu and Kashmir in September, 1965. Operations such as this tied down large numbers of Indian troops.

Below: Indian troops, some armed with 7.62mm Ishapore rifles prepare to attack a Pakistani post on the Kasur sector during the 1965 Indo-Pakistan War.

liberated Burma, the fighting in Indonesia against the brief British postwar occupation and afterwards against the Dutch, the wars in French Indo-China, the attempted Chinese communist take-over known as the 'Malayan Emergency' in 1948–60, and the Indonesian-Malaysian 'Confrontation' of 1961–5 were all purely guerrilla wars in one sense or another, except in Indo-China. There one of history's most extraordinary conflicts took place, embracing an external, conventional war between states, a civil war and an undeclared but full-scale war fought between one of the Asian parties to the war and an external belligerent; the whole being fought simultaneously on several different levels extending from rural insurgency to full-scale conventional campaigns using every form of modern lethal equipment and the full gamut of air power short of nuclear weapons.

These post-imperial wars were fought for three distinct classes of objective, sometimes two or even three simultaneously, and the ultimate object was often blurred. The fighting in Java and Indo-China, for instance, arose spontaneously as wars of liberation. The Indonesians understandably believed that the British, who had arrived to liquidate the Japanese occupation, were going to hand them back to the Dutch, and in the bizarre operations that resulted the British actually recruited Japanese PoWs into their ranks to reinforce their own diminishing strength.

Then there were what might be called the 'wars of colonial disengagement', when the imperial occupying forces remained only to hold the ring long enough to create a politically stable situation and to hand over to a viable government; preferably one well-disposed to its former suzerain. This was sometimes apt to lead to three-cornered contests, very disagreeable for the so-called 'security forces'. It was from just such a situation that the United Kingdom finally despairingly withdrew from its self-imposed commitment in Aden. The question of whether to go or stay was always acutely difficult and raised formidable moral problems. Britain withdrew from India because no other course was open, as it did from Burma. The fearful massacres of 1947 in the Punjab resulted from the one decision, and a period of anarchy – not yet completely cured – from the other. The Malays, who for various reasons had always had harmonious relations with the British, accepted the proffered independence while the 'Emergency' was still in full blast and sensibly agreed to British military aid and a military presence for as long as necessary.

The third category of war developed when the firm hand of the imperial power was removed and the newly independent states reverted enthusiastically to their ancient enmities. India and Pakistan achieved their independence on 15 August 1947, and on 29 August a force of armed 'volunteers' invaded the semi-independent

state of Kashmir with the connivance of the Pakistan government, thus beginning a costly and useless state of belligerence which has, sadly, continued ever since.

Kashmir was one of the many 'princely' states which the British had left to decide for themselves whether to accede to India or to Pakistan. It was ruled by a Hindu prince, but its population was 75 percent Moslem. For Pakistan, whose boundaries had been drawn so as to include Moslem majorities, this single factor was conclusive, but apart from the religious basis for its claim, the Pakistan government was understandably opposed to seeing a territory from which the flow of water to its vital irrigation could be controlled, gave strategic access

M24 Chaffee light tank

Crew: 5. **Weight:** 40,500lb (18,370kg). **Length:** 18' (5.486m). **Length hull:** 16' 5¾" (5.028m). **Width:** 9' 8" (2.95m). **Height: (w/o A/A MG):** 8' 1½" (2.463m). **Road speed:** 34mph (55kmh). **Range:** 106 miles (173km). **Engines:** Two Cadillac Model 44T24, V-8, water-cooled petrol developing 110 HP at 3400rpm. (each). **Ground pressure:** 11.09psi (.78kg/cm²). **Vertical obstacle:** 3' (.914m). **Trench:** 8' (2.438m). **Gradient:** 60%. **Armour:** 12.7 to 38mm.

The Chaffe was designed as a replacement for the earlier Stuart light tank. The first prototype, which was known as the T24, was completed in October 1943. Production commenced early in 1944 and 4,070 were built by the end of the war, manufacturers being Massey-Harris and Cadillac.

The M24 saw action in Europe in the last year of the war. Some were also sent to the Far East and since World War II it has seen action in many parts of the world including Korea, Indochina and Pakistan. Recently, the Norwegian Army had their Chaffees rebuilt with a new 90mm gun, engine, transmission and fire control system to extend them until 1985 – at least 40 years after they were built.

The chassis of the M24 was the basis for a whole "Light Combat Team" which included the M19 twin 40mm anti-aircraft gun system, M37 105mm Howitzer Motor Carriage and the M41 155mm Howitzer Motor Carriage.

The Chaffee has a crew of five – commander, gunner, loader, driver and radio-operator/assistant driver/bow machine gunner. Its main armament consists of a 75mm gun, a co-axial .30 (7.62mm) machine gun. A .30 (7.62mm) machine gun is mounted in the bow and there is a .50 (12.7mm) Browning machine gun on the commander's cupola for use in the anti-aircraft role. It carries 48 rounds of 75mm, 440 rounds of .50 and 3,750 rounds of .30 machine gun ammunition.

by snow in the winter, where untrained and unacclimatised men can, and did, die of fatigue, exposure and lack of oxygen. Air transport and air support are the key to modern mountain tactics, but before these techniques could be perfected they were to be tested by a totally unexpected enemy, who had only recently been chanting the slogan '*Hindi Chini Bhai Hai*' – that Indians and Chinese were brothers.

After the Chinese had reoccupied their alienated province of Tibet in 1950 (with scant regard for any views that the Tibetans might have had on the subject) they took a legalistic and unfraternal look at the old British-defined frontier – the 'MacMahon Line' and decided that it wrongly favoured India. This would hardly appear to be a *casus belli*, or the scanty pastures for goats or yaks worth the cost of a war, but nevertheless Chinese encroachment backed by minor military moves continued all through 1961, and in 1962 a general war broke out.

The Chinese, after careful preparation, attacked in two sectors. In Ladakh they had actually built the strategic Aksai-Chin road across the wedge of Indian territory which protrudes to the north-east and mounted an offensive to clear its trace by cutting off the whole salient. Far away to the east the Chinese attacked southwards from the Tibetan border just east of the frontier between India and Bhutan, driving the Indian troops down the road running from Tawang to Bomdi La and Rupa, and not stopping until they had virtually driven in and broken the Indian 4th Division, when they suddenly declared a unilateral cease-fire, on 21 November 1962, as inscrutably as they had begun operations on 20 October.

The Chinese showed considerable tactical skill in deep penetration, arriving undetected in the middle or rear of the Indian defended localities in decisive strength, and similar skill in close combat, 'bunker-busting' with hand-held rocket-launchers in the most disconcerting manner. But occasionally they delivered their 'human wave' attacks in the fashion seen in Korea and were mown down whenever the excellent Indian artillery was deployed in any strength.

For the Indian army the defeat was humiliating but beneficial. Their units and junior leaders had fought as bravely as ever, but there had been serious faults in the higher command which were now corrected. The army was reorganised so that a proportion of divisions was properly equipped and trained for fighting on India's mountainous land frontier. The balance of the total forces was adjusted so that every resource was not directed at the western front against Pakistan and the ability to fight on all likely fronts on 'interior lines' increased. This was a far-sighted move, as events in 1971 were to show.

Hostilities with Pakistan were to flare up again in 1965 after the Indian government unilaterally announced that Kashmir and Jammu were henceforth to be regarded as similar in status to the other Indian states. This resulted in some fierce, entirely orthodox fighting for local objectives. Apart from skirmishing in the Rann of Kutch (April–May), Pakistan began infiltration backed by artillery across the Kashmir cease-fire line which showed the effectiveness of guerrilla tactics in such terrain, some 10,000 irregu-

Left: Bangla Desh recruits being shown how to use a .303 Vickers heavy machine gun in April 1971. The Indian Army, assisted by Bangla Desh guerillas soon defeated the Pakistan Army.

to her northern flank and from which the important rail and road route from Lahore to Rawalpindi could be threatened along a 200 mile stretch, pass into any hands other than its own.

The Pakistanis, rather than use their regular forces, sent in some 4,000 (20,000 according to some) of those famous warriors who had kept the British busy for so long on the North-West Frontier, Mahsud, Wazir and Afridi tribesmen, bred to carry arms from adolescence and unsurpassed in the minor tactics of mountain warfare. It was hoped that these Pathan *lashkars* (little tribal armies made up of families, villages and clans) would sweep away the feeble Kashmir state forces, seize the capital Srinagar and its airfield, and so trigger off a general rising among the Kashmiri Moslems and, with luck, set up a government ready to accede to Pakistan before the Indians could intervene.

The Pakistanis correctly appreciated that any Indian counterattack must be by air in the absence of any routes from the south-east or east fit to take wheeled transport. It was a gamble that might just have come off 30 or 40 years before, but the tribesmen, good fighters as they were, lacked discipline and central direction, were armed only with rifles, and were without any form of tactical communication. They were, moreover,

pitted against a highly competent Indian staff wielding a well-tempered fighting machine. All the same, the *lashkars* had only to continue their initial rush, which began by tearing down the road to Srinagar in their overloaded civilian lorries until they hit a roadblock, whereupon they leapt out, scrambled up the hills on either side in their inimitable fashion to double-outflank and clinch the manoeuvre with a ferocious charge, fighting-knife and rifle in hand, to repeat the process at the next check. This brought them to within four miles of the capital and its vital airfield, but they had wasted 48 precious hours. They had paused for two days of terror in the little town of Baramula 30 miles back, massacring the non-Moslems and looting – some of the tribesmen in their traditional fashion went off home with what they could carry and as many girls as they could kidnap – and the delay was just enough for the Indians to fly in a battalion. The 1st Sikhs were roughly handled and lost their commanding officer, but the Sikhs are ancient enemies of the Pathans. They held the road doggedly and the Pakistani chance of taking Kashmir by *coup de main* was lost for good.

'Frontier warfare' and 'mountain warfare' had always been peculiar to the old North-West Frontier, but from now on the Indians had to adjust the intricacies of modern warfare to operations in the Himalayan foothills, where skilled light infantry remain supreme. These 'foothills' are magnificent ranges 12,000–18,000 feet high, without roads and with the trails and passes blocked

lars keeping 50,000 Indian regulars backed by over 200 guns and mortars fully occupied. Hoping that the Indians were sufficiently distracted in this way, on 1 September 1965 the Pakistanis attacked in the lightly-held Chamb sector north of Jammu where there was good tank country, in great armoured strength and with massive artillery support, and were checked by the Indians only after hard fighting. The Indians in turn mounted a limited offensive astride the axis Amritsar-Lahore on 6 September with the aim of drawing the Pakistani tanks away from Chamb and, as it got under way, the larger mission of inflicting decisive casualties on the Pakistani army. Offensive and counter-offensive followed for another fortnight and the fighting died down with little territorial advantage, but the score in terms of tanks clearly favouring the Indians who, the Pakistanis began to perceive, were no push-over.

What one can but hope will prove to be the final major campaign in this sterile conflict took place in 1971. This time the war centred round East Pakistan, which under political oppression and economic exploitation was becoming increasingly hostile to rule from West Pakistan. Instability in Bengal increased to a point at which the Indian government could not ignore. Humanity demanded military action, and self-interest argued that if Pakistan's most economically productive wing was detached, the aggressive West Pakistanis would have their economic teeth drawn and the danger

from that quarter would be substantially reduced. Politically the moment for military action had to be nicely judged, for if the Chinese chose to intervene on Pakistan's behalf there could be a war on three instead of two fronts, which would be embarrassing, for although reorganisation had produced a balanced deployment and a reserve, India's land defences were stretched in an enormous arc from Rajputana round to Assam. In any case some mountain troops would have to be pulled south from the Himalayan and north-eastern sectors for a campaign in Bengal. The risk was taken, for China was in the throes of becoming respectable as an international power and, moreover, its dangerous frontier was now the one with Soviet Russia, of whom it was secretly terrified.

As regards relative strengths, India had 24 divisions plus a number of armoured and infantry brigades (two of parachute troops) and its tank strength had been augmented by 450 Russian T-55s and T-56s and 300 Indian-built Vijayantas of Vickers design. Morale was high and the quality of the high command outstanding. The army was supported by an efficient air force equipped with Mikoyan-Gurevich MiG-21s, Sukhoi Su-7s, some serviceable home-constructed Folland Gnat interceptors and some old British Hawker Hunters and English Electric Canberras.

Against this the Pakistani army could muster only 12 infantry and two armoured divisions, plus an armoured brigade and an

air force weaker and less efficient than India's. As basic material Pakistani troops were excellent, but a corrupt regime had rotted the army's leadership and morale.

The war on two fronts took place as predicted. Pakistan attacked in the west in the hope of drawing some Indian strength away from the defenders of Bengal. The events of 1965 repeated themselves: very stiff fighting and limited gains and losses by both sides. But the Indians held firm in the west against heavy pressure, first parrying and then riposting with limited offensives. The operations of 1971 finally dispelled any vain dreams that the 'sword-arm' of old India could, despite its numerical inferiority,

Right: Indian and Pakistan officers signing the surrender documents for the surrender of all Pakistani Forces in East Pakistan. The State of Bangladesh was then formed.

Below right: A Mukti Bahini guerilla guarding Parulia Bridge in East Pakistan after it had been damaged by retreating Pakistani troops on November 23 1971.

Below: Indian troops move forward on the Western sector during the Indo-Pakistan campaign of 1971.

sweep aside the armies of the effete Hindus and win another battle of Panipat outside the walls of Delhi. Not an Indian brigade had to be moved west. General Jagjit Singh Aurora's daring concentric attack on West Pakistan went forward uninterrupted and on 16 December he received the surrender of the Pakistani commander in Dacca.

A close study of this campaign will edify military students for a long time to come. Bengal, now Bangla-Desh (literally Land of Bengal), is an eminently defensible country cut up by rivers five miles wide and obstructed by marshes. The Indian plan was a masterly combination of airborne, guerrilla and conventional forces, based on complete mobility and the bypassing of all centres of resistance. The advance was not held up for bridging operations; troops and guns were ferried over the rivers by helicopter, and 'supply and transport' was by air, boat, canoe or country cart as suitable. An

astonishing momentum was maintained from start to finish – it was a *Blitzkrieg* without tanks.

Now India's only remaining military problem is a small but intractable insurgency in the Naga area (the scene of the historic Kohima and Imphal battles of 1944 where the old British Indian Army so distinguished itself).

One Asian campaign remains to be mentioned, as it is of considerable tactical interest, lying as it does somewhere between the fields of pure insurgency and conventional warfare. This was the so-called 'Konfrontasi' or 'confrontation', the undeclared war between Indonesia and Malaysia resulting from a spurious claim by the Indonesians to Kalimantan Utara, or northern Borneo; the Indonesians arguing that they, and not the Malay government in Kuala Lumpur, were the lawful successor state to the former British colony of North

Borneo (Sabah) and the states of Brunei and Sarawak. The political ramifications are too complex to be described in a short space, but on the military side the Indonesian regular troops, purporting to be volunteers or freedom fighters (like the Pathans in Kashmir) infiltrated across the 1,000-mile border in the hope of igniting an anti-Malay insurgency. This was a failure, but the intruders were a dangerous nuisance.

The counter-strategy was highly sophisticated and, as it turned out, remarkably successful. Both operations and any publicity were kept at a low pitch and a low profile, the part played by British and Gurkha troops being deliberately minimised. The posture was, at least outwardly, defensive, Indonesian penetration being accepted so as to transfer the odium of being the aggressor to the Indonesians. Within these constraints a highly aggressive defence was conducted on unusual lines, outwardly

Vickers main battle tank

Crew: 4. **Weight, loaded:** 85,098lb (38,600kg). **Length, overall:** 31' 10⅞'' (9.728m). **Length, hull:** 25' 11¾'' (7.92m). **Width:** 10' 4⅞'' (3.168m). **Height (w/o A/A MG):** 8' 8'' (2.64m). **Road speed:** 34.8mph (56kmh). **Range:** 298 miles (480km). **Engine:** Leyland L60 Mk.4B, 6 cylinder water-cooled engine developing 650 BHP at 2670rpm. **Ground pressure:** 12.8psi (.9kg/cm²). **Vertical obstacle:** 3' (.914m). **Trench:** 8' (2.438m). **Gradient:** 60%. **Armour:** 25 to 80mm.

The Vickers Main Battle Tank was developed from 1961 to a specification laid down by the Indian Government. The first prototype was completed in England in 1963 followed by production examples in 1964. Some were delivered to India in 1965 and in the same year work started on India's first tank plant at Avadi, near Madris. In 1966, this plant completed its first Vickers MBT. Known to the Indians as the Vijayanta. Initially, many of the components were imported from England, but now over 80% of the tank is built in India. Over 600 Vijayantas have now been completed.

The Vickers MBT has the famous British 105mm rifled tank gun and the same engine and transmission as the Chieftain MBT and a GEC/AEI fire control system is provided. It is much lighter than the Chieftain and has better mobility, but somewhat thinner armour. The Vijayanta saw combat with the Indian Army during the last Indo-Pakistan conflict. About 50 Vickers MBTs have also been delivered to Kuwait.

The basic model is the Mk.1 with a ranging machine gun and a 7.62mm machine gun mounted co-axially with the main armament. There is a similar weapon on the commander's cupola for anti-aircraft defence and on each side of the turret are six smoke dischargers. Total ammunition supply consists of 44 rounds of 105mm, 600 rounds for the ranging machine gun and 3,000 rounds of 7.62mm machine gun ammunition. The latest model is the Vickers MBT Mk.3, which has numerous improvements including a new powerpack and a laser rangefinder.

155mm M1 gun (Long Tom)

Crew: 14. **Calibre:** 155mm. **Maximum range:** 25,700 yards (23,500m). **Weight, travelling:** 30,500lb (13,880kg). **Length, travelling:** 34' 3'' (10.434m). **Width, travelling:** 9' 11'' (3.02m). **Height, travelling:** 8' 6'' (2.59m). **Elevation:** −2 to +63°. **Traverse:** 30° left and right. **Rate of fire:** 1 round per minute.

The 155mm M1 gun was developed in the 1930s and was standardized in 1938, and on the outbreak of WWII, production was well under way. It served on all fronts and earned the name "Long Tom" as it had such a long and accurate range. Many armies still use the Long Tom today under the designation M59. A self-propelled model, the M40, was also developed and using a number of Sherman tank components in its chassis. The 8-inch (203mm) M1 howitzer used the same carriage as the M1 gun, which helped to standardize on carriage production.

The gun is mounted on a eight-wheeled carriage with a two-wheeled limber, and is normally towed by a 6x6 truck or a full-tracked prime mover. When in the firing position, it is supported on jacks and each of the trails is fitted with a spade. The recoil mechanism is of the hydropneumatic variable recoil type and the breech mechanism is of the interrupted screw type. The weapon fires an M101 HE projectile which weighs 95lb (43kg) or an AP round of 99lb (44.9kg).

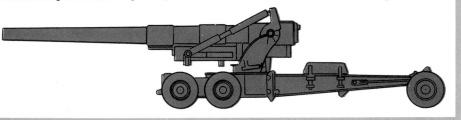

Above: Anti-tank gunner training in the Dutch East Indies, before their independence, which were every-ready to defend the islands against invasion.

ignoring the dangers of dispersion and a static defence. The support of villagers along the border was won over by a skilful 'hearts and minds' operation and they acted as an observer screen to report incursions. At strategic points tiny jungle forts sufficient to contain a company of infantry or so, a couple of pieces of light artillery and a helicopter landing strip were established, to serve as firm bases for patrols to provide artillery fire and supply and information centres. Ostensibly they were hostages to any determined attack: in reality they were bait for the Indonesian raiders, who were sometimes in battalion strength. The real defence was far out and based on counter-patrolling and well-judged ambushes, the troops being rapidly deployed on likely approach routes by helicopter. The unqualified success of the campaign, which tied up the aggressors in endless and unprofitable skirmishing until the fall of President Achmed Soekarno and the change of government in Jakarta, was due in great part to the British General Sir Walter Walker, who with great foresight had trained the British troops in Malaya to the highest pitch of skill-at-arms and jungle craft, and who as Director of Operations also designed the strategy. Ironically the last and most successful colonial, or rather post-colonial, campaign ever to be fought by Britain is also the least known.

'Civil' war in Korea

The only major 'peace-keeping' operation run by the United Nations, the Korean War showed America's determination to check communism and marked China's emergence as a major military power.

Even in the first exhilarating days of peace following World War II, a new world conflict was already beginning to emerge. The USSR, as Sir Winston Churchill warned early in 1946, was lowering an 'iron curtain' across the European continent along the western borders of territories occupied by its military forces during the war. In the four years following, the USSR attempted by subversion and intimidation to gain political influence beyond those borders.

The United States set out to block the extension of Soviet influence through international economic and military alliances, the most prominent of which was the North Atlantic Treaty Organisation (NATO). 'I believe,' President Harry S Truman declared, in what was to become known as

the Truman Doctrine, 'that it must be the policy of the United States to support free peoples who are resisting attempted subjugation . . . that we must assist free peoples to work out their own destinies in their own way . . . that our help should be primarily through economic and financial aid which is essential to economical stability and orderly political processes.' Thus there was evolving by mid-1950 a cold war between power blocs, nations aligned with the United States confronting those assembled under the leadership of the Soviet Union.

Although the new conflict was centred in Europe, it was also visible in Asia on the peninsula of Korea, jutting south-east from the central Asian mainland. Freed from 40 years of Japanese rule by the Allied victory in World War II, Korea by late 1948 had become a land divided at the 38th parallel of north latitude, crossing the peninsula at its waist. Immediately after the war, the 38th parallel had marked the boundary between American and Soviet forces taking the surrender of Japanese troops in Korea. It then divided US and USSR occupation zones, and finally became the border between the communist Democratic People's Republic of Korea (North Korea) created by the Russians in the north and the Republic of Korea (South Korea) established along democratic lines under US sponsorship in the south.

After Russian and American occupation forces had withdrawn from Korea in 1948 and 1949, the northern regime opened a cold war campaign to undermine the southern government. When its subversive efforts failed, North Korea launched a direct attack, sending its army south across

Using locally acquired transportation, men of the US Headquarters Company, 3rd Battalion, 187th Regimental Combat Team, move up to the front line 20 miles Northwest of Wonju, Korea, in February, 1951.

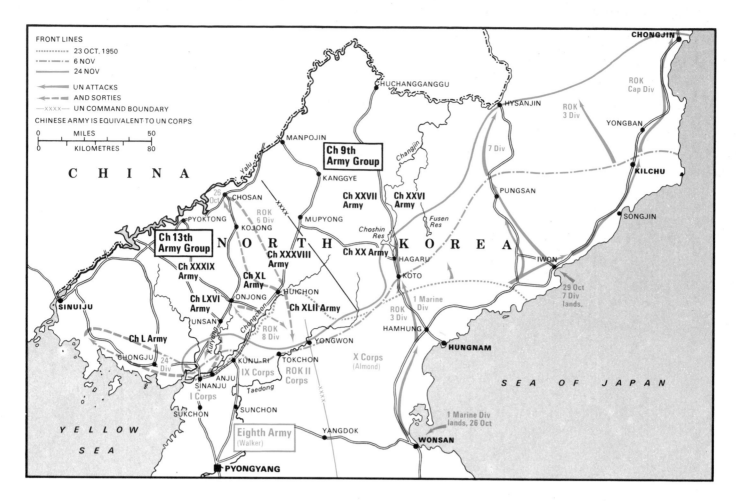

the 38th parallel at dawn on Sunday, 25 June 1950. In one sense, the invasion marked the beginning of a civil war between peoples of a divided country. In another, larger sense, the cold war had erupted in open hostilities.

The North Korean invasion force of seven well-trained divisions was fully equipped with Russian weapons of World War II vintage, including T-34 tanks, 122-mm howitzers and 76-mm guns. South Korea had eight partially-trained, understrength divisions lightly equipped with American World War II gear. In the entire army there were just 90 short-barrelled 105-mm howitzers. It had no tanks, and no anti-tank weapons effective against T-34s.

The immediate North Korean objective was Seoul, the South Korean capital city 35 miles south of the 38th parallel on the western side of the peninsula. Pusan, South Korea's principal port at the south-eastern tip of the peninsula, was the final prize.

The North Korean army quickly crushed the South Korean defences on the parallel. Its main force entered Seoul on 28 June while secondary spearheads kept pace in central and eastern Korea. During the four-day onslaught, the South Korean army lost almost half its men and equipment. While North Korean forces regrouped before crossing the Han river south of Seoul, the remaining South Korean forces attempted to set up new defences on the south bank of the Han.

At the instigation of the US, the Security Council of the United Nations Organisation (UNO), the world body formed in 1945 to promote peace through international co-operation, demanded on 25 June that North Korea cease its attack and withdraw its forces north of the 38th parallel. When this

demand was ignored, the council urged UN members to help South Korea repel the North Korean invasion. The USSR member of the council had boycotted its meetings since January 1950 in protest to the UN's refusal to seat the People's Republic of China, the newly-risen communist state on the Chinese mainland. Had the Soviet member been present, he would undoubtedly have vetoed any attempted council move against North Korea.

President Truman had already directed the US Far East Command (FEC) in Japan to deploy air and naval forces in support of the South Koreans. On 30 June, he authorised the FEC commander, General of the Army Douglas MacArthur, to commit all ground forces available in the Far East. But as firm as Truman was in his acts to help South Korea, he was equally determined to restrict the fighting to the Korean peninsula, and to take no steps that would bring the military forces of the USSR or of the People's Republic of China into the war to help North Korea. There was to be no use of the atomic bomb, and no wholesale commitment of other American military resources. The battle was to be a limited one, or in the president's terms a 'police action', fought solely to clear North Korean forces out of South Korea.

Because of drastic post-World War II reductions in manpower and defence budgets, the ground forces immediately available to MacArthur, as was true of most US Army units, were understrength, incompletely trained and only partially equipped with weapons and equipment left over from World War II. By any measurement MacArthur's forces were unprepared for battle.

The North Koreans had already crossed

the Han river when MacArthur received word to commit American ground troops. A westward North Korean attack had already captured Inchon, a Yellow Sea port 25 miles west of Seoul; and North Korean forces attacking south moved into the town of Suwon, 25 miles south of the capital city.

The speed of the North Korean drive, combined with the unreadiness of American forces, compelled MacArthur to trade space for time. He opened a delaying action on the main road below Seoul, which slanted south-east through Suwon, Osan and Taejon to Pusan. A small American force from the 24th Division took position astride the road at Osan, 10 miles below Suwon, near dawn on 5 July. A North Korean division supported by tanks attacked shortly afterward. Unable to stop the tanks and being too small to prevent North Korean infantry from flowing around both flanks, the American force was pushed into a disorganised retreat by mid-afternoon.

Although fought by larger forces of the 24th Division, the next several battles had similar results. By 13 July, the division was forced back on Taejon, 60 miles below Osan, where it took position along the Kum river above the town. Clumps of South Korean troops were strung out to the west and east to help delay the North Koreans.

Other countries meanwhile offered assistance. Ground, air and naval forces eventually sent to help South Korea represented 20 UN members and one non-member nation. The United States, Great Britain, Australia, New Zealand, Canada, Turkey, Greece, France, Belgium, Luxembourg, the Netherlands, Thailand, the Philippines, Colombia and Ethiopia furnished ground combat troops. India, Sweden, Norway, Denmark and Italy (the non-UN country)

supplied medical units. Air forces arrived from the United States, Australia, Canada and Union of South Africa; and naval forces came from the United States, Great Britain, Australia, Canada and New Zealand.

At the bidding of the UN, the United States established the United Nations Command (UNC) under MacArthur to take charge of these diverse forces. Super-imposing the headquarters of his new command over his existing Far East Command, MacArthur assigned incoming air units to the Far East Air Forces, naval units to Naval Forces, Far East, and all ground troops, including the South Korean army, to the US 8th Army commanded by Lieutenant-General Walton H. Walker.

Defeated at the Kum river and elsewhere, American and South Korean forces meanwhile steadily gave way. By August the 8th Army held only the south-eastern corner of Korea, where General Walker ordered a stand along a 140-mile line arching from the south coast to the east coast above Pusan. During the next six weeks, the North Koreans threw 13 infantry divisions and an armoured division against Walker's 'Pusan Perimeter', but by shuttling reserves to meet whatever threat appeared greatest at a given moment, Walker prevented

M26 Pershing tank

Crew: 5 (commander, gunner, loader, driver and bow gunner). **Weight:** 92,000lb (41,731kg). **Length, overall:** 28′ 10″ (8.788m). **Length, hull:** 21′ 2″ (6.45m). **Width:** 11′ 6″ (3.504m). **Height:** 9′ 11″ (3.022m). **Road speed:** 20mph (32kmh). **Range road:** 92 miles (148km). **Engine:** Ford eight cylinder petrol developing 500 HP. **Vertical obstacle:** 3′ 10″ (1.168m). **Trench:** 8′ 6″ (2.59m). **Gradient:** 60%. **Armour:** 13 to 102mm.

Early in 1944, the Americans built a medium tank known as the T26, followed by an improved model, the T26E1, a heavy tank. Late in 1944, approval was finally given to place the T26E3 (this being a further development of the T26E1) in limited production. The first 20 pre-production M26s were sent to Europe early in 1944, ten attached to the 3rd Armoured Division and ten to the 9th Armoured Division. They

gave a very good account of themselves as the troops at last had a tank which could take on the German Panther and Tiger tanks. Late in 1944 the Americans were losing about three tanks for every enemy tank destroyed. Approval for full production of the M26 was finally approved in January 1945, and 1,436 were built before the war ended. In addition to those sent to Europe, some also saw combat in the Pacific and post war, the Pershing fought in Korea.

The Pershing was armed with a 90mm gun with an elevation of + 20° and a depression of − 10°. A .30 Browning was mounted co-axially with the main armament and a similar weapon was mounted in the hull. A .50 Browning machine gun was also mounted on the turret for anti-aircraft defence. Ammunition carried was 70 rounds of 90mm, 5000 rounds of .30 and 500 rounds of .50-calibre. Other variants of the M26 included the M45 (with 105mm howitzer) close support tank, T31 cargo carrier, T84 8-inch Howitzer Motor Carriage, and T12 armoured recovery vehicle.

serious communist penetrations and inflicted telling losses on the North Koreans.

The strength of the 8th Army meanwhile grew as additional forces, more and stronger weapons, and better equipment reached Korea. By mid-September, Walker's forces possessed over 500 medium tanks (M26, M46 and M4A3 models), newly-developed 3.5-inch rocket-launchers to help handle enemy tanks, and full issues of 57-mm and 75-mm recoilless rifles, developed but not used to any great extent near the end of World War II.

At sea UNC warships wiped out enemy naval opposition and blockaded the Korean coast; and over Korea UNC air forces achieved air supremacy. Besides World War II models of fighters and bombers, UNC pilots were flying Lockheed F-80 Shooting Star jet aircraft. Other jet models that would be used as the war continued included US Air Force Republic F-84 Thunderjets and North American F-86 Sabres, US Navy carrier-based Grumman F9Fs and McDonnell F2Hs, and British Gloster Meteor 8s.

From the outset, MacArthur saw that the deeper the North Koreans drove, the more vulnerable they would become to an amphibious envelopment. He planned such a blow at Inchon, the port west of Seoul. A force landing at Inchon would have to move inland only a short distance to cut the main North Korean supply routes passing through Seoul. Combined with a northward attack by the 8th Army from the Pusan area, a landing at Inchon could produce decisive results since North Korean troops retiring before the 8th Army would be cut off by the amphibious force behind them or would be forced to make a difficult withdrawal through the Taebaek mountains farther east.

X Corps, a force of US Marine and army troops, swept into Inchon on 15 September, captured the port that day and pressed toward Seoul. The 8th Army rolled out of the Pusan Perimeter on 16 September and linked with X Corps 10 days later. By the end of the month, Seoul was in UNC hands and the remnants of the North Korean army had been driven out of South Korea.

A decision to destroy the remainder of the North Korean army, a decision encouraged by the opportunity to eliminate communist rule in the north and unite the country, took the UNC into North Korea in October. The 8th Army captured Pyongyang, the North Korean capital city 120 miles north of Seoul, on the 19th. A few days later, it crossed the Chongchon river only 65 miles south of the Yalu river, the border between North Korea and Communist China. As the 8th Army reached the Chongchon, the separate X Corps came in by sea at Wonsan, North Korea's major east coast port.

In an accelerated drive aimed at ending the war before winter, the 8th Army moved through western North Korea while X Corps sent columns up the east coast and through the Taebaek mountains toward the Changjin Reservoir and the Yalu. UNC forces moved steadily along both coasts. But almost everywhere else they encountered stout resistance, and on 25 October discovered that Communist China, as it had earlier threatened to do if American forces crossed the 38th parallel, had sent in forces to assist the North Koreans.

In the east, Chinese defences slowed X Corps' interior column moving toward the Changjin Reservoir. In the west, Chinese attacks forced the 8th Army back to the Chongchon river. Then, on 6 November,

Right: American infantrymen of Company D, 31st Infantry Regiment, 7th Infantry Division, watch as fighters attack North Korean positions on Hill 598, near Kumhua, Korea in October, 1952.

Below: An American 155mm howitzer firing against North Korean positions in August, 1950. Although the Allies had complete air superiority, it was the ground battles that proved decisive

the Chinese in both sectors abruptly broke off contact.

The UNC believed that the Chinese involved in these engagements numbered no more than 50,000 troops. Since Mac-Arthur was certain that the UNC could defeat these forces and that his air power could prevent major Chinese reinforcements from crossing the Yalu into Korea, Washington officials allowed him to try again to reach the northern border.

The UNC reopened its attack on 24 November and moved easily toward the Yalu. But during the night of 25 November, hard Chinese attacks hit the 8th Army; on the 27th the attacks engulfed X Corps forces at the Changjin Reservoir; and by the 28th UNC positions began to crumble. Not 50,000, it soon became clear, but more than 300,000 Chinese troops had entered the war with the objective of driving the UNC out of Korea.

Confronted by this great strength, the 8th Army withdrew in long, swift strides, outdistanced the Chinese and by the middle of December established a coast-to-coast defence line near the 38th parallel. X Corps initially pulled into a beach-head at the port of Hungnam, north of Wonsan, then withdrew by sea to Pusan, where it became part of the 8th Army. Lieutenant-General Matthew B. Ridgway meanwhile took command of the 8th Army following General Walker's death in a motor vehicle accident.

While formidable in numbers, the Chinese essentially constituted a mass of infantry with little artillery support, no tank support and only primitive logistical support. Their wide assortment of weapons and equipment, mostly of Japanese, American, German and Soviet manufacture, was neither balanced in kinds nor calibres nor plentiful. No more than a third of the members of some units possessed individual weapons. Although their numbers would grow even larger, they were, in sum, guerrilla forces not organised, equipped, trained or supported for sustained operations in conventional warfare.

In the air, on the other hand, the Chinese challenged UNC air forces with Russian-built Mikoyan-Gurevich MiG-15 jets, which were more manoeuvrable than the jets flown by UNC pilots. Chinese pilots, however, were less skilled, as was indicated on 8 November, when in the first all-jet air battle in history the pilot of a slower F-80 shot down one of the MiGs.

By the end of 1950, almost half a million communist forces stood opposite the 8th Army. Attacking on New Year's Eve, Chinese units drove toward Seoul while a number of rebuilt North Korean divisions pushed south in central and eastern Korea. The 8th Army gave up Seoul on 4 January 1951, and set up a new line 40 miles farther south. Communist pressure finally subsided in mid-January. Setting out light screening forces, most communist units withdrew to obtain replacements and new supplies.

The 8th Army moved north in a methodical attack on 25 January, wiping out each pocket of resistance before making another advance. Communist screening forces fought back vigorously; but the 8th Army recaptured Seoul in mid-March, reached the 38th parallel by early April and then began moving, once more, into North Korea. Informed by intelligence sources that the communists were preparing a new offensive, General Ridgway in mid-April issued plans for delaying actions to be fought when the counterattack materialised. This was his last

Russian SU-76 self-propelled gun

Crew: 4 (commander, gunner, loader and driver). **Weight:** 24,691lb (11,200kg). **Length:** 16′ 5″ (5m). **Width:** 9′ (2.74m). **Height:** 6′ 11″ (2.1m). **Road speed:** 30mph (45kmh). **Range:** 224 miles (360km). **Engines:** Two GAZ-202, 6 cylinder, in-line, water cooled petrol engines developing 70 HP at 3600rpm. **Ground pressure:** 8.1psi (.57kg/cm²). **Vertical obstacle:** 25″ (.65m). **Trench:** 6′ 6″ (2m). **Gradient:** 47%. **Armour:** 10-35mm.

The SU-76 entered production in 1942 and was based on the T-70 light tank chassis with a modified version of the 76mm (M1943) ZIS-3 anti-tank gun mounted at the rear. It was designed to be a tank destroyer but it was soon found that it lacked the necessary armour and firepower and was relegated to the support role. Since World War II, it has seen combat in Korea and it still remains in service with some countries today, including China and Yugoslavia.

The 76.2mm gun has an elevation of +25° and a depression of −5°, traverse being 20° left and 12° right. A total of 60 rounds of ammunition are carried, types available being HE, APHE, HVAP and HEAT. The 76mm gun has a maximum range of 12,248 yards (11,200m), with the gun at maximum elevation. Some SU-76s had a 7.62mm anti-aircraft machine gun mounted on the roof.

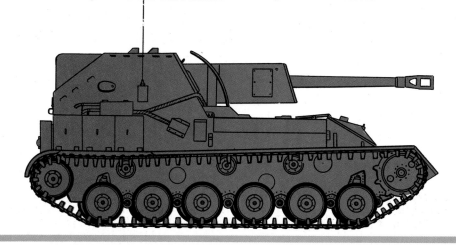

Centurion tank

Crew: 4 (commander, gunner, loader, driver). **Weight:** 114,247lb (51,820kg). **Length, overall:** 32′ 4″ (9.854m). **Length, hull:** 25′ 8″ (7.823m). **Width:** 11′ 1½″ (3.39m). **Height (w/o A/A MG):** 9′ 10⅜″ (3.009m). **Road speed:** 21.5mph (34.6kmh). **Range:** 118 miles (190km). **Engine:** Rolls Royce Mk.IVB, 12 cylinder, OHV, petrol engine developing 650 BHP at 2550rpm. **Ground pressure:** 13,5psi (.95kg/cm²). **Vertical obstacle:** 3′ (.914m). **Trench:** 11′ (3.352m). **Gradient:** 60%. **Armour:** 17 to 152mm.

The Centurion has been one of the most successful of all British tank designs. Development commenced in 1944 under the designation A41 and six prototypes were built by the end of the war, but did not see combat.

Over 4,000 Centurions were built, most by the Royal Ordnance Factory at Leeds, and Vickers. The Centurion has the right combination of armour, firepower and mobility and over the years has been both up-gunned and up-armoured. The first models had a 17-Pounder gun, followed by the 20-Pounder; late models had a 105mm gun which is now the standard NATO tank gun. Its main drawback was its Meteor petrol engine, but both Vickers and the Israelies now have programmes to replace this engine and its original transmission with a new powerpack and transmission which gives the Centurion both a higher speed and a greater radius of action.

Many other Centurion versions have been developed, including armoured recovery vehicles, three types of bridgelayer, a beach armoured recovery vehicle and an armoured engineer vehicle. There have been many projects, some of which reached prototype stage, including 120mm and 183mm tank destroyers, amphibious models, and a flamethrower. One of the more interesting projects was armed with twin 105mm howitzers in a new turret.

The Mk.13 Centurion is armed with a 105mm gun, a 7.62mm co-axial machine gun, a .50 (12.7mm) ranging machine gun, a 7.62mm anti-aircraft machine gun and six smoke dischargers are mounted on either side of the turret. Total ammunition carried is 64 rounds of 105mm, 600 rounds of .50 (12.7mm) and 4750 rounds of 7.62mm.

American Marines of the 1st Marine Division landing during the amphibious assault at Inchon, Korea, on September 15, 1950. These landings, behind enemy lines, were a complete success with very few casualties.

act as 8th Army commander. In one of the most controversial episodes of the war, President Truman relieved MacArthur of command for failing to give full support to US policies governing the conduct of the war and appointed Ridgway to take his place. Lieutenant-General James A. Van Fleet became the new 8th Army commander on 14 April.

The communists attacked a week later, again aiming their main effort at Seoul. Severely punishing the enemy while withdrawing slowly, the 8th Army stopped the push a few miles north of the capital city by the end of the month. Van Fleet postponed a counterattack after intelligence sources indicated that his forces had defeated only the first phase of the offensive. Having recouped their losses, the communists resumed their attack on 15 May, this time driving through the 8th Army's east-central positions. Van Fleet contained this attack after it had penetrated 30 miles, and struck back immediately. Disorganised by their May effort, the communist forces offered little resistance and suffered heavy losses as they retreated north. by mid-June, the 8th Army was slightly above the 38th parallel.

UNC forces having again pushed north of the parallel, the United States and other members of the UNC coalition were now willing, as they had not been during the past autumn, to accept the clearance of communist forces from South Korea as a suitable final result of operations. It was their decision to hold the 8th Army in defences along the line just gained and wait for a bid for armistice negotiations from the communist high command, to whom it should now be clear that their forces lacked the ability to conquer South Korea. It proved a valid decision. On 23 June 1951, Jacob Malik, USSR delegate to the United Nations, encouraged the opening of cease-fire discussions. Peking Radio endorsed Malik's proposal shortly afterward; and on 10 July military delegations from the opposing forces opened armistice negotiations at a neutralised site in no-man's land.

By 26 July, the armistice delegations fixed the points to be settled for bringing about an armistice. But the Chinese and North Korean delegates thereafter seemed concerned more with gaining advantages than with settling differences, and finally broke off negotiations on 22 August. The 8th Army then launched attacks to improve its defensive positions, capturing such heights as Bloody Ridge and Heartbreak Ridge in hard battles, as indicated by the names given the ground taken.

The 8th Army's successes may have convinced communist leaders to return to the armistice conference table. At their offer, negotiations resumed on 25 October. But discord over several issues, principally the terms of a prisoner-of-war exchange, delayed progress. While argument continued, battle action mounted to patrol clashes, raids and furious fights for outposts. The men who fought over oddly-shaped land masses, such as Sniper Ridge, the Hook, the T-Bone and Old Baldy, experienced all-out warfare, but the lines remained substantially unchanged at the end of 1952. In May 1952 General Mark W. Clark replaced General Ridgway as the UNC commander; and October of 1952 the armistice conference

again went into recess.

A notable development along the 8th Army front during this period was the use of helicopters. The pilots of Bell H-13s and Hiller H-23s picked up wounded men at the front and carried them to mobile army surgical hospitals (MASH) located near the front. The rapid evacuation and treatment saved many lives. Larger cargo helicopters, Sikorsky H-19s and Piasecki H-21s, were used to carry supplies to forces occupying positions in mountainous, nearly-roadless terrain.

Up to February 1953, when Lieutenant-General Maxwell D. Taylor replaced Van Fleet as commander of the 8th Army, and during the next three months, the front remained generally quiet. The armistice talks resumed in April; and the pace of battle quickened in May and June when communist forces opened hard, though limited attacks, which the 8th Army contained without losing any important ground. A similar communist attack and 8th Army counterattack in July proved to be the last major engagement of the war. By 20 July the armistice delegations finally reached full agreement. The armistice documents were signed at 1000 hours on 27 July and, as provided in the agreement, all fighting stopped 12 hours later.

During the 37 months of war, UNC casualties exceeded 550,000, including almost 95,000 dead. Estimated communist casualties totalled 1,500,000. In terms of territory, there was little gain or loss for either side. According to armistice terms, the front line existing at the final hour became the new boundary between North and South Korea. Slanting from a point 15 miles south of the 38th parallel in the west to a point 40 miles north of the parallel in the east, the new border differed only slightly from the prewar division.

Within three days of the armistice, the forces of each side withdrew two kilometres from the new border to establish a demilitarised zone that was not to be trespassed upon. To enforce the armistice terms, a Military Armistice Commission composed of an equal number of officials from each side was established. Assisting this principal group was a Neutral Nations Supervisory Commission with members from Sweden, Switzerland, Czechoslovakia and Poland.

The main scene then shifted to Geneva in Switzerland where, as required by the armistice agreement, a conference of the belligerent nations was to arrange the unification of Korea. From the first meeting on 26 April 1954, there was a complete impasse. The representatives of UNC nations wanted a government for all of Korea established through elections supervised by the UN. The communist delegation insisted that the UN had no authority to deal with the matter. The conference closed on 15 June 1954, with Korea still divided and with opposing forces still facing each other across the demilitarised zone, a situation that was to continue with little probability of resolution.

A North Korean Soviet-supplied T-34/85 Tank knocked out on a bridge south of Suwon, Korea, in October, 1950, as a result of an air attack by the USAF. The allies had complete air superiority during the Korean War.

Vietnam

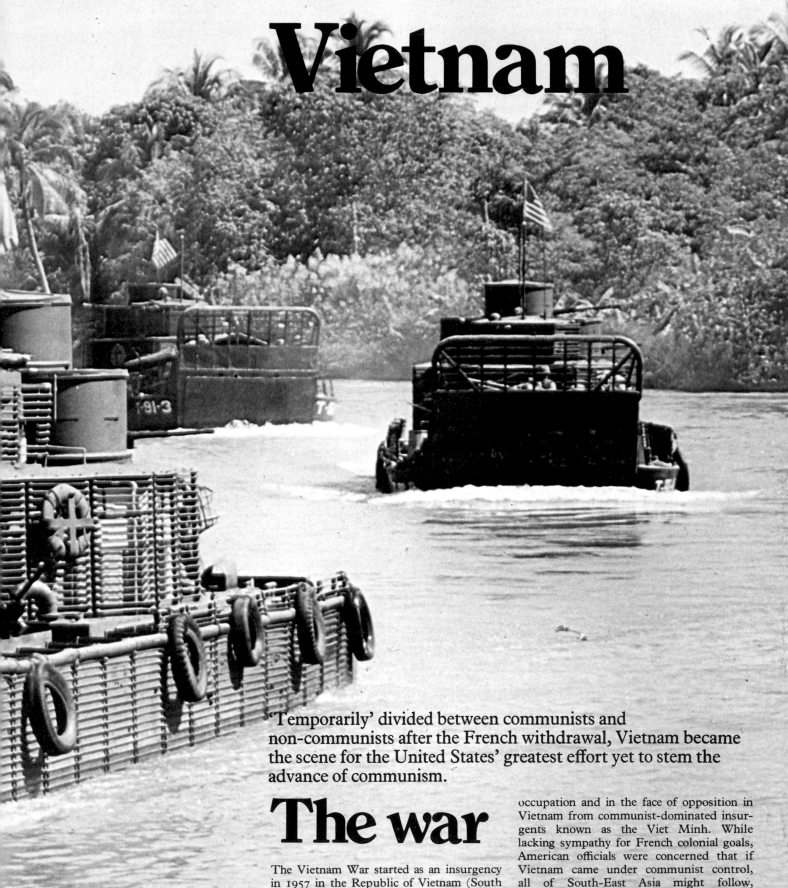

A heavily armed monitor leads landing craft of the United States Navy River Assault Flotilla One along the Mekong River during Operation Coronado Nine, Vietnam, December, 1967.

'Temporarily' divided between communists and non-communists after the French withdrawal, Vietnam became the scene for the United States' greatest effort yet to stem the advance of communism.

The war

The Vietnam War started as an insurgency in 1957 in the Republic of Vietnam (South Vietnam) with the insurgents supported by the Democratic Republic of Vietnam (North Vietnam). Lasting until 1975, it involved in the last 10 years active participation by North Vietnamese troops on the side of the insurgents, and for much of that time participation by Free World forces on the side of the South Vietnamese government.

The United States first became involved in Vietnam soon after World War II when France was seeking to re-establish hegemony over its Indo-Chinese colonies of Cambodia, Laos and Vietnam in the wake of Japanese occupation and in the face of opposition in Vietnam from communist-dominated insurgents known as the Viet Minh. While lacking sympathy for French colonial goals, American officials were concerned that if Vietnam came under communist control, all of South-East Asia might follow, leading to threats to Australia, the Philippines and other countries – what became known as the 'domino theory', in fact.

American concern increased early in 1950 after the Soviet Union and the People's Republic of China recognised the insurgent Viet Minh government, headed by a charismatic leader, Ho Chi Minh, and after the Chinese communists began providing military assistance to the Viet Minh. When France at last granted a measure of autonomy to French-sponsored governments in Cambodia, Laos and Vietnam, the US

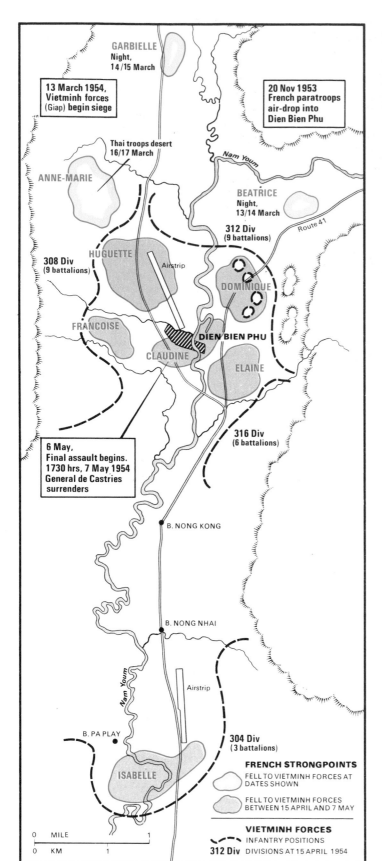

administration of President Harry S Truman on 2 February 1950, recognised the three governments. That of Vietnam was headed by the former Vietnamese emperor, Bao Dai.

Beginning in late spring of 1950, the United States began providing military and economic assistance to the three governments. Channeled through the French, most of it went to support the French war in Vietnam. By 1954 the United States was furnishing 78 per cent of the cost of the French war effort.

The French campaign nevertheless went badly. Partly because the French were unwilling to grant total independence to the Vietnamese, Bao Dai was unable to attract the popular following that Ho Chi Minh commanded. Beset by political opposition at home to a colonial war and subjected to a major tactical defeat between November 1953 and May 1954 at Dien Bien Phu, France in the spring of 1954 agreed to an international conference to settle the fighting. The agreements reached in the so-called Geneva Accords led to a cease-fire and what was meant to be a temporary division of the country by creation of a demiliterised zone (DMZ) along the 17th parallel. Ho Chi Minh's government presided over North Vietnam from Hanoi; Bao Dai's over South Vietnam from Saigon.

Soon after promulgation of the Geneva Accords, Bao Dai's premier, a staunch anti-communist, Ngo Dinh Diem, ousted the playboy emperor, took over the government and in the autumn of 1954 asked for American aid.

Although the Geneva Accords called for consultation in 1956 between the two

Top left: American aircrew shot down over North Vietnam are paraded through the capital of North Vietnam, Hanoi.

Left: Wounded Viet-Cong prisoners. One of the many problems encountered by the Americans was the positive identification of VC who often wore no uniforms.

Above right: Viet-Cong moving supplies through the jungle on bicycles. The Ho-Chi-Minh trail from N. Vietnam right down to S. Vietnam was kept open all through the year despite being under constant attack by American aircraft.

Vietnamese governments designed to lead to nationwide elections, Diem refused to participate on grounds that South Vietnam had not acceded to the Accords.

Foiled in taking over the entire country through elections, the communists turned to military means. A campaign of terrorism, begun in 1957 by former Viet Minh left behind in South Vietnam, intensified over the next few years as other South Vietnamese trained in North Vietnam joined in. The insurgents came to be known as the Viet Cong, or VC.

By mid-1961, after the North Vietnamese government had sponsored a National Front for the Liberation of South Vietnam, a communist-front organisation designed to attract anti-Diem nationalists, the VC had become a serious threat to the Diem regime.

In the face of the growing threat, a new US president, John F. Kennedy, decided to increase the numbers of American advisers but not to commit combat troops. In addition to the prior goal of assuring a non-communist South Vietnam, the American

purpose became to assure the credibility of the United States in its commitments. During 1962 American military strength in South Vietnam grew to more than 11,000.

The increased American military assistance included four US Army helicopter companies and substantial numbers of Air Force planes. With that assistance and a growth of South Vietnamese military and paramilitary forces to over 400,000 men, hope for defeating the insurgency grew; but that was reckoning without the turbulent political climate within the country. Disturbed by Diem's autocratic methods, a cabal of military leaders in November 1963 staged a *coup d'état* in which Diem was killed. A succession of unstable governments ensued.

Amid the political turmoil, the insurgency flourished. By 1964 VC strength had grown to 35,000 in military units and 100,000 overall, including political cadres, known as the 'infrastructure'. A government programme to relocate the rural population in supposedly secure 'strategic hamlets' collapsed. Although American military strength continued to increase, reaching 23,000 during 1964, including more helicopter companies but still no ground combat troops, the insurgency continued to grow. Avoiding for the time being the onus of violating the neutrality of the DMZ, the North Vietnamese sent arms and supplies provided by China and the Soviet Union down a series of routes through neighbouring Laos known collectively as the Ho Chi Minh Trail.

Following two incidents between American destroyers and North Vietnamese patrol-boats in the Gulf of Tonkin in August 1964, the US Congress by a near-

unanimous vote passed a resolution authorising President Kennedy's successor, Lyndon B. Johnson, 'to repel any armed attack against the forces of the United States and to prevent further aggression'. That resolution was for long to serve as the legal basis for American action in an undeclared war until subsequently repealed by a disenchanted Congress in 1970. For the time being President Johnson used it only as authority for retaliatory air strikes against North Vietnamese patrol-boat bases.

Beginning in the late autumn of 1964, the VC began to appear in regimental and divisional strength. Stretched thin trying to protect vital installations and populated areas, the Army of the Republic of Vietnam (ARVN, pronounced *arvin*) was unable to counter the growing threat. ARVN losses reached the equivalent of a battalion a week, leadership often failed and the desertion rate was high. The communists seized and temporarily held some district and province capitals, and US installations, including the embassy in Saigon, were for the first time direct targets of VC attack.

Following terrorist attacks on two American installations in February 1965, President Johnson authorised retaliatory air strikes against targets in North Vietnam, ordered the families of American soldiers sent home, deployed a Hawk missile air-defence battalion to an air base in the northern part of South Vietnam at Danang, and authorised US Air Force planes to assist ARVN ground units within South Vietnam. Yet the situation continued to deteriorate to the point that some observers were predicting that South Vietnam might fall within six months. Upon the advice of the American ambassador, Maxwell Taylor, and the

MACV commander, General William C. Westmoreland, that 'something new' had to be introduced if South Vietnam was to survive, President Johnson ordered a sustained bombing campaign against North Vietnam.

Lest a sudden, massive bombing attack provoke China and the Soviet Union into open assistance to North Vietnam, President Johnson directed that the aerial campaign develop gradually in intensity and that the capital of Hanoi and major port of Haiphong be excluded. The goal was not to defeat North Vietnam but to convince North Vietnamese officials to halt their support for the VC insurgency.

With the bombing campaign, a need developed for American ground combat troops to protect the air bases within South Vietnam. President Johnson first authorised two US Marine Corps battalions in March 1964, to defend the air base at Danang, followed by a military police battalion to protect installations in Saigon.

The arrival of the first ground combat troops led inevitably to more troops and increased American participation. In May a US Army airborne brigade arrived to protect an air base at Bien Hoa, and in late June General Westmoreland received authority for the airborne troops to launch the first American ground offensive, a brief foray into an enemy stronghold near the air base. General Westmoreland also received authority for B-52 strategic bombers, based on Guam and later in Thailand, to hit entrenched communist bases in remote regions of South Vietnam. At this time Australia and South Korea also agreed to contribute token ground forces.

At the same time political unrest continued in Saigon. In late June 1965 a new government took over, headed by General Nguyen Van Thieu as head of state and Air Vice-Marshal Nguyen Cao Ky as premier. It was not apparent at the time, but the government was at last to provide a measure of political stability for the country.

Regular troops of the North Vietnamese Army having been identified in the Central Highlands region of South Vietnam and the ARVN situation still being perilous, General Westmoreland concluded in June that if South Vietnam was to survive, sizable numbers of American ground troops would be required. After sending to Saigon a fact-finding mission headed by Secretary of Defense Robert McNamara, President Johnson agreed. In late July he announced pending commitment of an airmobile division with additional forces to be sent as required. By the end of 1965, 180,000 American troops would be in South Vietnam, a number eventually to increase to almost 550,000, plus another 65,000 from other Free World countries.

As more American troops arrived, the pattern of their commitment was soon set: US Marines in the northern provinces and US Army troops in the central provinces and around Saigon, leaving the ARVN fully responsible for the southern provinces of the Mekong river delta. Only in late 1966 were American troops introduced into the delta in the form of a Riverine Force with armoured gunboats, floating artillery platforms and barracks ships.

As the fire brigade phase passed by mid-1966 (despite infiltration of North Vietnamese troops raising total communist military strength to more than 225,000), General Westmoreland directed American troops to bear the main battle against the enemy's big units, thereby freeing most ARVN troops to protect villages and hamlets in support of a programme known as 'pacification'. Under this programme American and South Vietnamese civilian agencies brought government services to the people, while the police and the ARVN weeded out local guerrillas and the infrastructure. In the fight against the big units, American troops invaded long-sacrosanct enemy sanctuaries, such as War Zone D near Bien Hoa and War Zone C along the Cambodian border, and combed the mountainous jungle of the Central Highlands to bring the enemy to battle and keep him away from the densely populated regions along the coast.

It was a war without front lines, a chequerboard war in which American and ARVN troops might be swiftly set down almost anywhere by helicopters and one in which communist troops also could be almost anywhere, often intermingled with the population and indistinguishable from non-combatants.

This kind of war defied the usual standards for measuring progress, so that the military turned to imprecise statistics: number of enemy killed by 'body count', how many villages 'pacified', how many

Above: A wounded American is helped by his comrades. Helicopters were often able to evacuate casualities to hospital within an hour of them being wounded.

Above right: Viet Cong prisoners being taken aboard a US Hovercraft in the Mekong Delta, South Vietnam. The hovercraft proved very effective in the tough environment of the Delta.

Right: A UH-1B Huey helicopter lands at Fire Support Base Cunningham. Armed with 150mm howitzers, this base gave fire support to patrols moving around the surrounding countryside.

miles of highway opened. Under a policy of the Johnson administration to keep the war localised, American and South Vietnamese troops were forbidden to cross the borders of Laos and Cambodia, even though the VC and North Vietnamese established sanctuaries in those countries, ran supply routes through them and used the Cambodian port of Sihanoukville as a major port of entry for supplies.

Toward the end of 1967 General Westmoreland responded to a major move by North Vietnamese troops across the DMZ by sending some US Army units to reinforce the Marines in the northern provinces. Heavy fighting was underway there, including a big enemy build-up against a US

Marine Corps base at the remote village of Khe Sanh, when on 30 January 1968, the first day of the lunar new year holidays, known as Tet, the communists launched a countrywide offensive against towns and cities. Some 84,000 men attacked 125 localities and penetrated deeply into 10 cities. Although the ARVN cleared most of the cities in a matter of days, fighting in Saigon and Hué was protracted. The North Vietnamese simultaneously instituted a siege of the base at Khe Sanh, which was finally defeated by massive application of American firepower, including use of B-52 bombers.

Although American and South Vietnamese intelligence had detected indications of a coming offensive, the countrywide nature of it came as a surprise. Even though the communists lost 32,000 killed against 3,000 American and South Vietnamese dead, the offensive had a stunning effect on the American people, who had been impressed with reports of substantial progress in the war but among whom vocal and demonstrative anti-war sentiment had been growing. Confronted with the death and destruction of the Tet offensive on their television screens, they came to see the war as unwinnable. When General Westmoreland asked for substantial reinforcements to exploit what he saw as an enemy defeat, President Johnson was swayed by public opinion to deny them.

President Johnson opted instead for a partial halt in the bombing of North Vietnam in the hope of bringing the North Vietnamese to the negotiating table. Although the North Vietnamese agreed, and talks opened in Paris in May 1968, there was little to be negotiated. The North Vietnamese were determined to take over South Vietnam; the United States were determined to prevent it. Thus the talks dragged on unproductively for months lengthening into years.

A new US president, Richard M. Nixon, meanwhile decided on a policy of gradual American withdrawal through a programme called 'Vietnamization', of building up the South Vietnamese armed forces to a point where there could be reasonable expectation of their carrying the burden of the fighting alone. By early 1972 almost all American ground combat troops had departed. Meanwhile, to improve the ARVN's chances, President Nixon had authorised an incursion by American and South Vietnamese

Above left: A 175mm M107mm self propelled gun of A Battery, 2nd Battallion, 94th Artillery, fires in support of Marines fighting in the As Hua valley in Vietnam in 1967

Left: South Vietnamese soldiers using a shell hole for cover. Often in the jungle the opposing sides were so close that fire support could not be provided by aircraft or artillery.

Right: A wounded American being carried aboard a rescue helicopter for airlifting out of the battlefield. Helicopters were used in large numbers in Vietnam in a wide variety of roles, especially fire support.

forces against enemy sanctuaries in Cambodia in late spring of 1970 and a raid against the Ho Chi Minh Trail in Laos by the ARVN in early 1971.

In an apparent effort to influence negotiations in Paris, the North Vietnamese on 30 March 1972 launched a conventional invasion across the DMZ and subsidiary thrusts from Laos and Cambodia. Achieving surprise with heavy artillery and tanks, they made some gains near the Cambodian border and seized all the northernmost province of Quang Tri before the ARVN, with American tactical air support, rallied. In retaliation President Nixon ordered renewed bombing of North Vietnam, including the first use of B-52s against the north, and mining of Haiphong harbour.

Despite that punishment, the North Vietnamese still refused to make concessions until late in the year when they finally dropped a demand for President Thieu's ouster as a preliminary to a cease-fire agreement. Under heavy public and Congressional pressure to end the war, President Nixon dropped an American demand for withdrawal of all North Vietnamese troops from South Vietnam. The two sides thus were near agreement on a cease-fire by the end of 1972; but when President Thieu objected to some of the provisos, President Nixon made one more effort to force North Vietnamese concessions by a heavy 12-day bombing of North Vietnam with B-52s. When the North Vietnamese still refused to concede anything further, the two sides on 23 January 1973 initialed a cease-fire agreement to become effective five days later. Heavy fighting erupted in the interim as the North Vietnamese sought to extend their holdings before the cease-fire became effective.

As sporadic fighting continued after the cease-fire, the US Congress, apparently reflecting the mood of the American people, passed a resolution effective from 15 August 1973, forbidding funds for any more American military action, including bombing, in South-East Asia. That removed any deterrent to the North Vietnamese increasing their forces inside South Vietnam and in Laos and Cambodia, so that by early 1975 the South Vietnamese forces, stretched thin with their 13 divisions trying to protect all their elongated country, were at a sharp disadvantage confronting up to 400,000 North Vietnamese troops. The US Congress also sharply cut funds for military assistance to South Vietnam.

In January 1975 a North Vietnamese attack over-ran Phuoc Long province alongside Cambodia. When that provoked no American reaction, they opened a major offensive on 5 March in the Central Highlands and the northern provinces. Under heavy enemy pressure, ARVN forces began a withdrawal from the highlands that quickly turned into a rout.

Although President Thieu tried to form a new defence to save Saigon and the southern provinces, there appeared to be little hope of success in the face of 20 North Vietnamese divisions. In late April Thieu resigned amid a hastily-mounted American effort to evacuate remaining Americans and South Vietnamese officials. On 30 April Thieu's successor surrendered.

The weapons

In the 1950s, the American army was trained and equipped to fight a full scale conventional or nuclear conflict in any part of the world. It was not trained or equipped to fight a guerilla type conflict. American advisers had been in South Vietnam since the early 1950s but their average strength was only about 700 men and their role was to advise the South Vietnamese Army on equipment, training and tactics. The first major Army unit to arrive in Vietnam was the 57th Transportation Company (Light Helicopter) which was equipped with 32 H-21 helicopters. This arrived in December 1961 aboard the carrier USS *Card*. Within 12 days the unit was in action. Over the next few years additional specialised units were sent to Vietnam, but it was not until April 1965, that the first complete fighting unit was alerted for deployment to Vietnam. This was the 173rd Airborne Brigade from Okinawa. It should also be remembered that the US Air Force, Navy, Marines and Coast Guard had large numbers of men in Vietnam. The highest combined strength in South Vietnam was reached in January, 1969, when there were 542,400 men in Vietnam.

When the first troops were committed it soon became apparent that both tactics and equipment would have to be adopted for a guerilla type campaign. Without doubt, the helicopter played a vital role in Vietnam conflict.

Although helicopters had been used in numerous earlier guerilla campaigns in Algeria and Malaya, it was not until Vietnam that they were used in large numbers. Initially they were used for transporting cargo and wounded troops, but they were soon pressed into service for reconnaissance and assault. In the early days the CH-21 Shawnee was used in large numbers for both the cargo and assault roles but as the war progressed it was replaced by the Bell UH-1 Iroquois. This was used as a troop carrier, cargo carrier and as an escort helicopter. At first they were armed with 7.62mm machine guns, but later with a variety of weapons including 2.5 inch rockets, air-to-ground missiles (the French SS-11), .50 machine guns and 40mm chin-mounted grenade launchers.

It was found that when the additional armament was installed the assault helicopters often could not keep up with the troop-carrying helicopters which they were protecting. A special attack helicopter was

A Chinook hovers, waiting to evacuate the wounded during the last days of American involvement in the Vietnam War. When the Americans withdrew there were scenes of wild panic as South Vietnamese deserters fought with civilian refugees for places aboard the aircraft and warships used for evacuation.

in fact already being developed from components of the UH-I, this was the Bell AH-I HueyCobra. This first flew in September 1965 and by mid-1967 was being used in combat in Vietnam. This has a crew of two, and a top speed of 352km/h (218mph) and a maximum range of 580km (360 miles). Most common armament in Vietnam was a chin-mounted 40mm grenade launcher and a 20mm mini-gun. Additional rockets and machine guns could be fitted on stub wings on each side of the fuselage.

Before the assault helicopters could be deployed the land position had to be reconnoitred and this was carried out by the small LOH's (Light Observation Helicopter), such as the OH-6 Cayuse or the OH-58 Kiowa. These were normally armed with a single 7.62mm mini-gun.

The Boeing Chinook, the CH-47, was the heavy troop-lifter. It could carry up to 44 fully equipped troops and had a crew of three. It could also be used to carry up to 8000kg (17,636lb) of cargo, either in the cargo hold or slung under the fuselage. For lifting heavy loads and for rescuing downed fighters and helicopters, the Sikorsky CH-54, or Skycrane, was used. This has a crew of three and can lift up to 9000kg (19,840lb). It could also carry a special ambulance pod or a similar 'people pod' containing up to 87 combat troops. The US Marines used a variety of helicopters in Vietnam including the H-53 Sea Stallion, H-34 Seahorse (the Army equivalent being the Choctaw) and the Bell UH-I.

Initially, helicopters were organised into small units such as Assault Helicopter Companies, Surveillance Airplane Companies, and so on. These formed Combat Aviation Battalions which in turn formed Combat Aviation Groups. These Combat Aviation Groups then formed an Aviation Brigade, which also had the Heavy Helicopter Company and Air Traffic Control Detachments and others.

In 1963, the 11th Air Assault Division was formed for an extensive series of trials in the United States. The trials were a success and in March 1965 it was decided to convert the 11th Air Assault Division from a Test Division to an active division, so on 1 July 1965 the 1st Cavalry Division (Airmobile) was activated. This was soon alerted for Vietnam and the advance party arrived on 25 August 1965. The Division had a complement of 15,787 officers and men and just 1,600 vehicles. It had a total of 428 helicopters (93 Light Observation, 287 Utility/Assault and 48 Cargo), and a flight of 6 Mohawk reconnaissance aircraft. The Division had its own artillery which consisted of three battalions each with 18 105mm M102 howitzers as well as its own engineers and other supporting arms. The 1st Air Cavalry Division (Airmobile) was a success in Vietnam, although further changes were made in its training and equipment as a result of combat experience. On 1 July 1968, the 101st Airborne Division was redesignated the 101st Air Cavalry Division, and this, too, was deployed to Vietnam.

The build-up in helicopter strength of the US Army was remarkable. In 1960 the Army had an active strength of 2,895 fixed wing aircraft and 2,663 helicopters, ten years later, in 1970, it had 2,241 fixed wing aircraft and 9,903 helicopters. The arrival in Vietnam of large numbers of helicopters created severe problems, both maintenance and storage-wise.

The standard US Army rifle in the 1950s was the 7.62mm M14. However, this was found to be too heavy for use in Vietnam and the Army then adopted the much lighter 5.56mm M16, designed by Eugene Stoner. Initially, the gun gave a great deal of trouble but this was found to be mainly due to bad maintenance. The M16 is still the standard rifle of the American Army and over 4 million have been built so far. Since the Americans adopted the 5.56mm round, a number of countries have designed weapons to fire this round, although no NATO country has yet adopted the 5.56mm round. One main advantage of the round is its small

Right: A South Vietnamese infantryman heavily loaded with equipment. Although heli-borne troops were extensively used in Vietnam, it was the infantryman who bore the brunt of the fighting

Below: US Marine Ontos armed with six 106mm recoilless rifles in Vietnam in July 1966. The Ontos was a tank destroyer but was used in Vietman against VC forcifications.

size which allows the infantryman to carry more ammunition than usual, and the weapon itself is that much lighter than many other rifles.

The standard Army machine gun was the 7.62mm M60. The infantry used it on a bipod and it was also mounted on helicopters and armoured vehicles such as the M113 Armoured Personnel Carrier. The 40mm M79 grenade launcher was widely used and this fired a variety of ammunition, including HE and anti-personnel rounds, maximum range being 400m (437yards). The standard mortars used were the 81mm M29, with a maximum range of 3,350m (3,660yards), and the 107mm M30, with a range of 5,420m (5,925yards). These were mounted on standard infantry type mounts or in the rear of M113 APC's.

Both towed and self-propelled weapons were used by the Americans. Towed weapons included the 105mm M101 and M102 and the 155mm M114 Howitzers, all of these could be transported beneath a helicopter like the Chinook. Self-propelled models used included the 105mm M108, 155mm M109, 175mm M107 and the 203mm M110. Artillery was used in a variety of ways, for example in a static firebase or with an air assault. On one occasion, four howitzers, their crews and 280 rounds of ammunition were airlifted behind enemy lines. The guns fired all of the ammunition and were then airlifted out again—in just 17 minutes.

Initially it was thought that AFV's would be of limited use in Vietnam, and would only be used for convoy escort and defensive operations around air bases, fire bases and so on. It soon became apparent that armour could operate in most parts of Vietnam for most of the year. The two most common US AFV's were the M48 tanks armed with a 90mm gun and the M113 APC. The latter

Fire Support Base "6", operated by Detachment 244 of the 5th Special Forces Group, three miles north of Ben Het, Vietnam, was typical of many fire support bases throughout Vietnam.

was used in large numbers, not only as an APC but as a light tank. Many specialised models were developed as a result of combat experience in Vietnam. The M551 Sheridan was deployed to Vietnam at an early stage, in fact as soon as it was built. It was not so successful as the M48 and M113 and many faults soon became apparent.

Cadillac Gage Commando 4 × 4 Armoured Cars were used in large numbers for convoy escort duties and for patrolling airfields and other high-risk areas. The American Marines used their LVTP-5's in amphibious operations, especially in the Northern part of the country. They also used their M50 Ontos tank destroyers armed with six 106mm

Bell AH-1G HueyCobra helicopter

Crew: 2. **Weight:** 9500lb (4309kg). **Length of fuselage:** 44' 5'' (13.59m). **Rotor diameter:** 44' (13.41m). **Max speed:** 219mph (352kmh). **Maximum range:** 357 miles (574km). **Engine:** Lycoming T53-L13B turboshaft developing 1100 SHP.

Bell developed the AH-1 from the standard UH-1 Iroquois and the first prototype flew in September 1965. A production order was placed in April, 1966, and by mid 1967, the AH-1G was in action in Vietnam. The crew of two sat in tandem with the gunner in front and the pilot behind. A chin turret could have a single 20mm (three barrelled) cannon with 750 rounds, or a 7.62mm Minigun (with 4,000 rounds) and 40mm grenade launcher (300 rounds), or a 7.62mm Minigun with 8,000 rounds. On each side of the fuselage are stub wings, each with two hardpoints for a variety of weapons, including 6 or 8 TOW missiles, pods of 7 or 19 2.75 inch rockets, 7.62mm machine guns or 20mm cannon. To enhance its battlefield survival capabilities the HueyCobra has self-sealing fuel tanks, hydraulic boost system, the engine is protected by sheets of boron carbide, the tail pipe is shrouded so that the cooling air mixes with the exhaust to reduce the infra-red signature and the crew seats are also of boron carbide. So far about 1,000 HueyCobras have been built and are in service with the United States Army, United States Marines, Spain and Iran. At the present the Americans have a major programme to update the AH-1G to AH-1S standard.

Bell UH-1B Huey helicopter

Crew: 2 + 7. **Weight:** 8500lb (3856kg). **Length of fuselage:** 42' 7'' (12.98m). **Rotor diameter:** 44' (13.41m). **Maximum speed:** 138mph (222kmh). **Maximum range:** 212 miles (341km). **Engine:** Lycoming T63-L-11 turbine developing 1100 SHP.

When American troops arrived in Vietnam in large numbers the Bell UH-1 Iroquois was increasingly used and soon replaced older helicopter types previously in use. The Iroquois can be traced back to 1955 when Bell won a US Army competition for a utility helicopter known as the Model 204. First to enter service in 1959 was the UH-1A, which could carry a pilot and six passengers. This was followed by the UH-1B which had a larger cabin to take seven men and two crew members, and which saw extensive use in Vietnam, as did the UH-1D (Bell 205). The UH-1D had a more powerful engine and could carry between 12 and 14 troops. The UH-1E was an assault model for the US Marine Corps, whilst the UH-1F was built for the USAF.

Other models have since been built, for specialised roles such as anti-submarine warfare, trainers and air-sea rescue. In Vietnam, helicopters were initially used to transport men and supplies but they were soon taking on air assault role. A selected area would be softened up by air strikes on suspected enemy positions before the helicopters, with assault troops, were sent in. The Huey, as the UH-1B was called, was also used as a gunship armed with various combinations of 7.62mm and 12.7mm machine guns, 20mm cannon, 2.75 inch rockets, 40mm grenade launchers and French SS 11 missiles.

M113 armoured personnel carrier

Crew: 2 + 11. **Weight loaded:** 10.93t. **Length:** 15' 11¾'' (4.87m). **Width:** 8' 10'' (2.69m). **Height:** 8' 4'' (2.54m). **Road speed:** 42.5mph (68.4kmh). **Water speed:** 3.6 mph (5.8kmh). **Range:** 310 miles (500km). **Engine:** GMC Diesel developing 215 HP. **Ground pressure:** .77psi (.54kg/cm²). **Vertical obstacle:** 2' (.61m). **Trench:** 6' 6'' (1.68m). **Gradient:** 60%.

The M113 is the most widely used armoured personnel carrier in the West, if not the world. The prototype was built by the FMC Corporation of San Jose, California, in 1958, with the first production vehicles being completed just two years later. Since then over 60,000 have been built and it is in service with over 30 countries. First production M113s were powered by a petrol engine and were followed by the diesel-powered M113A1. This has a much larger radius of action as well as being safer, diesel fuel being less prone to fire than petrol. The APC has a crew of two—a commander who also acts as the gunner, and the driver—and can carry 11 fully equipped infantry who leave the vehicle by a hydraulically operated ramp in the rear of the hull. It is normally armed with a .50 (12.7mm) machine gun, although there are many local modifications, the most interesting being Australian M113s, some of which have the complete turret of the Saladin armoured car mounted behind the driver's position, and are known as M113 FS (Fire Support). There are over 100 different models of the M113 including the M106 (107mm) mortar carrier, M125 (81mm) mortar carrier, M132 flamethrower, M163 20mm Vulcan Air Defence System, M577 Command Post, the TOW equipped anti-tank vehicle and so on.

SA-7 anti-aircraft missile

Diameter of launcher: 3.9″ (100mm). **Length of launcher:** 4′ 5″ (1'346m). **Weight of launcher:** 23.3lb (10.6kg). **Weight of missile:** 20.25lb (9.2kg). **Maximum range:** 3790 yards (3500m). **Maximum altitude:** 6560′ (2000m). **Minimum altitude:** 164′ (50m).

So far the only known Soviet man-portable missile is the SA-7, or Grail. It was first encountered in the 1973 Middle East war but has not been very effective in combat as its warhead lacks killing power. The SA-7 is operated thus: the operator points the launcher at the target and presses a trigger to switch on the thermal battery. When the missile has picked up the target, an audible warning is given and a light comes on. The operator then presses the trigger again when the target is within range and the missile is launched. The SA-7 has three motors, the first ejecting the missile from the launcher, the second acting as a booster and the third being a sustainer. The missile has two cancard wings at the front, four spring loaded tail fins and the high explosive warhead has a graze fuse. Unlike the British Blowpipe the SA-7 has no IFF (Identification Friend or Foe) system, so unless the operator has a very high standard of recognition there is a risk that he will shoot down one of his own aircraft.

TOW anti-tank missile

Crew: 2. **Missile length:** 3′ 10″ (1.17m). **Missile diameter:** 6″ (.152m). **Missile weight at launch:** 39½lb (18kg). **Weight (launcher and missile):** 222½lb (102kg). **Minimum range:** 71 yards (65m). **Maximum range:** 4100 yards (3750m).

The TOW—Tube-launched, Optically-tracked, Wire-guided—anti-tank missile was developed in the early 1960s by Hughes Aircraft of California. Its official designation is MGM-71A and so far over 150,000 have been built for service with over 15 countries. TOW has been used in combat by both Israel and the United States (in Vietnam) and has achieved a very high kill rate.

The missile is available in three basic modes—mounted on a vehicle such as the M113 APC or the M151 Jeep, carried by a helicopter such as the Huey-Cobra which can mount eight or used by infantry.

The latter consists of a tripod mounting, traversing unit, launch tube, optical sight and the electronic guidance computer. All the operator has to do is to keep the cross-hairs of the sight on the target; sensors translate the movements of the target into electrical pulses which are fed into the computer, which automatically determines range and azimuth for firing. The missile itself has two motors; the first ejects the missile a short distance from the tube and then the in-flight motor is ignited. TOW is connected to the launcher by two fine wires and once launched, the computer continues to monitor inputs from the sensors regarding sight changes and feeds course directions to the missile.

TOW has a high explosive shaped charge warhead which will knock out any tank and most battlefield fortifications. Currently under development is a night sight to increase the combat effectiveness of the weapon.

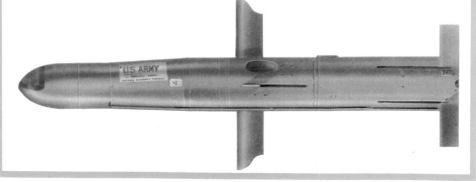

recoilless rifles to knock out VC bunkers. The Americans did not encounter North Vietnamese tanks in large numbers, although a number of bases with American advisers were attacked by Soviet-built PT-76 and T-54 tanks. Later in the War, the North Vietnamese used large numbers of AFV's when they attacked across the DMZ. These were dealt with by air strikes, M48 tanks and by US TOW helicopters.

Mines and booby traps were a constant source of trouble in Vietnam and according to some estimates they caused 70 per cent of all vehicle losses and 20 per cent of all personnel casualties. The VC used Russian and home-made mines as well as American bombs and ammunition that had not exploded. The Americans put a lot of work into developing mine clearance systems and techniques, but the answer to this problem in land warfare has yet to be found.

The Americans made extensive use of sensors in Vietnam. These were deployed either ground-mounted or mounted in aircraft. Sensors were also dropped behind enemy lines and these fed accurate information to a central command where artillery or air strikes were co-ordinated and before the suspected target was attacked. Since Vietnam, the United States Army has embarked on an ambitious new programme of sensor development under the name of REMBASS—or Remotely Monitored Battlefield Sensor System. Night vision systems were also developed for helicopters, fighting vehicles and infantry weapons, enabling the enemy to be located and attacked at night. Many new developments have been undertaken as a result of combat experience in Vietnam. Ground surveillance radars were also used in large numbers. Viet-Cong mortars were a continuous source of casualties in Vietnam, and there were insufficient mortar location radars to go around all of the bases.

Logistics played a major, and often-forgotten, role in Vietnam. The US and S. Vietnam forces consumed large quantities of food, ammunition, fuel, spare parts and other stores. These had to be transported from the United States to Vietnam and then inland to the individual bases. The vast majority of stores were sent to Vietnam by sea; very urgent equipment went by air. When the Americans first arrived in Vietnam there were hardly any port facilities at all, so the US Corps of Engineers were brought in to build the ports, roads, bridges and airfields required. Once ashore, they were transported inland by truck or plane; the latter were used to supply cut-off fire-bases and camps along the border. Transport aircraft used for this role included US Air Force C-130 and C-123s as well as Army CV-7s. The US Army 4 × 4 GOER high mobility truck was also tested in Vietnam with such success that it is now in widespread use by the Army for a variety of logistical roles.

Front line Vietnamese troops had similar equipment to the Americans. Towards the end of the war however, they were always

RPG-7 anti-tank grenade launcher

Calibre of launcher: 1½″ (40mm). **Calibre of round:** 3.3″ (85mm). **Length of launcher:** 3′ 3″ (.99m). **Weight of launcher:** 15.4lb (7kg). **Weight of grenade:** 4.95lb (2.25kg). **Range (stationary target):** 545 yards (500m). **Range (moving target):** 330 yards (300m).

Since the day the tank first appeared on the battlefield the infantry has had a requirement for a light weapon which could stop it. In World War I, the Germans used both a special bullet for their standard 7.92mm rifles and a heavy anti-tank rifle. During World War II, a variety of weapons such as the German Panzerfaust and the British PIAT were developed. The Soviet RPG-7V is the current Russian light anti-tank weapon and has now replaced the earlier RPG-2.

The RPG-7V basically consists of an open-ended tube provided with two grips, the forward one having the trigger mechanism. When the weapon is fired, the grenade leaves the barrel at a speed of about 328ft/sec (100m/sec). Four fins then unfold to stabilise it and a rocket motor cuts in, to increase its speed to about 900ft/sec (295m/sec). The grenade has a HEAT warhead which will penetrate 320mm of armour and its effective range is 300-500m and after 922 yards (920m) the rocket self-destructs if it does not hit the target. For daylight operations, an optical sight is fitted and an NSP-2 infra-red sight can be used for night operations. Its main drawbacks are that it is unstable in high winds and it is noisy.

7.62mm AK and AKM rifles

Weight: AK (loaded magazine) 10.58lb (4.8kg), (empty magazine) 9.47lb (4.3kg); AKM (loaded magazine) 8.0lb (3.64kg) (early version 8.4lb, 3.8kg), (empty magazine) 6.93lb (3.14kg) (early version 7.3lb, 3.31kg). **Length overall (no bayonet):** AK-47 (either butt), 34.25in (870mm); AKM, 34.5in (876mm). **Ammunition:** Standard M43 (M-1943). **Muzzle velocity:** 2,345ft/sec (715m/sec). **Effective range:** (semi-auto) 400m; (auto) 300m. **Rate of fire:** Cyclic, 600rds/min; auto, .90rds/min; semi-auto. 40rds/min.

Produced in greater quantity than any other modern small arms, the Kalashnikov AK and AKM can fairly be claimed to have set a new standard in infantry weapons. The original AK-47, with which Viet-long infantry were supplied, came with a wooden stock or (for AFV crews, paratroopers and motorcyclists) a folding metal stock. It owed much to German assault rifles, and like them uses a short cartridge firing a stubby bullet. A gas-operated weapon with rotating bolt (often chrome-plated), it can readily be used by troops all over the world of any standard of education, and gives extremely reliable results under the most adverse conditions. Versions with different designations have been licence-produced in at least five countries, and it is used in about 35. The standard Soviet military weapon today is the AKM, an amazingly light development making extensive use of plastics and stampings, and with a cyclic-rate reducer, compensator and other improvements. Either rifle can have luminous sights or the NSP-2 IR sight. Another fitment is a new bayonet which doubles as a saw and as an insulated wire-cutter. The AKM was used extensively by the Viet-Cong during the latter stages of the war in Vietnam.

M16 rifle

Calibre: 5.56mm. **Weight with magazine and sling:** 8.2lb (3.73kg). **Length:** 3′ 3″ (.99m). **Magazine capacity:** 20 or 30 rounds. **Muzzle velocity:** 3280fps (1000m/s). **Rate of fire:** 700/900rpm (cyclic). 150/200rpm (automatic). 45/65rpm (single shots). **Range:** 433 yards (400m).

The M16 (or AR-15 as it was originally known) was designed by Eugene Stoner and is a further development of the earlier 7.62mm AR-10. The weapon was first ordered by the United States Air Force and was then adopted by the United States Army for use in Vietnam. It has now almost replaced the 7.62mm M14 Rifle in the US Army and has been adopted by many countries around the world. Over 4 million M16s have been built and it is still being manufactured by Colt Industries of Hartford. The M16 was the first of the current range of lightweight rifles and fires a light 5.56mm round rather than the 7.62mm NATO round.

short of spare parts, fuel and ammunition. Their scale of equipment, in some cases, was far below the equivalent issue to an American battalion, especially in surveillance equipment. Second line units were equipped with a variety of weapons including M1 rifles and carbines, BAR's and .30 and .50 Browning machine guns.

Air Support was vital in Vietnam and a wide variety of US Air Force, Navy and Marine Corps aircraft were used. One aircraft specially developed for use in Vietnam was the Dakota DC3 Gunship. This was armed with three 7.62mm General Electric Miniguns, each capable of firing 6,000 rounds per minute. These proved highly effective against Viet-Cong positions. Later, C-119 and C-130 gunships were developed, the latter having special night vision equipment for use over Laos and Cambodia at night.

In the early days of the war, the Viet-Cong used a variety of French, American, British and Russian weapons which they obtained from a variety of countries. They also had many weapons of local manufacture. As the war progressed they received more modern weapons from both China and Russia, as well as captured weapons.

The standard Viet-Cong assault weapon was the AK-47 which had a 30 round magazine; later in the war the AKM was also used. A variety of machine guns were used, including the 7.62mm RP-46, the RPD and the RPK. They also had the Russian 12.7mm DShK machine gun for anti-aircraft use, and large numbers of Soviet 37mm guns. The VC took machine guns from shot-down US helicopters and used them in the anti-aircraft role.

The Viet-Cong had a variety of 50mm, 82mm and 120mm mortars and artillery rockets on single launchers and towards the end of the war they used artillery on a large scale, especially the 130mm M1946. With its range of 31,000m (33,883yards) it outranged everything the S. Vietnamese had. They also used SA-2 and SA-7 anti-aircraft missiles, the latter causing heavy initial losses to helicopters until the S. Vietnamese started 'nap of the earth flying'.

The VC used every type of anti-tank weapon in the Russian inventory, including the Sagger ATGW. The VC and North Vietnamese also used armoured vehicles in South Vietnam in large numbers during the closing months of the war, including T-54 and T-34/85 tanks, PT-76 light amphibious tanks and the BTR-50 and BTR-60 armoured personnel carriers.

Conflicts in the Middle East

Against a background of inter-Moslem struggles, the four wars fought between the Israelis and the Arabs for Palestine have proved some of the greatest threats to world peace since World War II.

The area known as the Middle East has been called the fertile triangle by historians, and from here developed the civilization of Europe. Since World War II, the area has been a more dangerous birthplace, for its continuous conflicts appear to some military writers to be trial runs for a future global battle. Without doubt the Arab–Israeli wars, coupled with the area's richness in oil resources, have produced a worldwide impact. In 1976 the former seems to have stabilised with the assistance of United States diplomacy, and the latter offers hope for the future by the massive wealth it brings to the Arab countries. Yet as the years since the end of World War II have shown, a storm may blow up at any time and the great military strength deployed by the countries who may find themselves in conflict gives little comfort.

The end of World War II saw the Arab countries determined to prevent the emergence of a Jewish state in Palestine while the two major powers, the United States and

Soviet Russia, found different reasons to support the Jews. Britain, the mandatory power, was basically pro-Arab but there were strong pro-Jewish elements in the Labour government, whose efforts were aided by a pan-European guilt feeling stemming from the Nazi genocide efforts. When it was announced that the prewar policy of limited immigration, limited to 1,500 Jews per month, was to be enforced, the secret Jewish armies (*Haganah, Irgun Zvai Leumi* and *Lehi* or 'Stern Gang') in Palestine embarked on a policy of cirumventing and harassing the British. The latter two groups in particular also commenced a policy of terrorism and murder that has since become only too common throughout the world.

With world opinion against it as a result of Jewish propaganda, Britain decided to place the problem in the hands of the United Nations. Here a committee studying the problem recommended the partition of the country between the Arabs and Jews. The Palestinians and their Arab supporters refused to accept this decision and during the months up to the final British withdrawal the former, assisted by the latter, continually attacked the Jewish settlers, while preparing for assault by regular forces once the British protecting power had gone.

Palestine's neighbours (Egypt, Trans-Jordan or Jordan, Syria, Iraq and Lebanon) were confident that they could crush the 600,000 Jews within a few days. There was no great faith among the Jews that they could defeat the expected Arab onslaught, but in the months of 1947 and 1948 they built up trained companies which they knew to be qualitatively better soldiers than their enemies. It was the necessary equipment which the future Israelis lacked. Although the Arab armies had only the cast-off clothing of the belligerents in the late conflict, this was far more sophisticated than anything the Jews had been able to obtain;

Sherman tanks of the Israeli Army moving up to the front in the 1973 Middle East Campaign. Although obsolete by today's standards, the Sherman continues to give good service with many armies around the world.

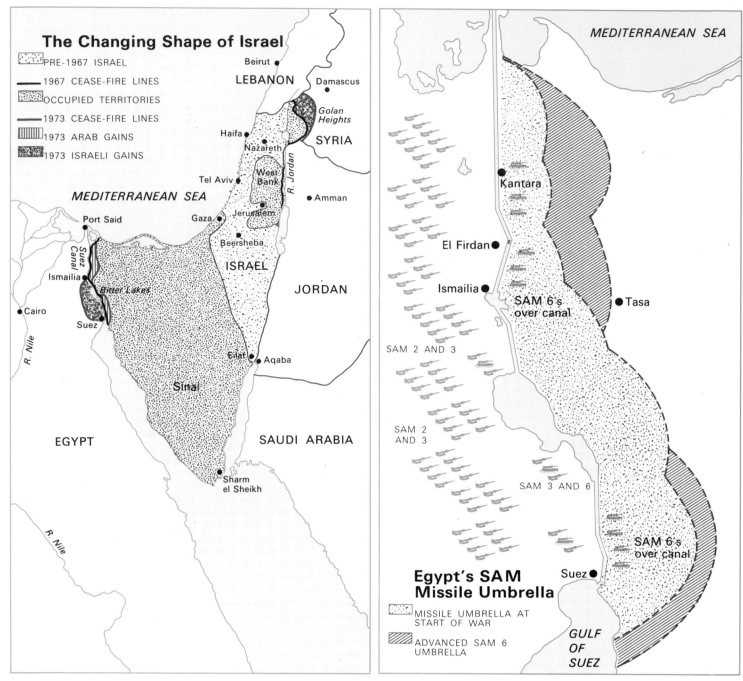

The Changing Shape of Israel

- PRE-1967 ISRAEL
- 1967 CEASE-FIRE LINES
- OCCUPIED TERRITORIES
- 1973 CEASE-FIRE LINES
- 1973 ARAB GAINS
- 1973 ISRAELI GAINS

Beirut
LEBANON
Damascus
Golan Heights
Haifa
SYRIA
Nazareth
West Bank
R. Jordan
MEDITERRANEAN SEA
Tel Aviv
Amman
Port Said
Jerusalem
Gaza
Beersheba
ISRAEL
Suez Canal
JORDAN
Ismailia
Bitter Lakes
Cairo
R. Nile
Suez
Eilat
Aqaba
Sinai
SAUDI ARABIA
EGYPT
Sharm el Sheikh
R. Nile

MEDITERRANEAN SEA
Kantara
El Firdan
Ismailia
SAM 6's over canal
Tasa
SAM 2 AND 3
SAM 2 AND 3
SAM 3 AND 6
SAM 6's over canal
Suez

Egypt's SAM Missile Umbrella

- MISSILE UMBRELLA AT START OF WAR
- ADVANCED SAM 6 UMBRELLA

GULF OF SUEZ

for although the latters' agents were active in secret purchases, it was found impossible to get major items through the British blockade.

Accepting that their only future lay in armed force, the Israelis produced 'Plan D', which was to defend the borders allocated to the new state by the UN and the Jewish population that lived outside them. In April 1948 the first major Jewish operation took place as the *Haganah* seized Arab villages and evicted their inhabitants to ensure communications between the coastal settlements and Jerusalem. Fighting now escalated and battles broke out in various towns: the Jews captured Tiberias and the important port of Haifa, while in Jerusalem the Arab Legion (of the Trans-Jordan or Jordanian Army) took the Jewish quarter.

When on 15 May 1948 the Israeli state officially came into being, the Jews had so far had the best of the fighting. But at once they were faced with invasion by the regular forces of Egypt, Trans-Jordan, Syria, Iraq, Lebanon and the independent Arab Liberation Army. So on its formation the *Zahal* or Israel Defence Force (IDF) found its

enemies had made deep incursions into its country.

The war that followed was basically that of the infantryman supported by some artillery and a few armoured cars. Although initially the Arabs had air superiority, Jewish volunteers flying German aircraft obtained from Czechoslovakia, the country that did most to help the new state, soon achieved mastery over their less sophisticated enemies.

When on 11 June a UN truce was arranged, it turned out to be a turning point for the Israelis, although it was equally welcomed by the Arab states, who had found the fighting far harder than they had expected. The Jews, however, ignored the ban on arms supply and were thus able to bring in many of the weapons they had been lacking, including tanks and artillery but perhaps most importantly of all large quantities of rifles and machine-guns with their ammunition. The IDF was reorganised and the IZL and Stern gang disbanded, although force had to be used. The *Palmach*, an elitist formation of the *Haganah*, was incorporated complete and its leaders were

Above right: An M60 Tank of the Israeli Army moving up on the Sinai front. The M60, armed with the British-designed 105mm gun, proved capable of taking on the Egyptian and Syrian T-54/T-55 and T-62 tanks supplied by Russia.

Right: Israeli troops taking up positions during the 1973 Middle East Campaign. After their initial setbacks the Israelis were eventually successful on both the Syrian and Suez fronts.

to play a vital part in the later fighting.

When fighting broke out again on 9 July the Israelis quickly seized the initiative with a series of offensives. The main battle to open the road to Jerusalem was only partially successful as the Arab Legion held on to the fortress of Latrun, but the Arab towns of Lod and Ramla were captured. Now on all fronts the Arabs were on the defensive and failed to co-ordinate any attacks to help the Arab Legion. A fresh truce came into force on 19 July.

The Egyptians gave the Israelis the excuse to break the truce when they fired on an official UN convoy in October, and at once a

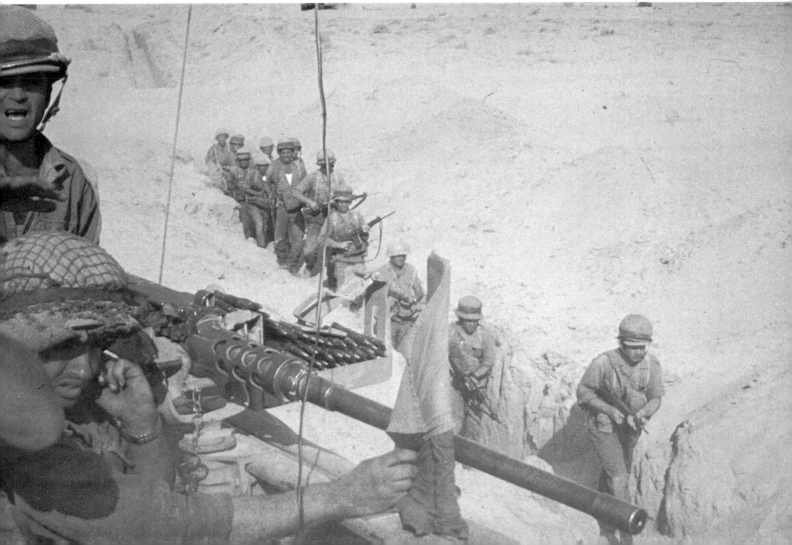

fresh series of operations commenced which drove the Egyptians back to the Gaza area except for a brigade which held out at Faluja. In the north the Arab Liberation Army was defeated and the Lebanese driven from the country. In January 1949 the Israelis drove the Egyptians from the Negev, apart from Gaza, and would have destroyed them except for a British ultimatum which stopped the invasion of the Sinai. The Arabs were now exhausted and armistice agreements were signed under UN auspices.

The armistices did not bring peace between the Jews and Arabs, the latter soon commencing raids on Israel; these in their turn provoked reprisals, which helped considerably in the foundation of a more efficient IDF. The raids were not masterminded by any central Arab organisation, but the initial failure of the reprisals resulted in the formation, under Ariel Sharon, of Unit 101 which was officially not part of the IDF. Later Unit 101 and a paratroop battalion were combined into Parachute Battalion 202.

Following the overthrow of the monarchy in Egypt in July 1952, the new military regime tried to extend its influence in the Arab world by supporting the attacks on Israel. Regular Egyptian forces also occupied positions in the demilitarised zone in Sinai and the scale of the fighting steadily escalated. Following the Egyptian seizure of the Suez Canal in July 1956, Britain and France came to an agreement with Israel to topple the Nasser regime by a joint attack. Israel had been considering for some time the need for such an attack following the Egyptian–Czech arms agreement of 1955. The basic plan was for the Anglo-French forces to intervene to 'separate' the combatants following a major Israeli offensive.

In October 1956 Egypt had some six brigades plus various other detachments in the Sinai, and the Israelis intended to cut them off from their base by dropping a paratroop force near the Mitla Pass on 29 October 1956. The paratroops were to be reinforced by the rest of Sharon's men, now a brigade strong, driving 125 miles from Kuntilla to Mitla, a task they were to achieve in 28 hours.

The main effort for the IDF was the attack on the Rafah-Kantara road, starting with a break-in at the Gaza Strip and an attack on the Egyptian defences in the area of the Umm Katef-Abu Agheila crossroads. At this time the Israeli chief-of-staff, Moshe Dayan, was relying mainly on his mechanised infantry to do the fighting, with his armoured brigades (the 7th and 27th equipped with Shermans and AMX-13 tanks) relegated to a supporting role. As it turned out, however, the tank force commanders took their own path and it was their units which decided the course of the battle. In the north, complying with the main plan the 27th Armoured Brigade broke through to the road and swinging west drove through to the Suez Canal area, leaving a brigade in its rear to mop up the enemy forces remaining in the Gaza Strip. All this was achieved with very few casualties.

The 7th Armoured Brigade was to advance on the area of the canal following the capture of the Umm Katef–Abu Agheila crossroads by the infantry. But the local commander allowed the tanks to attack 24 hours before planned, and it was the armour that succeeded in taking the Egyptian fortified positions while the infantry failed in their tasks. The 7th Armoured Brigade then drove west to link up with the paratroops. This 'enthusiasm' of subordinate commanders was not everywhere successful, as instance the paratroops' losses in an equally unauthorized battalion patrol through the Mitla Pass. But these breaches of discipline were not punished as the Israeli commanders' ability to press on and exploit success was part of the philosophy that Dayan desired to instil in the IDF. Before the cease-fire Israeli troops also occupied for the first time Sharm el Sheikh at the tip of the Sinai peninsula. For the loss of some 170 killed the Israelis had defeated two Egyptian divisions and had built-up a confidence in their army (particularly in their armoured forces) which was to dominate IDF tactics until the 1973 war.

Following pressure from the United Nations and the arrival of a United Nations 'peace-keeping' force, Israeli troops withdrew from the Sinai and the Gaza Strip. The latter was reoccupied by Egyptian forces within 48 hours, although Egypt had given an undertaking not to do so.

The Anglo-French invasion had not been a success, the two countries being stopped short in their tracks by world condemnation. Even their ability to deal with a much smaller power was brought into question by the difficulties experienced during the landings.

The next 10 years of uneasy peace were to see a tremendous arms build-up by both the Arabs and Israelis. Egypt and Syria obtained great quantities of Soviet equipment, while the Israelis built up a armoured force with British and American tanks.

The Israelis knew that the Egyptians were basing their training on the tactics of their Russian instructors, which suited their greater numbers, while they themselves had embraced the teachings of Liddell Hart advocating the 'indirect approach', spearheaded by the armoured fist of their battle-proved armoured formations.

1967 did not at first seem a year likely to see a fresh outbreak of fighting, but as incident built on incident the tension rose. In Israel and the Arab countries political uncertainty added to the pressure. When President Nasser ordered the UN to withdraw its buffer force, Israel felt that its only hope against the Arabs' larger numbers lay in striking first. The main enemy was seen as Egypt; Jordan was thought likely to remain neutral; and Syria was imagined to be a lesser danger. It was the Egyptian army of more than a quarter of a million that by its sheer numbers threatened the destruction of Israel.

The equipment of the two sides was still a mixture of World War II and postwar manufacture. The Egyptians had about 1,200 tanks (about 450 Russian T-34s with an 85-mm gun, 500 Russian T-54/55s with

A dying Israeli tank commander is lifted from his Centurion tank after it had been ambushed by a Syrian anti-tank team on the Golan Heights in the 1973 campaign.

a 100-mm gun and the remainder Josef Stalins with a 122-mm gun, American Shermans and a few British Centurions). The Syrians had about 500 tanks (T-34s, T-54/55s and Josef Stalins). Jordan had been equipped with M-48 Pattons and Centurions, and had some 100 of both types.

Israel was in the process of modernising her armoured force and had some 800 tanks, comprised of 250 Centurions, 200 Pattons, 150 AMX-13s with a 75-mm gun and 200 Super-Shermans with a French low-velocity 105-mm gun (some Shermans had not been refitted with the new gun and still had the original 75-mm weapon). The Pattons still had the American 90-mm gun, while the Centurions had the British high-velocity L7 105-mm gun. It was this last gun which was to leave its mark on the fighting that was about to take place, for it enabled the better-trained Israeli gunners to knock out their opponents at long ranges.

Like their Soviet mentors, the Egyptians had a great quantity of towed artillery, but no self-propelled weapons, while in keeping with their armoured philosophy the Israelis had 155-mm and 105-mm sp guns, as well as Sherman chassis fitted with large calibre mortars. Both sides had about the same number of jet aircraft, but it was the

destruction of the Egyptian air force on the first morning of the war that ensured the destruction of the Egyptian army in Sinai.

This army was drawn up in what has been called the sword and shield formation, with a strongly fortified line supported first by its own armour and artillery and then by a second armoured counterattack force. The Palestinian 20th and Egyptian 7th Infantry Divisions held such a position in the Gaza Strip. In the Abu Agheila area further south the 2nd Infantry Division was dug in with the 3rd Infantry Division behind it on the road to Ismailia. Further south, covering the Pilgrim's Way, which runs from Kuntilla near the Israeli border to Suez, was the 6th Infantry Division. To the west of the 3rd Division was the 4th Armoured Division with the latest Soviet tanks. The infantry division's tank battalion had T-34s. Between the 3rd and 6th Divisions was Shazli Force, made up of four tank battalions, a motorised infantry brigade, a commando battalion and four artillery regiments.

For their offensive the Israeli forces were organised into three *Ugdahs* or divisions. In the north for the attack on the Gaza Strip was an *ugdah* under Brigadier-General Israel Tal, the originator of Israel's

armoured philosophy, consisting of two armoured brigades and a force of paratroops supported by a tank battalion. The central *ugdah* of two armoured brigades was to drive through a gap between the Egyptian 3rd Division and the coast and seize the Mitla and Giddi Passes. The southern *ugdah*, commanded by General Sharon of Unit 101, had one infantry brigade and one armoured brigade plus two paratroop battalions, and was to attack the Egyptian 2nd Division in the area of the Umm Katef crossroads.

Tal's division attacked towards El Arish on the morning of 5 June 1967, the 7th Armoured Brigade with its Centurions and Pattons forcing its way into the Egyptian defence position, seizing the town of Khan Yunis then pressing on to Rafah, where it was engaged in heavy fighting with forces of the Egyptian 7th Division.

It has been part of the IDF's training that commanders should pull their men after them, and that tank commanders fight from the open turret of their vehicles. As a result the Israelis have always suffered high losses among their trained leaders, which in such a small country is something hard to afford.

Following the breakthrough at Rafah, the 7th Armoured Brigade advanced on El Arish with such speed that the plan for a paratroop drop and sea-landing was cancelled. So by the evening Tal had advanced some 40 miles. Meanwhile the central *ugdah*, commanded by Brigadier-General Avraham Yoffe, had moved across country the Egyptians considered impassable to Bir Lafhan to ambush forces advancing to counterattack Tal. In the morning the two *ugdahs* linked up at Bir Lafhan and the Egyptian forces in the Gaza Strip were trapped. The night battle fought by Yoffe seems to have been the only attempt made by the Egyptian 4th Armoured Division to intervene, for by morning Israeli aircraft made Egyptian movement nearly impossible.

Sharon's *ugdah* had moved across the border into Sinai in the morning, but the attack on the Egyptian position did not go in until after dark, although the armour had probed the defences and a battalion of Centurions had managed to block any withdrawal. The Egyptians were in a typical Soviet defensive situation: three lines of trenches behind a minefield, with artillery behind the infantry and then tanks as a mobile counterattack force. But the position's weakness lay in the fact that its flanks were 'secured' by 'impassable' ground. And it was from these flanks that the paratroops launched their attack against the Egyptian artillery and the infantry entered the trench system following a fierce barrage from the Israeli guns. The Egyptian artillery was soon silenced by the paratroopers and the infantry cleared a passage through the forward minefields for the Shermans to move through and engage the Egyptian tanks. As soon as the crossroads were clear, the second brigade of Yoffe's *ugdah* moved north-west to Bir Lahfan.

During 6 June Tal and Yoffe surrounded

AMX-13 light tank

Crew: 3. **Weight:** 33,089lbs (15,000kg). **Length, overall:** 20' 10½'' (6.36m). **Length, hull:** 16' (4.88m). **Width:** 8' 2½'' (2.5m). **Height:** 7' 6½'' (2.3m). **Road speed:** 37mph (60kmh). **Range:** 217/248 miles (350/400km). **Engine:** Sofam 8GXb 8 cylinder petrol developing 270 HP at 3200rpm. **Ground pressure:** 10.81psi (.76kg/cm²). **Vertical obstacle:** 2' 1½'' (.65m). **Trench:** 5' 3'' (1.6m). **Gradient:** 60%. **Armour:** 10mm to 40mm.

The AMX-13 was designed shortly after World War II by the Atelier des Constructions d'Issy-les-Moulineaux, to meet a French Army requirement for a light tank suitable for both reconnaissance and the tank destroyer role. It entered service with the French Army in 1952 and is now used by more than 30 countries. The basic AMX-13 chassis has been used for a whole family of vehicles which include armoured

personnel carriers, 105mm and 155mm self-propelled guns, mortar carriers, ambulances and cargo carriers. It has a crew of three men, comprising a commander, gunner and driver. No loader is required as the gun is fed from two six-round revolver type magazines, the empty cartridge cases being ejected through a hatch in the turret rear. Once these twelve rounds have been used however, the tank has to withdraw from the battle so that the crew can reload the magazines. The turret is of the oscillating type and has two halves, top and bottom, the gun being fixed in the top half which pivots on the bottom half.

When first built, the AMX-13 was armed with a 75mm gun but current models are armed with a 90mm gun which fires fin stabilised ammunition. The Dutch have examples with a 105mm gun whilst the French have many AMX-13s with two SS-11 anti-tank guided missiles mounted on each side of the gun barrel. A 7.5mm or 7.62mm machine gun is mounted co-axially with the main armament and there are two smoke dischargers on either side of the turret.

Right: An Israeli M113 APC moving up to the front in the 1973 Yom Kippur War. The M113 is the most widely used armoured personnel carrier in the western world.

and attacked the Egyptian airfield at Jebel Libni, but it was not until after a setpiece attack the next morning that the defenders finally gave in. The Israelis now set out to seize the three remaining routes to Suez: the Bir Gafgafa–Ismailia road, and the Giddi and Mitla Passes. The Israelis decided to achieve this by fighting their way up the road through the retreating Egyptians, but mechanical failure and lack of petrol proved more troublesome to Yoffe than the enemy. The battalion sent to the Mitla Pass arrived with only nine tanks, but these proved sufficient in conjunction with Israeli air attacks. Tal's tanks, ordered to block the northern route to Ismailia, had a harder battle as they had to fight the T-55s of the Egyptian 4th Armoured Division. However, by the evening of the 8th the pass was in Israeli hands and Tal's Patton drove through to reach the Suez Canal by the early hours of 9 June. Yoffe's tanks, forcing

the Mitla and Giddi Passes, were only a few hours later in reaching the canal.

While the other two *ugdahs* were pressing on to the canal, Sharon was clearing up what remained in the interior by setting up an ambush at Nakhl for the remnants of the Egyptian 6th Division. Sharm el Sheikh was easily captured by a paratroop force, and thus the whole of the Sinai had fallen into Israeli hands. The casualties suffered by the Israelis were given as 275 killed and 800 wounded. The Egyptians later stated that they had lost 1,500 officers and 10,000 men killed.

Jordanian forces commenced shelling Israeli positions in New Jerusalem during the morning of 5th June and occupied fresh positions in the truce zone. Israeli forces began to attack positions in the city. While they were doing this tanks were reported approaching from Jericho. Realising that if the Jordanians managed to occupy the

Ramallah Ridge his position would be seriously jeopardised Brigadier-General Uzi Narkiss, who commanded the Israeli forces in Jerusalem, sent the reserve armoured brigade which had assembled at Ramle to occupy the ridge. During the next day the brigade pushed on steadily, but had to fight hard for the ground it was gaining. South of Jerusalem, on the road to Bethlehem, the Jordanian village of Sur Behir was captured after 24 hours' heavy fighting. Meanwhile another Israeli *ugdah*, under Brigadier-General Elad Peled, which had been reserved to deal with any Syrian onslaught, was ordered to attack down the valley of the Jordan river from the north.

Before Peled's forces could reach the valley they were engaged in heavy fighting for two days in and around Jenin, and without total Israeli command of the air might have faced defeat by Jordan's 40th Armoured Brigade. While this battle had

Above left: Centurion tanks of the Israeli Army advancing in close formation towards the Golan Heights during the 1973 campaign.

Above: An Israeli Jeep armed with an American 106mm M40 recoilless rifle. Although recoilless rifles can knock out a tank at a range of 1000m, they create a large backblast when fired.

Left: Soviet-built SAM-6 missiles on display in Egypt. These, together with the ZSU-23-4 SP AA guns, shot down large numbers of Israeli aircraft in the early days of the 1973 war.

been going in Samaria, paratroops had been slowly making progress in Jerusalem, and by the evening of 6 June the city was surrounded. It was, however, the capture of Ramallah and Jericho that ended the Jordanian occupation of the area on the west bank of the Jordan river. At about 1000 hours on 7 June the Jews reached the Wailing Wall, the holiest of their holy places, which had last been in their hands 1,900 years before.

The Israelis hesitated to attack Syria, especially as that country had confined itself to shelling and small incursions by patrol groups easily repulsed by local militia. But the Syrian positions on the Golan Heights dominated Israeli settlements, and although the defences were formidable the Israeli attack started on 9 June, despite the fact that Syria had already accepted the UN cease-fire.

The Syrians had some 40,000 troops and 250 tanks manning the fortified line, and these now underwent the heaviest air attack of the war. Then the Israelis, attacking in four areas, slowly broke through the defence positions. The Syrians resisted well until the afternoon of the 10th, when they suddenly cracked and began to withdraw, leaving the Israelis in control of the Golan Heights and Kuneitra.

In six days the IDF had achieved all its aims and Israel now had secure frontiers, but not peace. In fact the failures of the war were to do more for improving the efficiency of the Arab armies than any peacetime training efforts.

Soviet Russia hastened to replace lost Egyptian and Syrian equipment with even more modern weapons, and during 1968 hundreds of guns were massed by Egypt along the Suez Canal. The first barrage of the 'War of Attrition' was fired on 8 September 1968 and the Israelis retaliated by sending a raiding force deep into Egypt. The canal front then remained quiet until March 1969, when the Egyptians restarted shelling. Not having the means to reply in kind, the Israelis resorted to their air force. Egypt attempted to reply in kind but suffered heavy losses. By early 1970 the IDF air force seemed able to range where it liked over Egypt, and Russia was forced to come to Egypt's aid. Early SAM-2 'Guideline' missiles were replaced by a later version and segmented by SAM-3 'Goa' batteries. These, together with hundreds of conventional anti-aircraft guns, increased Israeli losses and in August 1970 a cease-fire was agreed. This enabled the Egyptian missile batteries to be moved up to the canal bank.

During the months that followed, safe behind its new defences Egypt built up its army with Russian help. This help continued even after President Sadat, who had succeeded Nasser on the latter's death, had ordered many of the Russians to leave the country in July 1972. By 1973 Egypt was ready, and this time determined to strike first. The Egyptian high command saw as Israel's main advantage its air force and tank tactics, but thought that this could be offset by the new missiles. Egypt's manpower would enable the army to assault across the Suez Canal on a broad front.

Israeli's failure to be ready in October 1973 when warned of the joint attack about to be launched from south and north by Egypt and Syria had its roots in many causes, but its effects are all that can be considered. On the afternoon of 6 October 1973, under the cover of a massive artillery barrage and air strikes, the Egyptian forces struck across the canal, breaching the massive sand ramparts of the Bar Lev Line with high-powered water hoses. The Israeli strongpoints in the line were taken by surprise and when the armour moved up to their assistance, most of the tanks were put out of action by infantry armed with 'Sagger' missiles or RPG-7 anti-tank projectors. Meanwhile bridges were being placed across the canal by Soviet PNP mobile bridging equipment. By evening the Egyptians had 10 bridges across the canal and during the night five divisions with 500 tanks crossed over. On the morning of the 7th there were only about 100 Israeli tanks between the Egyptians and the main passes into the Sinai. But the Egyptians were worried about moving outside their SAM-2, SAM-3 and new SAM-6 'Gainful' missile cover on the west bank. There were also

many ZSU-23-4s SP anti-aircraft guns and SAM-7 'Grails', although it was the former type that was found to be the more effective weapon and caused the majority of Israeli losses.

Much has been made of the failure of Israeli tanks in the first few days. It was over-confidence and their use without supporting arms that was the reason, however, not the new magic of the anti-tank guided weapon. ATGWs will not stop a balanced force of tanks, guns and infantry. Following a second lesson in the attack on the Egyptian 2nd Army positions, which ended with unsupported tanks surrounded by hundreds of Egyptian infantry, the Israelis changed their tactics. Later the same day an Egyptian attack towards the Ismailia road was shot to pieces with even heavier losses by Israel tanks.

At this time the Israelis on the Sinai front were being forced to wait on the outcome of the fighting on the Syrian front, which was occupying the attention of their air force. But their forces were steadily building up as reserves arrived. When the Egyptian armour attacked on 14 October with nearly 1,000 tanks, some 250 were knocked out by the Israelis for so few losses (under 20) that no one would at first believe it.

The Israelis were now ready to counter-attack across the canal. During the night of 15–16 October paratroops under the command of Major-General Ariel Sharon, together with some tanks, got across to the west bank. During the 16th Egyptian forces fought fiercely to close the gap between their 2nd and 3rd Armies on the east bank

in the area of 'Chinese Farm'. The fight round the eastern bridgehead virtually cut Sharon off, but instead of consolidating these Israeli forces fanned out in all directions to attack SAM sites and any Egyptian position encountered. It is not clear why the Egyptian reaction was so slow, but it is apparent that they did not realise the full danger of the situation for at least 36 hours, by which time the battle round Chinese Farm had gone against them and a second Israeli division was ready to move across to the west bank. Russia, realising the danger better than Egypt, was now working hard for a cease-fire.

Although it was the canal battle that was to be decisive, it had been on the northern front the Israelies had been in most danger of defeat. With good co-ordination the Syrians had attacked at the same time as the Egyptians. But apart for the outpost on Mount Hermon the Israelis had been on the alert. Unlike the Egyptians, however, the Syrians were intending an armoured thrust right into the heart of Israel. The forces in the area on 6 October were the Israeli 7th Armoured Brigade in the north from Mount Hermon to Kuneitra and the Barak Brigade in the south from Kuneitra to El Al, while the Syrians deployed two armoured divisions and three mechanised infantry divisions, with a total of more than 800 tanks. It at once became a question of how long the two Israeli brigades could hold until reservist reinforcements reached them. (By their choice of the Jewish festival of Yom Kippur as the opening of their campaign the Arabs ensured that they had given

T-55 tank

Crew: 4 (commander, gunner, loader and driver). **Weight:** 79,366lb (36,000kg). **Length, overall:** 29' 6'' (9m). **Length, hull:** 20' 2'' (6.45m). **Width:** 10' 8¾'' (3.27m). **Height:** 7' 10½'' (2.4m). **Road speed:** 31mph (50km/h). **Range:** 310 miles (500km). **Engine:** V-55, 12 cylinder diesel developing 580 HP. **Ground pressure:** 11.52psi (.81kg/cm²). **Vertical obstacle:** 2' 7½'' (.8m). **Trench:** 8' 10½'' (2.7m). **Gradient:** 60%. **Armour:** 20 to 170mm.

The T-54/T-55 was a development of the T-44 which in turn was a development of the T-34 of World War II. The prototype T-54 was built in 1947 with the first production tanks being completed in 1949. Under the designation T-59 it is also built in China, Czechoslovakia and Poland. According to some estimates, up to 60,000 T-54/T-55 tanks were completed before it was replaced in production by the T-62 but at least 35 countries still use T-54s. The first T-55 was seen in 1961.

The main armament of the T-55 consists of a 100mm gun with an elevation of +17° and a depression of −4°; a 7.62mm SGMT (or PKT) machine gun is mounted co-axially with the main armament. Recently, some T-55s have been fitted with a 12.7mm DShK anti-aircraft machine gun. Total ammunition carried is 43 rounds of 100mm and 3,500 rounds of 7.62mm ammunition. In battle, the T-55, like the T-54, has two major disadvantages: a poor fire control system and very low depression for its main armament. The

latter places the tank at a considerable disadvantage when firing from a reverse slope as it must expose almost all its turret and hull in order to aim and fire. The T-55 has an NBC system, and night vision equipment and it can also be fitted with a schnorkel for deep wading.

Many T-54/T-55s are fitted with a dozer blade at the front of the hull for clearing battlefield obstacles. Other versions include bridgelayers, armoured recovery vehicles and special mineclearing tanks. The ZSU-57-2 anti-aircraft vehicle is based on a modified T-54 tank hull. The Israelies have rebuilt many T-54/T-55 tanks and fitted them with the British 105mm gun, new fire control system and a new American engine.

M60A1 main battle tank

Crew: 4 (commander, driver, gunner and loader). **Weight, combat:** 106,998lb (48.08t). **Length, with gun:** 30' 11½'' (9.436m). **Length, hull:** 22' 9½'' (6.946m). **Width:** 11' 11'' (3.631m). **Height:** 10' 8'' (3.251m). **Road speed:** 30mph (48kmh). **Range:** 310 miles (500km). **Engine:** V-12 diesel developing 750 HP at 2400rpm. **Ground pressure:** 11.23psi (.79kg/cm²). **Vertical obstacle:** 3' (.914m). **Trench:** 8' 6'' (2.59m). **Gradient:** 60%.

The M60 MBT is basically an M48 with many improvements including a new engine and the famous British 105mm tank gun in place of the earlier 90mm gun. First production M60s were completed in 1959, but were soon replaced by the M60A1, which has a redesigned turret for greater armour protection. So far well over 3,500 M60A1s have been built at the Detroit Tank Plant in Michigan. The 105mm gun of the M60A1 can fire a variety of different types of ammunition including High Explosive, High Explosive Anti-Tank (HEAT), Armour Piercing Discarding Sabot (APDS), Cannister and Smoke. A 7.62mm machine gun is mounted co-axially with the main armament and a 12.7mm machine gun is mounted in the commander's cupola, for use in both ground and anti-aircraft roles.

Other versions of the M60 include the M60A2 which has a new turret with a 152mm launcher, which can fire a Shillelagh missile with a range of 3000m, or an HE or HEAT round with a combustible cartridge case.

The M60A3, now in its final stages of development, is basically an M60A1 with modifications that include a laser rangefinder and suspension. The M728 Combat Engineer Vehicle (CEV) has a turret mounted 165mm demolition gun for use against field fortifications, dozer capability and an "A" frame on the turret for lifting heavy components. There is also a M60 Armoured Vehicle Launched Bridge (AVLB).

Left: Egyptian POWs being searched by Israeli soldiers during the Yom Kippur war. These POW's were eventually exchanged for the Israeli soldiers captured during the storming of the Bar Lev Line and some Israeli pilots.

the Israelies the one day of the year when the roads were clear for the reservists to join their units easily.) Destroying many times their own numbers, the Israeli brigades were slowly pushed back. Once again it was air power that had to be brought to their help, but this time only at great cost because of the SAM-6s and ZSU-23-4s. As each Israeli reserve battalion arrived it was pushed in to fill a gap. The most dangerous was at El Al, where a Syrian armoured brigade halted for some hours when all that was between it and a breakthrough was some half a dozen Israeli tanks. When the Syrians did attack a Centurion battalion was there to stop them.

Slowly, from 15 October onwards, the

Israelis began to push the Syrians back, it having been decided that this was to be the first priority. Yet the Syrians gave ground only slowly and at no time did they crack as they had in 1967. When Iraqi and Jordanian reinforcements arrived the Arabs attempted a fresh offensive. But the co-ordination of three national armies was too much for them, friend began to fire on friend and the offensive was called off. Further attacks were made by Syria's allies but they all failed as a result of basic mis-understandings. The front had by now stabilised, and the last battle before the final cease-fire was the retaking of Mount Hermon after bitter fighting on 22 October. Some 867 Syrians tanks were found on the Heights; the Israelis lost some 250, of which about 100 were a total loss. The death roll for the Israelis was given as 772 killed including pilots, and as ever it was the leaders and commanders who died.

Back in the south, when the second

division, under Major-General 'Bren' Adan, crossed over the canal and started to move south towards Suez, the Egyptian 3rd Army was in danger. When the division took the Genefa Hills, the 3rd Army's supply route was to all intents and purposes cut, as the Israelis dominated the Cairo–Suez road. When the first cease-fire came into force on the evening of the 22nd, the 3rd Army's position was hopeless and this is perhaps what caused its commanders to renew the fighting on the next day. They at least inflicted a defeat on the Israelis who tried to take Suez. However, when the second cease-fire came into force, Sharon was on the outskirts of Ismailia, threatening the city's links with Cairo and cutting the 3rd Army completely off. The whole war had ended in another Israeli victory, but this time without the Arabs being humbled. Perhaps the real losers were the European powers caught by the pan-Arab use of the 'oil weapon'.

Above: An Israeli artillery position on the Golan front in the 1973 Yom Kippir War. The Israelis had to halt the Syrian advance on the Golan front before they could turn their forces against the Egyptian Army in Sinai

Left: An Israeli Centurion tank moving up during the 1973 Campaign. Although outnumbered, the Israeli tanks had better guns and well-trained crews which gave them the edge over the Egyptian and Syrian tanks.

Although Arab–Israeli wars have dominated the military events in the Middle East since World War II, they have been only the largest pieces in a tapestry of discontent. Prior to World War II most of the states in the area were clients of the old imperial powers, but from 1945 onwards one by one they have become their own masters and this frequently led to a revolution to destroy the old regime and its connection with the former imperial power.

The Lebanon participated in the first war with Israel and, although it received 100,000 Palestinian refugees who commenced a terror campaign against the new state, it avoided being drawn into the later wars. Lebanon had in 1943 adopted a constitution which was supposed to represent the balance between Christian and Moslem Arab, but the former had a power advantage. This frequently led to violence, mainly inspired by neighbouring Syria. In 1958 the government asked the United States for help and Marines were landed in the face of a Syrian threat to invade.

It was in 1975 that the Lebanon collapsed into civil war brought about by the dissatisfaction of the left wing Moslem population and of the Palestinian refugees as together they now outnumbered the 'right-wing' Christians. Both sides had private armies which engaged in street battles and indiscriminate murder. It was the intervention of Palestinian forces from Syria (a sign that the United States is now really a 'paper tiger') that ensured the success of the left. Lebanon's future seems to be now as a satellite of Syria.

Jordan has also been threatened by Syria and in 1958, at the same time as the Lebanese trouble, British forces were flown in to support the monarchy. In 1970, following the blowing-up of three hijacked aircraft at Dawson's Field, the government forces turned on the guerrillas and expelled them from the country. An attempt by Syrian forces to intervene was repulsed by the Jordanian 40th Armoured Brigade. Later, following the threat of fresh intervention by Iraq and Syria, Saudi Arabia stationed troops in the country.

Iraq in a bloody coup in 1958 overthrew the monarchy and broke its alliance with the West (Baghdad Pact of 1955). For many years the government was engaged in a civil war with the large Kurdish minority. It commenced in 1961 and in 1970 the government granted many of the Kurds' demands. During the next four years, however, the Baath government was able to build up its army and when a disagreement developed during discussions on the boundaries of the autonomous Kurdish state, the government issued a 15-day ultimatum. Fighting broke out again in April 1974 and the Iraqi forces steadily drove the Kurds back into their mountain fastnesses, using T-62 tanks, plus MiG-21 and other modern Soviet aircraft. Following the agreement with Iran the Kurds lost their last support and the war ended with their collapse.

A result of the British decline was the outbreak of insurrections in the Arabian peninsula. In 1962 an Arab nationalist revolution overthrew the Imam of North Yemen. Fighting soon broke out between the royalists (the Imam had not been killed as the revolutionaries believed) and the new Yemen Arab Republic. The republican forces, aided by Egyptian officers, were facing defeat when Egyptian forces intervened. The Egyptians were full of confidence when they arrived but their troops were inexperienced in the mountain warfare of the territory and although they took the offensive, with more than 5,000 troops in February 1963, and captured the royalist towns of Marib and Harib and advanced into the mountains, they could not hold their gains. The royalists were receiving support from Saudi Arabia and by 1964 had driven the Egyptians back into the plains. A second Egyptian offensive was less successful and by 1965 they had given up the idea of a military victory and confined themselves to protecting the main towns. It has been said that they used poison gas during these operations, but this contention has never been proved for certain. What is certain is that many thousands died before the Egyptians withdrew and a compromise was reached between the moderates of both sides.

The revolution in North Yemen had repercussions for the British-controlled port of Aden and the South Yemen. Aden itself had proved a hotbed of radical Arab nationalism since the 1950s, and now the interior broke out into open revolt. An uprising in the Radfan brought about the use of British troops, and a policy similar to that employed on the North-West Frontier of India in the 1920s and 1930s was tried. Villages which supported the rebels were proscribed and after a warning so that their inhabitants could leave were bombed. But with the open border the inhabitants only withdrew to North Yemen, to return after the British troops had left.

In Aden itself terrorists assassinated British officials and Adenis who worked with them. With her withdrawal from a world role Britain announced the abandonment of Aden in 1966. The British departure brought about a complete collapse of the moderates and the formation of the Marxist People's Democratic Republic of Yemen.

The People's Democratic Republic of Yemen lent its support to the rebels in the neighbouring Sheikdom of Dhofar, part of Oman, and for the last few years there has been a continual guerrilla war going on, with British officers aiding the forces of the sultan. With the open support of a neighbouring country it is difficult to destroy the rebels, and although troops from Iran have assisted the rebels, who call themselves the Popular Front for the Liberation of Oman and the Arab Gulf, they continue to harass the sultanate.

Wars in Africa since 1945

Since World War II Africa has been torn by all manner of wars:
Black against Black, Black against White, tribal wars, political
wars, economic wars and several coups to set up or pull down
dictators.

The development of Africa's postwar states has been almost a tale of 'better the devil you don't know than the devil you do'. The untried attractions of independence or greater self-determination have consistently had more appeal than the rule of the government in power.

Former colonies have emerged from the relative security of colonial rule into an independence which sometimes resembles Western-style democracy but which can become a crude form of individual, tribal or party dictatorship. But these birth pangs are no worse than those in the history of many Western states. The difference is that ever since the days of the 18th century slavers, Africa has been regarded as fair pickings for powerful and well armed foreigners. With the decline of the colonial powers (Britain, France, Belgium and Portugal) there has been a rise in the influence of Russia, China, Cuba and some Middle Eastern states. These neo-colonialists are the patrons of the first of Africa's wars, the fight for self-determination.

Many of these wars have flourished in countries rich with natural resources. Here there is a two-fold incentive for war: the native populations resent the exploitation of these resources by the colonists or the central government; and the neo-colonists are happy to see exports to the West either redirected or cut off. The vast resources of Angola (coffee, cotton, fishmeal, maize, timber, iron ore, oil, and diamonds) have attracted both the Russians and the Cubans, while the copper and uranium of Katanga and the oil of Biafra drew in big business from the West as well as the major political powers.

Britain has been spared the worst of the colonial wars since it granted independence early and generally left behind some sort of African administration to take over. The colonial wars really began in earnest after France, Portugal and the White African states of the south found that they had neighbours who were newly independent Black states.

Angola had Zambia and Zaire, while Mozambique had Tanzania and Zambia as neighbours to shelter insurgents. The Portuguese could not cross these borders to any depth or in numbers, for the risk of attracting adverse international publicity was too great. This they discovered when they launched a seaborne raid on Senegal in an attempt to stamp out incursions into their colony of Guinea Bissau.

France hangs on to the little enclave of Djibouti, but has neighbours in the Somali Republic and Ethiopia.

Until Portugal pulled out of Africa, Rhodesia had only one hostile border, that with Zambia, while South Africa had the tiny Caprivi Strip. In 1976, without their Portuguese 'ally' the Whites of southern Africa face war on two new fronts.

Yet even after independence former colonies are often plagued by war. Some are torn by tribal struggles, others by racial, religious or political wars. Few are spared palace revolutions, coups or takeovers by the army.

Although Africa's wars may fall into a sort of pattern, the way in which they are waged varies from the near conventional with tanks, aircraft and artillery, through the classic guerrilla war of patrols, ambush and counter-ambush in jungle and elephant

A soldier of the Portuguese Army takes up a firing position with his 7.62mm Heckler and Koch Rifle during guerilla operations in Angola before the Portuguese withdrew and the civil war started.

grass, to tribal butchery with clubs, spears and *pangas* (the African *machete*).

In the background of many of these wars are the mercenaries. Not all are White, but most are. Many come from former colonies or southern Africa, but some are freebooters from Europe. Some are attracted by promises of high pay, but few receive it. Others simply cannot adjust to a normal life after service in their own countries' armies or in the French Foreign Legion. Their military standard varies from the solid professionalism of the ex-regular soldier to the erratic behaviour of a young man with a liking for guns. Their performance in the field depends on their equipment and the quality of the opposition. Perhaps the most successful mercenaries are those who are attached as instructors, as in the Biafran war, and who avoid being sent forward to the front.

To examine all of Africa's wars would be impossible, since some have gone virtually unreported in the West, but some bear study for they reflect a similarity in tactics, arms or objectives.

The Mau Mau rebellion in Kenya between 1952 and 1956 was not strictly a war of independence, but rather a revolt by the Kikuyu who were attempting to dominate their neighbouring tribes. It is significant that during the rebellion only 32 European civilians were killed in contrast with 1,817 Africans.

Although there was a political arm under Jomo Kenyatta, based in Nairobi, the security forces were able to isolate it from the military arm of the Mau Mau and so destroy it quickly. The creation of African home-guard units and protected villages in and around the Kikuyu Reserve, and the use of men of the King's African Rifles and of 'counter-gangs' of former Mau Mau terrorists, forced the Mau Mau into the remoter areas of the Aberdare mountains and deprived them of food and local support. By the end of the campaign 63 European, 3 Asian and 524 African, soldiers had been killed, but they had killed 11,503, captured

2,585 and received the surrender of 2,714 Mau Mau terrorists.

In 1957 the Gold Coast became the first British colony to gain its independence. It had set a precedent and three years later 17 French, British and Belgian colonies had followed this lead. On 30 June 1960 the Belgians pulled out of the Congo and left behind 17 Africans with university degrees and a population of 40 million unprepared for independence.

Almost from the first days there were inter-regional and inter-tribal disturbances; the feuding and war that followed lasted for over six years. It began when the *Force Publique*, the Congolese army, mutinied against its Belgian officers on the night of 5–6 July. The rebellion spread to the *Gendarmerie* and on 15 July the first elements of a United Nations peace-keeping force (ONUC) for the Congo were flown into Leopoldville.

Militarily the most significant phase of the operations that followed was the secession of the southern province of Katanga. It lasted from around 21 February 1961, when the UN demanded the withdrawal of mercenaries from the province, to 8 January 1962, when Katanga's President Moise Tshombe fled. He was to return to the Congo in 1964 and finally to leave a year later.

The UN moved against Katanga on 28 August 1961, occupying key points and attempting to arrest the foreign mercenaries. There was little success and a series of small-

Right: A heavily camouflaged Land Rover of the Federal Nigerian Army on patrol looking for rebel troops of the breakaway Eastern Region of Nigeria (Biafra)

Below: Captured Mau Mau terrorists are marched to local Home Guard Headquarters. Local Home Guards played a vital role in defeating the Mau Mau.

scale peace-keeping operations followed. After this period of stalemate the UN launched Operation 'Morthor' (Hindi for 'smash') in September, but it failed to break Tshombe's hold and further stalemate followed. There were sporadic outbreaks of fighting until December 1961 when heavy fighting flared up between the UN forces and the Katangese Gendarmerie and White mercenaries. This time ONUC deployed armoured cars and jet fighters and bombers. Again deadlock followed but finally a year later, after a clash between the Katangese and Indian and Ethiopian units of the UN, the secessionist troops were rolled up and Tshombe fled. The cost of the fighting for the UN was 126 killed and 138 wounded, with a further 109 deaths resulting from accidents and natural causes.

Although the UN forces left in June 1964 this was not the end of fighting in the Congo. Tshombe was invited back from Spain to become the prime minister of the Congo, in a last desperate effort to unify the country, and during his brief period in office in 1964–5 more than half the country was torn apart by an uprising which began as a small rebellion in Kwilu Province.

Headed by a rabblerouser named Pierre Mulele, and backed by supplies of arms from the communist world, the revolt began because of genuine grievances at the excesses of the central government and the Congolese army.

The fighting that followed was peculiarly savage. The rebel soldiers adopted the name Simba (Lion) and were initially tough but disciplined. However, by the end their barbarity appalled even battle-hardened mercenaries.

The most dramatic incident of the revolt was the airborne attack on the city of Stanleyville by a Belgian paratroop battalion. The rebels had captured the city and were holding 2,000 Americans and Europeans as hostages. The paratroops jumped at dawn on 24 November 1964 from five Lockheed C-130s of the US Air Force. Capturing the airfield they raced for central Stanleyville and reached it by 0720 hours. Although the Belgians were able to save most of the hostages, the Simbas killed 80 and seriously wounded 40, of whom five died later. A White mercenary column, Number 5 Commando under the English Colonel Mike Hoare, reached the city later that day. Fighting against the Simbas continued until late into 1965.

Mercenary troops had an important role in the fighting because the men of the Congolese National Army were terrified of the Simbas, to whom they attributed supernatural powers. The Simbas worked themselves into a frenzy before combat and, led by their witch-doctors, went to war motivated more by magic than politics.

White soldiers continued to influence Congolese politics when a revolt against President Joseph Mobutu in 1966 threw up a Belgian leader, 'Black Jack' Schramme.

His mercenaries (Number 10 Commando) were eventually bottled up on the border at Bukavu and forced over the border into Burundi in 1967.

But this little war had ceased to be of interest following a coup which took place in Nigeria on 14 January 1966. There were strong tribal influences at work here, and in the confusion that followed the coup there was a demand by the Ibos in the east that they secede from the previously dominant Moslem north. Ibos living in the north were massacred or fled east. Eventually Colonel Yakubu Gowon emerged as the leader of the north. A 'pagan', that is a non-Moslem from a minority group, he seemed an acceptable leader. In the east however a flamboyant bearded soldier, Colonel Odumegwu Ojukwu, assumed control of the little coastal enclave which became known as Biafra.

The Biafran War lasted from 7 July 1967 to 15 January 1970. At the beginning the

fighting was not severe, each side probing to see if by mere opposition it could bring down the opposing government. The Biafrans made some advances along the coast towards Lagos and even launched an air raid, using White mercenary pilots. In May 1968, however, the Nigerians captured Enugu and Onitsha and the Shell oil refinery at Port Harcourt in Biafra. The war should have ended that year, but logistic difficulties, the tough resistance and inventiveness of the Biafrans and a continued supply of arms from the Soviet Union and the West kept the fighting going. The Nigerians began to use aircraft to attack Biafran villages and also the airstrips that were being used both for relief by charity organisations and for re-supply of arms and ammunition.

On 23 December 1969 the Nigerians launched a four-pronged attack and on 11 January 1970 they captured Oweri, the Biafran capital. Four days later they accepted the Biafran surrender. Mercenary troops were used by both sides, by the Nigerians to fly their aircraft and by the Biafrans to train their soldiers. The 'underdog' situation of the Biafrans attracted some men like the Swedish Baron von Rosen who were not motivated by money. There were also reports of English voices heard during Biafran attacks shouting in the rear 'Come on you Black bastards, move!'

While this former colony was fighting to prevent a break-up into tribal sub-units,

Saladin armoured car

Crew: 4 (commander, gunner, loader and driver). **Weight:** 25,551lb (11,590kg). **Length, overall:** 17′ 4′′ (5.284m). **Length, hull:** 16′ 2′′ (4.93m). **Width:** 8′ 4′′ (2.54m). **Height:** 7′ 10′′ (2.39m). **Road speed:** 45mph (72kmh). **Range:** 250 miles (400km). **Engine:** Rolls-Royce B.80 Mk.6A 8 cylinder petrol engine developing 170 HP at 3750rpm. **Trench:** 5′ (1.52m). **Vertical obstacle:** 18′′ (.46m). **Gradient:** 42%.

The British Army has a 50-year tradition of using armoured cars for reconnaissance, the vehicles relying on their speed, mobility and quietness of operation and only fighting when necessary. They are also very useful for border patrols and a variety of internal security operations.

At the end of World War II, a requirement for a new range of armoured vehicles was issued, the result being the Saladin armoured car (FV601) and the Saracen APC (FV603). The Saracen was, however,

ordered first as it was urgently required for anti-guerilla operations in Malaya. The Saladin entered production at the Alvis factory at Coventry in 1958 and continued until 1972.

The Saladin has seen combat with the British Army in Aden, Brunei and Cyprus as well as with the Jordanian and Nigerian Armies. It has earned itself the reputation of being a well armed and well armoured vehicle and on a number of occasions it has even returned from a mission with wheels missing. Its main armament consists of a 76mm gun which can fire a variety of ammunition including HESH (High Explosive Squash Head for use against armour), High Explosive, Smoke, Canister (for use against infantry in the open) and Squash Head Practice. A .30 (7.62mm) machine gun is mounted co-axially with the main armament and there is a similar weapon on the roof for use in the anti-aircraft role. Six smoke dischargers are mounted either side of the turret. A total of 43 rounds of 76mm and 2750 rounds of .30 (7.62mm) is carried.

Portugal was fighting to retain a hold over the vast area of its African colonies.

In 1969 Portugal had 120,000 men committed in Guineau Bissau, Angola and Mozambique, and besides these conscripts there were home guard units and the *Groupes Especiales Paraquedistas* (GEP) and *Flechas* composed of guerrillas who had been 'turned round' to fight their former communist-trained comrades. Portugal tied up 50 per cent of its annual budget in these wars, and was forcéd to re-enlist specialists like doctors to serve in Africa for additional tours.

By 1973 Portugal had between 150,000 and 175,000 conscripts and regulars in its colonies. The opposition in Angola comprised 7,000 men of the *Movimento Popular de Libertaçao de Angola* (MPLA) under Dr Agostinho Neto, in Guineau Bissau 5,000 men of the *Partido Africano da Independência de Guiné e Cabo Verde* (PAIGC) under Aristide Pereira, while in Mozambique the *Frente de Libertaçao de Moçambique* (FRELIMO) under Samora Machel stood at between 3,000 and 4,000. Of all the colonial wars in southern Africa the Portuguese ones bore some resemblance to the French experience in Algeria. There was a large White population which included some very poor families, and there were also some wealthy African families who mixed with the upper crust of society in Angola and Mozambique.

Portugal fought its wars according to the classic principles of 'hearts and minds' and

that Portugal lost the war is no criticism of the formula. Portugal's abandonment of its colonies was the result of changes at home and not in Africa.

The operation of a 'hearts and minds' campaign is now widely known. Basicly the counter-insurgent government raises the standard of living within the country so that the promises of the guerrillas hold less attraction than the real benefits offered by the government. In conjunction with this operation the army wages a war of patrols, ambushes, food denial operations and sweeps against the guerrillas. If the neighbouring states can be persuaded to deny sanctuary to the guerrillas these tactics will succeed in time.

If Portugal had been rich enough and big enough to sustain the war and if its government at home had been less repressive, there is no reason why final victory should not have gone to it. Although the MPLA and FRELIMO had declared large areas of the jungle as liberated, the Portuguese still controlled the bulk of the population and the communications around the major towns. But as for the Americans in Vietnam and the French in Algeria, the war became too costly in blood and money, and for vast expenditure the Portuguese seemed to show little return. In the end it was the ability to last out a protracted war that led to the victory of the guerrillas.

Independence came in a rush in the wake of the Portuguese army revolt of 25 April 1974. Heavy pressure, on General Spinola and his successor General Costa Gomes, to withdraw from Africa led to negotiations with the guerrilla movements.

Throughout the following year there was confusion as the Portuguese army broke contact with the enemy and found that the White Angolans, in particular, were not keen to become part of Africa's newest independent Black state. Portuguese soldiers were involved in riots and a short-lived attempt by the colonists at UDI. Elements of the South African army moved over the southern border to protect a major hydro-electric dam system under construction at Calueque.

By 1976 Portugal was out of Africa. White refugees had fled over the border into South Africa or Rhodesia and fighting now flared up between rival factions in Angola.

The MPLA, holding the centre and east of the country, found themselves up against two rival factions. In the north-west there was the FNLA and in the south-east UNITA. Then Russian warships appeared

Above left: MPLA (People's Movement for the Liberation of Angola) soldiers take a wounded comrade across a river on an improvised raft.

Left: A solider of the Federal Nigerian Army with a German World War II 7.92mm MG42 machine gun complete with belts of ready-use ammunition

Above right: A Panhard EBR heavy armoured car of the Portuguese Army in Angola. The civil war followed the Portuguese withdrawal, and ended in defeat for pro-Western forces early in 1976

SOVIET ARMS AND INFLUENCE IN ANGOLA

There is scarcely a country in the world where the Soviet Union does not pursue some military, economic or political interest; and as, to a Soviet Marxist politician, economics and military affairs are merely different tools to achieve the same end, it is perhaps unwise to concentrate merely on military involvement as a measure of Soviet power or influence abroad. However, we give below a list of countries where representatives of the Soviet military are involved, as opposed to countries with whom arms deals have been concluded without direct involvement of Soviet personnel: Afghanistan, Algeria, Angola, Cuba, Egypt, Guinea, Indo China, Iraq, Libya, Somalia, Syria, Uganda, Yemen.

In their February 1976 issue, the *International Defence Review* quoted one source as having reported that the totals in weapons, vehicles and equipment supplied to MPLA forces in Angola included:

Infantry weapons and equipment: 10,000 AK-47 rifles; 10,000 AKM rifles; 10,000 SKS rifes; 2,000 Tokarev pistols; 80,000 hand grenades; 40,000 anti-tank and anti-personnel mines; 290 belt-fed heavy machine-guns; an unknown number of AT-3 *Sagger* anti-tank missiles; an unknown number of SA-7 SAMs; 1,100 RPG-2 anti-tank rocket launchers; 1,700 B-10 82 mm recoilless anti-tank guns; 1,000 82 mm mortars; 240 tactical communications sets;
Artillery: over 100 truck-mounted BM-21 40-tube 122 mm artillery rocket systems; 12,000 rounds for single-tube 122 mm rocket launchers; an unspecified number of old 76 mm ZIS-3 anti-tank cannon; 25 "heavy calibre" anti-aircraft guns; 300 AA guns "on armoured vehicles" (presumably either the ZSU-57-2 or ZSU-23-4);
Combat vehicles: at least 30 T-54 battle tanks; about 80 older T-34 battle tanks; 68 PT-76 amphibious light tanks; 92 BTR-50 amphibious tracked APCs; 74 BTR-60PA amphibious wheeled APCs; 20 BRDM armoured cars with heavy machine-guns; 32 old BRT-40 light armoured vehicles; 877 unspecified reconnaissance vehicles;
Logistics vehicles: 384 GAZ-51 trucks; 55 1¼ ton trucks; 80 ¼ ton trucks; 160 heavy trailers; 30 medium trailers; 40 generators;
Aircraft: 12 MiG-21 fighter-bombers; 3 MiG-15 fighter-bombers (a GCI net is reported to have been set up recently in MPLA territory by Russian "advisers");
Ships: 5 modified Soviet landing craft; 3 unspecified other ships (one from East Germany, 2 from Cuba); 5 smaller vessels bought with Soviet funds from the defunct Angola Shipping Co, SOTRAL.

Apparently all this equipment had been airlifted to Luanda and Henrique de Carvalho by Soviet Air Force Antonov An-12 and An-22 transport aircraft.

BM-21 multiple rocket launcher

Weight: 25,353lb (11,500kg). **Length:** 24' 1¼" (7.35m). **Width:** 8' 10" (2.69m). **Height:** 9' 4" (2.85m). **Road speed:** 46.6mph (75kmh). **Range:** 252 miles (405km). **Engine:** ZIL-375 8 cylinder petrol engine developing 175 HP.

Multiple Rocket Launchers have been used by the Soviet Army for some 40 years and during World War II they were known as Katyushas or Stalin Organs. Since then at least ten different types have been developed.

The main advantages of a Multiple Rocket System are that it can launch a large number of rockets in just a few seconds. Each Soviet tank and mechanized infantry division has three batteries of BM-21s, each with eight launchers. The BM-21 can fire at least three types of HE rocket—the long rocket, a 10' 7" long missile (3.226m) which weighs 170.86lb (77.5kg) at launch and has a maximum range of 22,418 yards (20,500m); the short rocket, 6' 3" (1.905m) long which weighs 100.96lb (45.8kg) and has a velocity of 1476fps (450m/s) and a maximum range of 12,904

yards (11,800m) and a third type, which is basically the short rocket with an additional motor which gives it a range almost approaching that of the long rocket.

Once the rockets have been fired, the launcher quickly moves to a new firing position, reloads in 5-10 minutes ready for firing again. The launcher is mounted on a standard URAL-375 6 × 6 truck which has a central tyre pressure regulation system fitted. The BM-21 has seen combat in the Middle East with Syrian and Egyptian forces, in Angola and in Vietnam. Its ability to bring a large amount of fire down in a few seconds has played a decisive role in many battles.

BRDM-2 reconnaissance vehicle

Crew: 4. **Weight:** 15,432lb (7.000kg). **Length:** 18' 10½" (5.75m). **Width:** 7' 8½" (2.35m). **Height:** 7' 7" (2.31m). **Road speed:** 62mph (100kmh). **Water speed:** 6.2mph (10kmh). **Range:** 466 miles (750km). **Engine:** GAZ-41, 8 cylinder water cooled developing 140HP. **Vertical obstacle:** 4' 1" (1.25m). **Gradient:** 60%. **Armour:** 10mm.

The BRDM-2 is one of the standard reconnaissance vehicles of the Warsaw Pact and has now replaced the earlier BRDM-1 in most front line units.

Its hull is of all-welded construction, with the driver at the front, the fighting compartment in the centre and the engine at the rear. The four tyres have a pressure regulation system which enables the driver to adjust the tyre pressure to suit ground conditions. In addition, there are four small belly wheels, two each side of the hull, which can be lowered when crossing very rough country and ditches. A winch is provided so that the BRDM-2 can recover itself from a bogged-down condition and the vehicle is amphibious and propelled through water by a single water jet mounted in the rear of the hull. It is armed with a turret-mounted 14.5mm KPV machine gun with a

7.62mm PKT MG mounted co-axially with the main armament. There are at least four known variants of the BRDM-2. In command configuration, the basic vehicle has the turret removed and additional radio installed; the radiological-chemical-reconnaissance vehicle is used to mark lanes through contaminated areas and the BRDM-2 (Sagger) is the basic vehicle with its turret removed and replaced by a launcher arm with overhead armour cover. Six Sagger missiles are carried in the ready-to-launch position with additional missiles inside the hull. The Sagger can be launched from within the vehicle, outside it with the aid of a separation cable and control box. The final model is the BRDM-2 SAM, or the SA-9 Gaskin as it is known in NATO. This has four surface-to-air missiles with a maximum effective range of 5470 yards (5km).

Left: The swift victory of the MPLA in Angola was the textbook example of Soviet political domination and arms supply. These MPLA recruits in Luanda in November 1975 have RPG-7 rocket launchers

off the coast and Cuban soldiers were flown in to assist the MPLA.

The appearance in Angola of Cuban soldiers fighting for the MPLA was something of a surprise. More significant was the deployment of T-34 and T-54 tanks, heavy mortars, recoilless guns, and single and multi-rail rocket-launchers. European mercenaries flown out to Angola were armed with little except small arms and by April 1976 the MPLA had complete control over Angola, although serious guerrilla activity seems to be continuing in the northern enclave of Cabinda.

About this time FRELIMO began to make threatening noises on the Rhodesian border with Mozambique. There were ambushes on the main roads leading to South Africa, and Rhodesia called up more men from reserve and territorial units.

Up to 1976 Rhodesia had fought a remarkably successful campaign against incursions over the Zambian border. Be-

tween the declaration of UDI in 1965 and 1973, of the 530 guerrillas who had crossed the border 499 had been killed, captured or surrendered. Rhodesia was helped by having the vast lake formed by the Kariba dam as part of its border. Its small air force covered free-fire zones in the Zambesi valley, patrols worked through the neighbouring bush and observation posts covered Lake Kariba.

The controversy about Rhodesia and the reluctance of the British government to take direct action against Salisbury after UDI is interesting in the light of British intervention in Kenya, Tanganyika and Uganda in January 1964 to supress mutinies by African troops.

In all since 1945 equatorial and southern Africa have had coups or attempted coups in 19 of their 30 odd states. Civil wars have been fought in the Sudan, Chad and Ethiopia and in 1976 France committed elements of the 13me *Demi-Brigade de la Légion Entrangère* and the 2me *Regiment Etrangère Parachutistes* as well as the special *Groupement Operational de Légion Etrangère* to protect the tiny colony of Djibouti.

Africa's wars and uprisings have been fought with weapons ranging from *pangas* to tanks and crude black-powder single-shot handguns to jet aircraft.

Small arms have come from the Eastern bloc, but Belgian FN rifles and machine-guns have been widely used. Ex-Belgian, British and French colonies use weapons, uniforms and vehicles supplied by or inherited from the former colonial government. Soviet armour and aircraft have been imported, but the aircraft are often piloted by crews on loan to train African pilots. South Africa and Rhodesia have some difficulties with spares and replacements for some of their aircraft and heavy weapons, but the French seem happy to fill these gaps when they appear.

Africa is an unstable continent and Black Africans a varied and volatile group of races, so it is hard to predict the future trends of warfare in the continent. Whether or not political expediency will triumph over anti-colonial fervour and impel the Black Africans to abandon their ideas of imposing majority rule in southern Africa is hard to say. But fears that African states will disappear into some kind of Marxist-Leninist communist power bloc are probably groundless. In war and politics Africans have a way of surviving the best and worst influences of alien intervention and then producing their own informal African version.

Guerilla warfare, insurgency and terrorism

Since World War II guerilla warfare, both urban and rural, together with terrorism by diverse groups have spread greatly, leaving their mark on North and South America, Europe and the Middle East.

A foot patrol of the Royal Highland Fusiliers on patrol in Belfast, North Ireland. The British Army has had more experience of Internal Security (IS) operations than any other army in the world today.

Apart from Korea, most military operations since 1945 have been reactions to the guerilla, the insurgent or the terrorist. This indicates how important in the nuclear age these protagonists and the 'war' they proclaim have become. In part this may be because this form of warfare has always been attractive to the communists and to the causes they espouse, but it is also the result of the limitation that the fear of nuclear holocaust puts on the use of force by major powers. Perhaps the most important reason of all is the climate of opinion which seems to accept violence and murder from the left-wing radical while condemning any reaction to it by government forces.

When discussing these forms of warfare Liddell Hart wrote: 'Campaigns of this kind are the more likely to continue because it is the only kind of war that fits the conditions of the modern age, while being at the same time well suited to take advantage of social discontent, racial ferment and nationalist fervours.' The problem of the armed forces was stated by a senior Canadian officer when preparing the security for the Montreal 1976 Olympics when he said that if nothing happened the public would complain he had over reacted and if there were attacks that he had not done enough.

Carlos Marighela, a leading guerilla writer, has said that part of the purpose of a campaign is to make life so unbearable for the ordinary public, because the government is forced to bring in ever more restrictive measures, that they become discontented and demand a change. This is where a government requires a strong nerve and the armed forces a heroic stoicism because if they are willing to accept casualties without over reacting, the public are likely to become thoroughly disenchanted with the rebels, and so there is a reasonable chance that the latter will wither away. In fact, for this type of warfare to succeed it is necessary for a large number of the public to be sympathetic to the rebels cause. Che Guevara believed that it was not necessary to have a large base but that a 'foco' or small group of armed idealists in the countryside would generate support from all discontents and revolutionaries. Both he and Castro, writing after the Cuban revolution of 1957–1959, say that it was fought by men of all ideas and all classes and that only later did the Marxists take power. This may be a warning to all 'liberals' who would ally themselves with a communist party. The insurrection worked in Cuba, but its target was a regime which was so rotten that it was hated by all. When Guevara tried his foco tactics in Bolivia they failed because there was no organisation to supply a back-up.

The vast majority of people in the world, including those in the third world, wish only for a stable government under which they may hope for greater prosperity and a 'better life'. The revolutionary with his vision must tear down even what they have to fulfil his purpose.

The list of 'the wars of liberation' since 1945 is a long one. There was the ELAS uprising in Greece in 1945 initially suppressed by the British only to break out again as a full-scale civil war. In this case it was a mistake on the communists' part as it led them to a military defeat in 1949 which kept them from positions of power for 30 years.

While this was happening, in China the greatest modern exponent of guerilla warfare was bringing his 'long march' to a successful conclusion. Mao Tse-tung has written how guerrilla forces can wage a long campaign during which the people are organised and indoctrinated to. support the cause, whereupon a regular revolutionary army can be brought into being to achieve the party's aims. Most 'Liberation Armies' have followed Mao's ideas to a greater or lesser extent, but they have operated in mainly backward rural countries. In an urban environment the revolutionary does not seek to engage in pitched battle with the government, but to bring it down by undermining the normal life of the country.

The French colonial empire was the scene of the strongest resistance, and hence the bloodiest battles, by any of the colonial powers except in certain ways Portugal. Indo-china and Algeria represent two different types of revolutionary war. The first, as in China, was that of a guerrilla army growing up into a regular force strong enough to defeat the central government. Again the people of Indo-China were involved by the communists in the cause for national freedom, and not in the formation of a communist state. Once the French had departed the communists had to fight an even longer and bloodier war until they could achieve their aim of political dominance of the whole of the former colony of Indo-China.

In Algeria (1954–1962) there was an attempt to fight the French army in battle with regimental teams more than 1,000

strong but, as in Greece, this only gave the government troops a better target and it had to be abandoned and a policy of harassment adopted. This succeeded where military efforts had failed. Some might argue that because they no longer have the stomach for mass slaughter, the only means to final victory in campaigns such as that in Algeria, the western nations are effete. One hopes rather that they show that mankind can progress.

It is this concern for human life, and particularly that of the innocent bystander, that has become the weapon of the terrorist. The most prominent users of terrorism have been the fighters for the 'liberation of Palestine'. For many years they confined their attacks to within the Jewish state and the world considered them largely an Israeli problem. But when they turned their attention to hijacking aircraft they hit the headlines in the world press. This, of course, was part of the reason for their action, as they felt that their cause was being allowed to wither away in the refugee camps. The first attack on an El Al (the Israeli national airline) aircraft took place in July 1968 when three members of the Popular Front for the Liberation of Palestine boarded in Rome a Boeing 707 bound for Tel Aviv. When the terrorists took over the aircraft they diverted it to Algiers. The Algerian authorities arranged the release of all the non-Israeli passengers and the Israeli women and children. The hijackers, however, demanded the release of 1,200 Arab guerilla held in Palestine as ransom for the 12 Israeli male passengers and crew. Eventually the aircraft and 12 hostages were released when the Israelis set free 16 Arab guerilla caught during the Six-Day

Above: Members of the French Anti-Gang Brigade surrounding a branch of the Société Centrale De Banque, Eastern Paris, where bank robbers had taken four people as hostages and demanded a ransom of 3 million Francs

Right: Aircraft hijackings have become increasingly common in recent years. Here, a hijacker covers an injured passenger off a Turkish DC-9 after four Turks hijacked the aircraft with 60 people aboard.

War of 1967. The PFLP began to attack El Al aircraft while they were on the ground at other European airports: at Athens in December 1968 and at Zurich in February 1969. On each occasion one Israeli was killed and several wounded. However, two terrorists were captured at Athens and three at Zurich, where a fourth was also killed by an Israeli guard.

Because of the tightening of Israeli security, the PFLP switched its attention to other airlines when a team hijacked a Trans-World Airlines' Boeing 707 bound for Tel Aviv in August 1969. The hijackers, among whom was the girl Leila Khaled, directed the aircraft to Damascus where, after the passengers had been disembarked, they tried to blow it up. The Syrians released all the passengers except two male Israelis whom they exchanged for 13 Syrians held by Israel.

In December 1969 five more PFLP terrorists were captured in Athens, two after attacking the El Al office and killing a baby and the other three when they were found to be carrying guns and explosives when trying to board a TWA Boeing 707. This

brought the number held in Athens to seven, with another three held in Switzerland.

In July 1970, when the trial of the baby killers was about to start, six PFLP terrorists hijacked an Olympic Airways Boeing 727 and forced it to land at Athens. Here they threatened to blow it up with its 55 passengers and crew if the seven PFLP prisoners were not released. Through the mediation of the Red Cross terms were agreed, by which the Greek government freed all seven PFLP terrorists.

This left six PFLP activists in custody, three in Switzerland and three more who had been arrested in an attempt to seize a El Al 707 at Munich. The leaders of the PFLP decided to organise their release and at the same time to embarrass King Hussein of Jordan, with whom they were at odds. So on 6 September 1970 a TWA 707 and a Swissair Douglas DC8 were hijacked and flown to Dawson's Field, a World War II RAF airstrip about 40 miles from Amman, the capital of Jordan. A third aircraft was to have been seized, but the attempt went wrong and the one male hijacker was shot dead by a security guard. The other, the girl Leila Khaled, was captured. The plane was forced to land at London's Heathrow Airport and Leila Khaled was taken to Ealing police station. Two other PFLP members who should have boarded the El Al aircraft had been refused seats by the Israelis, and had instead boarded a TWA Boeing 747 Jumbo-jet, hijacked it to Cairo and blew it up. They had not taken the 747 to Dawson's Field as they did not know if it could land there. While negotiations were getting under way for the release of the PFLP prisoners, a British BAC VC 10 on a flight from Bahrain to London was seized to force the British government to set free Leila Khaled.

The airstrip was besieged by troops of King Hussein's army, and under the leadership of the British government it was agreed to release the seven terrorists, but only after the 500 hostages had all been freed. Some 444 were set free at various times, and the remaining 56 taken to Palestinian refugee camps while the aircraft were blown up. Eventually the last hostages were released or rescued by the Jordanian army and when all were safe the seven PFLP prisoners were set free.

However, this was not a great victory for the PFLP as King Hussein immediately turned his army on them and drove them from the country they had hoped to take over. As a result, an even more extreme group of terrorists appeared in the Black September Organisation. This group was to indulge in such extremes that other Arab nations would become disillusioned with them.

During 1972, after a quiet period, there was a fresh outbreak with a Lufthansa 747 flown to Aden where it was released only after the payment of $5 million. At Lod Airport, Tel Aviv, a Sabena 707 from Brussels was held up by two men and two women who threatened to blow it up with explosives concealed in the girls' underwear unless 100 Arab prisoners were released by the Israelis.

A long period of negotiation started, although the Israeli government was determined not to give in, even at the risk of the passengers' lives. During the night the aircraft was immobilized by letting down the tyres and draining the undercarriage hydraulic fluid. So the terrorists were persuaded to allow 'mechanics' to approach the aircraft to repair the undercarriage.

Right: An engine of one of the three aircraft hijacked by Palestinian commandos burns at an airfield in Jordan after the commandoes had blown up the aircraft.

Below: French police with riot shields crowd behind a tree as students in the Rue de Lyon, Paris, shower them with missiles during the street battles of 1968.

Israeli commandos disguised in overalls seized the opportunity to assault the plane, shooting their way in. One passenger was shot dead when he got to his feet despite orders from the commandos to stay seated, and the same fate befell the two male terrorists. The two girls surrendered.

The sequel to this attempt was one of the most vicious attacks recorded. Three members of the Red Army Fraction, a Marxist organisation which had broken away from the Japanese communist party, arrived at Lod Airport as passengers on an Air France flight from Rome. While in Rome they had been given Kalashnikov rifles and grenades in special suitcases. Their baggage was not searched on leaving. At Lod they collected their suitcases, removed the rifles and opened indiscriminate fire. In the ensuing carnage 24 passengers were killed and 72 wounded. Two of the Japanese died, one by his own hand.

It is important to note here how more than one group of terrorists were co-

Right: A hooded Arab Black September Commando on the balcony of the Israeli building in the Olympic Village. Almost 20 people were killed in this attack

Below: German policemen, in track suits and armed with sub-machine guns, on the roof of a Munich Olympic Village building during the 1972 Black September Commando raid.

operating and how well organised they were. It is the terrorists' ability to find 'friends' that makes it very difficult for governments to defeat them and destroy their organisation. Their numbers are small, but air travel makes it possible for them to appear anywhere in the world. Money is no problem as they either have 'petro-dollars' or can get it by ransom demands.

The Black September Organisation carried out the revenge assassination of the Jordanian prime minister in Cairo and in September 1972 came the killings at the Munich Olympic Games. Eleven Israeli athletes and five terrorists were killed. Three terrorists were captured but they were later released after the hijacking of a German airliner.

In March 1973 eight members of the BSO seized the Saudi Arabian embassy in Khartoum where they took hostage one Belgian and two US diplomats. Their demand was for the release of 60 Palestinian prisoners held in Jordan and also that of Sirhan B. Sirhan, who had assassinated Senator Robert Kennedy in the United States. The United States refused to yield to the terrorists' demands and all three hostages were killed. The terrorists were arrested and convicted, but released by the Sudanese government after a year in prison.

Lately there has been an easing off in Arab efforts, perhaps as their political theorists may believe that time, and 'money', is on their side: it must never be forgotten how patient the communist is. An example of this is the Malayan Insurgency, which is often quoted as one of the most successful counter-operations. By 1960 this was considered to be finished but now, over 15 years later, the Malayan Races Liberation Army (MRLA) under Chin Peng is once more on the move from its hiding places over the border in Thailand. Now Malaysia is on its own and there is unlikely to be a British army to provide the stiffening and professionalism that it will need. For the true terrorist, his cause is a way of life and the fires that drive him are only damped down, never allowed to go out.

The danger of these damped down fires can no more clearly be seen than in Northern Ireland. Lord O'Neill, then Terence O'Neill, who became prime minister in 1963, sought to restore to the Catholics some of the rights an entrenched Protestant majority had removed from them during the years since the Anglo-Irish Treaty of 1921. The Civil Rights Association came into being to get the same standards of justice for all as existed in the rest of the United Kingdom. The Association was undoubtedly infiltrated by some extremists, but the reaction to it by the Protestants was even more extreme. In Londonderry rioting took place when the Royal Ulster Constabulary and the 'B Specials' used unnecessary violence. In Derry in August 1969 came the worst: Catholics, fearing police violence, barricaded themselves in the Bogside and flew the tricolour of the Irish Republic from their windows. Using CS gas and water cannon, the RUC attempted to break down the barricades but were beaten back and forced to withdraw. The Stormont government appealed to Westminster for help and British troops were sent into 'Free Derry',

9mm UZI sub-machine gun

Calibre: 9mm. **Weight:** 9.1lb (4.12kg). **Length, butt folded:** 18½'' (.45m). **Length, butt extended:** 25.2'' (.64m). **Range:** 219 yards (200m). **Muzzle velocity:** 400m/s. **Rate of fire:** 550/600rpm (cyclic).

130rpm (automatic). 64rpm (single shots). **Magazine capacity:** 25, 32 or 64 rounds.

The UZI sub-machine gun was designed in 1949 by a Major Uziel Gal, and since then has been built in large numbers by both Israel Military Industries and FN of Herstal, Belgium. Two models are available, one with a wooden stock and the other with a folding metal stock. The user can select either full automatic or single shot according to the tactical requirements.

7.65mm VZOR 61 pistol

Calibre: .32 (7.65mm). **Weight loaded:** 4.4lb (2.1kg). **Length, butt extended:** 20.2'' (.513m). **Length, butt retracted:** 10.6'' (.269m). **Magazine capacity:** 10 or 20 rounds. **Muzzle velocity:** 989fps (317m/s). **Rate of fire:** 40rpm (single shots). **Range:** 55 yards (50m) stock retracted. 219 yards (200m) stock extended.

The 7.65mm VZOR 61 (or Vz.61 Skorpion) is an unusual sidearm used by the Czech forces, although it has also been exported. The weapon uses the blowback method of operation and fires a standard .32 (7.65mm) round, on either single shot or full automatic. When not required, the wire stock folds forward through 180° so that it rests along the top of the weapon. A silencer can be fitted if required, although this reduces its effective range to about 110 yards (100m).

Belgian 7.62mm FN rifle

Calibre: 7.62mm. **Weight:** 11.12lb (5.06kg). **Length:** 43.3'' (2m). **Magazine capacity:** 20 rounds. **Muzzle velocity:** 2700fps (823ms). **Rate of fire:** 650/700rpm (cyclic). 120rpm (automatic). 60rpm (single shots). **Range:** 650 yards (600m).

The 7.62mm FN FAL (Fusil Automique Légère) was developed after the end of World War II by FN (Fabrique Nationale) of Herstal, Belgium, and has proved a great commercial success. So far the weapon has been adopted by over 70 nations and has been

built under licence in many countries including Argentina, Australia, Austria, Canada, India, Israel, Norway, South Africa and the United Kingdom. Many of these countries have carried out modifications of the rifle to meet their own special requirements.

The FN is gas operated and the user can select either single shots or full automatic. A number of armies however use the weapon for single shots only, as on full automatic, the high rate of fire is uneconomical. The sights are graduated from 219 yards (200m) to 650 yards (600m). A complete range of optional extras are available, including a heavy barrel, night sights and a periscope.

where they were greeted as liberators. However, following a speech by the Irish prime minister Jack Lynch 'that the reunification of the national territory can provide the only permanent solution....', the Protestants heard their worst fears realised.

They went on the rampage in Belfast while the RUC, seeming to believe they were dealing with an uprising, fired indiscriminately. In the course of three days seven people were killed and 500 homes burned down. Some 6,000 troops were sent to

Above: The Wheelbarrow Remote Handling Equipment can investigate an explosive device and remove it to a safe distance. It is shown here breaking a car window.

Right: Member of the IRA with a Soviet RPG-7V anti-tank rocket launcher. Guerilla forces in many parts of the world have these weapons and they were used by Egypt and Syria in the 1973 Campaign.

Belfast, with the task of separating and guarding the Protestant and Catholic areas. During the next months the army kept an uneasy peace, the B Specials were disbanded and the RUC reformed under a former head of the City of London Police. Then in June 1970 there was bad rioting in Belfast and five Protestants were killed. Soon after this the army searched the Catholic Lower Falls area for arms while a curfew was enforced. This marked the breaking point between the army and the Catholics, and the latter turned to the Irish Republican Army (IRA). Earlier the Provisional Army Council had been formed as a splinter group of the IRA. In February 1971 the first British soldier was killed and in March three young off-duty Scottish soldiers were murdered. The war had come.

As the situation in Northern Ireland developed, it was to show many 'urban guerrilla' theories to have a sound basis. With more troops and tougher laws for daily life the situation grew worse instead of better. The classic example of misjudgement was the policy of internment. It was sincerely believed by the government that it would help the situation, and so it and the army were horrified by the reaction. In the four months before internment (April to July 1971) four soldiers, no police and four civilians had been killed. In the four months after (August to November), 30 soldiers, 11 members of the RUC or Ulster Defence Regiment and 73 civilians were killed. There are some who say that this situation would have arisen in any event, and that internment only brought forward the time of the outbreak. This may be true, but without doubt internment was badly organised and there was unnecessary brutality in the interrogations which took place. The end was for the British government to step in and suspend the constitution.

There has been one lesson learned in the years that have followed: the security forces must not allow themselves to be provoked into extreme violence. When dealing with urban guerrillas the security forces must expect to take heavier casualties as they represent the larger target and they cannot take such action as 'Bloody Sunday', when 13 civilians were shot by paratroops in a riot in Derry. The Provisionals lost much of what they had gained by perpetrating their own 'Bloody Friday' when bomb attacks in Belfast killed 11, only two of whom were soldiers.

One point that the first internment raids proved was the need for good intelligence, and this is something that the free countries need to study today. The scenario of most revolutionaries is something like this: first the building up of cells; subversive operations such as strikes, demonstrations and riots; insurgency, with attacks by bomb and rifle on persons and property; as more sympathisers are gained, guerrilla groups take control of parts of the country; finally outright civil war followed by the collapse of the government, or the government's fall without civil war. The 'revolution' is at its weakest and most vulnerable in the initial stages, when it should be penetrated by agents. But there must be government will to do this. It is interesting and disturbing to note the attacks on such organisations as the CIA, FBI and Special Branch by left-wing writers, for these are the bodies which organisations who would take over a country have most cause to fear. Hence if such official bodies can be considered undemocratic, or limiting of personal liberty, then the task of those who would destroy freedom is that much easier.

The organisation of these revolutionary movements is to be fronted by an overt political party which also contains members of a subversive organisation. Lord George Brown has stated that this is true of the Parliamentary Labour Party. Then the subversive group contains a military member who organises the terrorists when needed. With these facts in mind the reader should watch the future activities of the Italian and Portuguese communists.

One result of the terrorist in Great Britain has been the involvement of the army in those activities on the borderline with police duties. Again note that the Canadian government also had to turn to their Defence Force for help in 'policing' the 1976 Olympics. In the Argentine the military took over the government of the country in the most well publicised coup in history. It was a most reluctant military take-over, but for months the country had been descending into anarchy as a result of the actions of the *Ejertico Revolucionario de Pueblo* or Peoples' Revolutionary Army. This is one of the largest and best organised groups of Trotskyites in the world, and it has strengthened its position by a series of kidnappings which have brought it an estimated $35 million in ransoms. The ERP has not had it all its own way in Argentina as there has been a backlash of the extreme right and there have been numerous murders of members of the left and right. By the middle of 1976 the new government does not seem to have managed to do anything to slow down the killing.

Modern methods of surveillance make it very difficult for any discontent to survive in a communist state, but against this 'modern war' the free nations are very vulnerable. Soldiers are at last studying this new 'battlefield', and are more ready now than before to cope with the techniques required.

Humber Pig

Crew: 2 + 6 (driver, commander and 6 men). **Weight:** 12,768lb (5790kg). **Length:** 16' 2'' (4.926m). **Width:** 6' 8½'' (2.004m). **Height:** 6' 11½'' (2.12m). **Road speed:** 40mph (64kmh). **Range:** 250 miles (402km). **Engine:** Rolls Royce B60 Mk.5A, six cylinder petrol developing 120 HP at 3750 rpm.

In the early 1950's, the Humber Company and the Fighting Vehicles Research and Development Establishment (now the Military Vehicles and Engineering Establishment) developed the FV1600 range of 1 ton trucks, both armoured and unarmoured. The armoured models included the FV1611 (APC), FV1612 (Radio), FV1613 (Ambulance) and the FV1620, a special anti-tank vehicle fitted with the Malkara long range missile. By the late 1960s most of these had been placed in reserve or sold as scrap. The troubles in Northern Ireland then started once again and the British Army found itself short of wheeled armoured personnel carriers. The armoured trucks were quickly brought back into service, as were quantities of the Alvis FV603 Saracen APC.

The correct name of the vehicle is Truck 1 Ton, Armoured, 4 × 4, Humber, and it is most commonly known as the Pig. It is widely used in Northern Ireland for transporting troops and supplies, but is not armed. Many Pigs have been fitted with teargas dischargers and barracade-removing equipment. In 1972/73 it was found that the IRA was using rifle bullets that could penetrate the armour of the Pig, all of which were then fitted with additional armour. Rear-axles and suspensions had also to be modified to take the added weight.

The military balance in Europe

Although no overt hostilities have taken place, the great struggle for supremacy between NATO and the Warsaw Pact in Europe continues to fascinate with its political, economic and tactical problems.

Over the past few years there has been much talk of *détente* between the Warsaw Pact and NATO. *Détente* is a French word, and the dictionary gives its meaning as 'unbending' or 'relaxing'. In the military sense a true *détente* means a relaxation of preparedness for war by all parties concerned. Unfortunately, the only relaxing carried out has been entirely on the part of NATO. The Soviet Union has not only not relaxed her military preparations in any way, but has greatly increased them.

Considerable efforts have been made by the United States to reduce the build-up of intercontinental nuclear missiles by the Soviet Union and itself under the SALT (Strategic Arms Limitation Talks) negotiations, and the US has succeeded in getting certain limits placed on the size of the strategic offensive forces (missile and bomber). In Europe there have been continuing talks between the Russians and NATO on what is known as Mutual Balanced Force

Reductions (MBFR) in central Europe, but nothing concrete has resulted. The Russians suggest a percentage cut of the forces on each side, but NATO, whose forces are already outnumbered by something like three to one by those of the Warsaw Pact, does not agree and would expect to see a larger reduction on the Warsaw Pact's side, in order that the opposing forces would be more evenly balanced.

In the NATO countries what has happened, however, has been a slow rundown of the armed services, largely because no country will expend the money necessary to keep them up, or indeed to improve them. That is not to say that defence budgets have not been increased: yearly increases have been made by all NATO countries, but they have barely kept pace with inflation, except possibly in the United States, and the increases have not been sufficient to develop or to buy the modern weapons which NATO needs to counter similar weapons now coming into service in the Warsaw Pact forces. Further, one of the biggest claims on a defence budget are the sums required to pay and maintain the men in the armed forces. Salaries all over the world have soared in the last few years, and the armed services have had to keep in step with the salaries in industry, with the result that a serviceman's pay is now some three times what it was 10 years ago. Defence budgets have not increased sufficiently to take this into account, with the result that nearly all the NATO forces have been reduced in size.

To take a few examples: Britain in 1971

The T-62 is the most modern Russian tank in widespread service. Although equipped with a very powerful 115-mm gun it is rather cramped and tiring to drive. The T-72, which can outfight all NATO tanks other than the Chieftain, is now replacing it.

NATO/Warsaw Pact forces located in Europe

In a general war situation, Warsaw Pact Forces committed against Nato might be allocated as follows:

Soviet Forces in the Leningrad Military District against Norway.

Soviet Ground and Naval and Air Forces from the Baltic Military District, plus Polish and East German airborne and amphibious forces against Denmark, the northern coast of West Germany and Holland.

Soviet Ground and Air Forces from the Group of Soviet Forces in Germany (GSFG) and the Soviet Northern Group of Forces (NGF) in Poland, and from the Moscow and Belorussian Military Districts, plus Ground Force elements of the East German and Polish armies, against North Germany (Hanover and the Ruhr); and (together with Czech army units and elements of the Soviet Central Group of Forces in Czechoslovakia (CGF) and Soviet troops from the Kiev Military District) against Central Germany (Frankfurt).

Soviet forces from GSFG, CGF and SGF (Soviet Southern Group of Forces in Hungary) plus elements of the East German, Czech and Hungarian Armies, and troops of the Kiev and Carpathian Military Districts, against Southern Germany (Stuttgart-Munich), Austria and Italy.

Against Southern Europe and Turkey Soviet troops of the Odessa and Causcasian Military Districts and elements of the Hungarian, Romanian and Bulgarian armies.

This would give a comparison of strengths as follows (Nato forces in parenthesis):
Warsaw Pact divisions 140-150(45) tanks 27,000 (10-11,000) artillery pieces 8-9,000 (6,000) men (under arms now) 1,240,000 (1,200,000).

Although the manpower under arms is approximately equal, the Warsaw Pact capacity for very rapid mobilisation would give them a 3-1 superiority in fighting troops after three weeks of mobilisation. Nato could only close the gap after a further month had elapsed.

To what extent the Soviet Union's Warsaw Pact allies can be relied upon depends, of course, on the political situation in which conflict occurs. The startling improvement in the quality and quantity of equipment with which the USSR has equipped the non-Soviet Warsaw Pact countries since 1970 would seem to indicate that these countries are increasingly being considered by the USSR as quite reliable allies. The German and Bulgarian Armies have particularly benefitted from this trend. The Poles, Czechs and Hungarian armies in addition use good quality domestically produced equipment. Only the Romanian army has failed to show a marked improvement since 1970. Presumably, due to Romania being the least controllable regime politically and having the least important position strategically, her army is accorded the lowest priority of resupply by the USSR.

It should be borne in mind that to ensure internal security in both peace and war, all Eastern European countries have very large forces under the control of their Ministries of the Interior or State Security organisations. These forces are, to all intents and purposes, military; being equipped with small warships, combat aircraft and armoured vehicles. To quote an example: A Polish conscript might find himself called up to do not two years national service in the army, but three years in the Border Troops of the Territorial Defence Force. Poland has 80,000 such troops, Romania 45,000, East Germany 80,-100,000, Hungary 20,000, Czechoslovakia 25,000 and Bulgaria 22,000. The USSR has in addition almost half a million such troops, many of whom would be used to ensure the stability of Eastern Europe in the event of war. In addition, all Eastern European countries have TA-style militia forces involving a very large percentage of their adult male populations.

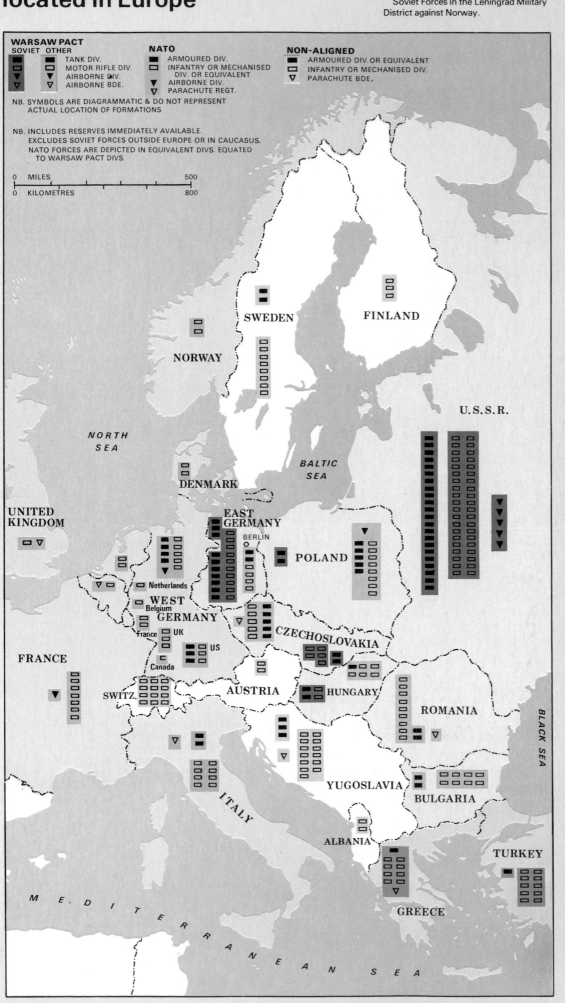

WARSAW PACT
SOVIET OTHER
TANK DIV.
MOTOR RIFLE DIV.
AIRBORNE DIV.
AIRBORNE BDE.

NATO
ARMOURED DIV.
INFANTRY OR MECHANISED DIV. OR EQUIVALENT
AIRBORNE DIV.
PARACHUTE REGT.

NON-ALIGNED
ARMOURED DIV. OR EQUIVALENT
INFANTRY OR MECHANISED DIV.
PARACHUTE BDE.

NB. SYMBOLS ARE DIAGRAMMATIC & DO NOT REPRESENT ACTUAL LOCATION OF FORMATIONS

NB. INCLUDES RESERVES IMMEDIATELY AVAILABLE. EXCLUDES SOVIET FORCES OUTSIDE EUROPE OR IN CAUCASUS. NATO FORCES ARE DEPICTED IN EQUIVALENT DIVS. EQUATED TO WARSAW PACT DIVS.

MILES 0 — 500
KILOMETRES 0 — 800

The Arms Race

US–USSR MILITARY PRODUCTION 1970–75

Approximate yearly average:

	USA	USSR
Tanks	450	2500
APC	1450	3800
Artillery	160	1400
Helicopters	600	1000
Tactical Aircraft	600	1000
Surface Ships	7–8	40
Missile Subs	less than 1	7

TOTAL HOLDINGS OF GROUND FORCE EQUIPMENT (excluding obsolete reserves)

	USA	USSR
Tanks	9000	42000
APCs	23000	41000
Artillery (including mortars and multiple rocket launchers)	9000	27000
Helicopters	9000	2300

PERSONNEL

	USA	USSR
Active	2.1 million	4.8 million
Reserve	1.9 million	7.2 million

DEFENCE EXPENDITURE (estimated) 1975

	USA	USSR
Percent of GNP	6%	15% (estimated)
Comparative figures of actual expenditure	100%	168% (estimated)

STRATEGIC FORCES 1975

	USA	USSR
ICBM	1054	1618
SLBM	656	784
Strategic Bombers	375	185
Intermediate Bombers	645	66

FIGHTER AND ATTACK AIRCRAFT

	USA	USSR
Fighter Interceptor Aircraft	374	2550
ABM Launchers	0	64
Strategic SAM Launchers	0	12000
Tactical Attack (incl Naval)	2300	5000

In general Soviet totals include more obsolescent hardware

had 381,000 persons in its armed services, and today has 345,000. The United States in the same period has reduced from 2,699,000 to 2,130,000.

Quite the reverse is the case in the Warsaw Pact countries. Every country has increased the numbers in their forces, particularly the Soviet Union whose forces in 1971 numbered 3,375,000 and now number 3,575,000, an increase of 200,000 men.

Apart from the increase in manpower, the Soviet Union's defence spending has risen from the equivalent of $84,400 million in 1972 to $103,800 million in 1975, an increase of roughly $19,000 million. Britain's expenditure in the same period was raised by only $2,500 million and that of the United States by $15,000 million.

Such enormous figures are difficult to comprehend, so perhaps an easier way of expressing what defence spending means to the individual is the amount it costs each citizen in taxes every year. In 1972 every Russian was paying $342 per year; in 1976 he is paying $409. Every American was paying $372; in 1976 the figure is $430. Every Briton was paying $141; in 1976 he is paying $185.

Tanks

Apart from salaries, public expenditure provides the armed forces' weapons, which are possibly of greater importance for the land forces in Europe today. Probably the most powerful and important weapon in conventional land warfare is the tank. In northern and central Europe, NATO can muster 7,000 main battle tanks (MBTs), against the Warsaw Pact's 19,000 (of which 11,500 belong to the Russians). In southern Europe the figures are NATO 3,500 and Warsaw Pact 7,750. These figures do not include the French army, because, as is well known, France does not at present belong to the military side of NATO. However, the chances are that France would be forced to come in on NATO's side should war ever break out, and this would add between 325 and 485 tanks to the NATO figure in central Europe.

Even with this French addition it will be seen that the Warsaw Pact's tanks greatly outnumber those of NATO. On the other hand the NATO tanks, principally British Chieftains, German Leopards, American M60s and French AMX-30s, are generally regarded as superior to those of the Warsaw Pact. The Russians have coming into service a new tank, the T-62, which is an improvement on their present T-55, but even so is probably not as good as NATO's more modern tanks. However, the Russians are developing a new tank, the T-72 (sometimes called the T-64), which may prove superior to any tank in service at present in NATO. But it is not ready yet and will not be in service for a few years, by which time NATO forces may also have an improved tank.

Anti-Tank Weapons

With such a preponderance of tanks against the Western Alliance, NATO has tended to concentrate on anti-tank weapons. The best defence against a tank is another tank with a powerful gun. NATO tanks have 90-mm, 105-mm and the British Chieftain's 120-mm guns. The new German tank, the Leopard II, which is not yet in full service, will also have a 120-mm gun. Rates of fire of tank guns are between seven and nine rounds per minute. The American M60 tank can fire from its 152-mm gun either a shell or a guided missile, the latter of which is the more accurate. On the whole, then, the NATO tanks should give a good account of themselves against other tanks.

The next best weapon against tanks is the helicopter armed with an anti-tank missile, and NATO is acquiring more and more of these, generally armed with the US TOW missile. Helicopters can hide below hills, suddenly pop up, launch their anti-tank missile and then duck down again under the protective cover of another hill. Similarly an anti-tank weapon mounted in a helicopter is much more mobile than one mounted on a vehicle, and mobility is all important to a force which is inferior in numbers of weapons.

For all that there are a considerable number of ground-based anti-tank missiles in, or coming into, service with NATO. Probably the most common is again the US TOW, which is made by the Hughes Aircraft Company. It has a range of 3,000 + metres and is automatically guided to a hit provided the operator keeps his sight on the target. Other types of missiles in use are the UK British Aircraft Corporation Swingfire and the Franco/German Hot and Milan, made by Aerospatiale and Messerschmitt-Bölkow-Blohm. Milan is a small missile, launched from the shoulder and Britain is to buy it for infantry use.

NATO's anti-tank missiles are good, although it is a pity from the logistics side that there are so many different types. They would undoubtedly inflict considerable casualties on the Soviet tanks in war, but unfortunately there are nothing like enough of them and reliance is still being placed on

T-64 or T-72 tank

Combat weight: Estimated at 39·3 tons (40,000kg).
Length: (Gun to front) about 32ft (10m). **Length:**
(Gun to rear) about 23ft (7m). **Width:** About 11ft
6in (3·5m). **Height:** Estimated at 7ft 2in (2200mm).
Engine: New engine of unknown type, but expected
to be water-cooled diesel of about 900hp. **Armament:**
New gun reported variously as having calibre of
122mm and of 125mm, with bore rifled at start and
smooth thereafter, firing fin-stabilized APDS
ammunition from 28-round automatic loader; probably one 7·62mm (co-axial) with large quantity of

ammunition. **Speed:** Up to 50mph (80km/h). **Range:**
Probably about 310 miles (500km). **Armour:** Probably
up to 120mm (more on mantlet). possibly of modern
type resistant to shaped charges.

Observers in the West have suggested that the new
turret of the T-62 was probably intended to be fitted
to a new chassis which was not ready in time. Continued progressive development led, by way of a
reported T-67 with the T-62 turret, to today's new
main battle tank now equipping armoured divisions of
the Soviet and other Warsaw Pact forces. Its designation has been reported to be T-64 and also T-72 (the
latter was accepted in the UK and USA at the time of
writing), and it is certainly an extremely formidable

tank able to outgun and out-fight any Western tank
except the British Chieftain. The completely new
chassis has small wheels and return rollers, a new
engine and transmission, and low-flash fuel stowage
as protection on each side. The ·heavily armoured
turret incorporates a superb new gun with mechanical
loading. This has allowed the crew to be reduced from
four to three, with the commander and gunner seated
high in the turret with no need to attend to the main
gun. The very latest IR, laser-ranging and NBC equipment are certain to be fitted, and it is reported that
driver fatigue has been greatly eased by reducing
engine vibration and driving work-load. Road speed is
remarkable.

FROG-7 surface to surface missile

Missile—Weight: 5071lb (2300kg). **Weight of warhead:** 992lb (450kg). **Length:** 29′ 10″ (9.1m).
Diameter: 21½″ (550mm). **Range:** 43.5 miles
(70,000m). **Vehicle—Crew:** 4. **Weight with missile:**
44,093lb (20,000kg). **Length:** 25′ 3¼″ (10.75m).
Width: 9′ 2″ (2.8m). **Height:** 12′ (3.66m). **Road
speed:** 40mph (65km/h). **Range:** 310 miles (500km).
Engine: two ZIL-375 water-cooled diesels developing
180 HP each.

The FROG-7 is the latest of the FROG—Free Rocket
Over Ground—missiles, and is carried on the rear of a
ZIL-135 8 × 8 high mobility truck. When reaching the
launch position, jacks are lowered at the sides and
rear to stabilise the truck when the missile is being
launched. Once the missile has been fired, the truck
moves off to a new position. A further ZIL-135 truck
carrying three reserve missiles is then brought up and
positioned alongside the launcher, which uses an
hydraulic crane to take a new missile from the re-supply
truck.

Soviet Tank and Motor Rifle Divisions each have a
FROG Battery with four launchers, plus command,
transport and missile resupply vehicles.

The FROG-7 is mainly used against known targets
such as troop concentrations, headquarters, supply
depots and ammunition dumps. A variety of warheads can be fitted, including High Explosive, Chemical
and Tactical Nuclear. The missile itself has a single
stage rocket and uses solid propellant.

The FROG-7 was used by both Egypt and Syria

against Israel during the 1973 war, but as a High
Explosive warhead was fitted, little damage was
caused. The missile is used by all members of the
Warsaw Pact.

---

small anti-tank guns or unguided rockets,
both of which are less efficient than guided
weapons.

The Warsaw Pact forces also have anti-
tank missiles with much the same ranges as
the NATO ones, but of course an anti-tank
missile is more of a defensive than an
offensive weapon and NATO should therefore be concentrating on them to a greater
extent than the Warsaw Pact, given that it is
NATO's intention never to carry out any
offensive act.

Apart from helicopters, fixed-wing aircraft can also be used against tanks and can
attack with rockets or bombs, including the
new self-homing bombs now coming into
service. A highly effective anti-tank weapon
is the cluster bomb, which is a bomb

carrying a number of small bomblets inside.
The latter are ejected from the main bomb
by gas pressure and spray the target. They
are particularly valuable against tank concentrations.

Another very useful weapon is the ground
mine. The Germans have two very effective
types, known as Medusa and Pandora,
which can be sown by helicopter. Britain
has also developed a quick method of sowing
mines from a vehicle. Apart from causing
casualties, minefields are of value in forcing
an enemy to take a different route and are
often used for this purpose where it is
desired to divert an advance into territory
more suitable for the defending forces.

In spite of the large number of tanks
available to the Warsaw Pact, the NATO

forces in central Europe would give them a
very hot reception, but of course, if the
Warsaw Pact is prepared to suffer heavy
casualties, sheer weight of numbers might
overcome the defences.

Artillery

Artillery includes both guns and rocket-
launchers. Here again the Warsaw Pact is
considerably stronger in northern and
central Europe, deploying a total of 5,600
guns, mortars and rocket-launchers against
NATO's 2,700. In southern Europe, for
once, the reverse is the case, NATO having
some 3,300 guns against the Warsaw Pact's
2,700.

The artillery situation in central Europe
is not quite as bad as it sounds because the

NATO guns' ammunition is of better quality and more lethal than that of the Warsaw Pact. Further, NATO's methods of supply of ammunition to the guns is probably superior, enabling them to keep up a higher rate of fire for a longer period. The Warsaw Pact is, however, improving its logistic arrangements and this slight degree of superiority may not last much longer.

However, there is one point very much in NATO's favour so far as artillery is concerned. The Americans have developed, and other NATO nations are following suit, a precision guided shell which results in extremely accurate fall of shot. It is a shell fitted with a laser seeker which will enable the shell to home onto any target reflecting laser light. The target is illuminated by a ground observer by means of a laser, and the shell's laser seeker picks up the beam's reflections and homes on the source of the reflections. The new shell's principal value is against tanks, but it can be used against other targets.

Missiles

Guns are not the only means of delivering explosives. Apart from aircraft, which are mentioned below, both NATO and the Warsaw Pact have tactical missiles. They are primarily intended to deliver nuclear warheads, but they can be fitted with conventional high-explosive warheads.

Most land-based tactical missiles have ranges of under 100 miles, but there are two longer range missiles: the US Pershing with a range of 400 miles and the Russian 'Scaleboard' with a range of 500 miles. The normal tactical missiles to be found on the battlefield are the Russian 'Frog' (35 miles) and 'Scud' (150 miles), while NATO relies on Honest John (22 miles), an American missile shortly to be replaced by another American missile, the Lance (70 miles). France has its own missile in the Pluton (75 miles).

The use of tactical nuclear missiles has long been a subject of controversy. NATO has some 7,000 such missiles in Europe, but they are American made, as are their nuclear warheads. Their use is rigidly controlled for fear that even a small nuclear explosion might unleash full-scale nuclear war. Up to the present the size of the warheads carried have been in the range of 1 kiloton (KT) to 100 KT, although the 'Scaleboard' is reported to be able to deliver 1 megaton (MT). Even 1 KT of nuclear explosive is far larger than any HE shell and would do considerable damage, not only to the target but to surrounding buildings. Its radioactive fall-out might extend over a number of square miles and many innocent civilians might be killed or maimed for life. To the enemy troops near the blast it would be difficult, if not impossible, to estimate the size of the explosion and it might well be reported as a major nuclear explosion. Thus it is easy to see how such an event might trigger off full-scale nuclear response. It is small wonder, then, that the Americans insist on deciding themselves whether tactical nuclear weapons should be used or not.

However, a new type of nuclear warhead, called the 'mini-nuke', has been developed by the Americans. This gives a much smaller nuclear explosion, of the order of a fraction of a kiloton, and is more controllable as regards fall-out. In other words, one 'mini-nuke' might have the same effect as that produced by a large number of HE shells, but it would affect only the target area and not the surrounding countryside and villages. Militarily it is a far more effective weapon than the present kiloton tactical missile. 'Mini-nukes' can be fitted to shells and bombs and can also have the terminal homing devices mentioned above.

So far not many 'mini-nukes' have been produced, but when they come into general use they should lead to reduced inhibition

about the use of nuclear weapons on the battlefield. The Russians, so far as is known, have not yet developed 'mini-nukes', so the inhibition on their side will remain. They do not, however, have as many tactical missiles as NATO.

Chemical Warfare

There is another form of weapon which the Russians are known to possess: chemical warfare (CW). NATO, with the possible exception of the Americans, has no offensive capability in CW, but most NATO nations have developed defensive measures against this very effective form of attack. Troops in the field are issued with special protective suits and respirators (gas masks), and in most NATO exercises chemical attacks are simulated and the troops made to wear their protective clothing for long periods.

Modern chemical agents are far more sophisticated than those used in World War I (the last time that chemical warfare was used in Europe). There is a new set of agents, called nerve agents, which are extremely toxic, one drop on the skin being enough to kill. There is also another agent, discovered by the Americans and called BZ, which affects the brain. Its effect is only temporary and the victim normally recovers after a day or so, but while he is under the influence of the agent he has no willpower and an attacker can do with him what he wishes. It is not known whether the Russians possess BZ or not, but its advantages are obvious and it is in effect a reasonably humane way of waging war. Mustard gas is still used; if breathed it is fatal, and if some of it comes in contact with the skin it causes terrible burns and incapacitates the victim.

The Warsaw Pact armies advancing into Europe might well use chemical agents ahead of their troops. The agents could be disseminated by shells, rockets or bombs, or could be sprayed from aircraft. If the advancing troops were about to occupy the

Lance surface to surface missile

Weight: 2834lb (1286kg). **Weight of warhead:** 465lb (210kg). **Length:** 20′ 5¾″ (6.242m). **Diameter:** 22″ (.609m). **Range:** 87 miles (45,720m). **Altitude:** 150,000′ (45,720m).

The Lance, or to give its correct designation, the MGM-52C, is a surface-to-surface missile which is now in service with the United States Army. Eight battalions are in service each with three batteries, each in turn having three firing platoons. Lance is replacing both the Honest John and Sergeant missiles and is manufactured by the Vought Corporation at Sterling Heights, Michigan.

The missile itself has two stages, powered by liquid fuel. Its guidance system is known as DC-Automet (Directional Control, Automatic Meteorological Compensation) and is invulnerable to all known countermeasures.

A variety of warheads can be fitted including High Explosive, tactical nuclear and cluster anti-tank type. Several years ago trials were carried out with TGSMs (Terminally Guided Sub-Missiles). The basic idea is that Lance would be launched into known concentrations of enemy armour, the TGSMs would be dispersed over the target and then homed onto the enemy tanks.

In the self-propelled role, the launcher ramp and missile are mounted in a chassis developed from the M548 cargo carrier, and is known as the M752. It has a top road speed of 40mph (64.3kmh) and is fully amphibious being propelled in the water by its tracks. It is supported in action by a M668, which is also a

development of the M548, and carries two spare Lance missiles and a crane for transferring a new missile to the M752. A lightweight M740 launcher is

also available, and this can towed behind a 4 × 4 or 6 × 6 truck, or is airtransportable under CH-47 Chinook helicopter.

T-62 main battle tank

Crew: 4 (commander, gunner, loader and driver). **Weight:** 80,436lb (36,500kg). **Length overall:** 32' 0⅝'' (9.77m). **Length, hull:** 22' 0¼'' (6.715m). **Width:** 11' (3.35m). **Height:** 7' 10½'' (2.4m). **Road speed:** 31mph (50kmh). **Range:** 310 miles (500km). **Engine:** V-12 diesel developing 700 HP at 2200 rpm. **Ground pressure:** 10.24psi (.72kg/cm²). **Vertical obstacle:** 2' 7½'' (.8m). **Trench:** 9' 2'' (2.8m). **Gradient:** 60% **Armour:** 20 tp 170mm.

The T-62 MBT was first seen in public during 1965 and is a direct development of the earlier T-54/T-55 MBT, but with a more powerful engine, longer and slightly wider hull, and a new turret with a new gun. According to some reports, over 50,000 have now been built. The T-62 was used in large numbers by the Egyptian and Syrian Armies during the 1973 Middle East war where it was found to be inferior to the Israeli M60A1 and Centurion tanks. Its main drawbacks are a slow rate of fire, poor fire control system and lack of range of the 115mm U-5TS smooth bore gun, which has an elevation of +17° and a depression of −4°. Three types of ammunition can be used: — High Explosive, Armour Piercing Fin-Stabilised Discarding Sabot (this has a muzzle velocity of 1500/1680 m/s and according to some American reports, can penetrate 300mm of armour at a range of 1500m, and High Explosive Anti-Tank (HEAT), the latter has a m/v of 1000 m/s and will penetrate 450mm of armour at a range of 1000m. The empty cartridge cases are ejected through a hatch in the rear of the turret. A 7.62mm PKT machine-gun is mounted to the right of the main armament and some T-62s have a 12.7mm anti-aircraft machine gun. A total of 40 rounds of 115mm and 3,500 rounds of 7.62mm ammunition are carried. Like all modern Soviet tanks, the T-62 is provided with infra-red driving and fighting equipment and a NBC system.

same ground, nerve agents would probably not be used as they tend to persist for some time. More likely would be mustard gas attack, or BZ if they have it. Nerve agents might be used to deny ground to enemy troops.

The protective clothing and respirators used by NATO troops give absolute protection provided they are donned in time. The problem is, however, to provide sufficient warning. Chemical shells could be mixed with HE shells and, since most of the agents are odourless, they are unlikely to be detected until their effect is felt.

The United States is thought to have a stockpile of nerve agents in America and possibly also in Europe, and there is no reason why chemical warfare should not be used in defence as well as in attack, but whether or not the Americans would use it

Right: The FH 70 155mm howitzer being tested in Sardinia. The FH 70 is a joint development by Germany, England and Italy and should enter service in the late 1970's. It has a range of 24,000m with standard ammunition and 30,000m with a rocket-assisted projectile.

Below: 'Sagger' ATGW is launched from a BRDM1 AFV. This missile is reasonably effective up to nearly 2 miles and was responsible for destroying many Israeli tanks during the Yom Kippur war

in Europe is a closely guarded secret.

Aircraft

Aircraft, of course, play a large part in land warfare, and the fast tactical strike plane can be used to attack such things as tanks, troops, bridges and headquarters. The Russians have recently produced some new and formidable tactical strike aircraft, in particular the Sukhoi Su-19 (NATO code-name 'Fencer') which has a maximum speed of Mach 2.3, a range of 900 miles and a weapon load of 8,000 pounds.

NATO has a variety of types, but the principal strike aircraft are the Lockheed F-104 Starfighter with a maximum speed of Mach 2.2, range of 1,550 miles and a weapons load of 4,000 pounds; and the McDonnell Douglas F-4 Phantom (Mach 2.2, range 1,860 miles, load 16,000 pounds). Britain, Germany and Italy are shortly to get the Panavia Multi Role Combat Aircraft (MRCA), now named Tornado, one of whose roles will be tactical strike, and whose performance should outshine those of both the F-104 and the F-4.

The Warsaw Pact greatly outnumbers NATO in tactical aircraft in service. In northern and central Europe it has a total of 4,020 aircraft, of which 1,325 are for ground-attack, as opposed to NATO's 2,050 aircraft, of which 1,250 are for ground-attack. In southern Europe the comparable figures are: Warsaw Pact 930 aircraft of which 200 are for ground-attack, NATO 858 of which 450 are for ground-attack. However, NATO has a greater proportion of multi-purpose machines (and when the MRCA comes into service the figure will be higher still) and some of these have a better range and payload than those of the Warsaw Pact. In addition many of the NATO aircraft have more sophisticated weapon delivery systems than have the Warsaw Pact types. For example there are the various types of guided bombs (laser and television) and air-to-ground missiles.

The Warsaw Pact air forces are more widely dispersed than are those of NATO, which has too few airfields. Great efforts are being made to 'harden' what airfields there are, by the building of reinforced runways and concrete aircraft shelters for resisting conventional bomb or missile attack.

On the credit side, NATO has more reinforcement aircraft, particularly in America. The total American tactical aircraft available as reinforcements amount to about 5,000, while those in the Soviet Union are about 4,500.

Air Defence

Both sides take air defence very seriously and both have radar chains to give early warning of approaching aircraft, coupled with long-range surface-to-air missiles (SAMs) and interceptor aircraft. However, there are gaps in the radar chains, particularly in the detection of low-flying aircraft. Low-level strikes on or immediately behind the battlefield are more than possible. As noted, the Warsaw Pact aircraft outnumber those of NATO in central Europe, so NATO is taking energetic steps to update its ground defences against low-level strikes.

NATO now has a number of close-range air defence missiles, the most prominent being the British Rapier, the Franco-

Leopard main battle tank

Crew: 4 (commander, gunner, loader and driver) **Weight:** 88,160lb (40,000kg). **Length overall:** 31' 4'' (9.543m). **Length hull:** 23' 3'' (7.09m). **Width:** 10' 8'' (3.25m). **Height:** 8' 8'' (2.64m). **Road speed:** 40mph (65kmh). **Range:** 372 miles (600km). **Engine:** MTU MB 838 Ca.M500, 10 cylinder multi-fuel diesel developing 830 HP at 2200rpm. **Vertical obstacle:** 3' 9'' (1.15m). **Trench:** 9' 10'' (3m). **Gradient:** 60%. **Armour:** 10—70mm.

The Leopard has been one of the most successful tanks developed since World War II. The first prototype was completed in 1960, followed by a pre-production batch. The first production Leopard was completed by Krauss-Maffei of Munich in 1965 and since then over 5,600 have been built or ordered by Australia, Belgium, Denmark, Germany, the Netherlands and Norway. In addition, Italy purchased 200 and is building a further 600. The first model to enter service was the Leopard A1, followed by the Leopard A2, A3 and most recently, the A4, the latter with a new turret of spaced armour.

The Leopard is armed with the British L7 105mm gun, which has an effective range of 2000m. A 7.62mm MG3 machine gun is mounted co-axially with the main armament and there is a similar weapon on the roof for anti-aircraft defence. Four smoke dischargers are mounted either side of the turret. A total of 60 rounds of 105mm and 5500 rounds of machine gun ammunition are carried. The Leopard has exceptional mobility and is easy to maintain—a complete power-pack, consisting of the engine and transmission, can be replaced in 20-30 minutes under field conditions. A full range of night vision equipment is provided, as is a NBC system. The tank can ford to a depth of 7' 4'' (2.25m) without preparation or a schnorkel can be quickly fitted which enables it to ford rivers up to 13' (4m) in depth.

M109 155mm self-propelled howitzer

Crew: 6. **Weight loaded:** 52,438lb (23.786t). **Length overall:** 21' 8'' (6.612m). **Length hull:** 20' 6¼'' (6.256m). **Width:** 10' 9¼'' (3.285m). **Height:** 10' 9½'' (3.289m). **Road speed:** 35mph (56kmh). **Range:** 224 miles (360km). **Engine:** Turbocharged diesel developing 405 HP at 2300rpm. **Ground pressure:** 10.8psi (.766kg/cm²). **Vertical obstacle:** 1' 9'' (.533m). **Trench:** 6' (1.828m). **Gradient:** 60%.

World War II proved the superiority of self-propelled artillery in many, but by no means all, roles and after the war, the United States developed a range of artillery which included the M44 (155mm), M52 (105mm), M53 (155mm) and the M55 (203mm). These however proved too difficult to maintain, were heavy and had a limited radius of action and in the mid-1950s a new series of light-weight self-propelled weapons was tested—the M108 (105mm)/M109 (155mm) and the M107 (175mm/M110 (203mm). The M108 and M109 entered production at the Cleveland tank plant in 1962 and the US Army soon decided to concentrate production on the M109. The M108 was phased out in 1963. Since then, over 3,200 M109s have been built and the type is now in service with many countries. Recently, the M109A1 has been developed. This model has a much longer gun barrel than the standard M109 and can fire a shell to a range of 18,000m against the 14,700m of the earlier M109. The M109 can fire a variety of ammunition (28 rounds are carried) including High Explosive, Nuclear, Smoke, Illuminating and Canister. A .50 (12.7mm) machine gun with 500 rounds is mounted on the commander's cupola.

Above: A US Army AH-1G helicopter launches a Rockwell Hellfire launch-and-leave anti-tank missile. Still under development, the missile is laser guided

Right: The Mi-24 Hind is the first Soviet helicopter gunship: Fire support during assault landings is its primary role.
(1) Pitot head. (2) 12.7-mm machine gun.
(3) Perspex bullet-proof shield. (4) Engine exhaust. (5) Laser rangefinder on gun camera mount. (6) Pods holding 32.57-mm unguided rockets. (7) Rails for Swatter semi-automatic ATGW.

German Roland II (which has also been bought by the Americans) and the French Crotale. The missiles are all very similar and can be either towed behind vehicles or mounted on armoured cars. Anti-aircraft guns are still used, and in fact in the Yom Kippur War (October 1973) the Israelis found to their cost that the Soviet-made AA guns used by the Egyptians were extremely efficient. They have a rate of fire of 4,000 rounds per minute, which surpasses anything that NATO has, although the Americans have the Vulcan gun with six barrels and a rate of fire of 3,000 rounds per minute.

Flexible Response

NATO's policy in Europe is to avoid the use of nuclear weapons as long as possible. A policy of 'Flexible Response' has therefore been adopted. This means that it is NATO's determination to meet any attack mounted by the other side with the same weapons as those used by the attackers.

Unfortunately an attacker always has the initial advantage since he can choose his place, timing and mode of attack. The defender has no such choice and must be ready to meet attacks at any time and along the whole of his front. NATO has always hoped that intelligence reports will be good enough to give it adequate warning of a coming onslaught and that they would enable it to mass its forces at the right place. One cannot help but wonder if this is really so. Large-scale troop movements can be so easily disguised under the guise of 'exercises' that it seems quite possible that NATO could one day be caught completely 'on the hop'.

NATO's forces are by no means strong enough to cover the whole of central Europe at one time. This means that it requires great mobility so that troops can be rushed to any threatened area with the minimum of delay. Helicopters could play a vital role in this; more troop-carrying helicopters are required and of course the strike helicopters with their anti-tank weapons are invaluable. In addition, all tanks, guns, armoured vehicles and headquarters must not only be completely mobile but must be able to move fast over any type of terrain. In fact NATO's armour is reasonably fast moving; the tragedy is that NATO does not possess sufficient armour or troops to enable it to

BMP-1 mechanised infantry combat vehicle

Crew: 2+8. **Weight:** 26,456lb (12t). **Length:** 20′ 8″ (6.3m). **Width:** 10′ (3.05m). **Height:** 6′ (1.83m). **Road speed:** 36mph (60kmp). **Range:** 310 miles (500km). **Engine:** Six cylinder diesel developing 280 HP. **Vertical obstacle:** 3′ 7″ (1.1m). **Trench:** 6′6″ (2m). **Gradient:** 60%.

The BMP-1 has the distinction of being the first Mechanised Infantry Combat Vehicle (MICV) to enter service in the World. Previously the APC (ie the American M113 or British FV432) simply carried infantry across the battlefield, but the MICV also enables troops to fight from within the vehicle, using firing ports in the hull sides and rear.

Since the BMP-1 entered service in 1967, it has been exported to many countries and saw combat with both Egyptian and Syrian forces in the 1973 Middle East campaigns. The Germans also have the Marder MICV in service, whilst the French have the AMX-10P and the Americans are developing a similar vehicle known as the XM723, which will enter service in 1980.

The BMP-1 has an aluminium and magnesium hull and carries a crew of three (commander, gunner and driver), and up to eight fully equipped infantrymen. The vehicle is fully amphibious, being propelled in the water by its tracks at a speed of 3.7mph (6kmh). A NBC system is provided as well as a full range of night vision equipment. The vehicle is armed with a turret-mounted 73mm gun which has an effective range of 1500/2000m, fed by an automatic loader; a 7.62mm PKT machine gun is mounted co-axially with the main armament. Over the 73mm gun is a launching rail for the Sagger wire-guided anti-tank guided missile, which has a maximum range of 2500m.

carry out a real policy of flexible response.

Another point which must be borne in mind is that NATO's reserves are largely drawn from the United States, some 3,000 miles away across the Atlantic. Exercises are held at intervals to see how long it would take to get the reserves into action in Europe, but although the troops can arrive fairly quickly by air, some of the heavy equipment, tanks and guns may have to come by sea, which takes time, and also raises the question of the control of the Atlantic in the initial stages of a war. The Soviet Union on the other hand has reserves stationed in Russia only a day's driving away by road and with adequate road and rail transport.

Standardisation

The Warsaw Pact has another great advantage over NATO. All its weapons and equipment are standardised, whether used by the Russians, Poles, East Germans or the rest. In NATO this is by no means the case. Each NATO nation has developed its own weapons and equipment, largely because each nation needs the work for its factories and wants its own engineers and scientists to keep abreast of technical know-how.

As a result NATO has numerous different equipments in the field, all requiring their own logistic support. For example, in 1973 a count was made of the different anti-tank weapons and it was found that there were no less than 31 in service in the NATO armies; there are four different types of

A Chieftain tank (foreground) and a Centurion tank (background) of the British Royal Armoured Corps on exercise in Dorset, England. The Centurion was replaced by the Chieftain in the 1960's.

main battle tank, each with different guns; seven types of combat aircraft, each with its own weapons system and its own considerable logistic support organisations; seven close-range air defence missiles; and there are hundreds of other similar examples.

NATO is doing its best to introduce some form of standardisation within its forces, but it is an uphill struggle, although it is estimated that something in the region of $2,000 million a year could be shaved off defence budgets if standardisation were fully implemented.

Finally, there is the question of morale, an important question, for with the best equipment in the world, wars are won or lost largely by the morale of the men in the field. Little is known of the morale of the Warsaw Pact troops, the majority of whom are conscripts, but NATO troops' morale is good and it must not be forgotten that they would be fighting for their very existence, and fighting over territory which they know and in which the majority of the civilians would be friendly. The Warsaw Pact might achieve considerable initial successes, but whether it could hold onto the captured territory against determined guerrilla type of resistance is open to question.

The picture painted is not a happy one for NATO, but it represents a situation which must be faced. The military know their shortcomings only too well, but they are powerless unless the politicians and the public in all the NATO nations realise the position and vote enough money to rectify matters. NATO could be strong, as strong or stronger than the Warsaw Pact, but strength will never be achieved without considerable financial sacrifices being made by every citizen in all the member nations of the Western Alliance.

Picture Credits

Photographic Research: Jonathan Moore

The publishers wish to thank the following photographers and organisations who have supplied photographs for this book.

Photographs have been credited by page number. Where more than one photograph appears on the page, references are made in the order of the columns across the page and then from top to bottom.

Some references have, for reasons of space, been abbreviated as follows:

The Imperial War Museum: IWM.
Ministry of Defence, London: MOD.
United States Marine Corps: USMC.

Jacket front: MOD. Jacket flaps and end papers: Photographers International (T. Fincher). Half title poster: IWM. Full title: Photographers International. Opposite credits page: USMC. Foreword page: IWM. Pages **10-11**: IWM. **13-15**: IWM. **16-17**: IWM. **18-22**: Novosti. **24-31**: IWM. **32-37**: Novosti. **38-61**: IWM. **62**: US Government. **64-66**: IWM. **68-70**: Fujiphotos. **71**: Novosti. **72-73**: Fujiphotos. **74-77**: IWM. **78**: Novosti. **80-81**: USMC. **82**: (top) IWM, (bottom) Novosti. **84**: (top) Süddeutsch, (bottom) US Signal Corps. **85**: IWM. **76**: Süddeutsch. **87**: Keystone. **88**: (top) Keystone, (bottom) IWM. **89**: J. G. Moore Collection, London. **90**: IWM. **91**: Keystone. **92-93**: J. G. Moore Collection, London. **94**: Blitz. **97**: Blitz. **99**: Bapty. **100-101**: Novosti. **102**: Blitz. **104**: Novosti. **105**: Bapty. **108-109**: IWM. **110**: Bapty. **111**: IWM. **113**: Bapty. **115-117**: IWM. **118**: US Army. **119**: Bapty. **120**: (top) US Army. **120-121**: (bottom) Bapty. **123**: Blitz. **124-125**: Novosti. **127**: Blitz. **128** Bapty. **129**: (top) IWM, (bottom) US Army. **131**: Blitz. **134-135**: (top) Blitz, (bottom) IWM. **136**: US Navy. **137**: USMC. **138**: (top and bottom) Fujiphotos. **141**: IWM. **142-145**: USMC. **146-148**: IWM. **152-153**: USMC. **154**: Popperfoto. **155**: USMC. **156-158**: US Army. **159**: (top) USMC, (bottom) Popperfoto. **160-163**: USMC. **164-165**: Keystone. **167-168**: Keystone. **171-172**: Keystone. **174-179**: US Army. **181**: USMC. **182-183**: US Army. **184-185**: USMC. **186**: (bottom) Photographers International. **194**: USMC. **195**: Photographers International. **196-198**: USMC. **200-201**: Photographers International. **203**: (top) Photographers International, (bottom) Camera Press. **204-212**: Photographers International. **213-216**: Camera Press. **217-220**: Popperfoto. **221**: Camera Press. **224-225**: Camera Press. **226**: Popperfoto. **227**: Keystone. **228** : Camera Press. **229-230** : Keystone. **232**: MOD. **233**: Camera Press. **234-235** and **240**: Educational and Television Films. **241**: MOD. **243**: (top) Rockwell Missile System Division. **244**: MOD.

The publishers wish to acknowledge their indebtedness to Andre Deutsch, publishers of **Insight on the Middle East War** by the Insight Team of the Sunday Times/Times Newspapers Limited (diagrams and maps on the Middle East wars).

proost Turnhout (Belgium)